THE MANDRAKE ROOT
AN ANTHOLOGY OF FANTASTIC TALES

Selected and arranged
by
JEREMY SCOTT

ACKNOWLEDGMENTS

I wish to thank Kathleen Farrell but for whom I might have missed the delightful irony of *The Stranger* by Richard Hughes; Reginald Moore for drawing my attention to *Pickle My Bones* by Arthur Calder-Marshall; Hsiao Chi'en for having introduced me to Sir Herbert Giles's *Strange Stories from a Chinese Studio* among many other Chinese curiosities. Finally I would like to express my appreciation towards my agents, Messrs. Gilbert Wright Limited, who coped with the extremely difficult question of copyright.

My appreciation for the very kind permission to include in this volume copyright material is due to the following authors (or their executors, trustees or representatives) and publishers:

To Messrs. Edward Arnold for "Oh, Whistle and I'll Come", by Dr. M. R. James, from *The Collected Ghost Stories of M. R. James*; to Mr. John Atkins (and Resurgam Books) for extracts from *The Diary of William Carpenter*; to Messrs. Ernest Benn for "Who Knocks at the Door", by Olive Schreiner, from *Stories, Dreams and Allegories*; to Messrs. Curtis Brown for "An Air-Raid Seen From Above", by Stella Benson, from *Living Alone*, published by Messrs. Macmillan; to Mr. Algernon Blackwood (and Messrs. A. P. Watt) for "The Man Who Was Milligan", from *Selected Stories*, published by William Heinemann, Ltd.; to Mr. Arthur Calder-Marshall (and Messrs. Jonathan Cape) for "Pickle My Bones", from *A Date With A Duchess*; to Messrs. Jonathan Cape for an extract from *A Portrait of the Artist as a Young Man*, by James Joyce; to Dr. Alex Comfort (and *Life and Letters Today*) for "The Lemmings"; to Mr. Walter De La Mare (and Messrs. Selwyn & Blount) for "Winter", from *Ding Dong Bell*; to Mr. E. M. Forster (and Messrs. Sidgwick & Jackson) for "The Story of a Panic", from *The Celestial Omnibus*; to Mr. Wrey Gardiner for *The White House*; to Miss Dorothy K. Haynes (and Mr. Reginald Moore) for "Changeling", from *Modern Reading*, No. 8; to Mr. Richard Hughes (and Messrs. Chatto & Windus) for "The Stranger", from *A Moment of Time*; to The Hogarth Press for "The Lady in the Looking-Glass", by Virginia Woolf, from *The Haunted House and Other Stories*; to Miss Pamela Hansford Johnson (and the Editor of the *English Review*) for *Altarwise*; to Messrs. John Lane, The Bodley Head, for "The Bell of Saint Euschemon", by Richard Garnett, from *The Twilight of the Gods*, and for "The Open Window", by H. H. Munro from *The Complete Stories of "Saki"*; to Mr. James Laver (and Messrs. Pearn, Pollinger & Higham) for "Mr. Hopkins and Galatea" from *The Laburnum Tree*, published by The Cresset Press; to Mrs. Frieda Lawrence (and Messrs. Pearn, Pollinger & Higham) for "The Last Laugh", by D. H. Lawrence, from *The Woman Who Rode Away*, published by William Heinemann Ltd.; to Mr. Fred Marnau for *The Wrinkled Women of St. Nepomuk*; to Mr. T. F. Powys (and Messrs. Chatto & Windus) for "No Room", from *The House with the Echo*; to Mr. Brian Rhys (and Messrs. J. M. Dent) for the translation of *The Horla*, by Guy de Maupassant; to Mr. William Sansom (and The Hogarth Press) for "The Peach-House-Potting-Shed", from *Fireman Flower*; to Sir Osbert Sitwell (and Messrs. Gerald Duckworth) for "The Greeting", from *Triple Fugue*.

I should further like to acknowledge use of text from: Messrs. Peter Davies for "The Familiar", by J. Sheridan Le Fanu, from *In A Glass Darkly*; Messrs. J. M. Dent for "The Leech of Folkestone", by Thomas Ingoldsby from *The Ingoldsby Legends*; Messrs. The Nonesuch Press for an extract from Thomas De Quincey from *The Selected Writings of Thomas De Quincey*, edited by Philip Van Doren Stern; Messrs. Simpkin, Marshall, Hamilton, Kent & Co., for *The Haunted and the Haunters*, by Lord Lytton.   J. S.

CONTENTS

	PAGE
ACKNOWLEDGMENTS	5
INTRODUCTION	8

*

"The wits go wool-gathering"

"Goe, and catche a falling starre,
Get with child a mandrake root,
Tell me, where all past yeares are,
Or who cleft the Divels foot. . . ."
JOHN DONNE.

THE EXTRAVAGANT

EVERLASTING FIRE. By *James Joyce*	11
THE MAN WHO WAS MILLIGAN. By *Algernon Blackwood*	13
THE STRANGER. By *Richard Hughes*	19
CHANGELING. By *Dorothy K. Haynes*	23
THE LAST LAUGH. By *D. H. Lawrence*	29

THE GROTESQUE

THE LEECH OF FOLKESTONE. By *Thomas Ingoldsby*	39
THE HAUNTED AND THE HAUNTERS. By *Edward Bulwer Lytton*	54
THE WRINKLED WOMEN OF ST. NEPOMUK. By *Fred Marnau*	75
PICKLE MY BONES. By *Arthur Calder-Marshall*	79
THE LEMMINGS. By *Alex Comfort*	83

THE BIZARRE

CONFESSIONS OF AN ENGLISH OPIUM-EATER. By *Thomas De Quincey*	87
THE HORLA. By *Guy de Maupassant*	89
THE LADY IN THE LOOKING-GLASS: A REFLECTION. By *Virginia Woolf*	97
THE PEACH-HOUSE-POTTING-SHED. By *William Sansom*	100
THE WHITE HOUSE. By *Wrey Gardiner*	106
WHO KNOCKS AT THE DOOR. By *Olive Schreiner*	108

*

"Never was seen, or heard, or known the like"

"Some hang above the tombs,
Some weep in empty rooms,
I, when the iris blooms,
Remember.

I, when the cyclamen
Opens her buds again,
Rejoice a moment—then
Remember."
MARY COLERIDGE.

THE FANCIFUL

AN AIR-RAID SEEN FROM ABOVE. By *Stella Benson*	110
THE OPEN WINDOW. By *H. H. Munro ("Saki")*	116
THE BELL OF SAINT EUSCHEMON. By *Richard Garnett*	118
THE STORY OF A PANIC. By *E. M. Forster*	124

THE QUAINT

	PAGE
"OH, WHISTLE AND I'LL COME, MY LAD." *By M. R. James*	137
NO ROOM. *By T. F. Powys*	148
ALTARWISE BY OWL-LIGHT. *By Pamela Hansford Johnson*	150
WINTER. *By Walter De La Mare*	157

THE EERIE

THE FAMILIAR. *By J. Sheridan Le Fanu*	163
MR. HOPKINS AND GALATEA. *By James Laver*	185
THE DIARY OF WILLIAM CARPENTER. *By John Atkins*	195
THE GREETING. *By Sir Osbert Sitwell*	204

*

A SELECTIVE BIBLIOGRAPHY (chiefly of shorter pieces) for the enthusiast . . 221

INTRODUCTION

THIS is not merely a collection of ghost stories, or a spate of horrors selected to thrill, nor again can the following tales be classified as unsolved mysteries. I have tried to embody all these classifications under my "fantastic" grouping, and attempted at the same time to go one step further by suggesting something even more indefinable.

The idea of the fantastic is one which has attracted mankind, and especially writers, since the beginning of time. All folklore can be called fantastic since all folklore is a strange plethora of fact and legend.

In choosing the well-known and popular lines from John Donne:

"Goe, and catche a falling starre,
Get with child a mandrake root,
Tell me, where all past yeares are,
Or who cleft the Divels foot. . . ."

as a motif for this anthology I am trying to trace the whole question of the reality of fantasy. The fantastic, as I see it, is not the impossible but rather the possibly-impossible born out of long-forgotten facts; for example the growth of the mandrake legend.

To most of us the mandrake is a legendary plant which we never expect to see in our gardens; indeed, we often doubt its existence. We may perhaps remember the Shakespearean references. "Give me to drink mandragora," cried Cleopatra to Charmian, "that I might sleep out this great gap of time my Antony is away." And Juliet, did she not tell her fear at the thought of waking before her time in the dark vault of the dead? Fear of hearing "shrieks like mandrakes torn out of the earth, that living mortels, hearing them run mad".

A plant which shrieks when pulled out of its ground; that is the main feature of the mandrake myth. We shiver at the queer fantasy of such a thought, yet we seldom delve deeper because most of us enjoy this particular and strange belief.

Behind every fantasy lies the solid root of fact. There is a mandrake plant of commonplace ancestry; we find it to be a mere relative of the potato family, Solanaceaa, a native of the Mediterranean region. A short-stemmed plant bearing a tuft of ovate flowers, with a thick, fleshy and often forked root. Its flowers are solitary, each carrying a purple bell-shaped corolla; its fruit a soft orange berry. A gaudily coloured creature of the plant world known for many poisonous properties and promising, like the witchs' spells, many virtues.

The natives of the African and Eastern continents knew the mandrake as an emetic, a purgative, a narcotic (*vide* Cleopatra's faith); and though today it has fallen into disrepute, in olden times it was valued highly and was used in many instances as an anaesthetic.

Its curious mythical qualities grew perhaps from the bizarre shape of its roots: a physical resemblance to the lower limbs of a man which resemblance often led to it being used as a love philtre, while its fruit was supposed (and in the East is still supposed) to facilitate pregnancy. With this superstition in mind one can better understand Donne's "get with child a mandrake root".

The borderline between the fantastic and the real becomes more illusive as one attempts to circumscribe the boundaries. Each man carries within himself his own fantasy, whether he knows this as day-dreaming or metaphysical speculation. Usually he leaves this inner world quite untouched in a corner of his brain; its fantastic properties are too much opposed to his mundane routine.

INTRODUCTION

The unknown is a terrible word; its associations are too ephemeral for the humanly acclimatized mind to recognize, let alone live with. To a certain extent man is sure of life; it holds familiar landmarks, pointers to the common behaviour, in themselves reassuring. One can anticipate certain results and conclusions. There are houses, streets, people, all in a more or less familiar form: one can recognize and label these, and they provide more than enough incident on which to focus attention and thought.

The unknown is linked with death and the living man is too preoccupied with his own personal living to wish to explore the mystery of what might or might not be. "Let the dead bury their own dead" we often say, breaking our connection with them as sharply as our minds will allow. Yet, to quote Walter de la Mare, "at the least living thought of them they (the dead) will awaken. The dry bones live, they walk again". To think is to give birth, give reality; thus the unknown becomes real when our minds apprehend it.

The oldest fear is that of the unknown. The most unsettling thought which is evaded and which carries with it a flavour of evil. Evil because it is unknown. The familiar, whether loved or hated, cannot wholly be evil since one is equipped by experience to deal with it. Yet the familiar itself is a mystery; life as we know it a fantasy in which we play a certain yet mysterious part:

> "This experience of life, which admits of no explanation even in its most simple moments, calls, in fact, for narration and not for criticism. It is possible to depict its tendencies. The inner and unconscious workings of that machinery form a mystery of which only the outer edges have been reached. The more it is probed, the more mysterious it becomes. From birth to death it is unending mystery."*

I have taken six well-known interpretations of the word fantastic and grouped my selected stories under these particular sub-divisions, contriving to endow the whole with a certain continuity.

Beginning with the "extravagant" I have chosen stories which can properly be described as passing the bounds of reason, being both wild and exorbitant in the circumstances they would have us believe. I have started off with the James Joyce extract from *A Portrait of the Artist as a Young Man.* Joyce's "Everlasting Fire" must precede all fantasies; it is the orthodox Catholic giving full rein to his horrific imagination and stimulating fear in others. The very idea of hell is fantastic. All evil, all sin, all devilry is found in man's idea of hell. The strongest primitive instinct in man. His idea of heaven is secondary; he apprehends heaven in order to dispel the horrors of hell. Hell passes all the bounds of reason, it is wild and completely exorbitant since its potentialities can never be fully imagined.

From the "extravagant" I have passed on to the "grotesque" where all is comically distorted and over-imagined. I believe I am right in saying that modern collectors of the fantastic often overlook Edward Bulwer Lytton's stories, and I have included his tale *The Haunted and the Haunters*. Edward Bulwer Lytton's career was a strange gothic romantic episode. He is mainly known for his historical novels such as *The Last Days of Pompeii* and his *Pelham*, portrait of a period dandy. His attraction towards the mysterious might almost be said to have been inherited. The family home, Knebworth in Hertfordshire, had many ghostly associations and was a legendary lair of phantoms. As a child Bulwer Lytton spent the larger part of his time soaking up all the curious knowledge to be found in Knebworth's extensive library of mediaeval books on astrology, necromancy, chiromancy, geomancy, aeromancy and similar strange subjects. In 1860 Bulwer Lytton compiled a geomantic figure for the purpose of forecasting Disraeli's career which proved to be exact in almost every detail. An ancestor of Bulwer Lytton's, a Dr. Bulwer, was known

---

* *Dance of the Quick and the Dead*, by Sacheverell Sitwell. (Faber.)

as an eccentric who studied the Black Art and expounded on the influence of stars on human destiny. Bulwer Lytton was attracted to mesmerism, clairvoyance and spiritualism and wrote to Dickens on these subjects. The tale which appears here was first published in *Blackwood's Magazine*.

The third section is the "bizarre", which is mainly concerned with a contrast of elements, and I have been surprised to find that the stories I eventually selected are all similar in one respect: they are all stories concerned with personal haunting and all tales of man being possessed by his own ghosts and his fight against them. The drug in de Quincey's *Opium Eater*; the madness in de Maupassant and Wrey Gardiner's tales; the ivory tower danger in William Sansom's *Peach-House-Potting-Shed*; the war in Olive Schreiner's dream. In the Virginia Woolf story we see the contrast within man himself; the devil which is the personal devil.

The "fanciful" is the lighter side of the fantastic and is whimsical and capricious in its irony. The "quaint" borders very much on to the "fanciful" for it touches on the piquantly unfamiliar, the curiously old-fashioned, the odd. My last section is the "eerie" where all is superstitiously weird and timid and uncertain.

The whole tone of these six sub-divisions of the fantastic is concentrated on the inexplicable in the known—the fact behind the legend, the reality behind the fantasy.

JEREMY SCOTT.

THE EXTRAVAGANT

EVERLASTING FIRE

By James Joyce

THE preacher's voice sank. He paused, joined his palms for an instant, parted them. Then he resumed: Now let us try for a moment to realize, as far as we can, the nature of that abode of the damned which the justice of an offended God has called into existence for the eternal punishment of sinners. Hell is a strait and dark and foulsmelling prison, an abode of demons and lost souls, filled with fire and smoke. The straitness of this prison is expressly designed by God to punish those who refused to be bound by his laws. In earthly prisons the poor captive has at least some liberty of movement, were it only within the four walls of his cell or in the gloomy yard of his prison. Not so in hell. There, by reason of the great number of the damned, the prisoners are heaped together in their awful prison, the walls of which are said to be four thousand miles thick: and the damned are so utterly bound and helpless that, as a blessed saint, Saint Anselm, writes in his book on similitudes, they are not even able to remove from the eye a worm that gnaws it.

They lie in exterior darkness. For, remember, the fire of hell gives forth no light. As, at the command of God, the fire of the Babylonian furnace lost its heat but not its light, so, at the command of God, the fire of hell, while retaining the intensity of its heat, burns eternally in darkness. It is a never-ending storm of darkness, dark flames and dark smoke of burning brimstone, amid which the bodies are heaped one upon another, without even a glimpse of air. Of all the plagues with which the land of the Pharaohs were smitten one plague alone, that of darkness, was called horrible. What name, then, shall we give to the darkness of hell which is to last not for three days alone but for all eternity?

The horror of this strait and dark prison is increased by its awful stench. All the filth of the world, all the offal and scum of the world, we are told, shall run there as to a vast reeking sewer when the terrible conflagration of the last day has purged the world. The brimstone, too, which burns there in such prodigious quantity fills all hell with its intolerable stench; and the bodies of the damned themselves inhale such a pestilential odour that, as Saint Bonaventure says, one of them alone would suffice to infect the whole world. The very air of this world, that pure element, becomes foul and unbreathable when it has been long enclosed. Consider then what must be the foulness of the air of hell. Imagine some foul and putrid corpse that has lain rotting and decomposing in the grave, a jellylike mass of liquid corruption. Imagine such a corpse a prey to flames, devoured by the fire of burning brimstone and giving off dense choking fumes of nauseous loathsome decomposition. And then imagine this sickening stench, multiplied a millionfold and a millionfold again from the millions upon millions of fetid carcasses massed together in the reeking darkness, a huge and rotting human fungus. Imagine all this, and you will have some idea of the horror of the stench of hell.

But this stench is not, horrible though it is, the greatest physical torment to which the damned are subjected. The torment of fire is the greatest torment to which the tyrant has ever subjected his fellow-creatures. Place your finger for a moment in the flame of a candle and you will feel the pain of fire. But our earthly fire was created by God for the benefit of man, to maintain in him the spark of life and to help him in the useful arts, whereas the fire of hell is of another quality and was created by God to torture and punish the unrepentant sinner. Our earthly fire also consumes more or less rapidly according as the object which it attacks is more or less combustible, so that human ingenuity has even succeeded in inventing chemical preparations to check or frustrate its action. But the sulphurous brimstone which burns in hell is a substance which is specially designed to burn for ever and for ever with unspeakable fury.

Moreover, our earthly fire destroys at the same time as it burns, so that the more intense it is the shorter is its duration; but the fire of hell has this property, that it preserves that which it burns, and, though it rages with incredible intensity, it rages for ever.

Our earthly fire again, no matter how fierce or widespread it may be, is always of a limited extent; but the lake of fire in hell is boundless, shoreless and bottomless. It is on record that the devil himself, when asked the question by a certain soldier, was obliged to confess that if a whole mountain were thrown into the burning ocean of hell it would be burned up in an instant like a piece of wax. And this terrible fire would not afflict the bodies of the damned only from without, but each lost soul will be hell unto itself, the boundless fire raging in its very vitals. O how terrible is the lot of those wretched beings! The blood seethes and boils in the veins, the brains are boiling in the skull, the heart in the breast glowing and burning, the bowels a red-hot mass of burning pulp, the tender eyes flaming like molten balls.

And yet what I have said as to the strength and quality and boundlessness of this fire is as nothing when compared to its intensity, an intensity which it has as being the instrument chosen by divine design for the punishment of soul and body alike. It is a fire which proceeds directly from the ire of God, working not of its own activity but as an instrument of Divine vengeance. As the waters of baptism cleanse the soul with the body, so do the fires of punishment torture the spirit with the flesh. Every sense of the flesh is tortured and every faculty of the soul therewith: the eyes with impenetrable utter darkness, the nose with noisome odours, the ears with yells and howls and execrations, the taste with foul matter, leprous corruption, nameless suffocating filth, the touch with red-hot goads and spikes, with cruel tongues of flame. And through the several torments of the senses the immortal soul is tortured eternally in its very essence amid the leagues upon leagues of glowing fires kindled in the abyss by the offended majesty of the Omnipotent God and fanned into everlasting and ever increasing fury by the breath of the anger of the Godhead.

Consider finally that the torment of this infernal prison is increased by the company of the damned themselves. Evil company on earth is so noxious that the plants, as if by instinct, withdraw from the company of whatsoever is deadly or hurtful to them. In hell all laws are overturned—there is no thought of family or country, of ties, of relationships. The damned howl and scream at one another, their torture and rage intensified by the presence of beings tortured and raging like themselves. All sense of humanity is forgotten. The yells of the suffering sinners fill the remotest corners of the vast abyss. The mouths of the damned are full of blasphemies against God and of hatred for their fellow sufferers and of curses against those souls which were their accomplices in sin. In olden times it was the custom to punish the parricide, the man who had raised his murderous hand against his father, by casting him into the depths of the sea in a sack in which were placed a cock, a monkey and a serpent. The intention of those lawgivers who framed such a law, which seems cruel in our times, was to punish the criminal by the company of hurtful and hateful beasts. But what is the fury of those dumb beasts compared with the fury of execration which bursts from the parched lips and aching throats of the damned in hell when they behold in their companions in misery those who aided and abetted them in sin, those whose words sowed the first seeds of evil thinking and evil living in their minds, those whose immodest suggestions led them on to sin, those whose eyes tempted and allured them from the path of virtue. They turn upon those accomplices and upbraid them and curse them. But they are helpless and hopeless : it is too late now for repentance.

Last of all consider the frightful torment to those damned souls, tempters and tempted alike, of the company of the devils. These devils will afflict the damned in two ways, by their presence and by their reproaches. We can have no idea of how horrible these devils are. Saint Catherine of Siena once saw a devil and she has written that, rather than look again for one single instant on such a frightful monster, she would prefer to walk until the end of her life along a track of red coals. These devils, who were once beautiful angels, have become as hideous and ugly as they once were beautiful. They mock and jeer at the lost souls whom they dragged down to ruin. It is they, the foul demons, who are made in hell the voices of conscience. Why did you sin ? Why did you lend an ear to the temptings of friends ? Why did you turn aside from your pious practices and good works ? Why did you not shun the occasions of sin ? Why did you not leave that evil companion ? Why did you not give up that lewd habit, that impure habit ? Why did you not listen to the counsels of your confessor ? Why did you not, even after you had fallen the first or the second or the third or the fourth or the hundredth time, repent of your evil ways and turn to God who only waited for your repentance to absolve you of your sins ? Now the time for repentance has gone by. Time is, time was, but time shall be no more ! Time was sin in secrecy, to indulge in that sloth and pride, to covet the unlawful, to yield to the promptings of your lower nature, to live like the beasts of the field, nay worse than the beasts of the field, for they, at least, are but brutes and have not reason to guide them : time was, but time shall be no more. God spoke to you by so many voices, but you would not hear. You would not crush out that pride and anger in your heart, you would not restore those ill-gotten goods, you would not obey the precepts of your holy church nor attend to your religious duties, you would not abandon those wicked companions, you would not avoid those dangerous temptations. Such is the language of those fiendish tormentors, words of taunting and of reproach, and hatred and of disgust. Of disgust, yes ! For even they, the very devils, when they sinned, sinned by such a sin as alone was compatible with such angelical natures, a rebellion of the intellect ; and they, even they, the foul devils must turn away ; revolted and disgusted, from the contemplation of those unspeakable sins by which degraded man outrages and defiles the temple of the Holy Ghost, defiles and pollutes himself.

THE MAN WHO WAS MILLIGAN

By Algernon Blackwood

MILLIGAN looked round the dingy rooms with an appraising air, while the landlady stood behind him, wondering whether he would decide to take them. She stood with her arms crossed ; her eye was observant. She, in her turn, was appraising Milligan, of course. He was a clerk in a tourist agency, and in his spare time he wrote stories for the cinema. What attracted him just now in the very ordinary lodgings was the big folding-doors. All he really needed was a bed-sitting-room, with breakfast, but he suddenly saw himself sitting in that front room writing his scenarios—successfully at last. It was rather tempting. He would be a literary man—with a study !

"Your price seems a trifle high, Mrs.—er——?" he opened the bargain.

"Bostock, sir, Mrs. Bostock," she informed him, then recited her tale of woe about the high cost of living. It was unnecessary recitation, for Milligan was not listening, having already decided in his mind to take the rooms.

While Mrs. Bostock droned monotonously on, his eye fell casually upon a picture that hung above the plush mantelpiece—a Chinese scene showing a man in a boat upon a little lake. He glanced at it, no more than that. It was better than glancing at Mrs. Bostock. The landlady, however, instantly caught that glance and noticed its direction.

"Me 'usband"—she switched off her main theme—"brought it 'ome from China. From Hong-Kong, I *should* say." And the way she aspirated the "H" in Hong made Milligan smile. He perceived that she was proud of the picture evidently.

"It's wonderful," he said. "Probably it's worth something, too. These Chinese drawings—some of 'em—are very rare, I believe."

The little picture was worth perhaps two shillings, and he knew it; but he had found his way to Mrs. Bostock's heart, and, incidentally, had persuaded her to take a shilling off the rent. The picture, he felt sure, had been stolen by her late husband, a sea captain. To her it was a kind of nest-egg. If she ever found herself in difficulties, it would fetch money. Milligan, by chance, had stumbled upon what he called a "good line".

Being an honest creature, he had no wish to use his knowledge, but every week thereafter, almost every day, indeed, some remark concerning the Chinese drawing passed between them: with the natural result that, while it bored him a good deal, he cultivated the theme, and in so doing gazed much and often at the Chinaman. That Celestial, sitting in the boat with his back to the room, rowing, rowing, eternally across the placid lake without advancing, he came to know in every detail.

Every time Mrs. Bostock chatted with him, his eye wandered from her grimy visage to the drawing. He used it to end the chat with:

"I like your picture so much," he observed. "It's nice to live with." He put it straight, he flicked dust from the frame with his handkerchief. "It's so much better than these modern things. It's worth a bit—I dare say——"

It chanced, at the time, that Lafcadio Hearn, the writer about Japan, was in his mind. He had once arranged a successful trip to Japan for a client of his firm, and the client had made him a present of one of Hearn's strange and wonderful books. It was hardly in the line of Milligan's reading, for it had no "film value", and he had sold the book—a collection of Chinese stories—to a second-hand bookseller for a shilling. But he had glanced at it first, and a story in it had remained sharply in his mind; a story about a picture of a man in a boat. An observer, watching the picture, had seen the man move. The man actually began to row. Finally, the man rowed right out of the picture and into the place—a temple—where the observer stood.

Milligan thought it foolish, yet his memory retained the details vividly. They stuck in his head. The graphic description was realistic. Milligan caught himself thinking of it every time he met a Chinaman in the street, every time he sold a ticket to China or Japan. It rose, it flitted by, it vanished. The memory persisted. And the moment his eye first saw Mrs. Bostock's treasure over the plush mantelpiece, this vivid memory of Hearn's story had again risen, flitted by, and vanished. It betrayed its vitality, at any rate. Wonderful chap, that Hearn, thought Milligan.

All this was natural enough, without mystery, without a hint of anything queer or out of the ordinary. What was a little queer—it struck Milligan so, at any rate—was an idea that began to grow in him from the very first week of his tenancy.

"That *might* be the very drawing the fellow wrote about," occurred to him one night as he laboured at a lurid scenario which was to make his fortune.

"Not impossible at all. It's an old picture probably. Exactly what Hearn described, too. I wonder! Why not?"

Why not, indeed? A fellow—especially a literary fellow—should use his imagination. Milligan used his. Sometimes he used it in prolonged labour till the early hours. The gas-light flickered across his pages, across that lake in China, across the boat, across the back and arms and pigtail of that diminutive Chink who rowed eternally over a placid Chinese lake without advancing an inch. The scenario of the moment brought in China, aptly enough. A glance at the picture, he found, was not unhelpful in the way of stimulating a flagging imagination.

Milligan glanced often. The gas-light was always flickering. Shadows were for ever shifting to and fro across Mrs. Bostock's worthless nest-egg. It was easy to imagine that the boat, the water, even the figure moved. Those dancing shadows! How they played about the arms, the back, the outline of the boat, the oars!

And when it was two in the morning, and the London streets lay hushed, and a great stillness blanketed the whole city, Milligan felt even a little thrilled. It was, he thought, "imaginative", to catch these slight, elusive movements in the drawing. He imagined the fellow rowing about, changing his position, landing. It helped his own mood, his incidents, his atmosphere. He had read Thomas Burke, of course. His scenarios always referred to Chinamen as "Chinks".

"That Chink's alive!" he whispered to himself. "By Jove! He moves in the picture. His place changes. It's an inspiration. I must use it somehow——!" And imagination, eerily stimulated in the deep silence of the sleeping city, was at work again.

This was the beginning of the strange adventure which befell the literary Milligan, whose imagination worked in the stillness of the small hours, but whose scenarios were never used.

"For why write scenarios," he said to me, "when you can *live* them?"

In Peking, ten or twelve years later, he said this to me, and I am probably the only person to whom this scenario he "lived" was ever confided.

In Peking his name was not Milligan at all. He was not working in a tourist agency. He was a rich man, aged thirty-eight, a "figure" in the English community there, a man of influence and position. But all that does not matter. What matters is the story of how he came to be in China at all—and this he does not know. He does not know how he came to be in China at all. There is no recollection of the journey even. Nor can he state precisely how he began the speculations and enterprises that made him prosperous, beyond that he suddenly found himself concerned in big, fortunate undertakings in the Chinese city.

There is this deep gap in the years.

"Loss of memory, I suppose they call it," he mentioned, after our chance acquaintanceship had grown into a friendship that gave me his confidence. What he *could* tell he told me frankly and without reserve, glad to talk of it, I think, to someone who did not mock, and making no condition of secrecy, moreover.

There was some link, apparently, between myself and the man who had been Milligan. Chance, that some call destiny, revealed it. And, as I listened to his amazing tale, I swore that on my return to London I would visit Mrs. Bostock and buy the picture. I wanted that Chinese drawing badly. wanted to examine it myself. Her nest-egg at last should be worth something, as Milligan, ten years before, had told her.

What happened was, apparently, as follows: Milligan, first of all, discovered in himself, somewhat suddenly it seemed, a new interest in China and things Chinese. If the birth of this interest was abrupt, its growth was extremely rapid.

China fairly leapt at him. He read books, talked with travellers, studied the map, the history, the civilization of China. The psychology of the Celestial race absorbed him. The subject obsessed him. He longed to go to China. It became a yearning that left him no peace day or night. In practical terms of time, money and opportunity the journey was, of course, impossible. He lived on in London, but actually he lived already in China, for where a man's thought is there shall his consciousness be also.

All this I could readily understand, for others, similarly, have felt the call and spell of countries like Egypt, Africa, the desert. There was nothing incomprehensible nor peculiar in the fascination China exercised upon the imaginative Milligan. It was his business, moreover, to sell exciting tickets to travellers, and China happened to have fired his particular temperament. Natural enough!

Natural enough, too, that, through this, the picture in his lodgings should have acquired more meaning for him, and that he should have studied it more closely and more frequently. It was the only Chinese object he had within constant reach, and he told me at wearisome length how he knew every tiniest detail of the drawing, and how it became for him a kind of symbol, almost a kind of sacred symbol, upon which he focused his intense desires—frustrated desires. Wearisome, yes, until he reached a point in his story that suddenly galvanized my interest, so that I began to listen with uncommon, if a rather creepy, curiosity.

The picture, he informed me, altered. There was movement among its details that he already knew by heart.

"*Movement!*" he half-whispered to me, his eyes shining, a faint shudder running through his big body.

The sincerity of deep conviction with which he described what happened left a lasting impression on my mind. His words, his manner, conveyed the truth of a genuine experience. Hitherto only the back of the Chink's head had been visible. Then, one night, Milligan saw his profile. The face was turned. It now looked a little over the shoulder, and towards the room.

From this moment, though he never detected actual movement when it occurred, the alteration in the drawing was marked and rapid. The face retained its new position; the angle of the profile did not widen, but the position of oars and boat, the attitude of arms and back, their size as well, these now changed from day to day.

There was a dreadful rapidity about these changes. The figure of the Chink grew bigger; the boat grew bigger, too. They were coming nearer. "I had the awful conviction," whispered the man who had been Milligan, "that they were coming—to fetch me. I used to get all of a sweat each time I saw the size and nearness grow. It was appalling, but also it was delightful somehow——"

I permitted myself a question: "Did your landlady notice it, too?" I inquired, concealing my scepticism.

"Mrs. Bostock was ill in bed the whole time. She never came into the room once."

"The servant?" I persisted. "Or any of your friends?"

He hesitated. "The girl who did the room," he said honestly, "observed nothing. She gave notice suddenly without a reason. So did the next girl. I never asked them anything. As for my friends"—he smiled faintly—"I was too scared—to bring them in."

"You were afraid they might *not* see what you saw?"

He shrugged his shoulders. "It scared me," he repeated, looking past me towards the shuttered windows of his study where we sat.

The account he gave of it all made my flesh creep even in that bright Peking sunshine. He certainly described what he saw, or believed he saw, as, day after day, night after night, that Chink rowed his boat slowly, slowly, surely, surely, very gradually, but with remorseless purpose, nearer, nearer—and nearer. The lodger watched. He also waited.

"The man," he whispered, "was rowing into the room. It was his purpose to row into the room. He was *coming to fetch me*." And he mopped his forehead at the thought of what had happened ten years ago.

Suddenly he leant forward.

"In the end," his thin voice rattled almost against my face, "he—did fetch me. I'm in that picture with him now. I'm not in China, as *you* think I am. This"—he tapped his chest, the chest of a successful business man—"is not me. I'm not Milligan. Milligan is in that picture with the Chink. He's in that boat. Sitting beside that Chink. Motionless. Being stared at by a succession of lodgers. Sitting in that stiff little boat. Very tiny. Not dead, but captive. Sitting without breath. Without feeling. Painted, yet alive. Caught on the surface of that placid Chinese lake until time or death dissolve the drawing——"

I thought he was going to faint, but, oddly enough, I did *not* think him merely mad. His mood, his crawling horror, his intense sincerity took me bodily into his own deep nightmare. He recovered quickly. He was a man who had himself always well in hand. He told me the end at once.

He had been to a dance and he came home tired, sober, having well enjoyed himself, it seems; about four in the morning. The time was early spring, and dawn was just giving faint signs of breaking, but the hall and passage of the house were still dark.

He entered his room and lit the gas, going at once to the mirror to have a look at himself. This was the first thing he did, he assured me, and in the mirror he saw, behind himself, the boat and the Chinaman, both of them—gigantic.

Gigantic was the word he used, though he used it, of course, relatively. The Chinaman was standing in the room. He was in the lake in front of the plush mantelpiece. The wall was gone—there was a sort of hazy space. Close at the Chinaman's heels lay the boat, both oars resting sideways on the water, their heads still in the rowlocks. Water was up to his feet, to Milligan's feet, for he not only felt his shoes soaked through, but he also heard the lapping sound of diminutive wavelets on the "shore".

He gave a great sigh. No cry, either of terror or surprise, he said, escaped him. His only sound was this great sigh—of acceptance, of resignation, of a mind benumbed and yet secretly delighted. The big Chink beckoned, smiled, nodded his yellow face, retreating very slowly as he did so. And Milligan obeyed. He followed. He stepped into the boat. The Chink took up the oars, and rowed him slowly, very slowly, across the placid lake, into the picture and out of his familiar, known surroundings, rowed him slowly, very slowly, into the land of his heart's deep desire.

. . . . . .

All the way home to England in the steamer this strangest of strange narratives haunted me. I still saw the man who was Milligan sitting in the study of his big, expensive house as he told it to me. His shrewd business brain had built that house; the fortune he had made provided the good lunch and cigars we had enjoyed together. From the moment of entering the boat his memory had remained a blank. Continuity of personality though still, it seemed to me, rather uncertain somewhere, had revived only when he was already a rich man who had spent years in China. This big gap in the years remains.

In my mind lay every detail of the story; in my pocket-book lay the address of Mrs. Bostock's rooms. I prayed heaven she might still be living, even if aged and crumpled by ten more English winters.

I had arranged to cable "Milligan" at once; we had selected the very words I was to use: "Two figures in boat", or "One figure in boat". He asked for the message in these words. Fortune favoured me; I found the rooms; Mrs. Bostock was alive; the rooms were unoccupied; I looked over them; I saw—the picture.

Before visiting Mrs. Bostock, however, I had visited the newspaper files in the British Museum, and the "Disappearance of James Milligan" was there for all to read. Millions had evidently read it. It had been *the* news of the day. Columns of space were devoted to it; dozens of false clues were started; crime was suggested, of course. His disappearance was complete. Milligan was a case of "sunk without trace", with a vengeance.

It was in the dingy front room that I experienced what was perhaps the most vivid thrill of wonder life has ever given me. I stood, appraising the room as a would-be lodger. Behind me, her arms crossed, appraising me in turn just as she had appraised her former lodger of ten years ago, stood Mrs. Bostock. Probably I looked more prosperous than he had looked; her attitude, at any rate, was attentive to a fault. Why I should have trembled a little is hard to say, but self-control was certainly not as full as it might have been, for my voice shook a trifle as, at length, I drew her attention with calculated purpose to the picture above the plush mantelpiece. I praised it.

"Me 'usband brought it back from Hong-Kong," I heard her say.

My breath caught a little, so that there was a slight pause before I said the next thing. My voice went slightly husky.

"I have a collection of Chinese drawings," I mentioned. "If you cared to sell, perhaps——"

"Oh, many 'as wanted to buy it," she lied easily, hoping to increase its value.

I mentioned five pounds. I mentioned another figure, too—the figure in the boat.

"That single figure," I explained in as calm a tone as I could muster, "is so good, you see. The Chinese artists never overcrowded their paintings. Now, if—instead of that single figure—there were two"—I moved closer to the picture, hoping she would follow—"the value," I went on, "would, of course, be less."

Mrs. Bostock had followed me. I had tempted her greed; I had tested her truth as well. We stood side by side immediately beneath the drawing. We examined it together.

At the mention of five pounds the woman had given a little gasp, jerking her body at the same time. Now, at such close quarters with the thing she hoped to sell me, her voice was dumb at first. At first. For a moment later a strange sound escaped her lips, a sound that was meant to be a cry, but only succeeded in being a wheezy struggle to get her breath. Her mouth opened wide, her eyes popped almost from her face. She staggered, recovered her balance by putting a hand on my arm for support, then stepped still nearer to the mantelpiece and thrust her head and shoulders close against the drawing. Her blind eyes peered. Her skin was already white.

"Two of 'em!" she exclaimed in a terrified whisper. "Two of 'em, so 'elp me, Gawd! And the other's *him*!"

I was ready to support. I had expected her to collapse perhaps. I felt rather like collapsing myself. She swayed, turning her horror-stricken countenance to mine.

"Mr. Milligan!" she screamed aloud, then, her voice returning in full volume: "It's Mr. Milligan. All this time that's where 'e's been. And I never noticed if till now!"

She swooned away.

The second figure faced the room, for the boat was in the position of being pushed by the oars, not rowed. The features were unmistakable. . . . Half an hour later I sent a cable to Peking: *Two figures in boat.*

The real climax, I think, came three days later, when, with the picture safely in my rooms, I had arranged for "specialists" to call and examine it. A chemist, an experienced dealer, and a sort of expert psychic investigator were already upstairs when I reached my flat.

The picture was in my bedroom. I had examined it myself—examined Milligan's face and figure—hour after hour, my flesh crawling, my hair almost rising as I did so. My guests were in the sitting-room, the servant informed me, handing me a telegram as I hurried up in the lift. My three friends were already known to each other, and, after apologizing for the delay, I brought in the drawing and laid it before them on the small table. I intended to tell them the story after their examination, the psychic investigator I meant to keep when the other two had left. Setting the drawing in front of them, I looked over their shoulders at it.

There was only one figure—the Chink. He sat alone in the little boat. He was rowing, not pushing; his back was to the room.

The dealer said the drawing was worth a shilling; the chemist said nothing; I, too, said nothing; but the psychic investigator turned sharply and complained that I was hurting him. My hand, it seems, had clutched the shoulder nearest to me, and it happened to be his. I allowed him to leave when the other two left. . . .

I was alone. I remembered the telegram. More to steady my mind than for any interest I felt in it, my fingers tore it open. It was a cablegram from—Peking, signed by a friend of Milligan and myself:

Milligan died heart failure yesterday.

THE STRANGER

By Richard Hughes

THE street in Cylfant was so steep that if you took a middling jump from the top of the village you would not touch ground again till you reached the bottom: but you would probably hurt yourself. The houses sat on each other's left shoulder, all the way up, so that the smoke from Mrs. Grocery-Jones' chimney blew in at Mrs. Boot-Jones' basement, and out through her top windows into the cellar of the Post Office, and out through the Post Office Daughter's little bedroom casement into that of the Butchery Aunt (who was paralysed and lived downstairs): and so on, up the whole line like a flue, till it left soot on the stomachs of the sheep grazing on the hill-side above.

But that does not explain why the Stranger came to Cylfant village, unless it was through curiosity: nor, indeed, what he was doing in such a Sabbath-keeping little anabaptist hamlet at all, where he might have known he would meet with an accident: nor what he was doing so far from home.

Mr. Williams was the rector of Cylfant, and perhaps thirty miles round: such an old fat man that he had difficulty in walking between his different churches on Sundays. His face was heavy, his eyes small but with a dream in them, and he kept sticky sweet things ready in his pocket. He was stone-deaf, so that now he roared like a bull, now whispered like a young lover. He might be heard roaring across a valley. He had one black suit, with patches on it; and one surplice, that he darned sometimes. He lived by letting the rectory in the summer: and when the Disestablishment Bill wiped away his stipend of eight pounds, he made up for it by taking in washing: you would see him in front of the rectory, legs set well apart, both heavy arms plunged up to the elbows in suds, a towel pinned to each shoulder to save his black coat, roaring a greeting to all who might pass.

Cylfant was very proud of the smallness of his congregation: for in Wales to have many church-people in a village is a great disgrace. They are always the scallywags, the folk who have been expelled from their chapels; and who hope, even if they cannot expect heaven, that things will not be quite so uncomfortable for them in the next world as if they gave up religion altogether. There were only three families, except for the Squire's governess, that ever came to Cylfant church. Mr. Williams hated verse, but he preached them pure poetry: he had such an imagination that if he meditated on the anatomy of angels there seemed to be strange flying things about his head; and the passionate roaring and whispering of his voice could hang Christ even on the polished brass altar-cross.

Presently he married the girl who played the harmonium: but she had one leg.

It was she, Minnie, that took in the Stranger. They were sitting one night in the rectory parlour, and Mr. Williams was reading a book of sermons with great fixity of mind, in order to forget his Loss: for that day the little ring on his watch-chain had opened, and he had lost the gold cross that he had always carried. Minnie was sure that it had been there when they started to climb the village: but they had no lantern: the wind was a fleet howling darkness, so they could not search till the morning, even if it lay on their very doorstep. Mr. Williams read three sermons at a gulp, and closed the book. It was always a thing of amazement that a man who read such dull sermons with such avidity could put so much thrill and beauty, so little of the moralities, into his own preaching.

He shut the book, and, giving a great sigh, puffed out his cheeks, while he squinted along the broad shirt-front under his chin. Minnie went to turn down the lamp—as she always did, for reasons of thrift, when her husband was not actually reading; and all at once she heard a cry in the night, sharp as a child's, and full of terror and innocence. She opened the door, and saw a small huddled figure in the roadway. There was a little light shining from it, bluish and fitful: and she knew at once it was something more than natural. She set her wooden leg firmly against the doorstep, and, bending down, caught the Stranger up in her arms, and lifted him over the threshold. He lay there, blinking in the lamplight: a grotesque thing, with misshapen ears and a broad, flat nose. His limbs were knotted, but the skin at his joints was yellow and delicate as a snake's belly. He had crumpled wings, as fine as petrol upon water: even thus battered, their beauty could not but be seen. He seemed in pain: and there was a small cross-shaped weal burnt on his side, as if he had stumbled on a little red-hot iron.

"Poor little thing," said Mr. Williams, looking at it sideways from his chair. "What is it?"

"It is more ugly than anything I have ever seen," said Minnie. "Perhaps it is an angel: for it was never born of woman."

"We should be more humble, Minnie," said her husband. "Who are we that God should send His angels to try us?"

"At any rate, I think it is not," said Minnie. "We will see."

She took up the book of sermons, and touched him on the forehead with it. He gave a shrill yell of pain.

"God forgive me for my cruelty," she exclaimed. "It must be a——"

"It is a Stranger," said Mr. Williams quickly.

Minnie turned and looked at him.

"What shall we do?" she shouted in his ear. "For if we harbour it we shall surely be damned. We must not help God's enemies."

"We are taught to love our enemies," whispered Mr. Williams. "And who is God's enemy is ours, too."

"But it can feel no gratitude," said Minnie. "It will return us evil for good."

"If we do good in the hope of gratitude we have our reward," roared Mr. Williams.

"You mean you will keep him?" said Minnie.

"I mean"—the old man groaned—"I do not know what to do, indeed, whatever."

But the visitor settled that question for them himself. He crawled over to the fireplace, and sitting himself on one of the reddest coals, smiled out at them with a grin that stretched from ear to ear.

* * *

That was how the little devil came to Cylfant rectory. He had great natural charm, and when the cross-shaped weal on his side was better—for it healed quickly under the action of fire—his spirits returned to him. One was led to forget the grotesque beauty of his form by the generous amiability of his expression. He took to the old rector at once; and Mr. Williams himself could not but feel a secret liking for him. That night he followed them up to bed: Mr. Williams had to shut and lock the bedroom door on him. But hardly were they inside when they saw a bluish light on the panel: and presently the little devil was sitting perched upon the bed-rail, watching with a sober interest Minnie unstrap her wooden leg: and even when she said her prayers—which she did in a shamefast fashion, for fear of giving him pain—he showed no embarrassment whatever. When they were both fast asleep, he took down Minnie's old peg from the shelf where she had laid it, and did something to it in the corner. He then lay down in a pool of moonlight, and was still sleeping soundly when the rector heaved himself out of bed in the morning. The old man woke Minnie, who scrambled out of bed, and began to strap on her leg preparatory to getting the breakfast: but a wonderful thing happened, for no sooner had she fitted her scarred stump into the leather socket than the leather changed to flesh, and the wood to flesh, and there she was with the most elegant and seductive leg that ever troubled a man's eye: and, moreover, there was a silk stocking on it, and a high-heeled Paris shoe on it, before she could recover from her surprise. As she drew on her old ringed black-and-white cotton oddment over the other stocky red ankle she thought that never had such a pair of legs been seen together on one body. She looked round in a guilty fashion: but her husband was balanced in front of the looking-glass shaving himself. He had not seen. She pulled on her dress all in a hurry and danced away downstairs. She let up the blinds and swept the floor; and all the time her new leg behaved as well as if she had known it all her life: but directly she flung open the front door to shake the mat, it began all at once to drag, and jib: she got pins and needles in it: it jumped and kicked like a thing quite out of control. And she saw the reason: for there in the roadway, where she had found the Stranger the night before, was the rector's gold cross.

"There is no mistaking," said Minnie to herself, "where *that* leg came from."

And, indeed, there was not. She sidled up to the cross with difficulty, and recovered it: and all at once heard steps on the cobbles. It was Scraggy Evan, the postman. Minnie's first thought was to hide the leg, for it would take some explaining away. But it would not be hidden: the shameless thing thrust the delicate turn of its ankle right under Scraggy Evan's nose. Scraggy's cheery "bore da!" was lost in a gasp, and poor Minnie fled into the house scarlet with shame, the damnable leg giving coquettish little kicks into the air as she went.

What Scraggy told the village we can only guess: but he must have told them something, or why should Mrs. Williams have received so many callers that morning? The first came when breakfast was hardly over: and the Stranger was sitting quietly on the hob picking his teeth with his tail. Minnie had great presence of mind. She ran to her work-box, and taking from it a red-flannel petticoat that she had been mending, wrapped the Stranger in it and crammed him quickly into a wooden box, begging him in a staccato whisper to lie still. Upon the face of Mr. Williams there was a look of much courage and resignation. Devil or no, he was prepared to justify his guest to all comers. Minnie opened the door, and Mrs. Grocery-Jones stood there.

"Good morning," said she. "I was calling to ask if you are driving over to Ynysllanbedrbachdeudraethgerylan today."

She paused and sniffed; then sniffed again.

There was no doubt of it: somewhere sulphur was burning.

"We are not," said Minnie. "We are too busy here, indeed, with the plaguey wasps. Mr. Williams has hardly smoked out one nest, but bad are they as they were before, indeed."

Mrs. Jones gave a gasp of surprise.

"Wasps in the winter-time?" she said.

"I did not say *wasps*," said Minnie, "I said the *wall-paper*, which the doctor thinks may have the scarlet-fever lurking in it, so have we fumigated the whole house."

It was lucky, thought Minnie, that her husband was so deaf. He would never have forgiven her.

"Well, good gracious!" said Mrs. Jones. As her eyes got used to the dim light she caught sight of a broad head with two beady yellow eyes, peering at her from a soap-box. "And is that a cat you have there, Mrs. Williams?"

"It is a *pig*!" she cried with sudden heat; for her new leg showed an obvious desire to kick Mrs. Jones out of the house. "It has the wind," she explained, "so we thought it would be best in the house, indeed."

"Well, good gracious me!" repeated Mrs. Jones.

Minnie's leg was quivering, but she managed to control it. Mrs. Jones was staring past her at the pig, as if she could not take her eyes off it. As, indeed, she could not: for suddenly she shot half across the road, backwards, with the force of a bullet: and when released she scrambled down the street, as she herself explained it, "as if the devil was after me": and there was the Stranger, wrapped still in the red-flannel petticoat, sitting on the window-sill and grinning amiably at her back.

. . . . .

If Mr. Williams had lived longer, a few curious things might have happened in Cylfant village: but he did not. There was a buzzing feeling in his head all that day, and when he went to bed at night he lay quietly on his back staring at the ceiling. It had turned a bright green. Presently, with his eyes open still, he began to snore. Minnie did not notice anything queer; and in the small hours of the morning, after two or three loud snorts, he stopped altogether.

When he felt better, he found that his soul was outside his body. It was not at all the kind of thing he had expected it to be, but was fairly round, and made of some stuff like white of egg. He gathered it gently into his arms, and began to float about: his body had disappeared. Presently he was aware that the Stranger was still watching him.

"You'll be damned for this: double-damned even, for giving place to the devil—and you a priest." He sighed. "It is so hard," he went on seriously, "even for devils to conquer their better nature. Oh, I *try* hard enough. I surely try. The seeds of goodness have lurked in us ever since the Fall: try as we will, they *sprout*.

"With a fork drive Nature out,
She will ever yet return."

"Temptation is always lurking ready for us: it is a long and a hard fight: the Forces of Evil against the Forces of Good. But we shall conquer in the end:

with Wrong on our side, we *must* conquer." There was an elation in his face that transcended all earthly ugliness. "At last," he went on, "I have done a really immoral act : an act with no trace of good in it, either in motive or effect. You will be damned, and Minnie will be damned too, even if she has to hop to hell on the leg I gave her. But it was hard, hard."

Old Williams floated over on to the other side.

"I am a sinful man," he said; "a very sinful man. Heaven was never my deserts, whatever."

The devil looked at him in surprise.

"Oh, you were not!" he said earnestly. "Indeed, you were not! You were the truest——"

He stopped suddenly. Williams was aware of the presence of some very unpleasant personality. He looked round: and behind him stood a tall figure with thin, tight lips and watery eyes, who began speaking at once—rapidly, as if by rote.

"As a matter of form," said he, "I claim this soul."

"As a matter of form," replied the devil in a sing-song voice, "he is mine."

The angel rapped out : "*De qua causa ?*"

"*De diabolo consortando*," chaunted the little devil, in even worse Latin.

"*Quae sit evidentia ?*"

"*Tuos voco oculos ipsos.*"

"*Quod vidi, vero, atque affirmo—Satis*," continued the angel. "*Tuumst.*" And he turned to go.

"Stop!" cried the Stranger suddenly, all his bad resolutions breaking down.

"Stop!" he cried, and began speaking rapidly. "I'm a backslider, I know, but the strain is too much: there's no true devilry in me. Take him: take him: there never was better Christian in Wales, I swear it: and to that alone his damnation is due : pure charity——"

"What are you talking about ?" snapped the angel petulantly. "The case is settled : I have withdrawn my claim."

"So do I!" cried the devil excitedly. "I withdraw mine."

The angel shrugged his wings.

"What's the use of making a scene ?" he said. "Never, in all my office, have I known a fiend break down and forget himself like this before. You are making an exhibition of yourself, sir! Besides, if we both withdraw, he can't go anywhere. It's none of my business."

He shrugged his wings and soared away.

"*Heaven or Hell or the Land of Whipperginny*," murmured Williams to himself, vague memories of Nashe rising to the surface of his astonishment. Together they watched the angel's purple pinions bearing him from sight: the Stranger cocked a snook at his straight back.

"Where now ?" asked the rector.

"Where now ? Heaven! Wait till he's out of sight."

He turned and winked broadly at Williams, making a motion on his bare shanks as if to thrust his hand in a pocket.

"You come with me," he said. "I know how I can get things fixed for you!"

CHANGELING

By Dorothy K. Haynes

THE witch had been sitting on the gargoyle all day. Moreen had watched, saying nothing, while mother combed her hair and tied the ribbon and said, "There! Now stand quiet at the window till Mummy gets ready." She had kept quite still, crushing flies under the curtain, and sometimes looking at the people in the street; but always she looked again at the gargoyle, where the witch sat drowsing, with her hair like nettle blossom, and her shoulders hunched high like wings.

"What are you always looking at?" said her mother, abstract in a haze of face powder and two kinds of perfume.

"That gargoyle," said Moreen, and her voice caught with a sound like a sob. "Isn't it funny?"

Her mother went over. "Oh, that one? Can you see its face from here, darling? Your eyes must be better than mine. I'll borrow daddy's opera-glasses and look some time."

Moreen knew that there was something queer about her. Her mother had never mentioned the witch, and yet there it was, a black hump arching out into the sky. And it was nonsense not to be able to see the gargoyle's face. It was grinning, with whiskers parallel to the wide lips. It had a face like a door-knocker, and round ears. The witch was even clearer. Moreen knew that the eyes were looking at her, even though they were shut, and that the hands were green as verdigris and crippled with warts. Moreen did not like the thought of the witch being feminine. You could not think of it. Undressing a witch, there would be nothing under the black clothes, nothing but a broom-stick and a short stalk for the head to go on.

In the afternoon, at tea in Mrs. Black's house, she sometimes forgot. There was a bronze canopy over the fire, and it was nice to see the fire, even though it was too warm. The carpet at Mrs. Black's was fawn, and everything else was fawn and new, and not used very much. Mrs. Black had only been in her bungalow a little while. The bungalow was different from Moreen's house, new and uncracked, but not nearly so solid.

Biting her chocolate biscuit at tea, or whispering to her mother and being led to the bathroom, Moreen had quick, sickening memories of what might be waiting on top of the gargoyle when she saw it again, but she put the thought away from her. At five o'clock, Mrs. Black said good-bye to them at the gate. After the quiet of the new road, with its villas and rockeries, the High Street was Bedlam, with red buses and red freestone houses, and the sun soon to be red with setting. Moreen looked up at the church clock. "Half past five," she said, but what she wanted to say was, "Oh, Mother, the witch is still there!" Her mother could not see the witch. She had shifted a little, but was still asleep, like a lump of black carrion festering on a rock.

Moreen wanted her mother to sit with her at bedtime. She looked so feverish that she got her own way. Mother spoke about sending for the doctor. "I don't like it," she kept saying. "Can't you tell Mummy what's wrong? Is your head aching? Your eyes are far too bright, dear." At last sleep came, breathing in from the open window in dark sighs. The child looked very young and babyish. The woman put the night-light on the table and stood still, watching the dull orange tongue lapping up the gloom. Ten o'clock. Moreen should have been asleep hours ago. One had to be firm with children. The woman yawned. Ten o'clock.

The moon was a thin rind curled low in the sky. The spire was squint on the church, and all the houses were leaning backwards. The lighted windows were at all angles, like red postage stamps. Smoke went sideways, a dim, black flag in the night.

"I'm seeing things, as if my eyes were crossed," thought Moreen. The bare cliff of the steeple shot out the gargoyle like a dangerous ledge. There was no witch, nothing but space, and a sky the deep colour of bluebells. But below the window came a scrabbling, like knives scratching along a plate, and a green hand like verdigris clutched at the sill. It was a palsied hand, crippled with warts, but it clung with nail and sinew, and raised the witch's head over the sill.

Moreen choked into a little whimper, because the witch's eyes were open now and looking at her.

"I'm old," said the witch, getting her knee over the sill. "I'm nearly done. I had to climb that last bit."

"Yes," said Moreen, but she wanted to scream for her mother.

The wind clutched the candlewick and tweaked off the waving tongue. "You were watching me," said the witch. "You looked up at me at half past five."

"Yes," said Moreen. Her hands and feet were cold under the covers.

"I've come for you," said the witch. "I don't want to frighten you. It's not me that wants you, it's the little people."

"No. I don't want to go! I'll scream!" The witch was horrible with the many horrors of the old, the shawlies who swear at closes and smell of gin, the cretins who gape and do not understand, and the fusty poor who never wash. "I'll scream for my mother, and she'll push you out into the street, you nasty old pig!"

The witch stepped back and did not fall. Solid pillars of air held her level in space. "You'll have to come," she said. "Your mother can't help. I thought all little girls wanted to go to fairyland!"

"I want my mother!"

"Your mother won't wake till morning."

"I don't want to go!"

"No, dearie, and the changeling they've put in your little bed doesn't want to come here, either. She'll have to, though, like it or not. Your mother won't know the difference, but she won't love her the same. It's not me that says it has to be, it's the little people."

"I want my mother. Go *away*, you dirty witch! I don't like you!"

"It's not my fault. See, the changeling's there already. She doesn't want to come here, but she's taking it better than you."

There was a head on the pillow, a strange, fair head like her own reflection. She hated it. The face smiled from the frills, pale and stupid, the kind of face that always did as it was told. A heavy body was beside her bed, seeming to sweat, suety. There was no room for her. She edged away, and the cold blue linoleum pressed her bare feet. The window swung towards her; the floor dropped away. The moon, curled low in the sky, dangled over the chequered tiles, and all the dogs in the street seemed to be howling. She screamed, "Mother, Mother, I don't want to go! Oh, Mother!" But the witch was the person who caught her hand. "All right, dearie, I'm rested now. I won't let you fall. You won't need to see me again, unless you want to, after we get to the little people."

She screamed. Nobody listened.

.   .   .   .   .

She had resisted the witch? "Yes," she said. They did not scold her, but she felt afraid of the way they talked. She hated the little people, sharp as thorns and shrill as treble chanters. She was afraid when they said she would forget. "I don't want to forget!" she screamed. "I want my mother! I want my mother!" She was very brave for seven years old, but she was afraid.

"You will forget your mother!" they said, chirping and dancing round about, and clapping their hands on the soles of their feet. "You will forget your mother! You'll forget yourself, you'll forget your house, you'll forget everything! You'll forget everything. But you'll always try to remember, and never quite find out what you want to remember. Serves you right!"

They were cruel and slight, nipping her on the arms out of curiosity. "Why does it serve me right?" she sobbed. "I want to go home! I haven't done any harm. I didn't want to come here! It was the witch brought me."

"We went for you, and you struggled with the witch! You struggled! You should have come when you were told!"

"I didn't want to. I didn't want to leave my mother."

"You'll forget your mother! You'll forget everything, but you'll never stop trying to remember. Serves you right!" They were hostile, these dark little red and brown people, hostile, and far too old for her. The youngest had age written on their faces; the oldest were spry and dreadful. They resented her, resented her youth and her strangeness, and the way she did not want to stay. They tormented her in little stabs of spite. She wept, and they gathered round in squeaking wonder. None of them understood how much she wanted her mother; none of them liked her.

She forgot. She forgot about everything. She sat beside a lake, thinking of summer, and the work they had made her do. She had had heavy labour among the spiked petals and the drugging scent of flowers and she had had unpleasant tasks with bees, whose legs were clogged and clarted with pollen. It was a lifeless, hot summer, a season in a sealed sphere of glass. Beyond the glass was something she could not call to mind, and round the sphere mist was quiet and thick. She lived in a land of twilight, of low stars and dim, green woods. Everything was low. Sometimes she felt as if the sky was no higher than a ceiling.

Once the sphere had cracked and the mist had thinned. It had been on the brightest day of summer, when the sky was the colour of stone and the sun a dull lamp burning in one corner. The sky gradually turned white. She heard a shaking rumble and a pounding, regular thud which jarred her body. Shadows sketched lightly on the mist pall, moving large like ferns magnified to fir trees. Something flickered. She was in a green-and-yellow landscape, with strong white light glaring on grass. Pink flowers stared at her from a bush, laughing above a collar of green leaves and thorns. She was choking as thoughts rushed over her like water.

The rumbling and pounding passed. A huge animal with a cart had gone by; its shadow inked over the view, and for a moment, very dimly, superimposed on the air and the ground, she could see the lake and the wee people scurrying along, all unconscious. They were frail and transparent, and vanished again as the sun shone on them. She did not know which world was real.

Dog roses and vetch bloomed bright among the green, and the road smelt of nettles and cow-dung and honeysuckle. These were strange things to her, but safe and comforting. She wanted to sob. She was very near to what she wanted to remember. Then a little boy in blue trousers tumbled through the hedge, stared at her, and said, "Ooh!" His fat hand, with black-rimmed nails, bulged above her in fleshy pillows, his fingers cut the light into four sections. The light strips grew narrower as the sound of the cart faded into flat air. It seemed as if the sky was closing with his fingers. She was sitting by the lake, with the waves like grey syrup under the mist, and the sun sinking into the crawl of the tide, to sizzle like a black ember.

· · · ·

It was autumn. Yellow leaves soaked sodden into the lake, and rain and frost raced each other over the brilliant berries. She would not work. She felt sick when she moved from the lake, and her head was a hollow iron ball, with words rolling round and knocking into each other. What the words were she did not know. She sat by the lake and poked her fingers between the pebbles, waiting for the mist to break again. The little pixie things were angry with her because she sat and dreamed all day. They grumbled. She watched them frisking and cheeping as they worked, and turned her back on them till they were tired of her sulking, and then they tried to be kind. They had wanted her to come to them, and during the long winter she would have to play with them. She would have to. Sad or dull, she would have to sing and play and be lively.

"The harvest's in!" they screamed, when the wind crisped and freshened over the gathered grain. "The harvest's in, and you never helped us! You never helped! If you were afraid of work, it's all done now, and all we have to do in winter is to have fun. Oh, we'll have jolly fun, when the snow comes! There won't be any flowers left, but we'll hang icicles on the branches, and sweep the snow away from under the trees, and dance mad on the bare ground. Dance like this, like this, like this!" They stamped about in front of her, clapping their hands on the soles of their feet. She turned away from them. "I don't want to dance! I want——" She had nearly said it that time, the words that were knocking in her head. "What—what do you want?" piped the little people, tweaking their fingers at her, deeving her. "Oh, I hate it here! I *hate* it!" she sobbed, and they all ran away.

She went with them into the forest, the dark forest where they danced. It was blue midnight, but the frost shone white. They swept up the hoar with twigs and bristles, and danced to the snap of dry branches, clapping their hands on the soles of their feet. They danced fast and jerky, and the Northern Lights swept fans and floods of mauve and crimson above the pines. Everything outside the dance was silent, except when a fir cone trembled and dropped, or the lush firs lifted bloomy layers and sighed. They dragged her into the circle and spun her round. She felt cold. Her feet went heavy with desire for rest, and she tripped clumsily. They pushed her on and on; she sank to the ground and screamed at them. "She is no good to us," they muttered among themselves. "She is no good. We'd be better without her." They turned to her and scolded. "You could have been happy here, but you'll never be happy now. It's your own fault; you struggled with the witch. You struggled too much!"

"What witch?" she said. "I don't remember a witch. There's something—I don't know."

"She's no good," said the little people. "She won't play. She won't work, and she won't play. We will send her back again."

So they let her sit by the lake a while longer. One day the witch appeared, older and a little more weary. The nettle blossom of her hair had blight on it, and the warts on her fingers were mildewed. She grinned, lolling her tongue about like lard in a hot pan. "Moreen!" she crooned. "It has been a long, long time, Moreen!"

The child did not know her name. The witch snatched her by the wrist and circled her in the air above the excited fairies. The little red and brown people threw stones after them, and bits of gravel pinging and stinging at their legs. Moreen wept. She hated them.

They flew through grey, choking tunnels of cloud, where the thunderclaps sulked and rested. Moreen was tired, too tired to see where she was going.

. . . . . .

Where—what place? There was an emptiness, a shabbiness about it, but the line of the houses was the same. She felt inside as if she ought to know where she was, but she could not remember. The house at the corner had its windows misted over with damp, and there were lace curtains, and geraniums gasping for air against the panes. She did not want to go to that house, but there was a bell-pull at the door, and letters on a brass plate, and she knew she would have to put her hands on the bell and tug it a little sideways. She knew how her fingers would grip on the black handle, but she did not understand or wonder what made her know.

She rang the bell, and her eyes went squinting over the curlicues on the stained name plate. A shadow moved behind the curtain on the glass door.

When the door opened, there was an old woman standing in a long skirt, a fat, square-looking woman, with her hair piled grey over her head, all knobs and pins and the concealed teeth of combs. Her blouse was frilled, high at the neck so that it should have choked her, but it only made her sweat. The child could smell the dirty scent of her and the shut-in smell of the house. There seemed to be mice there.

"Well," snapped the woman, "what do you want?"

"I—I don't know."

"Come, come; don't be silly. You wouldn't have rung the bell if you hadn't wanted something. Are you a new pupil?"

"Pupil . . .?"

"Yes. A music pupil. Do you want to learn the piano?"

"No. I don't know."

"Tut-tut! Who sent you? What's your name?"

"I don't remember."

"Oh dear, tiresome child! You'd better come in till I find out what you want. Wipe your feet, now!"

It was a sad, dark house. Somebody in a room was playing a monotonous little jig on a piano. The woman opened the door and leaned in, pressing her weight on the handle, and the child knew without seeing that the piano was black with a musty smell, and a girl in a pink dress sitting at it.

"Clara! You are not yet ready for the jig. Get on with your scales as I ordered you!"

A flat, sunless voice said, "Yes, Miss Moreen."

They went upstairs, on a red-and-blue carpet. On the landing a she-dog dragged her tired body to a basket. The woman opened a door to a room where there was a big bed and a desk. It was a dirty room, full of furniture. "Now!" she said, sitting down and wiping her moist hands, "I suppose you *have* come for music lessons. Did your mother send you?"

"No." She began to cry. "I was away. They took me to a place where there was a lake, and woods, and——"

"Oh, you've been on holiday? Well, don't waste all the afternoon. If you don't want lessons, what do you want? What's your name? Where do you come from?"

The piano was faint behind the closed door—doh me soh doh, soh me doh, arpeggios crawling like the fat she-dog. The child did not know what to say. She looked at the closed, steamy window. There was a dead fly on the sill, but beyond was the sky, like blue enamel, with a steeple stretching towards it. High in the stonework was a clock, and above that a gargoyle, jutting out as if it wanted to be sick. Astride its back was a witch, loose and insecure as a piece of burnt paper. The child opened her mouth and screamed.

"This is my house! I remember it by the witch sitting on the gargoyle! It's my house."

The woman's face was like dirty suet. "Here, that's enough! You're not well. This isn't your house. I've lived here all my life, and my mother lived here before she died. You sit quiet and I'll get you a drink of water. It's that hot—I thought there was something not quite right about you. . . ."

"But it's my house. I know it by the witch! Don't you see it?"

"No. There's no witch, dearie, it's just in your own mind you're seeing it. You sit quiet and I'll see what I can do for you. Oh, dear, such a bother . . .!"

She went out of the room, leaving the door open, and the old dog waddled in. The piano was still tumbling out notes—doh me soh doh, soh me doh—but it stopped on a black key and the door banged. The child was watching the witch, but she could see things happening in the street. A little girl in a pink frock ran over to the doctor at the corner. Soon the window was too steamy to see any more.

THE LAST LAUGH

By D. H. Lawrence

THERE was a little snow on the ground, and the church clock had just struck midnight. Hampstead in the night of winter for once was looking pretty, with clean white earth and lamps for moon, and dark sky above the lamps.

A confused little sound of voices, a gleam of hidden yellow light. And then the garden door of a tall, dark Georgian house suddenly opened, and three people confusedly emerged. A girl in a dark blue coat and fur turban, very erect: a fellow with a little dispatch-case, slouching: a thin man with a red beard, bareheaded, peering out of the gateway down the hill that swung in a curve downwards towards London.

"Look at it! A new world!" cried the man in the beard, ironically, as he stood on the step and peered out.

"No, Lorenzo! It's only whitewash!" cried the young man in the overcoat. His voice was handsome, resonant, plangent, with a weary sardonic touch. As he turned back his face was dark in shadow.

The girl with the erect, alert head, like a bird, turned back to the two men.

"What was that?" she asked, in her quick, quiet voice.

"Lorenzo says it's a new world. I say it's only whitewash," cried the man in the street.

She stood still and lifted her woolly, gloved finger. She was deaf and was taking it in.

Yes, she had got it. She gave a quick, chuckling laugh, glanced very quickly at the man in the bowler hat, then back at the man in the stucco gateway, who was grinning like a satyr and waving good-bye.

"Good-bye, Lorenzo!" came the resonant, weary cry of the man in the bowler hat.

"Good-bye!" came the sharp, night-bird call of the girl.

The green gate slammed, then the inner door. The two were alone in the street, save for the policeman at the corner. The road curved steeply downhill.

"You'd better mind your *step*!" shouted the man in the bowler hat, leaning near the erect, sharp girl, and slouching in his walk. She paused a moment, to make sure what he had said.

"Don't mind me, I'm quite all right. Mind yourself!" she said quickly. At that very moment he gave a wild lurch on the slippery snow, but managed to save himself from falling. She watched him, on tiptoes of alertness. His bowler hat bounced away in the thin snow. They were under a lamp near the curve. As he ducked for his hat he showed a bald spot, just like a tonsure, among his dark, thin, rather curly hair. And when he looked up at her, with his thick black brows sardonically arched, and his rather hooked nose self-derisive, jamming his hat on again, he seemed like a satanic young priest. His face had beautiful lines, like a faun, and a doubtful martyred expression. A sort of faun on the Cross, with all the malice of the complication.

"Did you hurt yourself?" she asked, in her quick, cool, unemotional way.

"No!" he shouted derisively.

"Give me the machine, won't you?" she said, holding out her woolly hand. "I believe I'm safer."

"Do you *want* it?" he shouted.

"Yes, I'm sure I'm safer."

He handed her the little brown dispatch-case, which was really a Marconi listening machine for her deafness. She marched erect as ever. He shoved his hands deep in his overcoat pockets and slouched along beside her, as if he wouldn't make his legs firm. The road curved down in front of them, clean and pale with snow under the lamps. A motor-car came churning up. A few dark figures slipped away into the dark recesses of the houses, like fishes among rocks above a sea-bed of white sand. On the left was a tuft of trees sloping upwards into the dark.

He kept looking around, pushing out his finely shaped chin and his hooked nose as if he were listening for something. He could still hear the motor-car climbing on to the Heath. Below was the yellow, foul-smelling glare of the Hampstead Tube station. On the right the trees.

The girl, with her alert pink-and-white face looked at him sharply, inquisitively. She had an odd nymph-like inquisitiveness, sometimes like a bird, sometimes a squirrel, sometimes a rabbit: never quite like woman. At last he stood still, as if he would go no farther. There was a curious, baffled grin on his smooth, cream-coloured face.

"James," he said loudly to her, leaning towards her ear. "Do you hear somebody *laughing*?"

"Laughing?" she retorted quickly. "Who's laughing?"

"I don't know. *Somebody!*" he shouted, showing his teeth at her in a very odd way.

"No, I hear nobody," she announced.

"But it's most *extraordinary*!" he cried, his voice slurring up and down. "Put on your machine."

"Put it on?" she retorted. "What for?"

"To see if you can *hear* it," he cried.

"Hear what?"

"The *laughing*. Somebody laughing. It's most *extraordinary*."

She gave her odd little chuckle and handed him her machine. He held it while she opened the lid and attached the wires, putting the band over her head and the receivers at her ears, like a wireless operator. Crumbs of snow fell down the cold darkness. She switched on: little yellow lights in glass tubes shone in the machine. She was connected, she was listening. He stood with his head ducked, his hands shoved down in his overcoat pockets.

Suddenly he lifted his face and gave the weirdest, slightly neighing laugh, uncovering his strong, spaced teeth and arching his black brows, and watching her with queer, gleaming goat-like eyes.

She seemed a little dismayed.

"There!" he said. "Didn't you hear it?"

"I heard *you*!" she said, in a tone which conveyed that *that* was enough.

"But didn't you hear *it*?" he cried, unfurling his lips oddly again.

"No!" she said.

He looked at her vindictively, and stood again with ducked head. She remained erect, her fur hat in her hand, her fine bobbed hair banded with the machine-band and catching crumbs of snow, her odd, bright-eyed, deaf nymph's face lifted with blank listening.

"There!" he cried, suddenly jerking up his gleaming face. "You mean to tell me you can't——" He was looking at her almost diabolically. But something else was too strong for him. His face wreathed with a startling, peculiar smile, seeming to gleam, and suddenly the most extraordinary laugh came bursting out of him, like an animal laughing. It was a strange, neighing sound, amazing in her ears. She was startled, and switched her machine quieter.

A large form loomed up: a tall, clean-shaven young policeman.

"A radio?" he asked laconically.

"No, it's my machine. I'm deaf!" said Miss James quickly and distinctly. She was not the daughter of a peer for nothing.

The man in the bowler hat lifted his face and glared at the fresh-faced young policeman with a peculiar white glare in his eyes.

"Look here!" he said distinctly. "Did you hear someone laughing?"

"Laughing? I heard you, sir."

"No, *not* me." He gave an impatient jerk of his arm, and lifted his face again. His smooth, creamy face seemed to gleam, there were subtle curves of derisive triumph in all its lines. He was careful not to look directly at the young policeman. "The most extraordinary laughter I ever heard," he added, and the same touch of derisive exultation sounded in his tones.

The policeman looked down on him cogitatingly.

"It's perfectly all right," said Miss James coolly. "He's not drunk. He just hears something that we don't hear."

"Drunk!" echoed the man in the bowler hat, in profoundly amused derision. "If I were merely drunk——" And off he went again in the wild, neighing, animal laughter, while his averted face seemed to flash.

At the sound of the laughter something roused in the blood of the girl and of the policeman. They stood nearer to one another, so that their sleeves touched and they looked wonderingly across at the man in the bowler hat. He lifted his black brows at them.

"Do you mean to say you heard nothing?" he asked.

"Only you," said Miss James.

"Only you, sir!" echoed the policeman.

"What was it like?" asked Miss James.

"Ask me to *describe* it!" retorted the young man, in extreme contempt. "It's the most marvellous sound in the world."

And truly he seemed wrapped up in a new mystery.

"Where does it come from?" asked Miss James, very practical.

"*Apparently*," he answered in contempt, "from over there." And he pointed to the trees and bushes inside the railings over the road.

"Well, let's go and see!" she said. "I can carry my machine and go on listening."

The man seemed relieved to get rid of the burden. He shoved his hands in his pockets again and sloped off across the road. The policeman, a queer look flickering on his fresh young face, put his hand round the girl's arm carefully and subtly, to help her. She did not lean at all on the support of the big hand, but she was interested, so she did not resent it. Having held herself all her life intensely aloof from physical contact, and never having let any man touch her, she now, with a certain nymph-like voluptuousness, allowed the large hand of the young policeman to support her as they followed the quick wolf-like figure of the other man across the road uphill. And she could feel the presence of the young policeman, through all the thickness of his dark-blue uniform, as something young and alert and bright.

When they came up to the man in the bowler hat, he was standing with his head ducked, his ears pricked, listening beside the iron rail inside which grew big black holly trees tufted with snow, and old, ribbed, silent English elms.

The policeman and the girl stood waiting. She was peering into the bushes with the sharp eyes of a deaf nymph, deaf to the world's noises. The man in the bowler hat listened intensely. A lorry rolled downhill, making the earth tremble.

"There!" cried the girl, as the lorry rumbled darkly past. And she glanced round with flashing eyes at her policeman, her fresh soft face gleaming with startled life. She glanced straight into the puzzled, amused eyes of the young policeman. He was just enjoying himself.

"Don't you see?" she said, rather imperiously.

"What is it, miss?" answered the policeman.

"I mustn't point," she said. "Look where I look."

And she looked away with brilliant eyes, into the dark holly bushes. She must see something, for she smiled faintly, with subtle satisfaction, and she tossed her erect head in all the pride of vindication. The policeman looked at her instead of into the bushes. There was a certain brilliance of triumph and vindication in all the poise of her slim body.

"I always knew I should see him," she said triumphantly to herself.

"Whom do you see?" shouted the man in the bowler hat.

"Don't you see him, too?" she asked, turning round her soft, arch, nymph-like face anxiously. She was anxious for the little man to see.

"No, I see nothing. What do you see, James?" cried the man in the bowler hat, insisting.

"A man."

"Where?"

"There. Among the holly bushes."

"Is he there now?"

"No! He's gone."

"What sort of a man?"

"I don't know."

"What did he look like?"

"I can't tell you."

But at that instant the man in the bowler hat turned suddenly, and the arch, triumphant look flew to his face.

"Why, he must be *there*!" he cried, pointing up the grove. "Don't you hear him laughing? He must be behind those trees."

And his voice, with curious delight, broke into a laugh again, as he stood and stamped his feet on the snow, and danced to his own laughter, ducking his head. Then he turned away and ran swiftly up the avenue lined with old trees.

He slowed down as a door at the end of a garden path, white with untouched snow, suddenly opened, and a woman in a long-fringed black shawl stood in the light. She peered out into the night. Then she came down to the low garden gate. Crumbs of snow still fell. She had dark hair and a tall dark comb.

"Did you knock at my door?" she asked of the man in the bowler hat.

"I? No!"

"Somebody knocked at my door."

"Did they? Are you sure? They can't have done. There are no footmarks in the snow."

"Nor are there!" she said. "But somebody knocked and called something."

"That's very curious," said the man. "Were you expecting someone?"

"No. Not exactly expecting anyone. Except that one is always expecting. Somebody, you know." In the dimness of the snow-lit night he could see her making big, dark eyes at him.

"Was it someone laughing?" he said.

"No. It was no one laughing, exactly. Someone knocked, and I ran to open, hoping as one always hopes, you know——"

"What?"

"Oh—that something wonderful is going to happen."

He was standing close to the low gate. She stood on the opposite side. Her hair was dark, her face seemed dusky, as she looked up at him with her dark, meaningful eyes.

"Did you wish someone would come?" he asked.

"Very much," she replied, in her plangent Jewish voice. She must be a Jewess."

"No matter who?" he said, laughing.

"So long as it was a man I could like," she said in a low, meaningful, falsely shy voice.

"Really!" he said. "Perhaps, after all, it was I who knocked—without knowing."

"I think it was," she said. "It must have been."

"Shall I come in?" he asked, putting his hand on the little gate.

"Don't you think you'd better?" she replied.

He bent down, unlatching the gate. As he did so the woman in the black shawl turned, and, glancing over her shoulder, hurried back to the house, walking unevenly in the snow, on her high-heeled shoes. The man hurried after her, hastening like a hound to catch up.

Meanwhile the girl and the policeman had come up. The girl stood still when she saw the man in the bowler hat going up the garden walk after the woman in the black shawl with the fringe.

"Is he going in?" she asked quickly.

"Looks like it, doesn't it?" said the policeman.

"Does he know that woman?"

"I can't say. I should say he soon will," replied the policeman.

"But who is she?"

"I couldn't say who she is."

The two dark, confused figures entered the lighted doorway, then the door closed on them.

"He's gone," said the girl outside on the snow. She hastily began to pull off the band of her telephone-receiver, and switched off her machine. The tubes of secret light disappeared, she packed up the little leather case. Then, pulling on her soft fur cap, she stood once more ready.

The slightly martial look which her long, dark-blue, military-seeming coat gave her was intensified, while the slightly anxious, bewildered look of her face had gone. She seemed to stretch herself, to stretch her limbs free. And the inert look had left her full soft cheeks. Her cheeks were alive with the glimmer of pride and a new dangerous surety.

She looked quickly at the tall young policeman. He was clean-shaven, fresh-faced, smiling oddly under his helmet, waiting in subtle patience a few yards away. She saw that he was a decent young man, one of the waiting sort.

The second of ancient fear was followed at once in her by a blithe, unaccustomed sense of power.

"Well!" she said. "I should say it's no use waiting." She spoke decisively.

"You don't have to wait for him, do you?" asked the policeman.

"Not at all. He's much better where he is." She laughed an odd, brief laugh. Then glancing over her shoulder, she set off down the hill, carrying her little case. Her feet felt light, her legs felt long and strong. She glanced over her shoulder again. The young policeman was following her, and she laughed to herself. Her limbs felt so lithe and strong, if she wished she could easily run faster than he. If she wished she could easily kill him, even with her hands.

So it seemed to her. But why kill him? He was a decent young fellow. She had in front of her eyes the dark face among the holly bushes, with the brilliant mocking eyes. Her breast felt full of power, and her legs felt long and strong and wild. She was surprised herself at the strong, bright, throbbing sensation beneath her breasts, a sensation of triumph and of rosy anger. Her hands felt keen on her wrists. She who had always declared she had not a muscle in her body! Even now, it was not muscle, it was a sort of flame.

Suddenly it began to snow heavily, with fierce frozen puffs of wind. The snow was small, in frozen grains, and hit sharp on her face. It seemed to whirl round her as if she herself were whirling in a cloud. But she did not mind. There was a flame in her, her limbs felt flamey and strong, amid the whirl.

And the whirling, snowy air seemed full of presences, full of strange unheard voices. She was used to the sensation of noises taking place which she could not hear. This sensation became very strong. She felt something was happening in the wild air.

The London air was no longer heavy and clammy, saturated with ghosts of the unwilling dead. A new, clean tempest swept down from the Pole, and there were noises.

Voices were calling. In spite of her deafness she could hear someone, several voices, calling and whistling, as if many people were hallooing through the air:

"He's come back! Aha! He's come back!"

There was a wild, whistling, jubilant sound of voices in the storm of snow. Then obscured lightning winked through the snow in the air.

"Is that thunder and lightning?" she asked of the young policeman, as she stood still, waiting for his form to emerge through the veil of whirling snow.

"Seems like it to me," he said.

And at that very moment the lightning blinked again, and the dark, laughing face was near her face, it almost touched her cheek.

She started back, but a flame of delight went over her.

"There!" she said. "Did you see that?"

"It lightened," said the policeman.

She was looking at him almost angrily. But then the clean, fresh animal look of his skin, and the tame-animal look in his frightened eyes amused her, she laughed her low, triumphant laugh. He was obviously afraid, like a frightened dog that sees something uncanny.

The storm suddenly whistled louder, more violently, and, with a strange noise like castanets, she seemed to hear voices clapping and crying:

"He is here! He's come back!"

She nodded her head gravely.

The policeman and she moved on side by side. She lived alone in a little stucco house in a side street down the hill. There was a church and a grove of trees and then the little old row of houses. The wind blew fiercely, thick with snow. Now and again a taxi went by, with its lights showing weirdly. But the world seemed empty, uninhabited save by snow and voices.

As the girl and the policeman turned past the grove of trees near the church, a great whirl of wind and snow made them stand still, and in the wild confusion they heard a whirling of sharp, delighted voices, something like seagulls, crying:

"He's here! He's here!"

"Well, I'm jolly glad he's back," said the girl calmly.

"What's that?" said the nervous policeman, hovering near the girl.

The wind let them move forward. As they passed along the railings it seemed to them the doors of the church were open, and the windows were out, and the snow and the voices were blowing in a wild career all through the church.

"How extraordinary that they left the church open!" said the girl.

The policeman stood still. He could not reply.

And as they stood they listened to the wind and the church full of whirling voices all calling confusedly.

"*Now* I hear the laughing," she said suddenly.

It came from the church: a sound of low, subtle, endless laughter, a strange, naked sound.

"Now I hear it!" she said.

But the policeman did not speak. He stood cowed, with his tail between his legs, listening to the strange noises in the church.

The wind must have blown out one of the windows, for they could see the snow whirling in volleys through the black gap, and whirling inside the church like a dim light. There came a sudden crash, followed by a burst of chuckling, naked laughter. The snow seemed to make a queer light inside the building, like ghosts moving, big and tall.

There was more laughter, and a tearing sound. On the wind, pieces of paper, leaves of books, came whirling among the snow through the dark window. Then a white thing, soaring like a crazy bird, rose up on the wind as if it had wings, and lodged on a black tree outside, struggling. It was the altar-cloth.

There came a bit of gay, trilling music. The wind was running over the organ-pipes like pan-pipes, quickly up and down. Snatches of wild, gay, trilling music, and bursts of the naked low laughter.

"Really!" said the girl. "This is most extraordinary. Do you hear the music and the laughing?"

"Yes, I hear somebody on the organ!" said the policeman.

"And do you get the puff of warm wind? Smelling of spring. Almond blossom, that's what it is! A most marvellous scent of almond blossom. *Isn't* it an extraordinary thing!"

She went on triumphantly past the church, and came to the row of little old houses. She entered her own gate in the little railed entrance.

"Here I am!" she said finally. "I'm home now. Thank you very much for coming with me."

She looked at the young policeman. His whole body was white as a wall with snow, and in the vague light of the arc-lamp from the street his face was humble and frightened.

"Can I come in and warm myself a bit?" he asked humbly. She knew it was fear rather than cold that froze him. He was in mortal fear.

"Well!" she said. "Stay down in the sitting-room if you like. But don't come upstairs, because I am alone in the house. You can make up the fire in the sitting-room, and you can go when you are warm."

She left him on the big, low couch before the fire, his face bluish and blank with fear. He rolled his blue eyes after her as she left the room. But she went up to her bedroom, and fastened her door.

In the morning she was in her studio upstairs in her little house, looking at her own paintings and laughing to herself. Her canaries were talking and shrilly whistling in the sunshine that followed the storm. The cold snow outside was stil clean, and the white glare in the air gave the effect of much stronger sunshine than actually existed.

She was looking at her own paintings, and chuckling to herself over their comicalness. Suddenly they struck her as absolutely absurd. She quite enjoyed looking at them, they seemed to her so grotesque. Especially her self-portrait, with its nice brown hair and its slightly opened rabbit-mouth and its baffled, uncertain rabbit eyes. She looked at the painted face and laughed in a long, rippling laugh, till the yellow canaries like faded daffodils almost went mad in an effort to sing louder. The girl's long, rippling laugh sounded through the house uncannily.

The housekeeper, a rather sad-faced young woman of a superior sort—nearly all people in England are of the superior sort, superiority being an English ailment—came in with an inquiring and rather disapproving look.

"Did you call, Miss James?" she asked loudly.

"No. No, I didn't call. Don't shout, I can hear quite well," replied the girl.

The housekeeper looked at her again.

"You knew there was a young man in the sitting-room?" she said.

"No. Really!" cried the girl. "What, the young policeman? I'd forgotten all about him. He came in in the storm to warm himself. Hasn't he gone?"

"No, Miss James."

"How extraordinary of him! What time is it? Quarter to nine! Why didn't he go when he was warm? I must go and see him, I suppose."

"He says he's lame," said the housekeeper censoriously and loudly.

"Lame! That's extraordinary. He certainly wasn't last night. But don't shout. I can hear quite well."

"Is Mr. Marchbanks coming in to breakfast, Miss James?" said the housekeeper, more and more censorious.

"I couldn't say. But I'll come down as soon as mine is ready. I'll be down in a minute, anyhow, to see the policeman. Extraordinary that he is still here."

She sat down before her window, in the sun, to think a while. She could see the snow outside, the bare, purplish trees. The air all seemed rare and different: as if some skin or integument had broken, as if the old, mouldering London sky had crackled and rolled back, like an old skin, shrivelled, leaving an absolutely new blue heaven.

"It really is extraordinary!" she said to herself. "I certainly saw that man's face. What a wonderful face it was! I shall never forget it. Such laughter! He laughs longest who laughs last. He certainly will have the last laugh. I like him for that: he will laugh last. Must be someone really extraordinary! How very nice to be the one to laugh last. He certainly will. What a wonderful being! I suppose I must call him a being. He's not a person exactly.

"But how wonderful of him to come back and alter all the world immediately! *Isn't* that extraordinary. I wonder if he'll have altered Marchbanks. Of course Marchbanks never *saw* him. But he heard him. Wouldn't that do as well, I wonder!—I *wonder*!"

She went off into a muse about Marchbanks. She and he were *such* friends. They had been friends like that for almost two years. Never lovers. Never that at all. But *friends*.

And after all, she had been in love with him: in her head. This seemed now so funny to her: that she had been, in her head, so much in love with him. After all, life was too absurd.

Because now she saw herself and him as such a funny pair. He so funnily taking life terribly seriously, especially his own life. And she so ridiculously *determined* to save him from himself. Oh, how absurd! *Determined* to save him from himself, and wildly in love with him in the effort. The determination to save him from himself.

Absurd! Absurd! Absurd! Since she had seen the man laughing among the holly bushes—*such* extraordinary, wonderful laughter—she had seen her own ridiculousness. Really, what fantastic silliness, saving a man from himself! Saving anybody. What fantastic silliness! How much more amusing and lively to let a man go to perdition in his own way. Perdition was more amusing than salvation, anyhow, and a much better place for most men to go to.

She had never been in love with any man, and only spuriously in love with Marchbanks. She saw it quite plainly now. After all, what nonsense it all was, this being-in-love business. Thank goodness she had never made the humiliating mistake.

No, the man among the holly bushes had made her see it all so plainly: the ridiculousness of being in love, the *infra dig* business of chasing a man or being chased by a man.

"Is love *really* so absurd and *infra dig*?" she said aloud to herself.

"Why, of course!" came a deep, laughing voice.

She started round, but nobody was to be seen.

"I expect it's that man again!" she said to herself. "It really *is* remarkable, you know. I consider it's a remarkable thing that I never really wanted a man, *any* man. And there I am over thirty. It *is* curious. Whether it's something wrong with me, or right with me, I can't say. I don't know till I've proved it. But I believe, if that man kept on laughing something would happen to me."

She smelt the curious smell of almond blossom in the room, and heard the distant laugh again.

"I do wonder why Marchbanks went with that woman last night—that Jewish-looking woman. Whatever could he want of her?—or she of him? So strange, as if they both had made up their minds to something! How extraordinarily puzzling life is! So messy, it all seems.

"Why does nobody ever laugh in life like that man? He *did* seem so wonderful. So scornful! And so proud! And so real! With those laughing, scornful, amazing eyes, just laughing and disappearing again. I can't imagine him chasing a Jewish-looking woman. Or chasing any woman, thank goodness. It's all *so* messy. My policeman would be messy if one would let him: like a dog. I do dislike dogs, really I do. And men do seem so doggy!——"

But even while she mused, she began to laugh again to herself with a long, low chuckle. How wonderful of that man to come and laugh like that and make the sky crack and shrivel like an old skin! Wasn't he wonderful! Wouldn't it be wonderful if he just touched her. Even touched her. She felt, if he touched her, she herself would emerge new and tender out of an old, hard skin. She was gazing abstractedly out of the window.

"There he comes, just now," she said abruptly. But she meant Marchbanks, not the laughing man.

There he came, his hands still shoved down in his overcoat pockets, his head still rather furtively ducked, in the bowler hat, and his legs still rather shambling. He came hurrying across the road, not looking up, deep in thought, no doubt. Thinking profoundly, with agonies of agitation, no doubt about his last night's experience. It made her laugh.

She, watching from the window above, burst into a long laugh, and the canaries went off their heads again.

He was in the hall below. His resonant voice was calling, rather imperiously;

"James! Are you coming down?"

"No," she called. "You come up."

He came up two at a time, as if his feet were a bit savage with the stairs for obstructing him.

In the doorway he stood staring at her with a vacant, sardonic look, his grey eyes moving with a queer light. And she looked back at him with a curious, rather haughty carelessness.

"Don't you want your breakfast?" she asked. It was his custom to come and take breakfast with her each morning.

"No," he answered loudly. "I went to a tea-shop."

"Don't shout," she said. "I can hear you quite well."

He looked at her with mockery and a touch of malice.

"I believe you always could," he said, still loudly.

"Well, anyway, I can now, so you needn't shout," she replied.

And again his grey eyes, with the queer, greyish phosphorescent gleam in them, lingered malignantly on her face.

"Don't look at me," she said calmly. "I know all about everything."

He burst into a pouf of malicious laughter.

"Who taught you—the policeman?" he cried.

"Oh, by the way, he must be downstairs! No, he was only incidental. So, I suppose, was the woman in the shawl. Did you stay all night?"

"Not entirely. I came away before dawn. What did you do?"

"Don't shout. I came home, long before dawn." And she seemed to hear the long, low laughter.

"Why, what's the matter?" he said curiously. "What have you been doing?"

"I don't quite know. Why?—are you going to call me to account?"

"Did you hear that laughing?"

"Oh yes. And many more things. And saw things, too."

"Have you seen the paper?"

"No. Don't shout, I can hear."

"There's been a great storm, blew out the windows and doors of the church outside here, and pretty well wrecked the place."

'I saw it. A leaf of the church Bible blew right in my face: from the Book of Job——" She gave a low laugh.

"But what else did you see?" he cried loudly.

"I saw *him*."

"Who?"

"Ah, that I can't say."

"But what was he like?"

"That I can't tell you. I don't really know."

"But you must know. Did your policeman see him, too?"

"No, I don't suppose he did. My policeman!" And she went off into a long ripple of laughter. "He is by no means mine. But I *must* go downstairs and see him."

"It's certainly made you very strange," Marchbanks said. "You've got no *soul*, you know."

"Oh, thank goodness for that!" she cried. "My policeman has one, I'm sure. *My policeman!*" And she went off again into a long peal of laughter, the canaries pealing shrill accompaniment.

"What's the matter with you?" he said.

"Having no soul. I never had one really. It was always fobbed off on me. Soul was the only thing there was between you and me. Thank goodness it's gone. Haven't you lost yours? The one that seemed to worry you, like a decayed tooth?"

"But what are you *talking* about?" he cried.

"I don't know," she said. "It's all so extraordinary. But look here, I *must* go down and see my policeman. He's downstairs in the sitting-room. You'd better come with me."

They went down together. The policeman, in his waistcoat and shirt-sleeves, was lying on the sofa, with a very long face.

"Look here!" said Miss James to him. "Is it true you're lame?"

"It is true. That's why I'm here. I can't walk," said the fair-haired young man as tears came to his eyes.

"But how did it happen? You weren't lame last night," she said.

"I don't know how it happened—but when I woke up and tried to stand up, I couldn't do it." The tears ran down his distressed face.

"How very extraordinary!" she said. "What can we do about it?"

"Which foot is it?" asked Marchbanks. "Let us have a look at it."

"I don't like to," said the poor devil.

"You'd better," said Miss James.

He slowly pulled off his stocking, and showed his white left foot curiously clubbed, like the weird paw of some animal. When he looked at it himself, he sobbed.

And as he sobbed, the girl heard again the low, exulting laughter. But she paid no heed to it, gazing curiously at the weeping young policeman.

"Does it hurt?" she asked.

"It does if I try to walk on it," wept the young man.

"I'll tell you what," she said. "We'll telephone for a doctor, and he can take you home in a taxi."

The young fellow shamefacedly wiped his eyes.

"But have you no idea how it happened?" asked Marchbanks anxiously.

"I haven't myself," said the young fellow.

At that moment the girl heard the low, eternal laugh right in her ear. She started, but could see nothing.

She started round again as Marchbanks gave a strange, yelping cry, like a shot animal. His white face was drawn distorted in a curious grin, that was chiefly agony, but partly wild recognition. He was staring with fixed eyes at something. And in the rolling agony of his eyes was the horrible grin of a man who realizes he has made a final, and this time fatal, fool of himself.

"Why," he yelped in a high voice, "I knew it was he!" And with a queer shuddering laugh he pitched forward on the carpet and lay writhing for a moment on the floor. Then he lay still, in a weird, distorted position, like a man struck by lightning.

Miss James stared with round, staring brown eyes.

"Is he dead?" she asked quickly.

The young poiceman was trembling so that he could hardly speak. She could hear his teeth chattering.

"Seems like it," he stammered.

There was a faint smell of almond blossom in the air.

THE GROTESQUE

THE LEECH OF FOLKESTONE

By Thomas Ingoldsby

READER, were you ever bewitched?—I do not mean by a "white wench's black eye", or by love potions, imbibed from a ruby lip;—but, were you ever really and bona fide bewitched, in the true Matthew Hopkins sense of the word? Did you ever, for instance, find yourself from head to heel one vast complication of cramps?—or burst out into sudorific exudation like a cold thaw, with the thermometer at zero?—Were your eyes ever turned upside down, exhibiting nothing but their whites?—Did you ever vomit a paper of crooked pins or expectorate Whitechapel needles?—These are genuine and undoubted marks of possession; and if you ever experienced any of them—why, "happy man be his dole!"

Yet such things have been: yea, we are assured, and that on no mean authority, still are.

The World, according to the best geographers, is divided into Europe, Asia, Africa, America, and Romney Marsh. In this last named, and fifth quarter of the globe, a Witch may still be occasionally discovered in favourable, i.e. stormy seasons, weathering Dungeness Point in an egg-shell, or careering on her broomstick over Dymchurch wall. A cow may yet be sometimes seen galloping like mad, with tail erect, and an old pair of breeches on her horns, an unerring guide to the door of the crone whose magic arts have drained her udder. I do not, however, remember to have heard that any Conjuror has of late been detected in the district.

Not many miles removed from the verge of this recondite region, stands a collection of houses, which its maligners call a fishing-town, and its well-wishers a Watering-place. A limb of one of the Cinque Ports, it has (or lately had) a corporation of its own, and has been thought considerable enough to give a second title to a noble family. Rome stood on seven hills; Folkestone seems to have been built upon seventy. Its streets, lanes and alleys—fanciful distinctions without much real difference—are agreeable enough to persons who do not mind running up and down stairs; and the only inconvenience at all felt by such of its inhabitants as are not asthmatic, is when some heedless urchin tumbles down a chimney, or an impertinent pedestrian peeps into a garret window.

At the eastern extremity of the town, on the sea-beach, and scarcely above high-water mark, stood, in the good old times, a row of houses then nominated

"Frog-hole". Modern refinement subsequently euphonized the name into "East-street"; but "what's in a name?"—the encroachments of Ocean have long since levelled all in one common ruin.

Here, in the early part of the seventeenth century, flourished in somewhat doubtful reputation, but comparative opulence, a compounder of medicines, one Master Erasmus Buckthorne; the effluvia of whose drugs from within, mingling agreeably with the "ancient and fish-like smells" from without, wafted a delicious perfume throughout the neighbourhood.

At seven of the clock, on the morning when Mrs. Botherby's narrative commences, a stout Suffolk "punch" about thirteen hands and a half in height, was slowly led up and down before the door of the pharmacopolist by a lean and withered lad, whose appearance warranted an opinion, pretty generally expressed, that his master found him as useful in experimentalizing as in household drudgery; and that, for every pound avoirdupois of solid meat, he swallowed, at least, two pounds troy-weight of chemicals and galenicals. As the town clock struck the quarter, Master Buckthorne emerged from his laboratory, and, putting the key carefully into his pocket, mounted the surefooted cob aforesaid, and proceeded up and down the acclivities and declivities of the town with the gravity due to his station and profession. When he reached the open country, his pace was increased to a sedate canter, which, in somewhat more than half an hour, brought "the horse and his rider" in front of a handsome and substantial mansion, the numerous gable-ends and bayed windows of which bespoke the owner a man of worship, and one well to do in the world.

"How now, Hodge Gardener?" quoth the Leech, scarcely drawing bit; for Punch seemed to be aware that he had reached his destination and paused of his own accord; "How now, man? How fares thine employer, worthy Master Marsh? How hath he done? How hath he slept? My potion hath done its office? Ha!"

"Alack! ill at ease, worthy sir—ill at ease," returned the hind; "his honour is up and stirring; but he hath rested none, and complaineth that the same gnawing pain devoureth, as it were, his very vitals: in sooth he is ill at ease."

"Morrow, doctor!" interrupted a voice from a casement opening on the lawn. "Good morrow! I have looked for, longed for, thy coming, this hour and more; enter at once; the pasty and tankard are impatient for thine attack!"

"Marry, Heaven forbid that I should baulk their fancy!" quoth the Leech *sotto voce*, as, abandoning the bridle to honest Hodge, he dismounted, and following a buxom-looking handmaiden into the breakfast parlour.

There, at the head and his well-furnished board, sat Master Thomas Marsh, of Marston Hall, a Yeoman well respected in his degree; one of that sturdy and sterling class which, taking rank immediately below the Esquire (a title in its origin purely military), occupied, in the wealthier counties, the position in sociey now filled by the Country Gentleman. He was one of those of whom the proverb ran:

> "A Knight of Cales,
> A Gentleman of Wales,
> And a Laird of the North Countree;
> A Yeoman of Kent,
> With his yearly rent,
> Will buy them out all three!"

A cold sirloin, big enough to frighten a Frenchman, filled the place of honour, counter-checked by a game-pie of no stinted dimensions; while a silver flagon of "humming-bub"—viz., ale strong enough to blow a man's beaver off—smiled opposite in treacherous amenity. The sideboard groaned beneath sundry massive cups and waiters of the purest silver; while the huge skull of a fallow deer, with its branching horns, frowned magestically above. All spoke of affluence, of comfort—all save the master, whose restless eye and feverish look hinted but too plainly the severest mental or bodily disorder. By the side of the proprietor of the mansion sat his consort, a lady now past the bloom of youth, yet still retaining many of its charms. The clear olive of her complexion, and "the darkness of her Andalusian eye", at once betrayed her foreign origin; in fact, her "lord and master", as husbands were even then, by a legal fiction, denominated, had taken her to his bosom in a foreign country. The cadet of his family, Master Thomas Marsh, had early in life become engaged in commerce. In the pursuit of his vocation he had visited Antwerp, Hamburg, and most of the Hanse Towns; he had already formed a tender connection with the orphan offspring of one of old Alva's officers, when the unexpected deaths of one immediate, and two presumptive, heirs placed him next in succession to the family acres. He married and brought home his bride; who, by the decease of the venerable possessor, heart-broken at the loss of his elder children, became eventually lady of Marston Hall. It has been said that she was beautiful, yet was her beauty of a character that operates on the fancy more than the affections; she was one to be admired rather than loved. The proud curl of her lip, the firmness of her tread, her arched brow and stately carriage, showed the decision, not to say haughtiness, of her soul; while her glances, whether lightening with anger, or melting in extreme softness, betrayed the existence of passions as intense in kind as opposite in quality. She rose as Erasmus entered the parlour, and, bestowing on him a look fraught with meaning, quitted the room, leaving him in unrestrained communication with his patient.

"For George, Master Buckthorne!" exclaimed the latter, as the Leech drew near. "I will no more of your pharmacy;—burn, burn—gnaw, gnaw—I had as lief the foul fiend were in my gizzard as one of your drugs. Tell me, in the devil's name, what is the matter with me!"

Thus conjured, the practitioner paused, and even turned somewhat pale. There was a perceptible faltering in his voice, as, evading the question, he asked, "What say your other physicians?"

"Dr. Phiz says it is wind—Dr. Fuz says it is water—and Dr. Buz says it is something between wind and water."

"They are all of them wrong," said Erasmus Buckthorne.

"Truly, I think so," returned the patient. "They are manifest asses; but you, good Leech, you are a horse of another colour. The world talks loudly of your learning, your skill, and cunning in arts the most abstruse; nay, sooth to say, some look coldly on you therefore, and stickle not to aver that you are cater-cousin with Beelzebub himself."

"It is ever the fate of science," murmured the professor, "to be maligned by the ignorant and superstitious. But a truce with such folly; let me examine your palate."

Master Marsh thrust out a tongue long, clear, and red as beetroot. "There is nothing wrong there," said the Leech. "Your wrist—no—the pulse is firm and regular, the skin cool and temperate. Sir, there is nothing the matter with you!"

"Nothing the matter with me, Sir 'Potecary? But I tell you there is the matter with me—much the matter with me. Why is it that something seems ever gnawing at my heart-strings? Whence this pain in the region of the liver? Why is it that I sleep not o' nights—rest not o' days? Why?"

"You are fidgety, Master Marsh," said the doctor.

Master Marsh's brows grew dark; he half rose from his seat, supported himself by both hands on the arms of his elbow-chair, and in accents of mingled anger and astonishment repeated the word "Fidgety!"

"Ay, fidgety," returned the doctor calmly. "Tut, man, there is nought ails thee save thine own overweening fancies. Take less of food, more air, put aside thy flagon, call for thy horse; be boot and saddle the word! Why, hast thou not youth?"

"I have," said the patient.

"Wealth and a fair domain?"

"Granted," quoth Marsh cheerily.

"And a fair wife?"

"Yea," was the response, but in a tone something less satisfied.

"Then arouse thee, man, shake off this fantasy, betake thyself to thy lawful occasions—use thy good hap—follow thy pleasures, and think no more of these fancied ailments."

"But I tell you, master mine, these ailments are not fancied. I lose my rest, I loathe my food, my doublet sits loosely on me—these racking pains. My wife, too, when I meet her gaze, the cold sweat stands on her forehead, and I could almost think——." Marsh paused abruptly, mused awhile, then added, looking steadily at his visitor, "These things are not right; they pass the common, Master Erasmus Buckthorne."

A slight shade crossed the brow of the Leech, but its passage was momentary; his features softened to a smile, in which pity seemed slightly blended with contempt. "Have done with such follies, Master Marsh. You are well, an' you would but think so. Ride, I say, hunt, shoot, do anything—disperse these melancholic humours, and become yourself again."

"Well, I will do your bidding," said Marsh thoughtfully. "It may be so; and yet—but I will do your bidding. Master Cobbe of Brenzet writes me that he hath a score or two of fat ewes to be sold a pennyworth; I had thought to have sent Ralph Looker, but I will essay to go myself. Ho, there!—saddle me the brown mare, and bid Ralph to be ready to attend me on the gelding."

An expression of pain contracted the features of Master Marsh as he rose and slowly quitted the apartment to prepare for his journey; while the Leech, having bidden him farewell, vanished through an opposite door, and betook himself to the private boudoir of the fair mistress of Marston, muttering as he went a quotation from a then newly published play:

> "Not poppy, nor mandragora,
> Nor the drowsy syrups of the world,
> Shall ever medicine thee to that sweet sleep
> Which thou own'dst yesterday."

Of what passed at this interview between the Folkestone doctor and the fair Spaniard, Mrs. Botherby declares she could never obtain any satisfactory elucidation. Not that tradition is silent on the subject—quite the contrary; it is the abundance, not paucity, of the materials she supplies, and the consequent embarrassment of selection, that makes the difficulty. Some have averred that the Leech, whose character, as has been before hinted, was more than threadbare, employed his time in teaching her the mode of administering certain noxious compounds, the unconscious partaker whereof would pine and die so slowly and gradually as to defy suspicion. Others there were who affirmed that Lucifer himself was there raised in *propria persona*, with all his terrible attributes of horn and hoof. In support in this assertion, they adduce the testimony of the aforesaid buxom housemaid, who protested that the hall smelt that evening like a manufactory of matches. All, however, seemed to agree that the confabulation, whether human or infernal, was conducted with profound secrecy, and protracted to a considerable length; that its object, as far as could be divined, meant anything but good to the head of the family: and the lady, moreover, was heartily tired of her husband; and that in the event of his removal by disease or casualty, Master Erasmus Buckthorne, albeit a great pholosophist, would have no violent objection to "throw physic to the dogs", and exchange his laboratory for the estate of Marston, its live-stock included. Some, too, have inferred that to him did Madame Isabel seriously incline; while others have thought, induced perhaps by subsequent events, that she was merely using him for her purposes; that one Jose, a tall bright-eyed, hook-nosed stripling from her native land, was a personage not unlikely to put a spoke in the doctor's wheel; and that, should such a chance arise, the Sage, wise as he was, would, after all, run no slight risk of being "bamboozled".

Master Jose was a youth well-favoured, and comely to look upon. His office was that of page to the dame; an office which, after long remaining in abeyance, has been of late years revived, as may well be seen in the persons of sundry smart hobbledehoys, now constantly to be met with on staircases and in boudoirs, clad, for the most part, in garments fitted tightly to the shape, the lower moiety adorned with a broad stripe of crimson or silver lace, and the upper with what the first Wit of our times has described as "a favourable eruption of buttons". The precise duties of this employment have never, as far as we have heard, been accurately defined. The perfuming of a handkerchief, the combing of a lap-dog, and the occasional presentation of a sippet-shaped *billet-doux*, are, and always have been, among them; but these a young gentleman standing five-foot ten, and aged nineteen "last grass", might well be supposed to have outgrown. Jose, however, kept his place, perhaps because he was not fit for any other. To the conference between his mistress and the physician he had not been admitted; his post was to keep watch and ward in the ante-room; and, when the interview was concluded, he attended the lady and her visitor as far as the courtyard, where he held, with all due respect, the stirrup for the latter, as he once more resumed his position on the back of Punch.

Who is it that says "little pitchers have large ears"? Some deep metaphysician of the potteries, who might have added that they have also quick eyes, and sometimes silent tongues. There was a little metaphorical piece of crockery of this class, who, screened by a huge elbow-chair, had sat a quiet and unobserved spectator of the whole proceedings between her mamma and Master Erasmus Buckthorne. This was Miss Marian Marsh, a rosy-cheeked laughter-loving imp of some six years old; but one who could be mute as a mouse when the fit was on her. A handsome and highly polished cabinet of the darkest ebony occupied a recess at one end of the apartment; this had long been a great subject of speculation to little Miss. Her curiosity, however, had always been repelled; nor had all her coaxing ever won her an inspection of the thousand and one pretty things which its recess no doubt contained. On this occasion it was unlocked, and Marian was about to rush forward in eager anticipation of a peep at its interior, when, child as she was, the reflection struck her that she would stand a better chance of carrying her point by remaining perdue. Fortune for once favoured her; she crouched closer than before, and saw that her mother had taken something from one of the drawers, which she handed over to the Leech. Strange mutterings followed, and words whose sound was foreign to her youthful ears. Had she been older, their import, perhaps, might have been equally unknown. After a while there was a pause; and then the lady, as in answer to a requisition from the gentleman, placed in his hand a something which she took from her toilet. The transaction, whatever its nature, seemed now to be complete, and the article was carefully replaced in the drawer from which it had been taken. A long, and apparently interesting conversation then took place between the parties, carried on in a low tone. At its termination, Mistress Marsh and Master Erasmus Buckthorne quitted the boudoir together. But the cabinet!—ay, that was left unfastened; the folding-doors still remained invitingly expanded, the bunch of keys dangling from the lock. In an instant the spoiled child was in a chair; the drawer, so recently closed, yielded at once to her hand, and her hurried researches were rewarded by the prettiest little waxen doll imaginable. It was a first-rate prize, and Miss lost no time in appropriating it to herself. Long before Madame Marsh had returned to her Sanctum, Marian was seated under a laurestinus in the garden, nursing her new baby with the most affectionate solicitude.

"Susan, look here; see what a nasty scratch I have got upon my hand," said the young lady, when routed out at length from her hiding-place to her noontide meal.

"Yes, miss, this is always the way with you! mend, mend, mend—nothing but mend! Scrambling about among the bushes, and tearing your clothes to rags. What with you, and with madam's farthingales and kirtles, a poor bower-maiden has a fine time of it!"

"But I have not torn my clothes, Susan, and it was not the bushes; it was the doll; only see what a great ugly pin I have pulled out of it! and look, here is another!" As she spoke, Marion drew forth one of those extended pieces of black pointed wire, with which, in the days of toupees and pompoons, our foremothers were wont to secure their fly-caps and head-gear from the impertinent assaults of "Zephyrus and the Little Breezes".

"And pray, miss, where did you get this pretty doll as you call it?" asked Susan, turning over the puppet, and viewing it with a scrutinizing eye.

"Mamma gave it me," said the child.—This was a fib!

"Indeed!" quoth the girl thoughtfully; and then, in half soliloquy, and a lower key, "Well! I wish I may die if it doesn't look like master! But come to your dinner, miss! Hark! the bell is striking One!"

Meanwhile Master Thomas Marsh, and his man Ralph, were threading the devious paths, then, as now, most pseudonymously dignified with the name of roads, that wound between Marston Hall and the frontier of Romney Marsh. Their progress was comparatively slow; for though the brown mare was as good a roadster as man might back, and the gelding no mean nag of his hands, yet the tracts, rarely traversed save by the rude wains of the day, miry in the "bottoms", and covered with loose and rolling stones on the higher grounds, rendered barely passable the perpetual alternation of hill and valley.

The master rode on in pain, and the man in listlessness; although the intercourse between two individuals so situated was much less restrained in those days than might suit the refinement of a later age, little passed in approximating to conversation beyond an occasional and half-stifled groan from the one, or a vacant whistle from the other. An hour's riding had brought them among the woods of Acryse; and they were about to descend one of those green and leafy lanes, rendered by matted and over-arching branches alike impervious to shower or sunbeam, when a sudden and violent spasm seized on Master Marsh, and nearly caused him to fall from his horse. With some difficulty he succeeded in dismounting, and seating himself by the road-side. Here he remained for a full half-hour in great apparent agony; the cold sweat rolled in large round drops down his clammy forehead, a universal shivering palsied every limb, his eyeballs appeared to be starting from their sockets, and to his attached, though dull and heavy serving-man, he seemed as one struggling in the pangs of impending dissolution. His groans rose thick and frequent; and the alarmed Ralph was hesitating between his disinclination to leave him, and his desire to procure such assistance as one of the few cottages, rarely sprinkled in that wild country, might afford, when after a long-drawn sigh, his master's features as suddenly relaxed; he declared himself better, the pang had passed away, and, to use his own expression, he "felt as if a knife had been drawn from out of his very heart". With Ralph's assistance, after a while, he again reached his saddle; and though still ill at ease, from a deepening and gnawing pain, which ceased not, as he averred, to torment him, the violence of the paroxysm was spent, and it returned no more.

Master and man pursued their way with increased speed, as, emerging from the wooded defiles, they at length neared the coast; then, leaving the romantic castle of Saltwood, with its neighbouring town of Hithe, a little on their left, they proceeded along the ancient paved causeway, and, crossing the old Roman road, or Watling, plunged again into the woods that stretched between Lympne and Ostenhanger.

The sun rose high in the heavens, and its meridian blaze was powerfully felt by man and horse, when, again quitting their leafy covert, the travellers debouched on the open plain of Aldington Frith, a wide tract of unenclosed country stretching down to the very borders of "the Marsh" itself.

Here it was, in the neighbouring chapelry, the site of which may yet be traced by the curious antiquary, that Elizabeth Barton, the "Holy Maid of Kent", had, something less than a hundred years previous to the period of our narrative, commenced that series of supernatural pranks which eventually procured for her head an unenvied elevation upon London Bridge; and though the parish had since enjoyed the benefit of the incumbency of Master Erasmus's illustrious and enlightened Namesake, still, truth to tell, some of the old leaven was even yet supposed to be at work. The place had, in fact, an ill name; and, though Popish miracles had ceased to electrify its denizens, spells and charms, operating by a no less wondrous agency, were said to have taken their place. Warlocks, and other unholy subjects of Satan, were reported to make its wild recesses their favourite rendezvous, and that to an extent which eventually attracted the notice of no less a personage than the sagacious Matthew Hopkins himself, Witchfinder-General to the British Government.

A great portion of the Frith, or Fright, as the name was then, and still, pronounces, had formerly been a Chase, with rights of Freewarren, &c., appertaining to the Archbishops of the province. Since the Reformation, however, it had been disparked; and when Master Thomas Marsh, and his man Ralph, entered upon its confines, the open greensward exhibited a lively scene, sufficiently explanatory of certain sounds that had already reached their ears while yet within the sylvan screen which concealed their origin.

It was fair-day; booths, stalls, and all the rude paraphernalia of an assembly that then met as much for the purposes of traffic as festivity, were scattered irregularly over the turf; pedlars, with their packs, horse-coupers, pig-merchants, itinerant vendors of crockery and cutlery, wandered promiscuously among the mingled groups, exposing their several wares and commodities, and soliciting custom. On one side was the gaudy riband, making its mute appeal to rustic gallantry; on the other, the delicious brandy-ball and alluring lollipop, compounded after the most approved receipt in the "True Gentlewoman's Garland", and "raising the waters" in the mouth of many an expectant urchin.

Nor were rural sports wanting to those whom pleasure, rather than business, had drawn from their humble homes. Here was the tall and slippery pole, glittering in its grease, and crowned with the ample cheese, that mocked the hopes of the discomforted climber. There the fugitive pippin, swimming in water not of the purest, and bobbing from the expanded lips of the juvenile Tantalus. In this quarter the ear was pierced by squeaks from some beleaguered porker, whisking his well-soaped tail from the grasp of one already in fancy his captor. In that, the eye rested, with undisguised delight, upon the grimaces of grinning candidates for the honours of the horse-collar. All was fun, frolic, courtship, junketing, and jollity.

Maid Marion, indeed, with her lieges, Robin Hood, Scarlet, and Little John, was wanting; Friar Tuck was absent; even the Hobby-horse had disappeared: but the agile Maurice-dancers yet were there, and jungled their bells merrily among stalls well stored with gingerbread, tops, whips, whistles, and all those noisy instruments of domestic torture in which scenes like these are even now so fertile. Had I a foe whom I held at deadliest feud, I would entice his favourite child to a Fair and buy him a Whistle and a Penny-trumpet.

In one corner of the green, a little apart from the thickest of the throng, stood a small square stage, nearly level with the chins of the spectators, whose repeated bursts of laughter seemed to intimate the presence of something more than usually amusing. The platform was divided into two unequal portions; the smaller of which, surrounded by curtains of a coarse canvas, veiled from the eyes of the profane the penetralia of this movable temple of Esculapius, for such it was. Within its interior, and secure from vulgar curiosity, the Quack-salver had hitherto kept himself ensconced; occupied, no doubt, in the preparation and arrangement of that wonderful panacea which was hereafter to shed the blessings of health among the admiring crowd. Meanwhile, his attendant Jack-pudding was busily employed on the proscenium, doing his best to attract attention by a practical facetiousness which took wonderfully with the spectators, interspersing it with the melodious notes of a huge cow's horn. The fellow's costume varied but little in character from that in which the late (alas! that we should have to write the word—late!) Mr. Joseph Grimaldi was accustomed to present himself before "a generous and enlightened public": the principal difference consisted in this, that the upper garment was a long white tunic of a coarse linen, surmounted by a caricature of a ruff then fast falling into disuse, and was secured from the throat downwards by a single row of broad white metal buttons; and his legs were cased in loose wide trousers of the same material; while his sleeves, prolonged to a most disproportionate extent, descended far below the fingers, and acted as flappers in the somersets and caracoles, with which he diversified and enlivened his antics. Consummate impudence, not altogether unmixed with a certain sly humour, sparkled in his eye through the chalk and ochre with which his features were plentifully bedaubed; and especially displayed itself in a succession of jokes, the coarseness of which did not seem to detract from their merit in the eyes of his applauding audience.

He was in the midst of a long and animated harangue explanatory of his master's high pretensions; and he had informed his gaping auditors that the latter was the seventh son of a seventh son, and of course, as they very well knew, an unborn Doctor; that to this happy accident of birth he added the advantage of most extensive travel; that in his search after science he had not only perambulated the whole of this world, but had trespassed on the boundaries of the next: that the depths of the Ocean and the bowels of the Earth were alike familiar to him; that besides salves and cataplasms of sovereign virtue, by combining sundry mosses, gathered many thousand fathom below the surface of the sea, with certain unknown drugs found in an undiscovered island, and boiling the whole in the lava of Vesuvius, he had succeeded in producing his celebrated balsam of Crackapanoko, the never-failing remedy for all human disorders, and which, a proper trial allowed, would go near to reanimate the dead. "Draw near!" continued the worthy, "draw near, every one of you. Fear not high and haughty carriage: though greater than King or Kaiser, yet is the mighty Aldrovando milder than mother's milk; flint to the proud, to the humble he is as melting was; he asks not your disorders, he sees them himself at a glance—nay, without a glance; he tells your ailments with his eyes shut!—Draw near! Draw near! the more incurable the better! List to the illustrious Dr. Aldrovando, first physician to Prester John, Leech to the Grand Llama, and Hakim in Ordinary to Mustapha Muley Bey!"

"Hath your master ever a charm for the toothache, an't please you?" asked an elderly countryman whose swollen cheek bespoke his interest in the question.

"A charm!—a thousand, and every one of them infallible. Toothache, quotha! I had hoped you had come with every bone in your body fractured or out of joint. A toothache! propound a tester, master o' mine—we ask not more for such trifles: do my bidding, and thy jaws, even with the word, shall cease to trouble thee!"

The clown, fumbling awhile in a deep leathern purse, at length produced a sixpence, which he tendered to the jester. "Now to thy master, and bring me the charm forthwith."

"Nay, honest man; to disturb the mighty Aldrovando on such slight occasion were pity of my life: areed my counsel aright, and I warrant thee for the nonce. Hie thee home, friend; infuse this powder in cold spring-water, fill thy mouth with the mixture, and sit upon thy fire till it boils!"

"Out on thee for a pestilent knave!" cried the cozened countryman; but the roar of merriment around bespoke the bystanders well pleased with the jape put upon him. He retired, venting his spleen in audible murmers; and the mountebank, finding the feelings of the mob enlisted on his side, waxed more impudent every instant, filling up the intervals between his fooleries with sundry capers and contortions, and discordant notes from the cow's horn.

"Draw near, draw near, my master! Here have ye a remedy for every evil under the sun, moral, physical, natural, and supernatural! Hath any man a termagent wife?—her is that will tame her presently! Hath any one a smokey chimney?—her is an incontinent cure!"

To the first infliction no man ventured to plead guilty, though there were those standing by who thought their neighbours might have profited withal. For the last-named recipe started forth at least a dozen candidates. With the greatest gravity imaginable, Pierrot, having pocketed their groats, delivered to each a small packet curiously folded and closely sealed, containing, as he averred, directions which, if truly observed, would preclude any chimney from smoking for a whole year. They whose curiosity led them to dive into the mystery, found that a sprig of mountain ash culled by moonlight was the charm recommended, coupled, however, with the proviso that no fire should be lighted on the hearth during its exercise.

The frequent bursts of merriment proceeding from this quarter at length attracted the attention of Master Marsh, whose line of road necessarily brought him near this end of the fair, he drew bit in front of the stage just as its noisy occupant, having laid aside his formidable horn, was drawing still more largely on the amazement of "the public" by a feat of especial wonder—he was eating fire! Curiosity mingled with astonishment was at its height; and feelings not unallied to alarm were beginning to manifest themselves, among the softer sex especially as they gazed on the flames that issued from the mouth of the living volcano. All eyes, indeed, were fixed upon the fire-eater with an intentness that left no room for observing another worthy who had now emerged upon the scene. This was, however, no less a personage than the *Deus ex machina*—the illustrious Aldrovando himself.

Short in stature and spare in form, the sage had somewhat increased the former by a steeple-crowned hat adorned with a cock's feather; while the thick shoulder-padding of a quilted doublet, surmounted by a falling band, added a little to his personal importance in point of breadth. His habit was composed throughout of black serge, relieved with scarlet slashes in the sleeves and trunks; red was the feather in his hat, red were the roses in his shoes, which rejoiced, moreover, in a pair of red heels. The lining of a short cloak of faded velvet, that hung transversely over his left shoulder, was also red. Indeed, from all that we could ever see or hear, this agreeable alternation of red and black appears to be the mixture of colours most approved at the court of Beelzebub, and the one most generally adopted by his friends and favourites. His features were sharp and shrewd, and a fire sparkled in his keen grey eye, much at variance with the wrinkles that ran their irregular furrows above his prominent and bushy brows. He had advanced slowly from behind the screen while the attention of the multitude was absorbed by the pyrotechnics of Mr. Merryman, and, stationing himself at the extreme corner of the stage, stood quietly leaning on a crutch-handle walking-staff of blackest ebony, his glance steadily fixed on the face of Marsh, from whose countenance the amusement he had insensibly begun to derive had not succeeded in removing all traces of bodily pain.

For a while the latter was unobservant of the inquisitorial survey with which he was regarded; the eyes of the parties, however, at length met. The brown mare had a fine shoulder; she stood pretty nearly sixteen hands. Marsh himself, though slightly bowed by ill health, and the "coming autumn" of life, was full six feet in height. His elevation giving him an unobstructed view over the heads of the pedestrians, he had naturally fallen into the rear of the assembly, which brought him close to the diminutive Doctor, with whose face, despite the red heels, his own was about upon level.

"And what makes Master Marsh here?—what sees he in the mummeries of a miserable buffoon to divert him when his life is in jeopardy?" said a shrill cracked voice that sounded as in his very ear. It was the Doctor who spoke.

"Knowest thou me, friend?" said Marsh, scanning with awakened interest the figure of his questioner: "I call thee not to mind; and yet—stay, where have we met?"

"It skills not to declare," was the answer; "suffice it we have met—in other climes perchance—and now meet happily again—happily at least for thee."

"Why truly the trick of thy countenance reminds me of somewhat I have seen before; where or when I know not: but what wouldst thou with me?"

"Nay, rather what wouldst thou here, Thomas Marsh? What wouldst thou on the Frith of Aldington?—is it a score or two of paltry sheep? or is it something nearer to thy heart?"

Marsh started as the last words were pronounced with more than common significance: a pang shot through him at the moment, and the vinegar aspect of the charlatan seemed to relax into a smile half compassionate, half sardonic.

"Grammercy," quoth Marsh, after a long-drawn breath, "what knowest thou of me, fellow, or of my concerns? What knowest thou——?"

"This know I, Master Thomas Marsh," said the stranger gravely, "that thy life is even now perilled, evil practices are against thee; but no matter, thou art quit for the nonce—other hands than mine have saved thee! Thy pains are over. Hark! the clock strikes One!" As he spoke a single toll from the bell-tower of Bilsington came, wafted by the western breeze, over the thick-set and lofty oaks which intervened between the Frith and what had been once a priory. Dr. Aldrovando turned as the sound came floating on the wind, and was moving, as if half in anger, towards the other side of the stage, where the mountebank, his fires extinct, was now disgorging to the admiring crowd yard after yard of gaudy, coloured riband.

"Stay! Nay, prithee stay!" cried Marsh eagerly. "I was wrong; in faith I was. A change, and that a sudden and most marvellous, hath indeed come over me; I am free; I breathe again; I feel as though a load of years had been removed; and—is it possible?—hast thou done this?"

"Thomas Marsh!" said the Doctor, pausing, and turning for the moment on his heel, "I have not: I repeat that other and more innocent hands than mine have done this deed. Nevertheless, heed my counsel well! Thou art encompassed; I, and I only, have the means of relieving thee. Follow thy courses; pursue thy journey; but as thou valuest life and more than life, be at the foot of yonder woody knoll what time the rising moon throws her first beam upon the bare and blighted summit that towers above its trees."

He crossed abruptly to the opposite quarter of the scaffolding, and was in an instant deeply engaged in listening to those whom the cow's horn had attracted, and in prescribing for their real or fancied ailments. Vain were all Marsh's efforts again to attract his notice; it was evident that he studiously avoided him; and when, after an hour or more spent in useless endeavour, he saw the object of his anxiety seclude himself once more within his canvas screen, he rode slowly and thoughtfully off the field.

What should he do? Was the man a mere quack? an impostor?—His name thus obtained—that might be easily done. But then his secret griefs; the doctor's knowledge of them; their cure; for he felt that his pains were gone, his healthful feelings restored!

True, Aldrovando, if that were his name, had disclaimed all co-operation in his recovery; but he knew, or he, at least, announced it. Nay, more, he had hinted that he was yet in jeopardy; that practices—and the chord sounded strangely in unison with one that had before vibrated within him—that practices were in operation against his life! It was enough! He would keep tryst with the Conjuror, if conjuror he were; and, at least, ascertain who and what he was, and how he had become acquainted with his own person and secret afflictions.

When the late Mr. Pitt was determined to keep out Bonaparte, and prevent his gaining a settlement in the county of Kent, among other ingenious devices adopted for that purpose, he caused to be constructed what was then, and has ever since been conventionally termed a "Military Canal". This is a not very practicable ditch, some thirty feet wide, and nearly nine feet deep—in the middle—extending from the town and port of Hithe to within a mile of the town and port of Rye, a distance of about twenty miles, and forming, as it were, the cord of a bow, the arc of which constitutes that remote fifth quarter of the globe spoken of by travellers. Trivial objections to the plan were made at the time by cavillers; and an old gentleman of the neighbourhood, who proposed as a cheap substitute to put down his own cocked-hat upon a pole, was deservedly pooh-pooh'd down; in fact, the job, though rather an expensive one, was found to answer remarkably well. The French managed, indeed, to scramble over the Rhine and the Rhone, and other insignificant currents, but they never did, or could, pass Mr. Pitt's "Military Canal". At no great distance from the centre of this cord rises abruptly a sort of woody promontory, in shape almost conical; its sides covered with thick underwood, above which is seen a bare and brown summit rising like an Alp in miniature. The "defence of the nation" not being then in existence, Master Marsh met with no obstruction in reaching this place of appointment long before the time prescribed.

So much, indeed, was his mind occupied by his adventure and extraordinary cure, that his original design had been abandoned, and Master Cobbe remained unvisited. A rude hostel in the neighbourhood furnished entertainment for man and horse; and here, a full hour before the rising of the moon, he left Ralph and the other beasts, proceeding to his rendezvous on foot and alone.

"You are punctual, Master Marsh," squeaked the shrill voice of the Doctor, issuing from the thicket as the first silvery gleam trembled on the aspens above. "'Tis well: now follow me and in silence."

The first part of the command Marsh hesitated not to obey, the second was more difficult of observance.

"Who and what are you? Whither are you leading me?" burst not unnaturally from his lips; but all question was at once cut short by the peremptory tones of his guide.

"Hush! I say; your finger on your lip, there he hawks abroad: follow me, and that silently and quickly." The little man turned as he spoke, and led the way through a scarcely perceptible path or track, which wound among the underwood. The lapse of a few minutes brought them to the door of a low building, so hidden by the surrounding trees that few would have suspected its existence. It was a cottage of rather extraordinary dimensions, but consisting of only one floor. No smoke from its solitary chimney; no cheering ray streamed from its single window, which was, however, secured by a shutter of such thickness as to preclude the possibility of any stray beam issuing from within. The exact size of the building it was, in that uncertain light, difficult to distinguish, a portion of it seeming buried in the wood behind. The door gave way on the application of a key, and Marsh followed his conductor resolutely but

D

cautiously along a narrow passage, feebly lighted by a small taper that winked and twinkled at its farther extremity. The Doctor, as he approached, raised it from the ground, and, opening an adjoining door, ushered his guest into the room beyond.

It was a dull and oddly furnished apartment, insufficiently lighted by an iron lamp that hung from the roof, and scarcely illuminated the walls and angles, which seemed to be composed of some dark-coloured wood. On one side, however, Master Marsh could discover an article bearing strong resemblance to a coffin; on the other was a large oval mirror in an ebony frame, and in the midst of the floor was described in red chalk a double circle about six feet in diameter, its inner verge inscribed with sundry hieroglyphics, agreeably relieved at intervals with an alternation of skulls and cross-bones. In the very centre was deposited one skull of such surpassing size and thickness as would have filled the soul of a Spurzheim or De Ville with wonderment. A large book, a naked sword, an hour glass, a chafing dish, and a black cat, completed the list of moveables; with the exception of a couple of tapers which stood on each side of the mirror, and which the strange gentleman now proceeded to light from the one in his hand. As they flared up with what Marsh thought a most unnatural brilliancy, he perceived reflected in the glass behind a dial suspended over the coffin-like article already mentioned: the hand was fast verging towards the hour of nine. The eyes of the little Doctor seemed riveted on the horologe.

"Now strip thee, Master Marsh, and that quickly: untruss, I say! discard thy boots, doff doublet and hose, and place thyself incontinent in yonder bath."

The visitor cast his eyes again upon the formidable-looking article, and perceived that it was nearly filled with water. A cold bath, at such an hour and under such auspices, was anything but inviting: he hesitated, and turned his eyes alternately on the Doctor and the Black Cat.

"Trifle not the time, man, an you be wise," said the former; "Passion of my heart! let but yon minute-hand reach the hour, and thou not immersed, thy life were not worth a pin's fee!"

The Black Cat gave vent to a single mew—a most unnatural sound for a mouser—it seemed as if it were mewed through a cow's horn.

"Quick, Master Marsh! Uncase or you perish!" repeated his strange host, throwing as he spoke a handful of some dingy-looking powders into the brazier. "Behold, the attack has begun!" A thick cloud rose from the embers; a cold shivering shook the astonished Yeoman; sharp pricking pains penetrated his ankles and the palms of his hands, and, as the smoke cleared away, he distinctly saw and recognized in the mirror the boudoir of Marston Hall.

The doors of the well-known ebony cabinet were closed; but fixed against them, and standing out in strong relief from the contrast afforded by the sable background, was a waxen image of himself! It appeared to be secured, and sustained in an upright posture, by large black pins driven through the feet and palms, the latter of which were extended in a cruciform position. To the right and left stood his wife and Jose; in the middle, with his back towards him, was a figure which he had no difficulty in recognizing as the Leech of Folkestone. The latter had just succeeded in fastening the dexter hand of the image, and was now in the act of drawing a broad and keen-edged sabre from its sheath. The Black Cat mewed again. "Haste or you die!" said the Doctor—Marsh looked at the dial; it wanted but four minutes of nine; he felt that the crisis of his fate was come. Off went his heavy boots; doublet to the right, galligaskins to the left; never was a man more swiftly disrobed; in two minutes, to use an Indian expression, "he was all face!" in another he was on his back, and up to his chin, in a bath which smelt strongly as of brimstone and garlic.

"Heed well the clock!" cried the Conjuror: "with the first stroke of Nine plunge thy head beneath the water, suffer not a hair above the surface: plunge deeply or thou art lost!"

The little man had seated himself in the centre of the circle upon the large skull, elevating his legs at an angle of forty-five degrees. In this position he spun round with a velocity to be equalled only by that of a tee-totum, the red roses on his insteps seeming to describe a circle of fire. The best buckskins that ever mounted at Melton had soon yielded to such rotatory friction—but he spun on—the Cat mewed, bats and obscene birds fluttered overhead; Erasmus was seen to raise his weapon, the clock struck!—and Marsh, who had "ducked" at the instant, popped up his head again, spitting and spluttering, half-choked wi th the infernal solution, which had insinuated itself into his mouth, and ears and nose. A disgust at his nauseous dip was, however, at once removed, when, casting his eyes on the glass, he saw the consternation of the party whose persons it exhibited. Erasmus had evidently made his blow and failed; the figure was unmutilated; the hilt remained in the hand of the striker, while the shivered blade lay in shining fragments on the floor.

The Conjuror ceased his spinning, and brought himself to an anchor; the Black Cat purred—its purring seemed strangely mixed with the self-satisfied chuckle of a human being. Where had Marsh heard something like it before?

He was rising from his unsavoury couch, when a motion from the little man checked him. "Rest where you are, Thomas Marsh; so far all goes well, but the danger is not yet over!" He looked again, and perceived that the shadowy triumvirate were in deep and eager consultation; the fragments of the shattered weapon appeared to undergo a close scrutiny. The result was clearly unsatisfactory; the lips of the parties moved rapidly, and much gesticulation might be observed, but no sound fell upon the ear. The hand of the dial had nearly reached the quarter; at once the parties separated; and Buckthorne stood again before the figure, his hand armed with a long and sharp-pointed misericorde, a dagger little in use of late, but such as, a century before, often performed the part of a modern oyster-knife, in tickling the osteology of a dismounted cavalier through the shelly defences of his plate armour. Again he raised his arm. "Duck!" roared the Doctor, spinning away upon his cephalic pivot: The Black Cat cocked his tail, and seemed to mew the word "Duck!" Down went Master Marsh's head; one of his hands had unluckily been resting on the edge of the bath: he drew it hastily in, but not altogether scatheless: the stump of a rusty nail, projecting from the margin of the bath, had caught and slightly grazed it. The pain was more acute than is usually produced by such trivial accidents; and Marsh, on once more raising his head, beheld a dagger of the Leech sticking in the little finger of the wax figure, which it had seemingly nailed to the cabinet door.

"By my truly, a scrape o' the narrowest!" quoth the Conjuror: "the next course, dive you not the readier, there is no more life in you than in a pickled herring. What! courage, Master Marsh; but be heedful; an they miss again, let them bide the issue!"

He drew his hand athwart his brow as he spoke, and dashed off the perspiration which the violence of his exercise had drawn from every pore. Black Tom sprang upon the edge of the bath, and stared full in the face of the bather: his sea-green eyes were lambent with unholy fire, but their marvellous obliquity of vision was not to be mistaken: the very countenance, too! Could it be?— the features were feline, but their expression was that of the Jack Pudding! Was the Mountebank a Cat?—or the Cat a Mountebank?—it was all a mystery: and Heaven knows how long Marsh might have continued staring at Grimalkin, had not his attention been again called by Aldrovando to the magic mirror.

Great dissatisfaction, not to say dismay, seemed now to pervade the conspirators: Dame Isabel was closely inspecting the figure's wounded hand, while Jose was aiding the pharmocopolist to charge a huge petronel with powder and bullets. The load was a heavy one; but Erasmus seemed determined this time to make sure of his object. Somewhat of trepidation might be observed in his manner as he rammed down the balls, and his withered cheek appeared to have acquired an increase of paleness: but amazement rather than fear was the prevailing symptom, and his countenance betrayed no jot of irresolution. As the clock was about to chime half past nine, he planted himself with a firm foot in front of the image, waved his unoccupied hand with a cautionary gesture to his companions, and, as they hastily retired on either side, brought the muzzle of his weapon within half a foot of his mark. As the shadowy form was about to draw the trigger, Marsh again plunged his head beneath the surface; and the sound of an explosion, as of firearms, mingled with the rush of water that poured into his ears. His immersion was but momentary, yet did he feel as though half suffocated: he sprang from the bath, and, as his eye fell on the mirror, he saw—or thought he saw—the Leech of Folkestone lying dead on the floor of his wife's boudoir, his head shattered to pieces, and his hand still grasping the stock of a bursten petronel.

He saw no more; his head swam; his senses reeled, the whole room was turning round, and, as he fell to the ground, the last impressions to which he was conscious were the chucklings of a hoarse laughter, and the mewings of a Tom Cat!

Master Marsh was found the next morning by his bewildered serving-man, stretched before the door of. the humble hostel at which he sojourned. His clothes were somewhat torn and much bemired! and deeply did honest Ralph marvel that one so staid and grave as Master Marsh of Marston should thus have played the roisterer, missing, perchance, a profitable bargain for the drunken orgies of midnight wassail, or the endearments of some rustic light-o'-love. Tenfold was his astonishment increased when, after retracng in silence their journey of the preceding day, the Hall, on their arrival about noon, was found in a state of uttermost confusion. No wife stood there to greet with the smile of bland affection her returning spouse; no page to hold his stirrup, or receive his gloves, his hat, and riding-rod. The doors were open, the rooms in most admired disorder; men and maidens peeping, hurrying hither and thither, and popping in and out, like rabbits in a warren. The lady of the mansion was nowhere to be found.

Jose, too, had disappeared; the latter had been last seen riding furiously towards Folkestone early in the preceding afternoon; to a question from Hodge Gardener he had hastily answered, that he bore a missive of moment from his mistress. The lean apprentice of Erasmus Buckthorne declared that the page had summoned his master, in haste, about six of the clock, and that they had rode forth together, as he verily believed, on their way back to the Hall where he had supposed Master Buckthorne's services to be suddenly required on some pressing emergency. Since that time he had seen nought of either of them: the grey cob, however, had returned late at night, masterless, with his girths loose, and the saddle turned upside down.

Nor was Master Erasmus Buckthorne ever seen again. Strict search was made through the neighbourhood, but without success; and it was at length presumed that he must, for reasons which nobody could divine, have absconded, together with Jose and his faithless mistress. The latter had carried off with her the strong box, divers articles of valuable plate, and jewels of price. Her boudoir appeared to have been completely ransacked; the cabinet and drawers stood open and empty; the very carpet, a luxury then newly introduced into England, was gone. Marsh, however, could trace no vestige of the visionary scene which he affirmed to have been last night presented to his eyes.

Much did the neighbours marvel at his story: some thought him mad; others, that he was merely indulging in that privilege to which, as a traveller, he had a right indefeasible. Trusty Ralph said nothing, but shrugged his shoulders; and falling, into the rear, imitated the action of raising a wine-cup to his lips. An opinion, indeed, soon prevailed, that Master Thomas Marsh had gotten, in common parlance, exceeding drunk on the preceding evening, and had dreamt all that he so circumstantially related. This belief acquired additional credit when they, whom curiosity induced to visit the woody knoll of Aldington Mount, declared that they could find no building such as that described, nor any cottage near; save one, indeed, a low-roofed hovel, once a house of public entertainment, but now half in ruins. The "Old·Cat and Fiddle"—so was the tenement called—had been long uninhabited; yet still exhibited the remains of a broken sign, on which the keen observer might decipher something like a rude portrait of the animal from which it derived its name. It was also supposed still to afford an occasional asylum to the smugglers of the coast, but no trace of any visit from sage or mountebank could be detected; nor was the wise Aldrovando, whom many remembered to have seen at the fair, ever found again on all that countryside.

Of the runaways nothing was ever certainly known. A boat, the property of an old fisherman who plied his trade on the outskirts of the town, had been seen to quit the bay that night; and there were those who declared that she had more hands on board than Carden and his sons, her usual complement; but, as the gala came on, and the frail bark was eventually found keel upwards on the Goodwin Sands, it was presumed that she had struck on that fatal quicksand in the dark and that all on board had perished.

Little Marion, whom her profligate mother had abandoned, grew up to be a fine girl, and a handsome. She became, moreover, heiress to Marston Hall, and brought the estate into the Ingoldsby family by her marriage with one of its scions.

Thus far Mrs. Botherby.

It is a little singular that, on pulling down the old Hall in my grandfather's time, a human skeleton was found enveloped in a tattered cloth that seemed to have been once a carpet, and which fell to pieces almost immediately on being exposed to the air. The bones were perfect, but those of one hand were wanting; and the skull, perhaps from the labourer's pick-axe, had received considerable injury; the worm-eaten stock of an old-fashioned pistol lay near, together with a rusty piece of iron which a workman, more sagacious than his fellows, pronounced a portion of the lock, but nothing was found which the utmost stretch of human ingenuity could twist into a barrel.

The portrait of the fair Marion hangs yet in the Gallery of Tappington; and near it is another, of a young man in the prime of life, whom Mrs. Botherby affirms to be that of her father. It exhibits a mild and rather melancholy countenance, with a high forehead, and the peaked beard and mustaches of the seventeenth century. The signet-finger of the left hand is gone, and appears, on close inspection, to have been painted out by some later artist; possibly in compliment to the tradition, which, teste Botherby, records that of Mr. Marsh to have gangreened, and to have undergone amputation at the knuckle-joint. If really the resemblance of the gentleman alluded to, it must have been taken at some period antecedent to his marriage. There is neither date nor painter's name; but, a little above the head, on the dexter side of the picture, is an escutcheon, bearing "Quarterly, Gules and Argent, in the first quarter a horse's head of the second;" beneath it are the words "AEtatis suae 26". On the opposite side is the following mark, which Mr. Simpkinson declared to be that of a Merchant of the Staple, and pretends to discover, in the monogram comprised in it, all the characters which compose the name of THOMAS MARSH, of MARSTON.

Respect for the feelings of an honourable family—nearly connected with the Ingoldsbys—has induced me to veil the real "sponsorial and patronymic appellations" of my next hero under a sobriquet interfering neither with rhyme or rhythm.* I shall merely add that every incident in the story bears, on the face of it, the stamp of veracity, and that many "persons of honour" in the county of Berks, who well recollected Sir George Rooke's expedition against Gibraltar, would, if they were now alive, gladly bear testimony to the truth of every syllable.

THE HAUNTED AND THE HAUNTERS

By Edward Bulwer Lytton

A FRIEND of mine, who is a man of letters and a philosopher, said to me one day, as if between jest and earnest: "Fancy! since we last met, I have discovered a haunted house in the midst of London."

"Really haunted?—and by what?—ghosts?"

"Well, I can't answer these questions; all I know is this—six weeks ago I and my wife were in search of a furnished apartment. Passing a quiet street, we saw on the window of one of the houses a bill, 'Apartments, Furnished'. The situation suited us: we entered the house—liked the rooms—engaged them by the week—and left them the third day. No power on earth could have reconciled my wife to stay longer; and I don't wonder at it."

"What did you see?"

"Excuse me—I have no desire to be ridiculed as a superstitious dreamer—nor, on the other hand, could I ask you to accept on my affirmation what you would hold to be incredible without the evidence of your own senses. Let me only say this, it was not so much what we saw or heard (in which you might fairly suppose that we were the dupes of our own excited fancy, or the victims of imposture in others) that drove us away, as it was an undefinable terror which seized both of us whenever we passed by the door of a certain unfurnished room, in which we neither saw nor heard anything. And the strangest marvel of all was, that for once in my life I agreed with my wife, silly woman though she be —and allowed, after the third night, that it was impossible to stay a fourth in that house. Accordingly, on the fourth morning I summoned the woman who kept the house and attended on us, and told her that the rooms did not quite suit us, and we would not stay out our week. She said dryly, 'I know why; you have stayed longer than any other lodger. Few ever stayed a second night; none before you a third. But I take it they have been very kind to you.'

" 'They—who?' I asked, affecting a smile.

" 'Why, they who haunt the house, whoever they are. I don't mind them; I remember them many years ago, when I lived in this house, not as a servant; but I know they will be the death of me some day. I don't care—I'm old, and must die soon, anyhow; and then I shall be with them, and in this house still.' The woman spoke with so dreary a calmness, that really it was a sort of awe that prevented my conversing with her further. I paid for my week, and too happy were I and my wife to get off so cheaply."

"You excite my curiosity," said I; "nothing I should like better than to sleep in a haunted house. Pray give me the address of the one which you left so ignominiously."

My friend gave me the address; and when we parted, I walked straight towards the house thus indicated.

---

* Pack o' nonsense!—Everybody as belongs to him is dead and gone—and everybody knows that the poor young gentleman's real name wasn't Sobriquet at all, but Hampden Pye, Esq., and that one of his uncles—or cousins—used to make verses about the king and the queen, and had a sack of money for doing it every year: and that's his picture in the blue coat and little gold-laced cocked hat, that hangs on the stairs over the door of the passage that leads to the blue room. Sobriquet!—but there!—The Squire wrote it after dinner! ELIZABETH BOTHERBY.

It is situated on the north side of Oxford Street, in a dull but respectable thoroughfare. I found the house shut up—no bill at the window, and no response to my knock. As I was turning away, a beer-boy, collecting pewter pots at the neighbouring areas, said to me : "Do you want anyone at that house, sir?"

"Yes, I heard it was to be let."

"Let!—why, the woman who kept it is dead—has been dead these three weeks, and no one can be found to stay there, though Mr. J—— offered ever so much. He offered Mother, who chars for him, £1 a week just to open and shut the windows, and she would not."

"Would not!—and why?"

"The house is haunted; and the old woman who kept it was found dead in her bed, with her eyes wide open. They say the devil strangled her."

"Pooh!—you speak of Mr. J——. Is he the owner of the house?"

"Yes."

"Where does he live?"

"In G—— Street, No.——."

"What is he?—in any business?"

"No, sir—nothing particular; a single gentleman."

I gave the pot-boy the gratuity earned by his liberal information, and proceeded to Mr. J——, in G—— Street, which was close by the street that boasted the haunted house. I was lucky enough to find Mr. J—— at home—an elderly man, with intelligent countenance and prepossessing manners.

I communicated my name and my business frankly. I said I heard the house was considered to be haunted—that I had a strong desire to examine a house with so equivocal a reputation—that I should be greatly obliged if he would allow me to hire it, though only for a night. I was willing to pay for that privilege whatever he might be inclined to ask. "Sir," said Mr. J—— with great courtesy, "the house is at your service, for as short or as long a time as you please. Rent is out of the question—the obligation will be on my side should you be able to discover the cause of the strange phenomena which at present deprives it of all value. I cannot let it, for I cannot even get a servant to keep it in order or answer the door. Unluckily the house is haunted, if I may use that expression, not only by night, but by day; though at night the disturbances are of a more unpleasant and sometimes of a more alarming character. The poor old woman who died in it three weeks ago was a pauper whom I took out of a workhouse, for in her childhood she had been known to some of my family, and had once been in such good circumstances that she had rented that house of my uncle. She was a woman of superior education and strong mind, and was the only person I could ever induce to remain in the house. Indeed, since her death, which was sudden, and the coroner's inquest, which gave it a notoriety in the neighbourhood, I have so despaired of finding any person to take charge of it, much more a tenant, that I would willingly let it rent-free for a year to anyone who would pay its rates and taxes."

"How long is it since the house acquired this sinister character?"

"That I can scarcely tell you, but very many years since. The old woman I spoke of said it was haunted when she rented it between thirty and forty years ago. The fact is that my life has been spent in the East Indies, and in the civil service of the Company. I returned to England last year, on inheriting the fortune of an uncle, amongst whose possessions was the house in question. I found it shut up and uninhabited. I was told that it was haunted, that no one would inhabit it. I smiled at what seemed to me so idle a story. I spent some money in repairing and roofing it—added to its old-fashioned furniture a few modern articles—advertised it, and obtained a lodger for a year. He was a colonel retired on half-pay. He came in with his family, a son and a daughter, and four or five servants : they all left the house the next day, and although they deponed that they had all seen something different, that something was equally terrible to all. I really could not in conscience sue, or even blame, the colonel for breach of agreement. Then I put in the old woman I have spoken of, and she was empowered to let the house in apartments. I never had one lodger who stayed more than three days. I do not tell you their stories—to no two lodgers have there been exactly the same phenomena repeated. It is better that you should judge for yourself, than enter the house with an imagination influenced by previous narratives; only be prepared to see and to hear something or other, and take whatever precautions you yourself please."

"Have you never had a curiosity yourself to pass a night in that house?"

"Yes. I passed not a night, but three hours in broad daylight alone in that house. My curiosity is not satisfied, but it is quenched. I have no desire to renew the experiment. You cannot complain, you see, sir, that I am not sufficiently candid; and unless your interest be exceedingly eager and your nerves unusually strong, I honestly add that I advise you *not* to pass a night in that house."

"My interest *is* exceedingly keen," said I, "and though only a coward will boast of his nerves in situations wholly unfamiliar to him, yet my nerves have been seasoned in such variety of danger that I have the right to rely on them—even in a haunted house."

Mr. J—— said very little more; he took the keys of the house out of his bureau, gave them to me—and thanking him cordially for his frankness, and his urbane concession to my wish, I carried off my prize.

Impatient for the experiment, as soon as I reached home I summoned my confidential servant—a young man of gay spirits, fearless temper, and as free from superstitious prejudice as anyone I could think of.

"F——," said I, "you remember in Germany how disappointed we were at not finding a ghost in that old castle, which was said to be haunted by a headless apparition?—well, I have heard of a house in London which, I have reason to hope, is decidedly haunted. I mean to sleep there tonight. From what I hear, there is no doubt that something will allow itself to be seen or to be heard—something, perhaps, excessively horrible. Do you think, if I take you with me, I may rely on your presence of mind, whatever may happen?"

"Oh, sir! pray trust me," answered F——, grinning with delight.

"Very well—then here are the keys of the house—this is the address. Go now—select for me any bedroom you please; and since the house has not been inhabited for weeks, make up a good fire—air the bed well—see, of course, that there are candles as well as fuel. Take with you my revolver and my dagger —so much for my weapons—arm yourself equally well; and if we are not a match for a dozen ghosts, we shall be but a sorry couple of Englishmen."

I was engaged for the rest of the day on business so urgent that I had not leisure to think much on the nocturnal adventure to which I had plighted my honour. I dined alone, and very late, and while dining, read, as is my habit. The volume I selected was one of Macaulay's Essays. I thought to myself that I would take the book with me; there was so much of healthfulness in the style, and practical life in the subjects, that it would serve as an antidote against the influences of superstitious fancy.

Accordingly, about half past nine, I put the book into my pocket, and strolled leisurely towards the haunted house. I took with me a favourite dog—an exceedingly sharp, bold, and vigilant bull-terrier—a dog fond of prowling about strange ghostly corners and passages at night in search of rats—a dog of dogs for a ghost.

It was a summer night, but chilly, the sky somewhat gloomy and overcast. Still there was a moon—faint and sickly, but still a moon—and if the clouds permitted, after midnight it would be brighter.

I reached the house, knocked, and my servant opened with a cheerful smile.

"All right, sir, and very comfortable."

"Oh!" said I, rather disappointed; "have you not seen nor heard anything remarkable?"

"Well, sir, I must own I have heard something queer."

"What?—what?"

"The sound of feet pattering behind me; and once or twice small noises like whispers close at my ear—nothing more."

"You are not at all frightened?"

"I! Not a bit of it, sir"; and the man's bold look reassured me on one point—viz., that, happen what might, he would not desert me.

We were in the hall, the street door closed, and my attention was now drawn to my dog. He had at first run in eagerly enough, but had sneaked back to the door, and was scratching and whining to get out. After patting him on the head, and encouraging him gently, the dog seemed to reconcile himself to the situation and followed me and F—— through the house, but keeping close at my heels instead of hurrying inquisitively in advance, which was his usual and normal habit in all strange places. We first visited the subterranean apartments, the kitchen and other offices, and especially the cellars, in which last there were two or three bottles of wine still left in a bin, covered with cobwebs, and evidently, by their appearance, undisturbed for many years. It was clear that the ghosts were not wine-bibbers. For the rest we discovered nothing of interest. There was a gloomy little back-yard, with very high walls. The stones of this yard were very damp—and what with the damp, and what with the dust and smoke-grime on the pavement, our feet left a slight impression where we passed. And now appeared the first strange phenomenon witnessed by itself in this strange above. I saw, just before me, the print of a foot suddenly form itself, as it were. I stopped, caught hold of my servant, and pointed to it. In advance of that footprint as suddenly dropped another. We both saw it. I advanced quickly to the place; the footprint kept advancing before me, a small footprint—the foot of a child: the impression was too faint thoroughly to distinguish the shape, but it seemed to us both that it was the print of a naked foot. This phenomenon ceased when we arrived at the opposite wall, nor did it repeat itself on returning. We remounted the stairs, and entered the rooms on the ground floor, a dining parlour, a small back parlour, and a still smaller third room that had been probably appropriated to a footman—all still as death. We then visited the drawing-rooms, which seemed fresh and new. In the front room I seated myself in an arm-chair. F—— placed on the table the candlestick with which he had lighted us. I told him to shut the door. As he turned to do so, a chair opposite to me moved from the wall quickly and noiselessly, and dropped itself about a yard from my own chair, immediately fronting it.

"Why, this is better than the turning-tables," said I, with a half-laugh—and as I laughed, my dog put back his head and howled.

F——, coming back, had not observed the movement of the chair. He employed himself now in stilling the dog. I continued to gaze on the chair, and fancied I saw on it a pale blue misty outline of a human figure, but an outline so indistinct that I could not distrust my own vision. The dog now was quiet.

"Put back that chair opposite to me," said I to F——; "put it back to the wall."

F—— obeyed. "Was that you, sir?" said he, turning abruptly.

"I—what!"

"Why, something struck me. I felt it sharply on the shoulder—just here."

"No," said I. "But we have jugglers present, and though we may not discover their tricks, we shall catch *them* before they frighten *us*."

We did not stay long in the drawing-rooms—in fact, they felt so damp and so chilly that I was glad to get to the fire upstairs. We locked the doors of the drawing-rooms—a precaution which, I should observe, we had taken with all the rooms we had searched below. The bedroom my servant had selected for me was the best on the floor—a large one, with two windows confronting the street. The four-poster bed, which took up no inconsiderable space, was opposite to the fire, which burned clear and bright; a door in the wall to the left, between the bed and the window, communicated with the room which my servant appropriated to himself. This last was a small room with a sofa-bed, and had no communication with the landing-place—no other door but that which conducted to the bedroom I was to occupy. On either side of my fireplace was a cupboard, without locks, flushed with the wall, and covered with the same dull-brown paper. We examined these cupboards—only hooks to suspend female dresses—nothing else; we sounded the walls—evidently solid—the outer walls of the building. Having finished the survey of these apartments, warmed myself a few moments, and lighted my cigar, I then, still accompanied by F——, went forth to complete my reconnoitre. In the landing-place there was another door; it was closed firmly. "Sir," said my servant in surprise, "I unlocked this door with all the others when I first came; it cannot have got locked from the inside, for it is a——."

Before he had finished his sentence, the door, which neither of us then was touching, opened quietly of itself. We looked at each other a single instant. The same thought seized both—some human agency might be detected here. I rushed in first, my servant followed. A small blank dreary room without furniture—a few empty boxes and hampers in a corner—a small window—the shutters closed—not even a fireplace—no other door, but that by which we had entered—no carpet on the floor, and the floor seemed very old, uneven, worm-eaten, mended here and there, as was shown by the whiter patches on the wood; but no living being, and no visible place in which a living being could have hidden. As we stood gazing round, the door by which we had entered closed as quietly as it had before opened: we were imprisoned.

For the first time I felt a creep of undefinable horror. Not so my servant. "Why, they don't think to trap us, sir; I could break that trumpery door with a kick of my foot."

"Try first if it will open to your hand," said I, shaking off the vague apprehension that had seized me, "while I open the shutters and see what is without."

I unbarred the shutters—the window looked on the little back-yard I have before described; there was no ledge without—nothing but sheer descent. No man getting out of that window would have found any footing till he had fallen on the stones below.

F——, meanwhile, was vainly attempting to open the door. He now turned round to me, and asked my permission to use force. And I should here state, in justice to the servant, that, far from evincing any superstitious terrors, his nerve, composure, and even gaiety amidst circumstances so extraordinary compelled my admiration, and made me congratulate myself on having secured a companion in every way fitted to the occasion. I willingly gave him the permission he required. But though he was a remarkably strong man, his force was as idle as his milder efforts; the door did not even shake to his stoutest kick. Breathless and panting, he desisted. I then tried the door myself, equally in vain. As I ceased from the effort, again that creep of horror came over me; but this time it was more cold and stubborn. I felt as if some strange and ghastly exhalation were rising up from the chinks of that rugged floor, and filling the atmosphere with a venomous influence hostile to human life. The door now very slowly and quietly opened as of its own accord. We precipitated ourselves into the landing-place. We both saw a large pale light—as large as the human figure, but shapeless and unsubstantial—move before us, and ascend the stairs that led from the landing into the attics. I followed the light, and my servant followed me. It entered, to the right of the landing, a small garret, of which the door stood open. I entered in the same instant. The light then collapsed into a small globule, exceedingly brilliant and vivid, rested a moment on a bed in the corner, quivered, and vanished. We approached the bed and examined it—a half-tester, such as is commonly found in attics devoted to servants. On the drawers that stood near it we perceived an old faded silk kerchief, with the needle still left in a rent half repaired. The kerchief was covered with dust; probably it had belonged to the old woman who had last died in that house, and this might have been her sleeping-room. I had sufficient curiosity to open the drawers; there were a few odds and ends of female dress, and two letters tied round with a narrow ribbon of faded yellow. I took the liberty to possess myself of the letters. We found nothing else in the room worth noticing—nor did the light reappear; but we distinctly heard, as we turned to go, a pattering footfall on the floor—just before us. We went through the other attics (in all four), the footfall still preceding us. Nothing to be seen—nothing but the footfall heard. I had the letters in my hand, just as I was descending the stairs, I distinctly felt my wrist seized, and a faint, soft effort made to draw the letters from my clasp. I only held them the more tightly, and the effort ceased.

We regained the bedchamber appropriated to myself, and I then remarked that my dog had not followed us when we had left it. He was thrusting himself close to the fire, and trembling. I was impatient to examine the letters; and while I read them, my servant opened a little box in which he had deposited the weapons I had ordered him to bring; took them out, placed them on a table close at my bed-head, and then occupied himself in soothing the dog, who, however, seemed to heed him very little.

The letters were short—they were dated; the dates exactly thirty-five years ago. They were evidently from a lover to his mistress, or a husband to some young wife. Not only the terms of expression, but a distinct reference to a former voyage indicated the writer to have been a seafarer. The spelling and handwriting were those of a man imperfectly educated, but still the language itself was forcible. In the expressions of endearment there was a kind of rough wild love; but here and there were dark unintelligible hints at some secret not of love—some secret that seemed of crime. *"We ought to love each other,"* was one of the sentences I remember, *"for now every one else would execrate us if all was known."* Again: *"Don't let anyone be in the same room with you at night—you talk in your sleep."* And again: *"What's done can't be undone; and I tell you there's nothing against us unless the dead could come to life."* Here there was underlined in a better handwriting (a female's), *"They do!"* At the end of the letter latest in date the same female hand had written these words: *"Lost at sea the 4th of June, the same day as——"*

I put down the letters, and began to muse over their contents.

Fearing, however, that the train of thought into which I fell might unsteady my nerves, I fully determined to keep my mind in a fit state to cope with whatever of marvellous the advancing night might bring forth. I roused myself—laid the letters on the table—stirred up the fire, which was still bright and cheerful—and opened my volume of Macaulay. I read quietly enough till about half past eleven. I then threw myself dressed upon the bed, and told my servant he might retire to his own room, but must keep himself awake. I bade him leave open the door between the two rooms. Thus alone, I kept two candles burning on the table by my bed-head. I placed my watch beside the weapons, and calmly resumed my Macaulay. Opposite to me the fire burned clear; and on the hearth-rug, seemingly asleep, lay the dog. In about twenty minutes I felt an exceedingly cold air pass by my cheek, like a sudden draught. I fancied the door to my right, communicating with the landing-place, must have got open; but no—it was closed. I then turned my glance to my left, and saw the flame of the candles violently swayed as by a wind. At the same moment the watch beside the revolver softly slid from the table—softly, softly—no visible hand—it was gone.

I sprang up, seizing the revolver with one hand, the dagger with the other; I was not willing that my weapons should share the fate of the watch. Thus armed, I looked round the floor—no sign of the watch. Three slow, loud, distinct knocks were now heard at the bed-head; my servant called out, "Is that you, sir?"

"No; be on your guard."

The dog now roused himself and sat on his haunches, his ears moving quickly backwards and forwards. He kept his eyes fixed on me with a look so strange that he concentrated all my attention on himself. Slowly he rose up, all his hair bristling, and stood perfectly rigid, and with the same wild stare. I had no time, however, to examine the dog. Presently my servant emerged from his room; and if ever I saw horror in the human face, it was then. I should not have recognized him had we met in the streets; so altered was every lineament. He passed by me quickly, saying in a whisper that seemed scarcely to come from his lips, "Run—run! It is after me!" He gained the door to the landing, pulled it open, and rushed forth. I followed him into the landing involuntarily, calling him to stop; but, without heeding me, he bounded down the stairs, clinging to the balusters, and taking several steps at a time. I heard, where I stood, the street door open—heard it again clap to. I was left alone in the haunted house.

It was but for a moment that I remained undecided whether or not to follow my servant; pride and curiosity alike forbade so dastardly a flight. I re-entered my room, closing the door after me, and proceeded cautiously into the interior chamber. I encountered nothing to justify my servant's terror. I again carefully examined the walls, to see if there were any concealed door. I could find no trace of one—not even a seam in the dull-brown paper with which the room was hung. How, then, had the THING, whatever it was, which had so scared him, obtained ingress except through my own chamber?

I returned to my room, shut and locked the door that opened upon the interior one, and stood on the hearth, expectant and prepared. I now perceived that the dog had slunk into an angle of the wall, and was pressing himself close against it, as if literally striving to force his way into it. I approached the animal and spoke to it; the poor brute was evidently beside itself with terror. It showed all its teeth, the slaver dropping from its jaws, and would certainly have bitten me if I had touched it. It did not seem to recognize me. Whoever has seen at the Zoological Gardens a rabbit fascinated by a serpent, cowering in a corner, may form some idea of the anguish which the dog exhibited. Finding all efforts to soothe the animal in vain, and fearing that his bite might be as venomous in that state as if in the madness of hydrophobia, I left him alone, placed my weapons on the table beside the fire, seated myself, and recommenced my Macaulay.

Perhaps, in order not to appear seeking credit for a courage, or rather a coolness, which the reader may conceive I exaggerate, I may be pardoned if I pause to indulge in one or two egotistical remarks.

As I hold presence of mind, or what is called courage, to be precisely proportioned to familiarity with the circumstances that lead to it, so I should say that I had been long sufficiently familiar with all experiments that appertain to the Marvellous. I had witnessed many very extraordinary phenomena in various parts of the world—phenomena that would be either totally disbelieved if I stated them, or ascribed to supernatural agencies. Now, my theory is that the Supernatural is the Impossible, and that which is called supernatural is only a something in the laws of nature of which we have been hitherto ignorant. Therefore, if a ghost rises before me, I have not the right to say, "So, then, the supernatural is possible," but rather, "So then, the apparition of a ghost is, contrary to received opinion, within the laws of nature—i.e., not supernatural."

Now, in all that I had hitherto witnessed, and indeed in all the wonders which the amateurs of mystery in our age record as facts, a material living agency is always required. On the Continent you will find still magicians who assert that they can raise spirits. Assume for the moment that they assert truly still the living material form of the magician is present; and he is the material agency by which, from sone constitutional peculiarities, certain strange phenomena are represented to your natural senses.

Accept, again, as truthful, the tales of Spirit Manifestation in America—musical or other sounds—writings on paper, produced by no discernible hand—articles of furniture moved without apparent human agency—or the actual sight and touch of hands, to which no bodies seem to belong—still there must be found the MEDIUM or living being, with constitutional peculiarities capable of obtaining these signs. In fine, in all such marvels, supposing even that there is no imposture, there must be a human being like ourselves, by whom, or through whom, the effects presented to human beings are produced. It is so with the now familiar phenomena of mesmerism or electro-biology; the mind of the person operated on is affected through a material living agent. Nor, supposing it true that a mesmerized patient can respond to the will or passes of a mesmerizer a hundred miles distant, is the response less occasioned by a material being; it may be through a material fluid—call it Electric, call it Odic, call it what you will—which has the power of traversing space and passing obstacles, that the material effect is communicated from one to the other. Hence all that I had hitherto witnessed, or expected to witness, in this strange house, I believed to be occasioned through some agency or medium as mortal as myself; and this idea necessarily prevented the awe with which those who regard as supernatural things that are not within the ordinary operations of nature, which have been impressed by the adventures of that memorable night.

As, then, it was my conjecture that all that was presented, or would be presented, to my senses, must originate in some human being gifted by constitution with the power so to present them, and having some motive so to do, I felt an interest in my theory which, in its way, was rather philosophical than superstitious. And I can sincerely say that I was in as tranquil a temper for observation as any practical experimentalist could be in awaiting the effects of some rare, though perhaps perilous, chemical combination. Of course, the more I kept my mind detached from fancy, the more the temper fitted for observation would be obtained; and I, therefore, riveted eye and thought on the strong daylight sense in the page of my Macaulay.

I now became aware that something interposed between the page and the light—the page was overshadowed: I looked up, and I saw what I shall find it very difficult, perhaps impossible, to describe.

It was a Darkness shaping itself out of the air in very undefined outline. I cannot say it was of a human form, and yet it had more resemblance to a human form, or rather shadow, than anything else. As it stood, wholly apart and distinct from the air and the light around it, its dimensions seemed gigantic, the summit nearly touching the ceiling. While I gazed, a feeling of intense cold seized me. An iceberg before me could not more have chilled me; nor could the cold of an iceberg have been more purely physical. I feel convinced that it was not the cold caused by fear. As I continued to gaze, I thought—but this I cannot say with precision—that I distinguished two eyes looking down on me from the height. One moment I seemed to distinguish them clearly, the next they seemed gone; but still two rays of a pale-blue light frequently shot through the darkness, as from the height on which I half believed, half doubted, that I had encountered the eyes.

I strove to speak—my voice utterly failed me; I could only think to myself, "Is this fear? It is *not* fear!" I strove to rise—in vain; I felt as if weighed down by an irresistible force. Indeed, my impression was that of an immense and overwhelming Power opposed to my volition—that sense of utter inadequacy to cope with a force beyond men's, which one may feel *physically* in a storm at sea, in a conflagration, or when confronting some terrible wild beast, or rather, perhaps, the shark of the ocean, I felt *morally*. Opposed to my will was another will, as far superior to its strength as storm, fire and shark are superior in material force to the force of men.

And now, as this impression grew on me, now came, at last, horror—horror to a degree that no words can convey. I still retained pride, if not courage; and in my own mind I said, "This is horror, but it is not fear; unless I fear, I cannot be harmed; my reason rejects this thing; it is an illusion—I do not fear." With a violent effort I succeeded at last in stretching out my hand towards the weapon on the table; as I did so, on the arm and shoulder I received a strange shock, and my arm fell to my side, powerless. And now, to add to my horror, the light began slowly to wane from the candles—they were not, as it were, extinguished, but their flame seemed very gradually withdrawn: it was the same with the fire—the light was extracted from the fuel; in a few minutes the room was in utter darkness. The dread that came over me, to be thus in the dark with that dark Thing, whose power was so intensely felt, brought a reaction of nerve. In fact, terror had reached that climax, that either my senses must have deserted me, or I must have burst through the spell. I did burst through it. I found voice, though the voice was a shriek. I remember that I broke forth with words like these—"I do not fear, my soul does not fear"; and at the same time I found the strength to rise. Still in that profound gloom I rushed to one of the windows—tore aside the curtain—flung open the shutters; my first thought was—LIGHT. And when I saw the moon high, clear, and calm, I felt a joy that almost compensated for the previous terror. There was the moon, there was also the light from the gas-lamps in the deserted slumbrous street. I turned to look back into the room; the moon penetrated its shadow very palely and partially—but still there was light. The dark Thing, whatever it might be, was gone—except that I could yet see a dim shadow, which seemed the shadow of that shade, against the opposite wall.

My eye now rested on the table, and from under the table (which was without cloth or cover—an old mahogany round table) there rose a hand, visible as far as the wrist. It was a hand, seemingly, as much of flesh and blood as my own, but the hand of an aged person—lean, wrinkled, small, too—a woman's hand. That hand very softly closed on the two letters that lay on the table: hand and letters both vanished. There then came the same three loud measured knocks I had heard at the bed-head before this extraordinary drama had commenced.

As those sounds slowly ceased, I felt the whole room vibrate sensibly; and at the far end there rose, as from the floor, sparks or globules like bubbles of light, many-coloured—green, yellow, fire-red, azure. Up and down, to and fro, hither, thither, as tiny Will-o'-the-wisps, the sparks moved, slow or swift, each at its own caprice. A chair (as in the drawing-room below) was now advanced from the wall without apparent agency, and placed at the opposite side of the table. Suddenly, as forth from the chair, there grew a Shape—a woman's shape. It was distinct as a shape of life—ghastly as a shape of death. The face was that of youth, with a strange mournful beauty, the throat and shoulders were bare, the rest of the form in a loose robe of cloudy white. It began sleeking its long yellow hair, which fell over its shoulders; its eyes were not turned towards me, but to the door; it seemed listening, watching, waiting. The shadow of the shade in the background grew darker; and again I thought I beheld the eyes gleaming out from the summit of the shadow—eyes fixed upon that shape.

As if from the door, though it did not open, there grew out another shape, equally distinct, equally ghastly—a man's shape—a young man's. It was in the dress of the last century, or rather in a likeness of such dress; for both the male shape and the female, though defined, were evidently unsubstantial, impalpable—simulacra—phantasms; and there was something incongruous, grotesque, yet fearful, in the contrast between the elaborate finery, the courtly precision of that old-fashioned garb, with its ruffles and lace and buckles, and the corpse-like aspect and ghost-like stillness of the flitting wearer. Just as the male shape approached the female, the dark Shadow started from the wall, all three for a moment wrapped in darkness. When the pale light returned, the two phantoms were as if in the grasp of the Shadow that towered between them; and there was a blood-stain on the breast of the female; and the phantom-male was leaning on its phantom-sword, and blood seemed trickling fast from the ruffles, from the lace; and the darkness of the intermediate Shadow swallowed them up—they were gone. And again the bubbles of light shot, and sailed, and undulated, growing thicker and thicker and more wildly confused in their movements.

The closet-door to the right of the fireplace now opened, and from the aperture there came the form of a woman, aged. In her hand she held letters —the very letters over which I had seen *the* Hand close, and behind her I heard a footstep. She turned round as if to listen, and then she opened the letters and seemed to read; and over her shoulder I saw a livid face, the face as of a man long drowned—bloated, bleached—seaweed tangled in its dripping hair; and at her feet lay a form as of a corpse, and beside the corpse there cowered a child, a miserable squalid child, with famine in its cheeks and fear in its eyes. And as I looked in the old woman's face, the wrinkles and lines vanished, and it became a face of youth—hard-eyed, stony, but still youth; and the Shadow darted forth, and darkened over these phantoms as it had darkened over the last.

Nothing now was left but the Shadow, and on that my eyes were intently fixed, till again eyes grew out of the Shadow—malignant, serpent eyes. And the bubble of light again rose and fell, and in their disordered, irregular, turbulent maze, mingled with the wan moonlight. And now from these globules themselves, as from the shell of an egg, monstrous things burst out; the air grew filled with them; the larvae so bloodless and so hideous that I can in no way describe them except to remind the reader of the swarming life which the solar microscope brings before his eyes in a drop of water—things transparent, supple, agile, chasing each other, devouring each other—forms like nought ever beheld by the naked eye. As the shapes were without symmetry, so their movements were without order. In their very vagrancies there was no sport, they came round me and round, thicker and faster and swifter, swarming over my head, crawling over my right arm, which was outstretched in involuntary command against all evil beings. Sometimes I felt myself touched, but not by them; invisible hands touched me. Once I felt the clutch as of cold soft fingers at my throat. I was still equally conscious that if I gave way to fear I should be in bodily peril; and I concentrated all my faculties in the single focus of resisting, stubborn will. And I turned my sight from the shadow—above, all from those strange serpent eyes—eyes that had now become distinctly visible. For there, though in nought else around me, I was aware that there was a WILL, and a will of intense, creative, working evil, which might crush down my own.

The pale atmosphere in the room began now to redden as if in the air of some near conflagration. The larvae grew lurid as things that live in fire. Again the room vibrated; again were heard the three measured knocks; and again all things were swallowed up in the darkness of the dark Shadow, as if out of that darkness all had come, into that darkness all returned.

As the gloom receded, the Shadow was wholly gone. Slowly as it had been withdrawn, the flame grew again into the candles on the table, again into the fuel in the grate. The whole room came once more calmly, healthfully into sight.

The two doors were still closed, the door communicating with the servant's room still locked. In the corner of the wall, into which he had so convulsively niched himself, lay the dog. I called to him—no movement; I approached—the animal was dead; his eyes protruded; his tongue out of his mouth; the froth gathered round his jaws. I took him in my arms; I brought him to the fire; I felt acute grief for the loss of my poor favourite—acute self-reproach; I accused myself of his death; I imagined he had died of fright. But what was my surprise on finding that his neck was actually broken—actually twisted out of the vertebrae. Had this been done in the dark?—must it not have been by a hand human as mine?—must there not have been a human agency all the while in that room? Good cause to suspect it. I cannot tell. I cannot do more than state the fact fairly; the reader may draw his own inference.

Another surprising circumstance—my watch was restored to the table from which it had been so mysteriously withdrawn; but it had stopped at the very moment it was so withdrawn; nor, despite all the skill of the watchmaker, has it ever gone since—that is, it will go in a strange erratic way for a few hours, and then comes to a dead stop—it is worthless.

Nothing more chanced for the rest of the night. Nor, indeed, had I long to wait before the dawn broke. Not till it was broad daylight did I quit the haunted house. Before I did so, I revisited the little blind room in which my servant and myself had been for a time imprisoned. I had a strong impression—for which I could not account—that from that room had originated the mechanism of the phenomena—if I may use the term—which had been experienced in my chamber. And though I entered it now in the clear day, with the sun peering through the filmy window, I still felt, as I stood on its floor, the creep of the horror which I had first there experienced the night before, and which had been so aggravated by what had passed in my own chamber. I could not, indeed, bear to stay more than half a minute within those walls. I descended the stairs, and again I heard the footfall before me; and when I opened the street door, I thought I could distinguish a very low laugh. I gained my own home, expecting to find my runaway servant there. But he had not presented himself; nor did I hear more of him for three days, when I received a letter from him, dated from Liverpool, to this effect:

Honoured sir,—I humbly entreat your pardon, though I can scarcely hope that you will think I deserve it, unless—which Heaven forbid!—you saw what I did. I feel that it will be years before I can recover myself; and as to being fit for service, it is out of the question. I am therefore going to my brother-in-law at Melbourne. The ship sails tomorrow. Perhaps the long voyage may set me up. I do nothing now but start and tremble, and fancy It is behind me. I humbly beg you, honoured sir, to order my clothes, and whatever wages are due to me, to be sent to my mother's, at Walworth—John knows her address.

The letter ended with additional apologies, somewhat incoherent, and explanatory details as to effects that had been under the writer's charge.

This flight may perhaps warrant a suspicion that the man wished to go to Australia, and had been somehow or other fraudulently mixed up with the events of the night. I say nothing in refutation of that conjecture; rather, I suggest it as one that would seem to many persons the most probable solution of improbable occurrences. My own theory remained unshaken. I returned in the evening to the house, to bring away in a hack cab the things I had left there, with my poor dog's body. In this task I was not disturbed, nor did any incident worth note befall me, except that still, on ascending and descending the stairs, I heard the same footfall in advance. On leaving the house, I went to Mr. J——'s. He was at home. I returned him the keys, told him that my curiosity was sufficiently gratified, and was about to relate quickly what had passed, when he stopped me, and said, though with much politeness, that he had no longer any interest in a mystery which none had ever solved.

I determined at least to tell him of the two letters I had read, as well as of the extraordinary manner in which they had disappeared, and I then inquired if he thought they had been addressed to the woman who had died in the house, and if there were anything in her early history which could possibly confirm the dark suspicions to which the letters gave rise. Mr. J—— seemed startled, and, after musing a few moments, answered: "I know but little of the woman's earlier history, except, as I before told you, that her family were known to mine. But you revive some vague reminiscences to her prejudice. I will make inquiries, and inform you of their result. Still, even if we could admit the popular superstition that a person who had been either the perpetrator or the victim of dark crimes in life could revisit, as a restless spirit, the scene in which those crimes had been committed, I should observe that the house was infested by strange sights and sounds before the old woman died—you smile—what would you say?"

"I would say this, that I am convinced, if we could get to the bottom of these mysteries, we should find a living human agency."

"What! you believe it is all an imposture? For what object?"

"Not an imposture in the ordinary sense of the word. If suddenly I were to sink into a deep sleep, from which you could not awake me, but in that sleep could answer questions with an accuracy which I could not pretend to when awake—tell you what money you had in your pocket—nay, describe your very thoughts—it is not necessarily an imposture, any more than it is necessarily supernatural. I should be, unconsciously to myself, under a mesmeric influence, conveyed to me from a distance by a human being who had acquired power over me by previous *rapport*."

"Granting mesmerism, so far carried, to be a fact, you are right. And you would infer from this that a mesmerizer might produce the extraordinary effects you and others have witnessed over inanimate objects—fill the air with sights and sounds?"

"Or impress our senses with the belief in them—we never having been *en rapport* with the person acting on us? No. What is commonly called mesmerism could not do this; but there may be a power akin to mesmerism, and superior to it—the power that in the old days was called Magic. That such a power may extend to all inanimate objects of matter, I do not say; but if so, it would not be against nature, only a rare power in nature which might be given to constitutions with certain peculiarities, and cultivated by practice to an extraordinary degree. That such a power might extend over the dead—that is, over certain thoughts and memories that the dead may still retain—and compel, not that which ought properly to be called the SOUL, and which is far beyond human reach, but rather a phantom of what has been most earth-stained on earth, to make itself apparent to our senses—is a very ancient though obsolete theory, upon which I will hazard no opinion. But I do not conceive the power would be supernatural. Let me illustrate what I mean from an experiment which Paracelsus describes as not difficult, and which the author of the *Curiosities of Literature* cites as credible: A flower perishes; you burn it. Whatever were the elements of that flower while it lived are gone, dispersed, you know not whither; you can never discover nor recollect them. But you can, by chemistry, out of the burst dust of that flower, raise a spectrum of the flower, just as it seemed in life. It may be the same with the human being. The soul has as much escaped you as the essence or elements of the flower. Still you may make a spectrum of it. And this phantom, though in the popular superstition it is held to be the soul of the departed, must not be confounded with the true soul; it is but the eidolon of the dead form. Hence, like the best-at-tested stories of ghosts or spirits, the thing that most strikes us is the absence of what we hold to be soul—that is, of superior emancipated intelligence. They come for little or no object —they seldom speak, if they do come; they utter no ideas above that of an ordinary person on earth. These American spirit-seers have published volumes of communications in prose and verse, which they assert to be given in the names of the most illustrious dead—Shakespeare, Bacon—heaven knows whom. Those communications, taking the best, are certainly not a whit of higher order than would be communications from living persons of fair talent and education; they are wondrously inferior to what Bacon, Shakespeare, and Plato said and wrote when on earth. Nor, what is more notable, do they ever contain an idea that was not on the earth before. Wonderful, therefore, as such phenomena may be (granting them to be truthful), I see much that philosophy may question, nothing that it is incumbent on philosophy to deny—viz. nothing supernatural. They are but ideas conveyed somehow or other (we have not yet discovered the means) from one mortal brain to another. Whether, in so doing, tables walk of their own accord, or fiend-like shapes appear in a magic circle, or bodyless hands rise and remove material objects, or a Thing of Darkness, such as presented itself to me, freeze our blood—still am I persuaded that these are but agencies conveyed, as by electric wires, to my own brain from the brain of another. In some constitutions there is a natural chemistry, and those may produce chemic wonders—in others a natural fluid, call it electricity, and these produce electric wonders. But they differ in this from Normal Science—they are alike objectless, purposeless, puerile, frivolous. They lead on to no grand results; and, therefore, the world does not heed, and true sages have not cultivated them. But sure I am, that of all I saw or heard, a man, human as myself, was the remote originator; and I believe unconsciously to himself as to the exact effects produced, for this reason: no two persons, you say, have ever told you that they experienced exactly the same thing. Well, observe, no two persons ever experience exactly the same dream. If this were an ordinary imposture, the machinery would be arranged for results that would but little vary; if it were a supernatural agency permitted by the Almighty, it would surely be for some definite end. These phenomena belong to neither class; my persuasion is, that they originate in some brain now far distant; that that brain had no distinct volition in anything that occurred; that what does occur reflects but its devious, motley, ever-shifting, half-formed thoughts; in short, that it has been but the dreams of such a brain put into action and invested with a semi-substance. That this brain is of immense power, that it can set matter into movement, that it is malignant and destructive, I believe: some material force must have killed my dog; it might, for aught I know, have sufficed to kill myself, had I been as subjugated by terror as the dog—had my intellect or my spirit given me no countervailing resistance in my will."

"It killed your dog! That is fearful! Indeed, it is strange that no animal can be induced to stay in that house; not even a cat. Rats and mice are never found in it."

"The instincts of the brute creation detect influences deadly to their existence. Man's reason has a sense less subtle, because it has a resisting power more supreme. But enough; do you comprehend my theory?"

"Yes, though imperfectly—and I accept any crotchet (pardon the word) however odd, rather than embrace at once the notion of ghosts and hobgoblins we imbibed in our nurseries. Still, to my unfortunate house the evil is the same. What on earth can I do with the house?"

"I will tell you what I would do. I am convinced from my own internal feelings that the small unfurnished room at right angles to the door of the bedroom which I occupied, forms a starting-point or receptacle for the influences which haunt the house, and I strongly advise you to have the walls opened, the floor removed—nay, the whole room pulled down. I observe that it is detached rrom the body of the house, built over the small back-yard, and could be femoved without injury to the rest of the building."

"And you think, if I did that——"

"You would cut off the telegraph wires. Try it. I am so persuaded that I am right, that I will pay half the expense if you will allow me to direct the operations."

"Nay, I am well able to afford the cost; for the rest, allow me to write to you."

About ten days afterwards I received a letter from Mr. J——, telling me that he had visited the house since I had seen him; that he had found the two letters I had described, replaced in the drawer from which I had taken them; that he had read them with misgivings like my own; that he had instituted a cautious inquiry about the woman to whom I rightly conjectured they had been written. It seemed that thirty-six years ago (a year before the date of the letters), she had married, against the wish of her relatives, an American of very suspicious character; in fact, he was generally believed to have been a pirate. She, herself, was the daughter of very respectable tradespeople, and had served in the capacity of a nursery governess before her marriage. She had a brother, a widower, who was considered wealthy, and who had one child of about six years old. A month after the marriage, the body of this brother was found in the Thames, near London Bridge; there seemed some marks of violence about his throat, but they were not deemed sufficient to warrant the inquest in any other verdict than that of "found drowned".

The American and his wife took charge of the little boy, the deceased brother having by his will left his sister the guardian of his only child—and in the event of the child's death, the sister inherited. The child died about six months afterwards—it was supposed to have been neglected and ill-treated. The neighbours deposed to have heard it shriek at night. The surgeon, who had examined it after death, said that it was emaciated as if from want of nourishment, and the body was covered with livid bruises. It seemed that one winter night the child had sought to escape—crept out into the back-yard, tried to scale the wall—fallen back exhausted, and been found at morning on the stones in a dying state. But though there was some evidence of cruelty, there was none of murder; and the aunt and her husband had sought to palliate cruelty by alleging the exceeding stubbornness and perversity of the child, who was declared to be half-witted. Be that as it may, at the orphan's death the aunt inherited her brother's fortune. Before the first wedded year was out, the American quitted England abruptly, and never returned to it. He obtained a cruising vessel, which was lost in the Atlantic two years afterwards. The widow was left in affluence; but reverses of various kinds had befallen her: a bank broke—an investment failed—she went into a small business and became insolvent—then she entered into service, sinking lower and lower, from housekeeper down to maid-of-all-work—never long retaining a place, though nothing peculiar against her character was ever alleged. She was considered sober, honest, and peculiarly quiet in her ways; still nothing prospered with her. And so she had dropped into the workhouse, from which Mr. J—— had taken her, to be placed in charge of the very house which she had rented as mistress in the first year of her wedded life.

Mr. J—— added that he had passed an hour alone in the unfurnished room which I had urged him to destroy, and that his impressions of dread while there were so great, though he had neither heard nor seen anything, that he was eager to have the walls bared and the floors removed as I had suggested. He had engaged persons for the work, and would commence any day I would name.

The day was accordingly fixed. I repaired to the haunted house—we went into the blind dreary room, took up the skirting, and then the floors. Under the rafters covered with rubbish, was found a trap-door, quite large enough to admit a man. It was closely nailed down, with clamps and rivets of iron. On removing these we descended into a room below, the existence of which had never been suspected. In this room there had been a window and a flue, but they had been bricked over, evidently for many years. By the help of candles we examined this place; it still retained some mouldering furniture—three chairs, an oak settle, a table—all of the fashion of about eighty years ago. There was a chest of drawers against the wall, in which we found, half-rotted away, old-fashioned articles of a man's dress, such as might have been worn eighty or a hundred years ago by a gentleman of some rank—costly steel buckles and buttons, like those yet worn in court dresses—a handsome court sword—in a waistcoat which had once been rich with gold-lace, but which was now blackened and foul with damp, we found five guineas, a few silver coins, and an ivory ticket, probably for some place of entertainment long since passed away. But our main discovery was in a kind of iron safe fixed to the wall, the lock of which it cost us much trouble to get picked.

In this safe were three shelves and two small drawers. Ranged on the shelves were several small bottles of crystal, hermetically stopped. They contained colourless volatile essences, of what nature I shall say no more than that they were not poisons—phosphor and ammonia entered into some of them. There were also some very curious glass tubes, and a small pointed rod of iron, with a large lump of rock-crystal, and another of amber—also a loadstone of great power.

In one of the drawers we found a miniature portrait set in gold, and retaining the freshness of its colours most remarkably, considering the length of time it had probably been there. The portrait was that of a man who might be somewhat advanced in middle life, perhaps forty-seven or forty-eight.

It was a most peculiar face—a most impressive face. If you could fancy some mighty serpent transformed into man, preserving in the human lineaments the old serpent type, you would have a better idea of that countenance than long descriptions can convey: the width and flatness of frontal—the tapering elegance of contour disguising the strength of the deadly jaw—the long, large, terrible eye, glittering and green as the emerald—and withal a certain ruthless calm, as if from the consciousness of an immense power. The strange thing was this—the instant I saw the miniature I recognized a startling likeness to one of the rarest portraits in the world—the portrait of a man of a rank only below that of royalty, who in his own day had made a considerable noise. History says little or nothing of him; but search the correspondence of his contemporaries, and you find reference to his wild daring, his bold profligacy, his restless spirit, his taste for the occult sciences. While still in the meridian of life he died and was buried, so say the chronicles, in a foreign land. He died in time to escape the grasp of the law, for he was accused of crimes which would have given him to the headsman. After his death, the portraits of him, which had been numerous, for he had been a munificent encourager of art, were bought up and destroyed—it was supposed by his heirs, who might have been glad could they have razed his very name from their splendid line. He had enjoyed a vast wealth; a large portion of this was believed to have been embezzled by a favourite astrologer or soothsayer—at all events, it had unaccountably vanished at the time of his death. One portrait alone of him was supposed to have escaped the general destruction; I had seen it in the house of a collector some months before. It had made on me a wonderful impression, as it does on all who behold it—a face never to be forgotten; and there was that face in the miniature that lay within my hand. True, that in the miniature the man was a few years older than in the portrait I had seen, or than the original was even at the time of his death. But a few years!—why, between the date in which flourished that direful noble and the date in which the miniature was evidently painted, there was an interval of more than two centuries. While I was thus gazing, silent and wondering, Mr. J—— said:

"But is it possible? I have known this man."

"How—where?" cried I.

"In India. He was high in the confidence of the Rajah of ——, and well-nigh drew him into a revolt which would have lost the Rajah his dominions. The man was a Frenchman—his name de V——, clever, bold, lawless. We insisted on his dismissal and banishment; it must be the same man—no two faces like his—yet this miniature seems nearly a hundred years old."

Mechanically I turned round the miniature to examine the back of it, and on the back was engraved a pentacle; in the middle of the pentacle a ladder, and the third step of the ladder was formed by the date 1765. Examining still more minutely, I detected a spring; this, on being pressed, opened the back of the miniature as a lid. Within-side the lid were engraved, "Mariana to thee— Be faithful in life and in death to——" Here follows a name that I will not mention, but it was not unfamiliar to me. I had heard it spoken of by old men in my childhood as the name borne by a dazzling charlatan, who had made a great sensation in London for a year or so, and had fled the country on the charge of a double murder within his own house—that of his mistress and his rival. I said nothing of this to Mr. J——, to whom reluctantly I resigned the miniature.

We had found no difficulty in opening the first drawer within the iron safe; we found great difficulty in opening the second: it was not locked, but it resisted all efforts, till we inserted in the chinks the edge of a chisel. When we had thus drawn it forth, we found a very singular apparatus in the nicest order. Upon a small thin book, or rather tablet, was placed a saucer of crystal; this saucer was filled with a clear liquid—on that liquid floated a kind of compass, with a needle shifting rapidly round, but instead of the usual points of a compass were seven strange characters, not very unlike those used by astrologers to denote the planets. A very peculiar, but not strong nor displeasing odour, came from this drawer, which was lined with a wood that we afterwards discovered to be hazel. Whatever the cause of this odour, it produced a material effect on the nerves. We all felt it, even the two workmen who were in the room—a creeping tingling sensation from the tips of the fingers to the roots of the hair. Impatient to examine the tablet, I removed the saucer. As I did so the needle of the compass went round and round with exceeding swiftness, and I felt a shock that ran through my whole frame, so that I dropped the saucer on the floor. The liquid was split—the saucer was broken—the compass rolled to the end of the room—and at that instant the walls shook to and fro, as if a giant had swayed and rocked them.

The two workmen were so frightened that they ran up the ladder by which we had descended from the trap-door; but seeing that nothing more happened, they were easily induced to return.

Meanwhile, I had opened the tablet: it was bound in plain red leather, with a silver clasp; it contained but one sheet of thick vellum, and on that sheet were inscribed, within a double pentacle, words in old monkish Latin, which are literally to be translated thus: "On all that it can reach within these walls— sentient or inanimate, living or dead—as moves the needle, so work my will! Accursed be the house, and restless be the dwellers therein."

We found no more. Mr. J—— burnt the tablet and its anathema. He razed to the foundations the part of the building containing the secret room with the chamber over it. He had then the courage to inhabit the house himself for a month, and a quieter, better-conditioned house could not be found in all London. Subsequently he let it to advantage, and his tenant has made no complaints.

But my story is not yet done. A few days after Mr. J—— had removed into the house, I paid him a visit. We were standing by the open window and conversing. A van containing some articles of furniture which he was moving from his former house was at the door. I had just urged on him my theory that all those phenomena regarded as supermundane had emanated from a human brain; adducing the charm or rather curse we had found and destroyed in support of my philosophy. Mr. J—— was observing in reply, "That even if mesmerism, or whatever analogous power it might be called, could really thus work in the absence of the operator, and produce effects so extraordinary, still could those effects continue when the operator himself was dead? and if the spell had been wrought, and, indeed, the room walled up, more than seventy years ago, the probability was, that the operator had long since departed this life"; Mr. J——, I say, was thus answering, when I caught hold of his arm and pointed to the street below.

A well-dressed man had crossed from the opposite side, and was accosting the carrier in charge of the van. His face, as he stood, was exactly fronting our window. It was the face of the miniature we had discovered; it was the face of the portrait of the noble three centuries ago.

"Good heavens!" cried Mr. J——, "that is the face of de V——, and scarcely a day older than when I saw it in the Rajah's court in my youth!"

Seized by the same thought, we both hastened downstairs. I was first in the street; but the man had already gone. I caught sight of him, however, not many yards in advance, and in another moment I was by his side.

I had resolved to speak to him, but when I looked into his face I felt as if it were impossible to do so. That eye—the eye of the serpent—fixed and held me spellbound. And withal, about the man's whole person there was a dignity, an air of pride and station and superiority, that would have made anyone, habituated to the usages of the world, hesitate long before venturing upon a liberty or impertinence. And what could I say? What was it I would ask? Thus ashamed of my first impulse, I fell a few paces back, still, however, following the stranger, undecided what else to do. Meanwhile he turned the corner of the street; a plain carriage was in waiting, with a servant out of livery dressed like a *valet-de-place* at the carriage door. In another moment he had stepped into the carriage, and it drove off. I returned to the house. Mr. J—— was still at the street door. He had asked the carrier what the stranger had said to him.

"Merely asked whom that house now belonged to."

The same evening I happened to go with a friend to a place in town called the Cosmopolitan Club, a place open to men of all countries, all opinions, all degrees. One orders one's coffee, smokes one's cigar. One is always sure to meet agreeable, sometimes remarkable, persons.

I had not been two minutes in the room before I beheld at a table, conversing with an acquaintance of mine, whom I will designate by the initial G——, the man—the Original of the Miniature. He was now without his hat, and the likeness was yet more startling, only I observed that while he was conversing there was less severity in the countenance; there was even a smile, though a very quiet and very cold one. The dignity of mien I had acknowledged in the street was also more striking; a dignity akin to that which invests some prince of the East—conveying the idea of supreme indifference and habitual, indisputable, indolent, but resistless, power.

G—— soon after left the stranger, who then took up a scientific journal, which seemed to absorb his attention.

I drew G—— aside. "Who and what is that gentleman?"

"That? Oh, a very remarkable man, indeed. I met him last year amidst the caves of Petra—the scriptural Edom. He is the best Oriental scholar I know. We joined company, had an adventure with robbers, in which he showed a coolness that saved our lives; afterwards he invited me to spend a day with him in a house he had bought at Damascus—a house buried amongst almond blossoms and roses—the most beautiful thing! He had lived there for some years, quite as an Oriental, in grand style. I half suspect he is a renegade, immensely rich, very odd; by the by, a great mesmerizer. I have seen him with my own eyes produce an effect on inanimate things. If you take a letter from your pocket and throw it to the other end of the room, he will order it to come to his feet, and you will see the letter wriggle itself along the floor till it has obeyed his command. 'Pon my honour 'tis true; I have seen him affect even the weather, disperse or collect clouds, by means of a glass tube or wand. But he does not like talking of these matters to strangers. He has only just arrived in England; says he has not been here for a great many years; let me introduce him to you."

"Certainly! He is English, then? What is his name?"

"Oh!—a very homely one—Richards."

"And what is his birth—his family?"

"How do I know? What does it signify?—no doubt some parvenue, but rich—so infernally rich!"

G—— drew me up to the stranger, and the introduction was effected. The manners of Mr. Richards were not those of an adventurous traveller. Travellers are in general constitutionally gifted with high animal spirits; they are talkative, eager, imperious. Mr. Richards was calm and subdued in tone, with manners which were made distant by the loftiness of punctilious courtesy—the manners of a former age. I observed that the English he spoke was not exactly of our day. I should even have said that the accent was slightly foreign. But, then, Mr. Richards remarked that he had been little in the habit for many years of speaking in his native tongue. The conversation fell upon the changes in the aspect of London since he had last visited our metropolis. G—— then glanced off to the moral changes—literary, social, political—the great men who were removed from the stage within the last twenty years—the new great men who were coming on. In all this Mr. Richards evinced no interest. He had evidently read none of our living authors, and seemed scarcely acquainted by name with our younger statesmen. Once and only once he laughed; it was when G—— asked him whether he had any thoughts of getting into Parliament. And the laugh was inward, sarcastic, sinister—a sneer raised into a laugh. After a few minutes G—— left us to talk to some other acquaintances who had just lounged into the room, and I then said quietly:

"I have seen a miniature of you, Mr. Richards, in the house you once inhabited, and perhaps built, if not wholly, at least in part, in —— street. You passed by that house this morning."

Not till I had finished did I raise my eyes to his, and then his fixed my gaze so steadfastly that I could not withdraw it—those fascinating serpent eyes. But involuntarily, and as if the words that translated my thought were dragged from me, I added in a low whisper: "I have been a student in the mysteries of life and nature; of those mysteries I have known the occult professors. I have the right to speak to you thus." And I uttered a certain pass-word.

"Well," said he dryly, "I concede the right—what would you ask?"

"To what extent human will in certain temperaments can extend?"

"To what extent can thought extend? Think, and before you draw breath you are in China!"

"True. But my thought has no power in China."

"Give it expression, and it may have: you may write down a thought which, sooner or later, may alter the whole condition of China. What is a law but a thought? Therefore thought is infinite—therefore thought has power; not in proportion to its value—a bad thought may make a bad law as potent as a good thought can make a good one."

"Yes; what you say confirms my own theory. Through invisible currents one human brain may transmit its ideas to other human brains with the same rapidity as a thought promulgated by visible means. And as thought is imperishable—as it leaves its stamp behind it in the natural world even when the thinker has passed out of this world—so the thought of the living may have power to rouse up and revive the thoughts of the dead—such as those thoughts *were in life*—though the thought of the living cannot reach the thoughts which the dead *now* may entertain. Is it not so?"

"I decline to answer, if, in my judgment, thought has the limit you would fix to it; but proceed. You have a special question you wish to put."

"Intense malignity in an intense will, engendered in a peculiar temperament, and aided by natural means within the reach of science, may produce effects like those ascribed of old to evil magic. It might thus haunt the walls of a human habitation with spectral revivals of all guilty thoughts and guilty deeds once conceived and done within those walls; all, in short, with which the evil will claims *rapport* and affinity—imperfect, incoherent, fragmentary snatches at the old dramas acted therein years ago. Thoughts thus crossing each other haphazard, as in the nightmare of a vision, growing up into phantom sights and sounds, and all serving to create horror, not because those sights and sounds are really visitations from a world without, but that they are ghastly monstrous renewals of what have been in this world itself, set into malignant play by a malignant mortal. And it is through the material agency of that human brain that these things would acquire even a human power—would strike as with the shock of electricity, and might kill, if the thought of the person assailed did not rise superior to the dignity of the original assailer—might kill the most powerful animal if unnerved by fear, but not injure the feeblest man, if, while his flesh crept, his mind stood out fearless. Thus, when in old stories we read of a magician rent to pieces by the fiends he had evoked—or still more, in Eastern legends, that one magician succeeds by arts in destroying another—there may be so far truth, that a material being has clothed, from its own evil propensities, certain elements and fluids, usually quiescent or harmless, with awful shape and terrific force; just as the lightning that had lain hidden and innocent in the cloud becomes by natural law suddenly visible, takes a distinct shape to the eye and can strike destruction on the object to which it is attracted."

"You are not without glimpses of a very mighty secret," said Mr. Richards composedly. "According to your view, could a mortal obtain the power you speak of, he would necessarily be a malignant and evil being."

"If the power were exercised as I have said, most malignant and most evil —though I believe in the ancient traditions that he could not injure the good. His will could only injure those with whom it has established an affinity, or over whom it forces unresisted sway. I will now imagine an example that may be within the laws of nature, yet seem wild as the fables of a bewildered monk.

"You will remember that Albertus Magnus, after describing minutely the process by which spirits may be invoked and commanded, adds emphatically that the process will instruct and avail only to the few—that a *man must be born a magician!*—that is, born with a peculiar physical temperament, as a man is born a poet. Rarely are men in whose constitution lurks this occult power of the highest order of intellect; usually in the intellect there is some twist, perversity, or disease. But, on the other hand, they must possess, to an astonishing degree, the faculty to concentrate thought on a single object—the energetic faculty that we call WILL. Therefore, though their intellect be not sound, it is exceedingly forcible for the attainment of what it desires. I will imagine such a person, pre-eminently gifted with this constitution and its concomitant forces. I will place him in the loftier grades of society. I will suppose his desires emphatically those of the sensualist—he has, therefore, a strong love of life. He is an absolute egotist—his will is concentrated in himself—he has fierce passions —he knows no enduring, no holy affections, but he can covet eagerly what for the moment he desires; he can hate implacably what opposes itself to his objects; he can commit fearful crimes, yet feel small remorse; he resorts rather to curses upon others, than to penitence for his misdeeds. Circumstances, to which his constitution guides him, lead him to a rare knowledge of the natural secrets which may serve his egotism. He is a close observer where his passions encourage observation, he is a minute calculator, not from love of truth, but where love of self sharpens his faculties, therefore he can be a man of science. I suppose such a being, having by experience learned the power of his arts over others, trying what may be the power of will over his own frame, and studying all that in natural philosophy may increase that power. He loves life, he dreads death; *he wills to live on.* He cannot restore himself to youth, he cannot entirely stay the progress of death, he cannot make himself immortal in the flesh and blood; but he may arrest for a time so prolonged as to appear incredible, if I said it—that hardening of the parts which constitutes old age. A year may age him no more than an hour ages another. His intense will, scientifically trained into system, operates, in short, over the wear and tear of his own frame. He lives on. That he may not seem a portent and a miracle, he *dies* from time to time, seemingly, to certain persons. Having schemed the transfer of a wealth that suffices to his wants, he disappears from one corner of the world, and contrives that his obsequies shall be celebrated. He reappears at another corner of the world, where he resides undetected, and does not revisit the scenes of his former career till all who could remember his features are no more. He would be profoundly miserable if he had affections—he has none but for himself. No good man would accept his longevity, and to no men, good or bad, would he or could he communicate its true secret. Such a man might exist: such a man as I have described I see now before me! —— Duke of ——, in the court of ——, dividing time between lust and brawl, alchemists and wizards; again, in the last century, charlatan and criminal, with name less noble, domiciled in the house at which you gazed today, and flying from the law you had outraged, none knew whither; traveller once more revisiting London, with the same earthly passions which filled your heart when races now no more walked through yonder streets; outlaw from the school of all the nobler and diviner mystics; execrable Image of Life in Death and Death in Life, I warn you back from the cities and homes of healthful men; back to the ruins of departed empires; back to the deserts of nature unredeemed!"

There answered me a whisper so musical, so potently musical, that it seemed to enter into my whole being, and subdue me despite myself. Thus it said:

"I have sought one like you for the last hundred years. Now I have found you, we part not till I know what I desire. The vision that sees through the Past, and cleaves through the veil of the Future, is in you at this hour; never before, never to come again. The vision of no puling fantastic girl, of no sickbed somnambule, but of a strong man, with a vigorous brain. Soar and look forth!"

As he spoke I felt as if I rose out of myself upon eagle wings. All the weight seemed gone from air—roofless the room, roofless the dome of space. I was not in the body—where I knew not—but aloft over time, over earth.

Again I heard the melodious whisper: "You say right. I have mastered great secrets by the power of Will; true by Will and by Science I can retard the process of years: but death comes not by age alone. Can I frustrate the accidents which bring death upon the young?"

"No; every accident is a providence. Before a providence snaps every human will."

"Shall I die at last, ages and ages hence, by the slow, though inevitable, growth of time, or by the cause that I call accident?"

"By a cause you call accident."

"Is not the end still remote?" asked the whisper, with a slight tremor.

"Regarded as my life regards time, it is still remote."

"And shall I, before then, mix with the world of men as I did ere I learned these secrets, resume eager interest in their strife and their trouble—battle with ambition, and use the power of the sage to win the power that belongs to kings?"

"You will yet play a part on the earth that will fill earth with commotion and amaze. For wondrous designs have you, a wonder yourself, been permitted to live on through the centuries. All the secrets you have stored will then have their uses—all that now makes you a stranger amidst the generations will contribute then to make you their lord. As the trees and the straws are drawn into a whirlpool—as they spin round, are sucked to the deep, and again tossed aloft by the eddies, so shall races and thrones be plucked into the charm of your vortex. Awful Destroyer—but in destroying, made, against your own will, a Constructor!"

"And that date, too, is far off?"

"Far off; when it comes, think your end in this world is at hand!"

"How and what is the end? Look east, west, south, and north."

"In the north, where you never yet trod—towards the point whence your instincts have warned you, there a spectre will seize you. 'Tis Death!—I see a ship, it is haunted—'tis chased, it sails on. Baffled navies sail after that ship. It enters the region of ice. It passes a sky red with meteors. Two moons stand on high, over ice-reefs. I see the ship locked between white defiles—they are ice-rocks. I see the dead strew the decks—stark and livid, green mould on their limbs. All are dead but one man—it is you! But years, though so slowly they come, have then scathed you. There is the coming of age on your brow, and the will is relaxed in the cells of the brain. Still that will, though enfeebled, exceeds all that man knew before you, through the will you live on, gnawed with famine: And nature no longer obeys you in that death-spreading region; the sky is a sky of iron, and the air has iron clamps, and the ice-rocks wedge in the ship. Hark how it cracks and groans. Ice will imbed it as amber imbeds a straw. And a man has gone forth, living yet, from the ship and its dead; and he has clambered up the spikes of an iceberg, and the two moons gaze down on his form. That man is yourself; and terror is on you—terror; and terror has swallowed your will. And I see swarming up the steep ice-rock, grey grisely things. The bears of the north have scented their quarry—they come near you and nearer, shambling and rolling their bulk. And in that day every moment shall seem to you longer than the centuries through which you have passed. And heed this —after life, moments continued make the bliss or the hell of eternity."

"Hush," said the whisper; "but the day, you assure me, is far off—very far. I go back to the almond and rose of Damascus!—sleep!"

The room swam before my eyes. I became insensible. When I recovered, I found G—— holding my hand and smiling. He said: "You who have always declared yourself proof against mesmerism, have succumbed at last to my friend Richards."

"Where is Mr. Richards?"

"Gone, when you passed into a trance—saying quietly to me, 'Your friend will not wake for an hour.'"

I asked, as collectedly as I could, where Mr. Richards lodged.

"At the Trafalgar Hotel."

"Give me your arm," said I to G——, "let us call on him; I have something to say."

When we arrived at the hotel, we were told that Mr. Richards had returned twenty minutes before, paid his bill, left directions with his servant (a Greek) to pack his effects, and proceed to Malta by the steamer that should leave Southampton the next day. Mr. Richards had merely said of his own movements, that he had visits to pay in the neighbourhood of London, and it was uncertain whether he should be able to reach Southampton in time for that steamer; if not, he should follow in the next one.

The waiter asked me my name. On my informing him, he gave me a note that Mr. Richards had left for me, in case I called.

The note was as follows: "*I wished you to utter what was in your mind. You obeyed. I have, therefore, established power over you. For three months from this day you can communicate to no living man what has passed between us—you cannot even show this note to the friend by your side. During three months, silence complete as to me and mine. Do you doubt my power to lay on you this command?—try to disobey me. At the end of the third month, the spell is raised. For the rest I spare you. I shall visit your grave a year and a day after it has received you."*

So ends this strange story, which I ask no one to believe. I write it down exactly three months after I received the above note. I could not write it before, nor could I show to G——, in spite of his urgent request, the note which I read under the gas-lamp by his side.

THE WRINKLED WOMEN OF ST. NEPOMUK*

By Fred Marnau

THE wrinkled women of St. Nepomuk's know nothing of the essence of the angelic or of the divine transition from one life to the other. Ghosts tumble about their waking and their sleeping, the witches of Macbeth call to them, in their imaginations dances the stranger who knocks at the kitchen doors at night: "I am the pestilence, you miserable wretch!" They know nothing of the holy sadness of Death, they have never heard Bach fugues.

They only know this awful horror. And they feed their fears, subtly and inventively. Once, a long time ago, there were quite a few of these fanatics, these connoisseurs of death. Now only seven remain. These seven, of course, are of one heart and soul, one harmonious world of ideas. Their daily meeting-place is the bench outside the morgue of the St. Nepomuk's Cemetery. The reason for this loyalty is a most carefully calculated one. The Dreadful Prince, papal and thin-as-thread, should very soon now have grown so used to the sevenfold apparition that finally, they believe, he will overlook them altogether. Whereby a great deal would be gained. Because the things we come across suddenly—a christening, a murder, a crumbling wall, hollow-sounding drums in a funeral-procession, dancing fools, a memory of far away, a rare guest—those things alone we never forget, they occupy our minds, they force us to act. Us, and the thin-as-thread Prince. The seven women have grandiose, masterly conceptions of dying and of Death. They have found a new language, foreign to everyone else, to inform each other of the tangled results of their systems. The seven experts outside the morgue are full of daring hopes. Have they not grown so very old, have not the others all died? Their clothes rot on their bodies, no one ever sees them eat or buy food. Perhaps they dig for worms at night. They cannot improve their lot, men will never again dance with them, their bodies are stiff and deformed, yet life pullulates somewhere within them like a gluttonous weed, and it will not let go of them. But they dare not talk to each other of that, it is their trade secret, their dangerous secret of which Death in his severity must not come to hear. If he did find out all their glory would be at an end, their loyalty to the cemetery unmasked as a cheap fraud. And who can tell the kind of dying Death would think up as punishment? O ghastly horror! Only to stay silent and unnoticed, ah, to stay unnoticed. Only busily to go to the cemetery, as if one had long been part of it. Usually when they leave for home the watchman is already turning the key in the lock. They creep to the next corner and only then dare to open their mouths again. Once more we are on the outside and they have had to stay behind, their hearts titter scornfully. And satisfied, the seven limp homewards, while gently and quietly the dead sleep on, tired of their heavy, sighful lives.

---
* Translated by E. O. Sigler.

On such afternoons at the cemetery they have many interesting topics of conversation, many experiences. The old woman in the centre, obviously president and leader of the union, had until a few years ago been in charge of the Municipal Public Convenience on the market square. None of the others had in her lifetime achieved such prominence. Envious and enthusiastic, they listen to the tales of this chosen one, who is sometimes even now employed in her former capacity, when her successor, an upstart of the ridiculous and dangerous age of sixty, cannot carry out her duties owing to illness.

She is just about to discuss with her lady friends the complete lack of talent of this young woman, when their attention is drawn to something much closer to their particular sphere of interest. A youth of enormous build, clad in a raven-black uniform much too tight for him, comes round the corner of the morgue. The sleeves of his coat fail to cover his fleshy lower arms, his hands are stuck into knitted gloves, also black; in his right he holds an ebony stick with a silver top. He evidently likes himself in this get-up. He swings the stick like a conductor leading his orchestra in soundless marching music. The silver tassels on his tunic jump up and down in time, and so does the bunch of feathers on his Napoleon hat.

"Ah, a first-class corpse!" lisps one old woman with joy and respect. The others are struck dumb with eagerness and curiosity. Their grey noses twitch as if they could hardly wait to find out the who and what of the newcomer: every corpse brings with it a different smell.

Even then appear on the scene, with slow, measured steps, the eight men, on their shoulders an important-looking oaken coffin. They file past the seven habitués and turn left into the first-class show-room. The fellow with the ebony cane takes up his post outside the glass door: guard of the great Sultan. The others inside, with refinement and pomp, set about the task of arranging the display. Many a good idea is envied and praised, certain changes are even made in the corpse's position. Finally the indoor palms are in their proper place, the electric candles alight; one has run to the tap for a pitcher of holy water, and another rearranged a little the medals on the velvet cushion. With justifiable satisfaction they look at their work.

The corpse-bearers have gone home, leaving behind only the fellow on guard who is paid extra for that. Already the sun throws long shadows of cross and stone over the hills, the crickets chirp in the grass, and the worms and green chafers vanish down their subterranean passages that draw through the dead as through rich old timber.

Now the seven become daring. The leader is to go first. "Yes, you go, perhaps he will let you have a look."

"I'll go . . . May I?" asks one very wrinkled one.

"Just exactly why you?" the leader wants to know.

"Poldy wouldn't send me away . . . even if he dare not know me in his uniform."

"Poldy? What Poldy?"—six want to know.

"That Poldy! My grandson there, with the ebony cane . . ." quivering with pride her voice proclaims.

Admiringly the six look from the old woman to Poldy, from Poldy to the old woman. "That your grandson?"

"Yesterday I gave him two crowns. And even if he dare not know me now —he is a good boy . . ." she describes her Marshal.

The leaders glory fades away; interest is concentrated on the corpse-guard's relative.

After a lengthy discussion the leader decides that she herself will inspect the corpse and that the old one may accompany her. The old one beams with importance.

Since they have previous experience of the guards they know just how to bypass their rudeness. They begin their tour far down the line where the cheap corpses are, with which they have been acquainted for a day or two already. Devoutly they stand before the glass doors of the poor dead. With a glance to the guard at the other end they take out their rosaries; the leader's voice becomes audible: soft, but loud enough for him to hear, she speaks in an affected manner to assure him of the piety of her doing.

Thus slyly and carefully they creep along the ranks of the dead; now and then stopping, hurrying on again the next moment; and when they reach an acquaintance from their street they stay long enough even for an obituary.

"Poor, poor Mr. Zapletal, just look at him lying there as though he's never been alive. And how he smiles, he must be with our Lord . . ."

The other one does not enter into this kind of talk, she can see no reason in it.

"And what about the sausages?"

"What sausages?"

"The rotten sausages."

"What are you talking about! You're thinking of Hajek. Mr. Zapletal never sold a bad sausage in his life. Where on earth did you get that idea?"

"From my Poldy, of course. . . ."

That hits home.

"Well, maybe so. But you know, he was such a pious man. How handsome he looked as sacristan of the Franciscans, just like St. Joseph himself. And he knew all the honourable gentlemen. After litany he even collected with the bell-purse . . . Well, well, Mr. Zapletal, and now there he lies. Just like the others, there he lies . . ." For all her pharisaical manner she cannot help gloating a little.

The other is more matter of fact, and impatient to reach their object. "If there he lies, there he lies; let's go," she says—frivolously loud, to the horror of her leader who had planned entirely different tactics. But her companion is thoughtless and a-quiver with curiosity.

At last they reach Poldy. Grandma winks at him with her lashless eyelids, encouraged by the memory of yesterday's gift of two crowns. Poldy is neutral, saying neither yes nor no. Probably in his brain there shines like the Neon sign of a cinema house, hope of a further two crowns.

It is unexpectedly easy: here they are already at the longed-for glass door; as children at the fair are awed by the terrible spectacle of Hadshi Cadabra, so the old one loses her *blasé* manner of speech and stands shyly at her leader's side.

"Just look, look at those rings. Why didn't they leave them at home? And cuff-links even! What a beautiful corpse! Almost alive! And all those candles! What show!" Enthusiastically she clicks her tongue, but shocked and mindful of the nearby Poldy she puts her hand to her mouth, as if that could undo the click.

The leader speaks not a word. She has a faraway look, no one could disturb her, only her lips mumble: "Twenty crowns . . . twenty crowns . . . that's the last straw . . . just like that . . . goes and dies . . . just like that . . . twenty crowns. . . ."

"Look at all those medals on the cushion! Probably a count he must be . . . or a baron . . . Did you see the medals?"

"Twenty crowns . . . twenty crowns . . . every time . . ."

The old one grows angry.

"What is all that silly talk of twenty crowns? Have you no heart?"

Her broken leader merely shakes her head. "Come, you shall hear."

She allows herself to be led back to the bench and the others.

"Twenty crowns . . . twenty crowns . . . rain or shine . . . now he's dead . . ."

The leader has cause enough to be sad and worried. With the rich man, gone where the seven women and the many dead have long been at home, her best source of income has died. So strange are the relations between humans that no one probably mourns as much over the death of the rich gentleman as this grey, nameless beggar-woman.

The gentleman in the oaken coffin had had a very odd friendship with her. Yes, people would gape if they knew of the many times the District Attorney had clandestinely climbed the dark land leading past the castle ruins, to visit the beggar-woman. Did the old woman realize that she was doing great services to society? Probably if she did, she would have been less enthusiastic about the shabby payment the District Attorney made her in exchange for her advice. No sentence, nothing was decided, until he had first sought her out in her cottage below the castle. He never noticed waiting in the doorways the girls with the silken legs when the evening was fanned by mellow summer's air, nor felt the ice-wind whistling from the Danube woods at Christmas time. Coughing, always bad-tempered, he climbed the steep steps, stick on his shoulder, his hat low on his brow. From the inn came drunken voices and the sound of mouth-organs. Fewer and fewer were the lights till he reached the castle and the tiny houses in its big shadow. At the poorest of them he stopped. Three times he knocked, short and clear. Slowly, but unexpectedly sudden, the door opened.

"Has your honour come again?"

The District Attorney raised his hat.

The old woman led him into her kitchen; her guest sat down on a sugar-box. With bent fingers she held a piece of candle into the glow of the hearth, patiently waiting for the wick to catch light. Her fingers are invulnerable. Out of a corner leapt a cat, frightening the District Attorney, but he suppressed the urge to run it through with his stick and stayed put on his box like a good boy. You never can tell, the cat might be the old woman's sister.

"Would your honour like a cup of coffee?"

He did not dare to say no. Obediently he gulped down a mugful of brown liquid, the old woman watching him like a mother.

"And what have you to tell me, my good woman?"

She shifted her chair closer to his.

"The Bishop is about again, your honour. When the sexton went to ring the bells at night he saw him at the altar. All the candles were lit, he was reading a mass. But he did not sing. Take note, your honour, he did not sing. He is worried. Perhaps he needs someone. Suddenly it was dark. Your honour, someone in the town will have to die!"

"Who, do you think?"

"The young die much easier than the old. A young one always helps an old one. Another cup of coffee, your honour?"

"Something to keep death away! Don't you know of anything yet?"

"Your honour, take care! You talk too much! Let the others die. Grow old, then all will be easier . . . Only hold on and grow old. Just let the others die . . ."

If the woman had only known the effect of her words. There had never been so many sentences of death in the town. For the theft of a goat the District Attorney called for the gallows. He let the others die. And his fame grew with the number of gallows that had been erected at his orders. The prelates sent him wine, the Jews sent him chickens. Like lean wolves the poor sinners broke under his wrath.

And the beggar-woman in the shadow of the castle put aside twenty crown note after twenty crown note, to take care of her endless future.

And now it is all over. There he lies now, the careless man dead, and she in her poverty would yet have to hire herself out as a candlewoman.

Oh, how stupid to make so much fuss of one's fear of death. It was just like calling to death to come and get him. She, of course, would be much more clever.

Suchlike are the memories of the seven wrinkled women. None of them has lived so important a life as her leader. The son of one had been a sergeant and once even seen the Emperor. And so she would describe the Emperor in detail, as if she had been the sergeant, not her son. As if she had said: "Listen, Emperor, when shall we two go hunting again?" But there is much less response to these Emperor stories than one might think. For, when all's said and done, what did he amount to? In life he had gone far, yes, but in the end, he, too, had died. Bah, the Emperor.

Much more interest is the annoyance caused them by one of their union. It so happened that somewhere in the cemetery an imaginary sweetheart of hers lay buried. None of the women succeeded in locating the grave of this seducer, although one or other of them often laid in wait for her among the tombstones, thus risking to miss some exciting event at the morgue. For it had become the habit of this disloyal one to disappear only when she believed the others busy, and to sneak to her lover, partly to tend his grave, partly, no doubt, to betray to him Heaven knows what secrets of the union. And in all probability, one night, when the others go home, she would have to stay behind. She is far too strongly drawn to the dead. She is an evil one, intent on the things of beyond. And the others are worried lest their own safety has been endangered by this madwoman.

But it seems there are no grounds for fear. Till winter comes, when the bench is empty. At winter-time the wrinkled women do not come out. At winter-time they mostly die. Then they lie in their scattered graves, aware of the majesty of death. Silent and proud, they lie as if they had never been acquainted with each other.

PICKLE MY BONES

By Arthur Calder-Marshall

'I KNOW," Charley said, taking Bimbo's arm in a firm hand. "If they don't want us, I know where we'll go." Split from the others, they turned downhill. "You met Ted Slaughter, didn't you, that night, Bimbo?"

"I know Slaughter," the young man answered, Bimbo the hawk, sweating beneath the eyes, "and his brothers, Plague and Pestilence. Not one of that family I haven't met. Huh!" His voice barked a laugh-cough. "Huh!. huh! that's funny, a joke, see?"

Street lamps revolved and stopped, reversed and stopped, swung back again. Night nibbles at faces. Take and grin and shake it off. "That's no joke, but symbology you're talking," said Charley, fat, white-skinned, with a voice that, coming from the coarse body, sounded rare and gentle. "But what I say is fact most wonderful, most curious fact, stranger than all fiction. Slaughter's the undertaker, a man setting his name to rights."

The sky was pricked out with stars, the road back netted with frost. "I knew a man in Lagos," Bimbo said. What song the sirens sang. "Yes, Lagos it was." Bathing in memory. "Name Christmas, a missionary by profession. Was that chance?" Hark, vault of heaven, was it chance? Discuss celestial bodies. Mars, are you warlike? Venus, true planet of love?

"What's in a name?" the older man pondered. "Why's Bun the Baker, why the Doctor Dose? Bim, boy, I tell you this. Mark it before I die. Should you want to plumb the profundity, interrogate the games of childhood. Explore

Tom Tiddler's Ground and cogitate the symbolosophy of Catch-as-Catch-can. What's Hunt the Slipper but what we all do, calling the slipper happiness, calling it truth?"

"Call it booze, Charley, and you're right. This Slaughter, has he got a cellar?"

The white face turned towards the hawk's eyes. "That's our reason. The purpose of our envoy. An's a fine chap, Slaughter, stands drinks with the best."

Swaying silence. Footsteps hammer tones in eternity. Silence stirred by street lamps. Sprang from a hoarding. ANDREWS THE LIVER SALT. Must have left it behind. Laugh, folks, at the fat man's bottom and he scratching his head, see. If he scratched his tail, he'd find it. Behind the hoarding was a broken house, cellars and rooms laid open like hollow teeth. The wind whipped at the sodden paper peeling from the walls. Where the December draught blows, men once warmed cold hands before a fire and women sewed in comfort.

"When you're dead, son," Charley said, "be balmed by Slaughter. His granny was Egyptian."

Bimbo stopped and separated himself from Charley as he swayed. His eyes stared down the light-pooled street, but they saw nothing. "The Egyptians drew the brain down through the nostrils." He hunched his shoulders, gestured with his hands. "Think, Charley, think of the hooked metal probing your cold nose to yoick the grey stuff down. Think of death, Charley. A man might blow his nose and see his cerebellum lying in his nose-rag. Ugh!" He shivered.

"Come along," said Charley. "I know you're going on the stage. You told me all that once this evening. It's not I don't believe you, but I just don't want to hear it over again."

A car, two cars, roared into, shot down the—"Cheerio, boys!"—street. Headlights piled up against a—"See those lights, Bim, that's Slaughter's"—shop-front. Then the cars wheeled, one behind the other, brakes grinding, turned right-angled down another street, humming away, away. The sound of a dying lamp glimmering, leaping up, down, up, but always farther down.

"You mustn't say that, Charley." Bim's voice trembled. "You mustn't make fun of that."

"I didn't mean it," Charley pressed his hand.

"You mustn't say it. You're my friend. There's some things sacred... I'll be a great actor. But if you don't believe in me, then who . . ."

"You'll be fine, Bimbo. You've got it in you. I know that."

The young man pushed him away. "You're just trying to comfort me." My God, how sad my voice, how sad the world is under a shivering sky! Harshening, his voice rose. "You don't believe in me. What you're saying now is just to comfort me."

"Slaughter's!" Charley distracted, pointing to the shop-front. "What monumental masonry! What venereal piles!" In the moonlight a blind angel stared at them winding a soundless horn. Before her feet were tussocks of immortelles. MY GOD HOW WONDERFUL THOU ART IN LOVING MEMORY OF . . . Inverted grave vases of porcelain. THE LORD HATH GIVEN . . . I wish he'd take away.

Staring up at higher stories, Adam's apple ripe in his throat, "No lights!" Charley gargled. "No one in."

Bim gazed at the vision in the dark shop, the rich coffins stacked behind glass along the walls until : "Try the side, Bim," Charley jerked his arm to follow. His knees were weak but his mouth was parched, tingling for liquor.

Through an arch slant shadowed from a wall-bracket, they now one mass, now two linked by an arm, lurched to where the backyard was trellised about. Here, concourse of angels and marble cherubs balanced on the balls of their feet like a frozen ballet class, stretched to, but never touched, God perhaps knew what paradise. Yearning maybe, merely to see a name sculped after IN LOVING MEMORY OF, ambitious only to stake first claim in the cemetery.

"No lights here, either," Charley said.

But Bim, "What matter? Come on," scrambled over the trellis sooner than wrestle with the gate latch.

Charley hesitated, cupped hands: "Hoy there. Anyone awake?" But no one answered.

"Found a door," called Bimbo. "But's locked." He pushed against it.

"No lights." Charley crossed the shadows of the angels. "No good. No lights."

Bim took a loose brick and—"You can't, Bim!"—smashed, the glass fell and clattered, the brick fell. "Can't do it, Bim." He got his hand through: "It's illegal." Bimbo turned the key in the lock, and, bending, drew the bolt.

"Oh, can't I just?" He swung the door back on a passage.

Pale in shadow, his face turned. "Come on, Charley." Blood, welling, clotted his hand and stuck his fingers together. "I've done this. Think I'm going back without a drink now?" He bound his handkerchief round the hand. "Enter the Slaughterhouse."

The older man followed, and they felt their way along in darkness. The sole noise was their footsteps on the brick floor. Then Charley's soft voice: "Here's a door." When he turned the handle, a grey rectangle dawned on the passage. He pushed down the switch and from the white shade light shot in a cone on to the floor. "Office," he said.

They looked round, dazed and silly. A desk, a chair, a flask of water and a glass. A safe, three filing cabinets, a hardwood book-case with account books and, on a shelf: "Bottles," said Charley. Bim said: "Booze."

Bim got on a chair and handed down a couple of bottles. Embalming fluid. Superior quality.

"What's good," Charley said. "I'm not dead yet."

"You will be soon. Jest pickle my bones in al-co-hol. It's alk. Got a corkscrew?"

"Use paper-knife." Charley leant against the side of the desk. Bimbo looked round. Charley flicked the knife with a finger. It swung on its shoulder. "Cut self?" he said. "You look white. Maybe's deep."

" 'S not deep," Bim said shivering. " 'S cold. Not enough alk. Carn get cork out."

"Get in then. Push home."

The young man tried, but his handkerchief got in his way. "Here, give it to me." Charley took the bottle, shoved the cork in, and smelt the bottle. "It's alk," he said, "and smells good." He raised the bottle and swigged.

Bim felt faint. Took glass of flask and said: "Fill." Charley poured glass full and Bim drank it down. "Jest pickle my guts in al-co-hol."

"Doan make that row," said Charles. "You'll wake the Slaughter household."

"Pretty funny idea getting pickled in pickling fluid."

" 'Member Nelson? England expects every man to do's duty. British Navy did theirs by un. Pickled him in rum and when they got to port, there wasn't a drop left. They'd tapped un."

"Was Colet, Dean St. Paul's. Know that story?" Bim said. "My God, room's cold. Give some more. 'S got kick."

He raised new brimmed glass and gulped half down. "What was I sayin'?"

Charley stared at his right foot. It moved up and down. Cracks in the toe were a toothless old man's face and the movement made him talk. St. Peter's bell chimed and struck once. "Last words, 'Room's cold!'" Charley answered.

Bim brushed hair back with hand. Flask on desk tilted, stood straight and

F

tilted. He rubbed eyes. "Yes and Colet, Dean St. Paul's. Now I remember, 'member. Fire of London. Think of the Great Fire, Charley. Think St. Paul's each stone of which was boun' wi' lead and gutter-pipes were lead. Know that? Know it melted in Great Fire and flowed down Ludgate Hill in molten stream?"

"Bottle's dead," Charley yawned. "Open other."

"You open. I talking. You listen an' open." Cigarette fell from fingers on to floor. Groped feeling for it. Hand tangled with leg. "Cig? Thanks, Charl." But didn't light, it stayed between fingers. "After Fire, two chaps came to Cathedral. Colet's coffin split, part melted in heat, maybe. Poked body with sticks. Bubbles came out."

"What's got to do . . .?" Charley held up bottle.

"Wait for point," Bim said. "Doan be impatient. No man ever got anywhere by impatience. Ole man pickled in liquor. They drank it. That proves it, doesn't it?"

Cigarette dropped Bim's fingers. Head sang what song sirens sang, sunk.

" 'S liquor's good, course."

"Drink't, prove't." Charley thrust bottle forward. But's head was sunken, drunken. "Drink." Charley thrust bottle at Bim's lips: "Drink."

Bim raised hand, held it in lax hand, dropped it from lax hand. It spilled across his legs.

"Wet here," Charley sprawled forward. "Where come liquor on trous?"

"Ge' 'way," Bim said. "Gray actor. Doan' b'lieve. What song the Sirens singling, circling sangled. Here we go roun' and down an' " . . . Raised eyes glazing, jutting lower lip forth. Slaver dried.

Charl clutched Bim roun' neck. "Ole man, sorry, ole man. Kiss me, Bim. Kiss. Kiss."

Both fell, heavy coats, on wood floor. Fell and lay. Charl tried rise, sank, on Bim's belly, pillowed his head. "Great actor, Bim. You'll act like . . . like some gray actor . . . name forgotten."

When Charley opened his eyes it was so dark that he could see nothing. His feet felt as if they were frozen and his fingers were numb. He shut his eyes again and tried to sleep. His head ached. Everything turned in his brain. He put his hand down and touched something wet. As he fell into half-sleep, he began to think: "Why is there water in my bed?" He thought: "It doesn't matter. There's water in my bed. It doesn't matter."

His brain swung round and he wanted to sleep, to stop feeling the pressure in his head. He thought: "Why in my bed?" When he opened his eyes, all was dark. He felt the mattress and it was wood. It was a floor. He felt his pillows. It was a warm coat. It was Bimbo.

"God, I've a head, Bimbo," he said. But Bimbo didn't answer. "Doesn't matter," he muttered. " 'S still dark." He went to sleep.

When he woke it was still dark. He struck his last match, but it gave no light. He threw it away.

He felt a bottle on the floor. It was so dark he couldn't see it. "Hold it up against the window." But there was no window. He lifted the bottle towards his eyes and hit himself on the nose. "Damn," he said, and put the bottle down.

His head was still splitting. There was a queer smell. He wanted to get back to his bed and sleep the blind off. "Bimbo," he said, "we'd better be going."

There was no answer. He pushed the body and said: "Wake up. Don't lie there dead drunk."

Bimbo did not move.

Charley groped in the darkness with his hand. He felt the shoulder and then the face. He drew his hand back. The skin was frigid.

He groped out again and touched Bimbo's lips with his fingers in the darkness. They were chilled stiff.

"Bimbo," he called, "wake up." He caught the boy's shoulders in his hands. "Wake up, for Christ's sake," he shouted. But the body was heavy and when he released his grip, it fell with a thud against the floor. He stood up staring into the darkness. "You're not dead, boy," he whispered. "Say you're not dead." But no sound came, no movement, no noise even of breathing.

Terror struck him, his pillow the cold body at his feet. He cupped his hands and bawled with his full lungs: "Ted! Ted! Ted! Come down here. Come, for God's sake. Ted! Ted!"

He heard a noise, a chair drawn back, a shout. "Who's there?"

"It's me. It's Charley. Come, for God's sake."

Footsteps hurried downstairs. "Where are you, Charley?"

"This way," he shouted. "In the cellar."

"Coming," the voice said. He heard a door open and Ted call: "You there, Charley?" But the voice was farther distant.

"Here," he shouted, "in this cellar place."

The sound of footsteps. A door open close to him. "My God," said Ted. "What are you doing here?"

Charley's voice trembled. "Turn on the light, Ted. I've got something awful to show you."

Ted did not speak, but Charley heard his breathing.

"Turn on the light, Ted. It's something. You can't think how terrible."

"I can't turn it on," said Ted softly. "It is on. And the sun's shining through the window."

THE LEMMINGS

By Alex Comfort

IT is an extremely long time since I was in that particular island, but I understand that what I am about to describe continues to occur periodically, though no longer regularly every five years as was formerly the case.

I had travelled a considerable distance from the nearest steamer port in a small boat rowed by native fishermen. Upon coming in sight of the island I noticed nothing unusual, but one of the rowers maintained that he could see greater activity than usual in the colony which extended along a line of yellow rocks running to westward. I could see the chimneys of the Keeper's house, however, and as we approached the jetty, which was constructed of bamboo poles and very flimsy, I noticed the Keeper himself hastening down a path through the woods to meet us. I also noticed that the path and the garden of the house was everywhere surrounded with high wire mesh fences, which, so far as I could judge by the recently turned earth at their bases, were continued to some depth underground. My anxiety to meet the Keeper was extremely great. I had heard the most remarkable stories on the boat both of the spectacle I had come so far to witness and of the extraordinary personality of this man—of his almost supernatural influence over his charges, who on account of the shortage of food on the island would probably have gnawed to death any other human visitor not under his protection—and of his alleged power of conversing with the creatures in their own language, an assertion which I am unable any longer to doubt.

"You are just in time," he remarked, shaking me by both hands as I stepped ashore. "Had you been a day late you might well have missed the whole performance. As it is we are in ample time. You will be able to lunch with me,

I think: I doubt if they will begin before tea-time. Please bring your bag to my house, and instruct the crew to fetch you in two days' time. Their arrival sooner might disturb the proceedings."

Examining the Keeper I found him to be a middle-aged man, bald, extremely —and at times, indeed, effusively—genial, wearing a blue uniform with red-piped edges, similar to that which postmen at home are accustomed to wear. The most singular feature of his attire, however, was a clerical collar, much soiled —owing, I suppose, to the infrequency of trade with that island: he also wore a stout leather belt, from which was suspended a whistle and an object which I took to be a sugar stick, but I saw upon closer inspection that it was a life-preserver, painted white with coloured spiral stripes like those upon a barber's pole. Seeing that my gaze rested upon these objects he smiled apologetically and explained their use.

"I assumed the collar," he said, "not out of religious conviction, but because, for some reason or other, I find it makes them less restive. You could imagine no shier animals. They take the most violent objection to some minor articles of dress—by the way, I must ask you if you have a watch or clock with you?"

I told him that I had.

"Then you will be so kind as to leave it at the house if we are to go down among them. It's a prejudice I have never been able to understand. As for this truncheon, I have to carry it, for even I am not entirely safe—their numbers are so great but I feel that to carry it openly might diminish their confidence in me. That confidence," he said, "is my major joy in life. I could never do anything which might diminish it. I have been on this island for nearly fifty years, alone, and I find these creatures my truest friends." A large tear ran down the piping on his collar.

"But what can have made you select so lonely and unremunerative an office?" I asked him.

"I do not know," he replied. "But the creatures chose me themselves."

"Chose you?"

"Yes, indeed. Please be careful of that hole. There are others near here, and my sight is not good enough to point them all out to you. The wire is defective. Very defective. Yes, you must know that formerly the office of keeper here was hereditary. When it was thrown open for applications, I was the first to submit my name together with a Scotsman. The retiring keeper stood us on the beach. There were thousands of them—the rocks and the sand were brown with them. Suddenly at a word from the Keeper they came forward, flowing over the rocks like hairy treacle. It was too much for the Scotsman. He turned to get behind the wire, but the old Keeper tripped him up, and they were all over him in a few seconds. He only managed to kill one. When they went away, his brain was the only part of him they had been unable to reach. My first duty, when the old Keeper had given me his whistle and truncheon and been rowed away, was to bury this separately. I have some of the bones in my study. They show the most interesting tooth-prints."

We were by now approaching the house, which was large and well built. It was surmounted by a watch-tower which, being the highest point of the island, dominated the shore in all directions. There was an elaborate system of trenches, nets, and wires crossing in every direction throughout the garden of the house, and upon coming accidentally in contact with one of these I was surprised to receive a sharp electric shock.

"I regret these defensive measures," said my host. "They are so unsightly. But I fear they are extremely necessary."

Having let us in with a key, my host guided me to my room and invited me to join him on top of the tower in a few minutes' time. From this eminence, as I have said, the entire island was revealed. I found my host leaning over the balcony examining a distant part of the coast through a pair of field-glasses.

Being unassisted by any such appliance, I could see nothing, except an appearance resembling a reddish-brown smoke which was passing along a small rocky valley among the trees to our right. There were a number of small bare hills of a sandy soil, and I noticed that these were studded in all directions with circular black mouths of holes, and with the mounds of yellow soil thrown up in the course of their excavation.

"I think," the Keeper was remarking, "they are going to start from that bay over there, Skull Bay. Yes, I am sure they are. You are going to be privileged. You will have a perfect view of the entire performance. Look over there, look over there. . . . They are assembling in their thousands."

As, however, he retained the glasses pressed closely to his eyes, I could be certain of nothing, only it appeared to me that along every defile a column of the same brownish smoke was making its way to the spot which he indicated. The spit of rocks at the far side of this bay, the same which I had remarked on approaching the island, was encrusted with a thick moving deposit of the same colour, like live fur. I mentioned this appearance to the Keeper, in the hope of getting the loan of his glasses.

"It is live fur," he remarked, retaining them. "You would never imagine the intelligence of the creatures, the love and patience which they have expended in preparing for this day. The females have swum for miles removing the weeds from the bay and the rocks. The males have been digging and refilling holes with almost human industry to prepare themselves. I ought to explain to you exactly what will happen. Very soon they will begin to gather in groups, as if to be addressed by their leaders. But they are waiting for me to give the signal. They have taken me into their confidence throughout. I have witnessed this event no less than nine times. I know by now what sort of things please them. I carve them little medals out of the tops of condensed milk tins and hang them from ribbons. For weeks beforehand they wait at my back door to drag the medals away to their holes. In their enthusiasm to make preparations they do irreparable damage to the island—that, I suppose, is partly responsible for the food shortage—but one has not the heart to stop them."

"But what exactly will they do?" I asked him.

"When they have been addressed by their leaders they will go down to the shore, all together, and stand at the edge of the sea. By that time it will be sundown, and they will call to me. I will then hoist a flag upon the pole which you see upon that hill. Then the leaders will enter the water, a few at a time. Gradually they will pass through the line of breakers and begin to swim out towards the setting sun and the open sea. Others will follow, squeaking with confidence. I tell you I have watched this spectacle no less than nine times, and on every occasion I have been struck and inspired by the expression of confidence upon the faces of every individual animal, even the females and the extremely young. You must forgive my sentimental and unscientific approach, but I have come to regard the creatures with affection, and I can interpret their expression as you can those of a man."

"And what then?" I asked.

"They continue to swim out to sea."

"For how long?"

"Until the last one has sunk. It is a most touching business. For weeks later the island is abnormally quiet, and I go round collecting and skinning the corpses with which the windward side is littered. The white sand on those beaches is almost entirely composed of pulverized bone."

I pondered for a moment this astounding biological phenomenon. "But how is it," I asked him, "that the species does not become extinct?"

"A certain number remain behind, of course," he told me. "The malformed and the sick, some of the extremely aged—though I have noticed the enthusiasm with which these lead the march to the shore, though hardly able to stagger along and quite unable to participate by swimming. And there are a certain number of abnormal adults who seem to have no urge to join in the migration. These are quite often killed by the others, though. I may be able to show you a few tonight." He put away the glasses, as by now the sun was not far from the water of the bay, and he found it dazzling. "If we go now," he said, "we shall have time for a meal before the migration begins."

Accordingly we went downstairs. The Keeper's imported food was excellent, and he diverted me throughout the meal with the exhibition and explanation of the curiosities with which the room was filled, including the Scotsman's bone, and a number of curious objects washed ashore by the sea. So much, however, was I wearied by my journey, that in the course of his talking I fell fast asleep.

I was wakened by my host bending over me and shaking me. I noticed, although the light was rapidly failing, that he had large tears running down his face. "Come," he said, "they are waiting for me." He removed a red flag from a small locker and opened the front door. We passed at a run through a gate in the high wire fence, which my host unlocked, and on among the trunks of the small trees with which the island is covered. On a number of occasions I fell as a result of catching my feet in holes or mounds of earth. The woods were entirely deserted, but I could detect a multiplicity of footprints all running the same way as we were running. My companion seemed to know every inch of the ground, for he never stumbled until we found ourselves on the summit of the small hole-riddled hill overlooking the bay, where the pole stood. "We are in time," he gasped.

I looked down on to the beach below me, utterly astounded by what I saw, a sight that in every way surpassed my expectations. The arena of white sand was illuminated by the oblique red light of the sun under a cloud bank, and both it and the spit of seaward rocks were flowing and undulating with an immense crowd of small red furry animals. They surged over the stones at the foot of the low cliffs, and fresh contingents continued to arrive in streams which poured out of several defiles and paths leading to the beach rather like a viscous fluid. There was a tide-mark of them creeping and climbing on the rocks. The beach itself was so congested that a number of the animals were jammed into cracks in the stones, while a long brown fringe undulated with each successive wave. My host was enraptured. "I never, never saw so many," was all he was capable of saying at first. Then he began to talk rapidly in my ear, pointing out to me facts which I would not otherwise have observed. I noted that the animals were engaged in crowding into groups, in the centres of which larger and older individuals could be seen. I could smell an overpowering smell of small rodent. The air was full of a minute shuffling and the dry noise of claws and tails crossing on stones. Turning my attention to individual animals closer to myself, I noticed that many were cleaning their fur, while the females brushed and licked their young and marshalled them in the direction of the shore. I noticed—or rather the Keeper pointed out to me with pride—that one of the larger lemmings was dragging a tin medal from a bedraggled ribbon between his prominent front teeth. I observed also the complacent, if not confident, expression upon the faces of the rodents, though being unfamiliar with their normal appearance I am unable to state its significance.

"Look there," said the Keeper, "that's the oldest animal I've seen. He's at the centre of a group. And do you see——' Here he broke off short, watching closely a small group of animals on the top of a low dune, separated from the rest. Their fur was noticeably less kempt than that of the others, and they were huddled into a group. As I watched, a larger lemming, passing, dragged one of them down into the crowd, and after a while his corpse was thrown out and rolled down the dune. "Those are some of the abnormals I told you of," said the Keeper. "They're apparently refusing to go."

Suddenly he stiffened, and caught my arm, pointing out to sea. The lower limb of the sun, elliptical in form, had touched the horizon. There was an instant cessation of movement below us, except where at the periphery of the crowd a few latecomers hastened to take their places. Then suddenly a shrill dry squeaking commenced at the end of the spit in the far distance and approached, until its volume was terrible. I put my hands to my ears, but could not exclude it. The Keeper spoke but I could not hear his words. With feverish hands he attached the flag to its halliard and hoisted it.

Instantly the sound ceased. There was a long quiet pause. And then the first lemming entered the water, and swam resolutely out, its head and paws jerking, and a red arrowhead of ripple coming from its chin. It swam about three yards alone, and then a second followed it, and another. Within a few moments the surface of the bay was covered with the minute black wedges of heads and intersecting V-shaped ripples, and the entire gathering began to crowd down the beach to the water, calling quietly to one another, the females administering a final preen to their young, the adults ruffling and smoothing their coats. They began to pass below us, headed out to sea. The Keeper took off his cap and held it before him, weeping and clapping his hands. After a while one or two of the animals ceased to swim and sank, many of them at a point immediately below our hill. I noticed that whenever one appeared on the point of sinking, two of the larger lemmings would rush towards him and attempt to reach him in time to hang round his neck one of the tin medals, the weight and encumbrance of which usually caused him to sink at once, though here and there the ribbon remained floating, suggesting that in these instances the medal was of wood. Before many moments had passed, there remained on the beach only the small group on their dune, and a solitary infant which rushed to and fro and finally entered the water, sinking just off the rocks below our viewpoint. The Keeper was shouting at the top of his voice, "Wonderful, wonderful!" By this time the squeaking was dying away, and the light fading. Only the net of ripples marked the progress of the lemmings out to sea.

The Keeper hauled down the flag, trembling with emotion. Already a few bodies were being returned by the water along the line of the tide. I gave him my promise to assist him the following day in the collection and preservation of the valuable skins, and thanked him for his hospitality and the unique opportunity I had enjoyed. By now it was dark, and the island extremely quiet.

THE BIZARRE

CONFESSIONS OF AN ENGLISH OPIUM-EATER

By Thomas De Quincey

THE Malay has been a fearful enemy for months. Every night, through his means, I have been transported into Asiatic scenery. I know not whether others share in my feelings on this point; but I have often thought that, if I were compelled to forego England, and to live in China, among Chinese manners and modes of life and scenery, I should go mad. The causes of my horror lie deep, and some of them must be common to others. Southern Asia, in general, is the seat of awful images and associations. As the cradle of the human race, if on no other ground, it would have a dim, reverential feeling connected with it. But there are other reasons. No man can pretend that the wild, barbarous, and capricious superstitions of Africa, or of savage tribes elsewhere, affect him in the way that he is affected by the ancient, monumental, cruel, and elaborate religions of Hindostan. The mere antiquity of Asiatic things, of their institutions, histories—above all, of their mythologies, etc.—is so impressive that to me the vast age of the race and name overpowers the sense of youth in the individual. A young Chinese seems to me an antediluvian man renewed. Even Englishmen, though not bred in any knowledge of such institutions, cannot but shudder at the mystic sublimity of *castes* that have flowed apart, and refused to mix, through such immemorial tracts of time; nor can any man fail to be awed by the sanctity of the Ganges, or by the very name of the Euphrates. It contributes much to these feelings that South-Eastern Asia is, and has been for thousands of years, the part of the earth most swarming with human life, the great *officina gentium*. Man is a weed in those regions. The vast empires, also, into which the enormous population of Asia has always been cast, give a further sublimity to the feelings associated with all oriental names or images. In China, over and above what it has in common with the rest of Southern Asia, I am terrified by the modes of life, by the manners, by the barrier of utter abhorrence placed between myself and *them*, by counter-sympathies deeper than I can analyse. I could sooner live with lunatics, with vermin, with crocodiles or snakes. All this, and much more than I can say, the reader must enter into before he can comprehend the unimaginable horror which these dreams of oriental imagery and mythological tortures impressed upon me. Under the connecting feeling of tropical heat and vertical sunlights, I brought together all creatures, birds, beasts, reptiles, all trees and plants, usages and appearances, that are found in all tropical regions, and assembled them together in China or Hindostan. From kindred feelings, I soon brought Egypt and her gods under the same law. I was stared at, hooted at, grinned at, chattered at, by monkeys, by paroquets, by cockatoos. I ran into pagodas, and was fixed for centuries at the summit, or in secret rooms; I was the idol; I was the priest; I was worshipped; I was sacrificed. I fled from the wrath of Brama through all the forests of Asia; Vishnu hated me; Siva lay in wait for me. I came suddenly upon Isis and Osiris: I had done a deed, they said, which the ibis and the crocodile trembled at. Thousands of years I lived and was buried in stone coffins, with mummies and sphinxes, in narrow chambers at the heart of eternal pyramids. I was kissed, with cancerous kisses, by crocodiles, and was laid, confounded with all unutterable abortions, amongst reeds and Nilotic mud.

Some slight abstraction I thus attempt of my oriental dreams, which filled me always with such amazement at the monstrous scenery that horror seemed absorbed for a while in sheer astonishment. Sooner or later came a reflux of feeling that swallowed up the astonishment, and left me, not so much in terror, as in hatred and abomination of what I saw. Over every form, and threat, and punishment, and dim sightless incarceration, brooded a killing sense of eternity and infinity. Into these dreams only it was, with one or two slight exceptions, that any circumstances of physical horror entered. All before had been moral and spiritual terrors. But here the main agents were ugly birds, or snakes, or crocodiles, especially the last. The ursed crocodile became to me the object of more horror than all the rest. I was compelled to live with him; and (as was always the case in my dreams) for centuries. Sometimes I escaped, and found myself in Chinese houses. All the feet of the tables, sofas, etc., soon became instinct with life: the abominable head of the crocodile, and his leering eyes, looked out at me, multiplied into ten thousand repetitions; and I stood loathing and fascinated. So often did this hideous reptile haunt my dreams that many times the very same dream was broken up in the very same way: I heard gentle voices speaking to me (I hear everything when I am sleeping), and instantly I awoke; it was broad noon, and my children were standing, hand in hand, at my bedside, come to show me their coloured shoes, or new frocks, or to let me see them dressed for going out. No experience was so awful to me, and at the same time so pathetic, as this abrupt translation from the darkness of the infinite to the gaudy summer air of highest noon, and from the unutterable abortions of miscreated gigantic vermin to the sight of infancy and innocent *human* natures.

THE HORLA

By Guy De Maupassant

8th May. What a perfect day! All the morning I lay stretched out on the grass in front of my house, under the towering plane-tree that spreads over the roof, giving protection and shade. I love this countryside, and love to live in this place, for here I am rooted fast by those deep and tender roots that bind a man to the soil where his forefathers lived and died, bind him to ways of thinking and eating, to customs and meat and drink, to the tones of the peasants' voices and turns of phrase, to the smell of the villages, the smell of the earth and of the air itself.

I love this house of mine where I have grown to manhood. From my windows I can see the Seine flowing by my garden, beyond the road, almost past my door—the broad River Seine, which goes from Rouen to Havre, laden with passing boats.

Away to the left lies the city of Rouen, blue-roofed beneath the throng of its pointed Gothic spires; above them all, slender but strong, rises the cathedral's iron shaft. They are innumerable, these spires—filled with bells that ring, under the azure of morning skies, sending forth their distant metallic humming, a brazen song blown by the breeze, stronger now and now fainter, as it rises and falls.

How lovely it was this morning!

Towards eleven, a long line of barges, drawn by a tug the size of a fly, groaning and straining and belching volleys of smoke, filed past my gates.

And after two English schooners, with red flags fluttering to the sky, came a noble Brazilian three-master, gleaming, spotlessly white from stem to stern. I saluted it; I don't know why the sight of this vessel gave me such pleasure.

12th May. For some days I have had a touch of fever; I feel unwell, or, rather, I feel depressed.

Whence come these mysterious influences, changing our happiness into gloom, our self-confidence into vague distress? One would think that the air, the transparent air, was full of unknowable powers, whose mysterious presence affected us. I wake up gay as a bird, feeling as though I must sing. Why? I go for a walk downstream; and suddenly, after strolling a little way, I turn back feeling disheartened, as if some misfortune awaited me at home. Why? Is it some cold shiver, passing over me, that has shaken my nerves, overshadowed my soul? Is it the shape of the clouds, or the colour of the day, the ever-changing hue of things, that has entered my eyes to trouble my thoughts? Who can say? Everything about us, everything we look at but do not see, everything we brush against but do not know, everything we touch but do not feel, has, on ourselves, on our senses, and through them, on our thoughts, on our very heart, effects that are sudden, surprising, inexplicable.

16th May. I am ill, undoubtedly! And I was so well last month! I have a fever, a dreadful fever, or rather a feverish attack of nerves, that afflicts my mind quite as much as my body. I have this constant, horrible feeling of a danger threatening, this apprehension of impending misfortune or approaching death, this presentiment which means no doubt the inroads of some disease, unknown as yet, at work in my blood and my flesh.

18th May. I have been to see my doctor, for I could not sleep any longer. He found that I had a quickened pulse, dilated pupils, and jangling nerves, but no disquieting symptom. I am to have douches and take bromide of potassium.

25th May. No change whatever! My condition is indeed strange. As evening draws on an unaccountable restlessness comes over me, as if the night held some dreadful menace in store for me. I dine quickly, then try to read; but I do not understand the words; I can hardly tell letter from letter. Up and down my room I go, oppressed by a vague and overmastering dread—dread of sleep, dread even of my bed.

Towards two I go to my bedroom. No sooner inside than I turn the key twice in the lock and shoot the bolts. I am frightened . . . of what? . . . I who have never been frightened before . . . I open my cupboards, look under my bed. I listen . . . listen . . . for what? Isn't it strange that a mere touch of something, a disturbed circulation, perhaps, some irritation of the network of the nerves, a slight congestion, a tiny interruption in the delicate and very imperfect working of the vital machine, can turn one of the bravest of men into a coward, one of the gayest into a victim of melancholia? Then I go to bed, and I wait for sleep as one might wait for the executioner. I wait in terror of its coming, with beating heart and trembling limbs; and my whole body shudders in the warmth of the blankets, up to the moment when I fall asleep of a sudden, as one would fall into a pit of stagnant water to drown.

I sleep—for some little time—two or three hours—then a dream—no, a nightmare, lays hold on me. I am quite aware that I am in bed and asleep—I feel it and know it—and I also feel that someone is drawing close to me, looking at me, feeling me, getting up on my bed, kneeling on my chest, taking my neck between his hands and squeezing . . . squeezing with all his strength . . . trying to strangle me.

And I struggle, bound down by that awful helplessness which paralyses us in dreams; I want to cry out—I cannot; I want to move—I cannot; with fearful efforts, gasping for breath, I try to turn over, to throw off this being who chokes and stifles me—I cannot!

Suddenly I wake, frantic, bathed in sweat. I light a candle. I am alone.

After this attack, which comes every night, I sleep peacefully until dawn.

2nd June. I am worse. What can be the matter with me? The bromide is useless, the douches are useless.

3rd June. An awful night. I am going away for a few days. No doubt a little holiday will set me right.

. . . . .

2nd July. Home again. I am quite myself now. And my little holiday has been delightful.

3rd July. Slept badly; clearly there is fever about, for my coachman is suffering from the same complaint as myself. Yesterday, as I came into the house, I noticed how unusually pale he looked.

"What's the matter with you, Jean?" I asked.

"It's like this, sir. I don't sleep now; me nights eat up me days. Ever since master left, it's been like an evil fate over me."

The other servants are well; but *I* myself live in dread of a fresh attack.

4th July. A fresh attack, and no mistake! The old nightmares have come back. Last night I felt someone crouching on top of me, who, with his mouth to mine, was drinking my life through my lips. Yes, he was draining it out of my throat, as would a leech. Then he got off me, gorged, and *I* woke up, so battered and bruised and exhausted that I couldn't stir. If this goes on for many more days I shall certainly leave home again.

5th July. Have I lost my reason? What happened last night is so extraordinary that my head feels queer when I think of it!

As is my habit every evening now, I had locked my bedroom door; then, feeling thirsty, I drank half a glass of water, and I happened to notice that my water-bottle was full to the glass stopper.

I then went to bed, dropping off into one of my frightful dreams. After about two hours I was awakened by a seizure more frightful than any before.

Imagine a man who is being assassinated in his sleep, who awakes to find a knife in his lungs, and lies there covered with blood, with the death-rattle in his throat, unable to draw his breath, on the verge of death, understanding nothing at all—and there you have it.

When at last I recovered my senses, I was again thirsty; I lit a candle and went towards the table where my water-bottle stood. I lifted it, tipping it over my glass; nothing came out. It was empty, entirely empty! At first I was mystified; then, all at once, such a terrible feeling came over me that I had to sit down, or rather, I tumbled into a chair! Then up I jumped again to gaze about me! In a bewilderment of astonishment and fear I sat down once more, before the transparent water-bottle. I stared at it fixedly, trying to solve the riddle. My hands were trembling! Someone, then, had drunk this water. Who? I? I, myself, no doubt! It could only be myself! Well, then, I was a somnambulist; unknown to myself, I was living that strange double life which makes us wonder whether there are two creatures in us; or whether an alien creature, unknowable, invisible, quickens our captive limbs at times, when our mind is asleep, and they obey this other creature, just as they would, more faithfully than they would, obey ourselves.

Ah! who can understand my anguish? Who can understand how a man feels when, wide awake, and wholly reasonable, he stares in terror through the sides of a glass bottle, looking for a pint of water that has disappeared during his sleep! I stayed there until dawn, not daring to go back to bed.

6th July. I am going mad. My water-bottle was drained again last night, or rather, I drained it!

But did I do it? Did I? Who could it be? Who? Ah, God above! I am going mad! Who can save me!

10th July. I have just been making the most remarkable tests. Most certainly I am mad! And yet . . .

On 6th July, before going to bed, I set out on my table wine, milk, water, bread, and strawberries. Someone drank—I drank—all the water and a little milk. The wine was left untouched, also the strawberries.

On 7th July I tried the same test, with the same result.

On 8th July I tried without the water and milk. Nothing was touched.

And on 9th July I replaced the water and milk on my table by themselves, taking care to cover the bottles in white muslin, and to tie down the corks. Then I rubbed my lips, beard, and hands, with black lead, and went to bed.

The same inexorable sleep took possession of me, followed soon after by the horrible awakening. I hadn't stirred; the sheets themselves had no stain. I hastened to the table. The muslin covering the bottles remained spotless. I untied the strings, panting with fear. Every drop of water was drunk! Every drop of milk was drunk! Ah, God above!

I am leaving for Paris this morning.

. . . .

30th July. I came home yesterday. All is well.

2nd August. Nothing new; beautiful weather. I spend my days watching the Seine flowing by.

4th August. Squabbles among my servants. They say that glasses are being broken in the cupboards at night. The butler accuses the cook, the cook accuses the washerwoman, and she accuses the other two. Who is the culprit? It would take a wise man to say!

6th August. This time I am not mad. I have seen! I have seen! . . . Doubts are no longer possible . . . I have seen! . . . I am still cold to the finger-tips, quaking to the marrow of my bones . . . I have seen!

At two o'clock, in bright sunlight, I was walking in my rose-garden . . . in the autumn rose-walk which is beginning to flower.

As I stopped to look at a *Géant des batailles* that bore three splendid blooms, I saw, I distinctly saw, quite close to me, the stem of one of these roses bend, as if some invisible hand had twisted it, and snap off, as if the hand had plucked it. Then the flower rose in the air, following the curve that an arm would make when carrying it to a mouth. And there it stayed, hanging in the translucent air, all by itself, motionless, a terrifying splash of red, three paces from my eyes.

Aghast, I darted out my hand to snatch it! My hand found nothing; it had vanished. I was seized with a violent fit of anger against myself, for it is not right that a serious-minded, reasonable man should have delusions like this.

But was it really a delusion? I turned round to look for the stem, and found it at once on the rose-tree, just freshly broken off, between the two remaining roses, still on their branch.

At that, I went indoors with my mind in a fearful state. For I am certain now, as certain as that night follows day, that living near to me is an invisible being, who feeds on water and milk, who can touch things, take them and move them about—governed therefore by physical laws, unperceived by our senses, and dwelling under my roof. . . .

7th August. A peaceful night. He drank the water in my bottle, but did not disturb my sleep.

I wonder if I am mad? While I was walking just now, in broad sunlight, along the river, doubts of my reason came to me—not vague doubts like those I have had so far; but doubts that were well defined, real. I have seen madmen; I have known some who remained quite intelligent, clear-headed, far-seeing even in all the things of life, save on one point only. And while they talked on any subject with clearness, penetration, and ease, suddenly their thought, striking on the reef of their madness, was rent in pieces there, scattered and foundered in that wild and terrible ocean, swept by the rushing waves and mists and squalls that we call insanity.

Certainly I should believe I was mad, quite mad, if I was not conscious of it all, well aware of my mental state, if I was not perfectly clear-headed, when probing down into its causes. Probably, then, I am only subject to delusions, and retain my reason. Some unknown disturbance must have taken place in my brain. Is it not possible that one of the imperceptible keys of the instrument within my brain has refused its work? An accident will sometimes deprive a man of his memory for proper names, or verbs, or figures, or simply dates. And the fact that these divisions of our thought are localized in the brain is well established today. What cause for surprise, then, if the faculty that records within me the unreality of certain delusions should be dormant just now?

These were my thoughts as I strolled along the river-bank. The sunshine flooded the water, made earth a delight to behold, filled my heart with the love of life—love of the swallows, that rejoiced my eyes with their swiftness; of the sedges that charmed my ear with their rustlings.

Little by little, however, a strange uneasiness came creeping through me. Some power, as it seemed, some occult power was paralysing me, stopping me, restraining me from going farther, was calling me back. I had the uncomfortable feeling that I must return, such as oppresses you when a beloved invalid is left behind at home, and you are seized with the presentiment that a turn for the worse has come.

Back, therefore, I came in spite of myself, sure that I would find bad news at home—a letter or telegram. But there was nothing, and I was left feeling more uneasy and more surprised than if I had again been through some strange experience.

8th August. A frightful evening, last night. He no longer declares himself. But I feel him near me, eyeing me, pervading me, dominating me—and more to be feared, hiding so, than if he was making his continual unseen presence known by supernatural signs.

Yet I slept well.

9th August. Nothing; but I am afraid.

11th August. Still nothing; I cannot stay at home any longer with this fear lodged in my mind; I am going away.

12th August, 10 p.m. All day I have been waiting to leave the house; I couldn't. It was so simple, so easy, the voluntary act that I wished to accomplish—simply to go out, get into my carriage to drive to Rouen. I couldn't. Why?

14th August. I am done for! Someone is master of my mind and controls it! Someone commands my every act, movement, thought. I count for nothing, now, within myself; I am merely a terrified, slave-like witness to my actions. I want to go out. I cannot. He does not wish it; trembling and panic-stricken, I stay in the arm-chair where he keeps me. I want to get up, that I may believe I am still my own master. I cannot! I am riveted to my chair, and my chair cleaves so fast to the ground that no power could lift us.

Then, all at once, I must, simply must, go to the end of my garden to pick strawberries and eat them. And I go. I pick the strawberries and I eat them. Ah, God, God, God! Is there a God? If God there be, save me! Help me! Deliver me! Mercy! Pity! Grace! Save me! Oh, what agony! What torture! What terror!

17th August. Ah, what a night! What a night! And yet it seems to me that I really should be rejoicing. I read until one in the morning! Hermann Herestrauss, doctor of philosophy and theogony, has written a book on the history and manifestations of every invisible being that hovers around mankind or is dreamed of in their dreams. He describes their origin, their domain, their powers. But not one of them resembles my familiar. One would say that man, ever since he has been able to think, has had some nervous foreknowledge of a new being—more powerful than himself, his successor in this world, and that, feeling him near but unable to foresee the nature of this over-man, in his terror he has created imaginary occult beings, shifting phantoms which have been born of fear.

After reading till one in the morning I went to sit by my open window to refresh my forehead and my mind with the gentle air of night.

The air was warm and sweet. How I would have enjoyed that night in days gone by!

No moon. The stars flashed and sparkled in the black deeps of the sky. Who dwells in those worlds? What forms, what living creatures, what animals, what plants are yonder? They who think in these far-off worlds, what know they beyond our knowledge? What powers have they transcending our own? What things do they see that are hidden from us? And may not one of their kind, passing one day through space, come down to this earth of ours to conquer it, as the Normans once crossed the sea to conquer weaker races?

We are so weak; so defenceless, so ignorant, so small are we, on this whirling spot of slime mingled with a rain-drop!

I dozed off, dreaming in this fashion, in the cool night air.

After sleeping for about forty minutes I opened my eyes, awakened by some vague and strange emotion. At first I saw nothing; then, all at once, it seemed to me that a page of the book lying open on my table had turned over of itself. Not a breath of air had passed in through my window. I waited. After about four minutes I saw, I saw—yes, with my eyes I saw one more page rise, then close down on to the one before, as if a finger had turned it over. My armchair was empty, *seemed* empty; but I understood that he was there, seated in my chair, and that he was reading. With one wild bound, the bound of an infuriated beast about to disembowel its tamer, I dashed across the room to seize him, throttle him, kill him! . . . But my chair, before I reached it, tipped over as if someone had fled before me . . . my table rocked, my lamp fell and went out, and my windows shut to as if some thief, caught in the act, had darted out into the night, grasping the frames with both hands.

He had fled then; *he* had been frightened, frightened of me!

Well then . . . well then . . . tomorrow . . . or after . . . one day or another, I shall be able to seize him with my fingers and crush him. Are not dogs sometimes known to bite, to choke the life out of their masters?

18th August. I have been thinking all day. Ah yes! I shall obey him, follow his suggestions, do everything that he wills, make myself humble, a slave, a craven. He has the upper hand. But the hour will come. . . .

19th August. I know . . . I know—all! I have just read this in the *Revue du Monde Scientifique*:

A curious item of news reaches us from Rio de Janeiro. An epidemic of madness, comparable to those waves of infectious insanity which attacked European peoples in the Middle Ages, is raging at the moment in the province of San Paulo. The frenzied inhabitants desert their houses, villages and fields, saying that they are pursued, possessed, and controlled, like human cattle, by beings which are invisible though tangible, a kind of vampire which feeds on them during their sleep and also drinks water and milk without appearing to touch any other food.

Professor Don Pedro Henriquez, accompanied by several distinguished doctors, has left for the province of San Paulo, to study *in situ* the causes and symptoms of this extraordinary madness and to propose to the emperor the most fitting measures to restore the raving inhabitants to reason.

Aha, I remember, I remember the lovely Brazilian three-master that passed below my windows on her way up the Seine, last 8th of May! I thought her so beautiful, so white, so pleasant! The Being was on board, coming from the land where his race was born! And he saw me! He saw my white house, too; and he leapt from the ship to the shore. Ah, God above!

And now I know, I foresee. Man's reign on earth is over.

HE has come, he that was feared in the innocent, trembling hearts of the early races. He who was exorcised by uneasy priests, whom sorcerers summoned on gloomy nights though invisible as yet to their sight, He whom the forebodings of earth's momentary masters clothed in the monstrous or pleasing shapes of gnomes, spirits, genii, fairies, and hobgoblins. After these first crude picturings of fearful minds, came men with greater insight, who foreshadowed him more clearly. Mesmer guessed at him; and, ten years since, doctors learned the precise nature of his power, before He himself had wielded it. They have toyed with this weapon of the coming Lord, the domination of a mysterious willpower over the enslaved human mind. They have called it magnetism, hypnotism, suggestion . . . and what not. I have seen them playing like thoughtless children with this horrible power! Woe upon us! Woe upon Man! He has come, the . . . the . . . what is his name to me . . . and I cannot hear . . . the . . . yes . . . he is calling it . . . I am listening! . . . I can't quite . . . again . . . Horla . . . I heard . . . the Horla . . . it is He . . . the Horla . . . he has come!

Ah, the vulture has devoured the dove, the wolf has devoured the lamb, and the lion the buffalo with his sharp-pointed horns; man has slain the lion with the arrow, the sword, and the gun; but the Horla will do unto Man what we have done unto the horse and the ox: his chattel, his servant, and his food, by the sole might of his will. Woe upon us!

. . . . . .

19th August. I shall kill him. I have seen him! I sat down at my table yesterday evening, and I pretended to be writing with concentration. I knew, right well, that he would come roaming round me, close, close, so close that perhaps I could touch him, seize him? And then! Then . . . I should have the strength of a desperate man. I should have my hands, my knees, my chest, my head, my teeth, to strangle him, crush him, bite him, rend him.

I was watching for him, with every nerve in my body tingling.

I had lit my two lamps and the eight candles over my mantelpiece, as if all this light would help me to make him out.

Facing me was my bed, my old four-poster of oak; to the right, my fireplace; to the left, my door, carefully shut now, after standing open a long time, to attract him; behind me, a great, high wardrobe with a mirror that I used every day for shaving and dressing and always glanced into from habit, to see myself at full length, whenever I passed before it.

So I pretended to be writing, to mislead him, for he was on the watch; and, all of a sudden, I felt, I *knew* that he was reading over my shoulder, that he was there, touching my ear.

I jumped up, with hands outstretched, wheeling round so quickly that I nearly fell. Well? . . . my mirror was as bright as in broad daylight, and I could not see myself reflected. It was clear and bright and luminous to its very depth! My reflection did not appear there . . . yet I was standing right in front! I could see every inch of the clear tall mirror! Wild-eyed, I stared; and I hadn't the courage to advance one foot or make a single movement, knowing well as I did that he was there, but that he would escape me once more, the invisible-bodied one, who had swallowed up my reflection.

Imagine my fear! And then, behold! all at once I began to see myself in a mist, deep down in the mirror, in a mist as though through a sheet of water; and it seemed to me that the water was slowly gliding from left to right, leaving my reflection clearer with the passing of each second. It was like the end of an eclipse. The thing that shut me out did not seem to have clearly marked outlines, but a kind of opaque transparence, thinning out by little degrees.

Then at last I was able to see myself perfectly, just as I do every day when I look in the glass.

So I had seen him! And the terror of it abides, making me shiver yet.

20th August. Kill him, but how? I cannot grasp hold of him. Poison? He would see me mixing it in the water; moreover, would our poisons have any effect on his imperceptible body? They would not, they would certainly not. What then? What then?

21st August. I have sent for a locksmith from Rouen, and have ordered iron shutters for my room, like those that certain private mansions in Paris have, before the lower storey windows, for fear of burglars. He is also making me a door to match. I have got the name of a coward, but what do I care!

. . . . . .

10th September. Rouen, Continental Hotel. It's done . . . it's done . . . but is he dead? My mind is still in a whirl after seeing it all.

Yesterday, then, after the locksmith had fitted my iron shutters and door, I left everything open until midnight, although it was beginning to be cold.

All at once I felt that he was there; and was overjoyed, crazy with joy. I rose in leisurely fashion and sauntered up and down for a long while, to prevent his suspecting a thing; then I took off my boots and put on my slippers with a careless air; then I closed my iron shutters, and, strolling back to the door, shut the door also, turning the key twice. Returning then to the window I made it fast with a padlock and pocketed the key.

Suddenly, I realized that he was following me about excitedly; that he in his turn was afraid, that he was commanding me to open and let him out. I all but gave way; yet did not quite give way. Instead, I stood with my back to the door, opened a crack, just wide enough to let me slip through backwards; and as I am very tall, my head grazed the lintel. I was certain that he could not have escaped; and I shut him in, alone, alone. Oh, joy, I had him! Then downstairs I went at a run; in the drawing-room below my bedroom I took my two lamps and emptied the oil out over the carpet, over the furniture, and all about; then I set light to it, and escaped, after carefully locking the big front door with two turns of the key.

I went to hide myself at the bottom of my garden, in a clump of laurels. What a time it took! What a time it took! All was dark, silent, motionless; not a breath of air, not a star; mountainous clouds, that I could not see, but which weighed on my mind with a great and heavy weight.

I watched my house and waited. What a time it took! I was already beginning to think that the fire had gone out of itself, or that *He* had put it out, when one of the lower windows, yielding before the thrust of the fire, fell out with a crash. A flame, a great tongue of flame, yellow and red, long, soft, caressing, climbed up the white wall, licking upwards to the roof. A gleam shot out into the trees, into the branches, into the leaves; and a shiver, too—a shiver of fear! The birds were waking; a dog began to howl; I thought day was dawning! Two other windows fell out the next moment, and I saw that the entire lower storey of my dwelling was one raging furnace. But a cry, a dreadful cry, the piercing scream of a woman rang out into the night, and two garret windows flew open! I had forgotten my servants! I saw their terrified faces, their arms waving! . . .

Then, wild with horror, I set off at a run for the village, yelling: "Help! Help! Fire! Fire!" I met people already on their way from the village, and turned back with them, to see.

But now the house was one vast, awe-inspiring bonfire, a monstrous bonfire that lit up the face of the earth; a bonfire in which human creatures were burning to death; and He, too, burned—He, my prisoner, the New Being, the new master, the Horla!

Suddenly the entire roof fell in, and a volcano of flames shot up sky-high. Through every window opening into the furnace I could see the cauldron of fire; and I thought of him there, in that oven, dead. . . .

Dead? Perhaps? . . . His body? His body that was transparent to the light of day, could it be destroyed by the means that are deadly to our own?

And if he was not dead? . . . Time only, perhaps, can lay hands upon that Terrible, Invisible Being. Why this transparent body, this unknowable body—if he, too, must fear pain, wounds, sickness, and untimely death?

Untimely death? All human terror lies therein! First Man, then Horla. First comes he that may die on any day, in any hour, at any minute, through any accident; thereafter, he that shall only die when his day and his hour and his minute have come, because he has attained his life's bourne!

No, no, no, no . . . there is no room for doubt, no doubt at all! . . . He is not dead.

Well then , . . well then . . . the only thing left to do is to kill—myself.

Translated by Brian Rhys.

THE LADY IN THE LOOKING-GLASS: A REFLECTION

By Virginia Woolf

PEOPLE should not leave looking-glasses hanging in their rooms any more than they should leave open cheque-books or letters confessing some hideous crime. One could not help looking, that summer afternoon, in the long glass that hung outside in the hall. Chance had so arranged it. From the depths of the sofa in the drawing-room one could see reflected in the Italian glass not only the marble-topped table opposite, but a stretch of the garden beyond. One could see a long grass path leading between banks of tall flowers until, slicing off an angle, the gold rim cut it off.

The house was empty, and one felt, since one was the only person in the drawing-room, like one of those naturalists who, covered with grass and leaves, lie watching the shyest animals—badgers, otters, kingfishers—moving about freely, themselves unseen. The room that afternoon was full of such shy creatures, lights and shadows, curtains blowing, petals falling—things that never happen, so it seems, if someone is looking. The quiet old country room with its rugs and stone chimney-pieces, its sunken book-cases and red and gold lacquer cabinets, was full of such nocturnal creatures. They came pirouetting across the floor, stepping delicately with high-lifted feet and spread tails and pecking allusive beaks as if they had been cranes or flocks of elegant flamingoes whose pink was faded, or peacocks whose trains were veiled with silver. And there were obscure flushes and darkenings too, as if a cuttlefish had suddenly suffused the air with purple; and the room had its passions and rages and envies and sorrows coming over it and clouding it, like a human being. Nothing stayed the same for two seconds together.

But, outside, the looking-glass reflected the hall table, the sunflowers, the garden path so accurately and so fixedly that they seemed held there in their reality unescapably. It was a strange contrast—all changing here, all stillness there. One could not help looking from one to the other. Meanwhile, since all the doors and windows were open in the heat, there was a perpetual sighing and ceasing sound, the voice of the transient and the perishing, it seemed, coming and going like human breath, while in the looking-glass things had ceased to breathe and lay still in the trance of immortality.

Half an hour ago the mistress of the house, Isabella Tyson, had gone down the grass path in her thin summer dress, carrying a basket, and had vanished, sliced off by the gilt rim of the looking-glass. She had gone presumably into the lower garden to pick flowers; or as it seemed more natural to suppose, to pick something light and fantastic and leafy and trailing, travellers' joy, or one of those elegant sprays of convolvulus that twine round ugly walls and burst here and there into white and violet blossoms. She suggested the fantastic and the tremulous convolvulus rather than the upright aster, the starched zinnia, or her own burning roses alight like lamps on the straight posts of their rose trees. The comparison showed how very little, after all these years, one knew about her; for it is impossible that any woman of flesh and blood of fifty-five or sixty should be really a wreath or a tendril. Such comparisons are worse than idle and superficial—they are cruel even, for they come like the convolvulus itself trembling between one's eyes and the truth. There must be truth; there must be a wall. Yet it was strange that after knowing her all these years one could not say what the truth about Isabella was; one still made up phrases like this about convolvulus and travellers' joy. As for facts, it was a fact that she was a spinster; that she was rich; that she had bought this house and collected with her own hands—often in the most obscure corners of the world and at great risk from poisonous stings and Oriental diseases—the rugs, the chairs, the cabinets

G

which now lived their nocturnal life before one's eyes. Sometimes it seemed as if they knew more about her than we, who sat on them, wrote at them, and trod on them so carefully, were allowed to know. In each of these cabinets were many little drawers, and each almost certainly held letters, tied with bows of ribbon, sprinkled with sticks of lavender or rose leaves. For it was another fact—if facts were what one wanted—that Isabella had known many people, had had many friends; and thus if one had the audacity to open a drawer and read her letters, one would find the traces of many agitations, of appointments to meet, of upbraidings for not having met, long letters of intimacy and affection, violent letters of jealousy and reproach, terrible final words of parting—for all those interviews and assignations had led to nothing—that is, she had never married, and yet, judging from the mask-like indifference of her face, she had gone through twenty times more of passion and experience than those whose loves are trumpeted forth for all the world to hear. Under the stress of thinking about Isabella, her room became more shadowy and symbolic; the corners seemed darker, the legs of chairs and tables more spindly and hieroglyphic.

Suddenly these reflections were ended violently and yet without a sound. A large black form loomed into the looking-glass; blotted out everything, strewed the table with a packet of marble tablets veined with pink and grey, and was gone. But the picture was entirely altered. For the moment it was unrecognizable and irrational and entirely out of focus. One could not relate these tablets to any human purpose. And then by degrees some logical process set to work on them and began ordering and arranging them and bringing them into the fold of common experience. One realized at last that they were merely letters. The man had brought the post.

There they lay on the marble-topped table, all dripping with light and colour at first and crude and unabsorbed. And then it was strange to see how they were drawn in and arranged and composed and made part of the picture and granted that stillness and immortality which the looking-glass conferred. They lay there invested with a new reality and significance and with a greater heaviness, too, as if it would have needed a chisel to dislodge them from the table. And, whether it was fancy or not, they seemed to have become not merely a handful of casual letters but to be tablets graven with eternal truth—if one could read them, one would know everything there was to be known about Isabella, yes, and about life, too. The pages inside those marble-looking envelopes must be cut deep and scored thick with meaning. Isabella would come in, and take them, one by one, very slowly, and open them, and read them carefully word by word, and then with a profound sigh of comprehension, as if she had seen to the bottom of everything, she would tear the envelopes to little bits and tie the letters together and lock the cabinet drawer in her determination to conceal what she did not wish to be known.

The thought served as a challenge. Isabella did not wish to be known—but she should no longer escape. It was absurd, it was monstrous. If she concealed so much and knew so much one must prize her open with the first tool that came to hand—the imagination. One must fix one's mind upon her at that very moment. One must fasten her down there. One must refuse to be put off any longer with sayings and doings such as the moment brought forth—with dinners and visits and polite conversations. One must put oneself in her shoes. If one took the phrase literally, it was easy to see the shoes in which she stood, down in the lower garden, at this moment. They were very narrow and long and fashionable—they were made of the softest and most flexible leather. Like everything she wore, they were exquisite. And she would be standing under the high hedge in the lower part of the garden, raising the scissors that were tied to her waist to cut some dead flower, some overgrown branch. The sun would beat down on her face, into her eyes; but no, at the critical moment a veil of cloud covered the sun, making the expression of her eyes doubtful—was it mocking or tender, brilliant or dull? One could only see the indeterminate outline of her rather faded, fine face looking at the sky. She was thinking, perhaps, that she must order a new net for the strawberries; that she must send flowers to Johnson's widow; that it was time she drove over to see the Hippesleys in their new house. Those were the things she talked about at dinner, certainly. But one was tired of the things that she talked about at dinner. It was her profounder state of being that one wanted to catch and turn to words, the state that is to the mind what breathing is to the body, what one calls happiness or unhappiness. At the mention of those words it became obvious, surely, that she must be happy. She was rich; she was distinguished; she had many friends; she travelled—she bought rugs in Turkey and blue pots in Persia. Avenues of pleasure radiated this way and that from where she stood with her scissors raised to cut the trembling branches while the lacy cloud veiled her face.

Here with a quick movement of her scissors she snipped the spray of travellers' joy and it fell to the ground. As it fell, surely some light came in, too, surely one could penetrate a little farther into her being. Her mind then was filled with tenderness and regret. . . . To cut an overgrown branch saddened her because it had once lived, and life was dear to her. Yes, and at the same time the fall of the branch would suggest to her how she must die, herself and all the futility and evanescence of things. And then again, quickly catching this thought up, with her instant good sense, she thought life had treated her well; even if fall she must, it was to lie on the earth and moulder sweetly into the roots of violets. So she stood thinking. Without making any thought precise—for she was one of those reticent people whose minds hold their thoughts enmeshed in clouds of silence—she was filled with thoughts. Her mind was like her room, in which lights advanced and retreated, came pirouetting and stepping delicately, spread their tails, pecked their way; and then her whole being was suffused, like the room again, with a cloud of some profound knowledge, some unspoken regret, and then she was full of locked drawers, stuffed with letters, like her cabinets. To talk of "prizing her open" as if she were an oyster, to use any but the finest and subtlest and most pliable tools upon her was impious and absurd. One must imagine—here was she in the looking-glass. It made one start.

She was so far off at first that one could not see her clearly. She came lingering and pausing, here straightening a rose, there lifting a pink to smell it, but she never stopped; and all the time she became larger and larger in the looking-glass, more and more completely the person into whose mind one had been trying to penetrate. One verified her by degrees—fitted the qualities one had discovered into this visible body. There were her grey-green dress, and her long shoes, her basket, and something sparkling at her throat. She came so gradually that she did not seem to derange the pattern in the glass, but only to bring in some new element which gently moved and altered the other objects as if asking them, courteously, to make room for her. And the letters and the table and the grass walk and the sunflowers which had been waiting in the looking-glass separated and opened out so that she might be received among them. At last there she was, in the hall. She stopped dead. She stood by the table. She stood perfectly still. At once the looking-glass began to pour over her a light that seemed to fix her; that seemed like some acid to bite off the unessential and superficial and to leave only the truth. It was an enthralling spectacle. Everything dropped from her—clouds, dress, basket, diamond—all that one had called the creeper and convolvulus. Here was the hard wall beneath. Here was the woman herself. She stood naked in that pitiless light. And there was nothing. Isabella was perfectly empty. She had no thoughts She had no friends. She cared for nobody. As for her letters, they were all bills. Look, as she stood there, old and angular, veined and lined, with her high nose and her wrinkled neck, she did not even trouble to open them.

People should not leave looking-glasses hanging in their rooms.

THE PEACH-HOUSE-POTTING-SHED

By William Sansom

THE old gardener was restive.

Perhaps, seeing him standing up there on the hothouse roof, clinging to the flag-pole with one rigid arm, motionless, peering silent, whitened by the moonlight till he looked like a plaster figure-head—perhaps you would never have thought his behaviour exactly "restive". But the very fact that he was up on the roof at all—and not asleep among his peaches in the hothouse—shows plainly that his old mind was troubled.

Of course, you would have required a telescope to see him in the first place. You would have had to peer through your telescope all the way over the vast formal garden, all the way along the avenues of rhododendron and tamarisk, past little grey stone statues entwined in their lovers' groves, over the sleeping lake, past lilies and pergolas and miniature bridges, until you finally saw the glass peach-house silhouetted against a dark and distant hedge. And even before that, it would have been necessary for you to have climbed to the top of the high brick wall that ran all of five kilometres round the great garden.

What was life like in the peach-house—isolated in that great empty garden? Many have wondered this. Many who have applied for a permit to visit the peach-house, perhaps even to live in it, or at any rate in a similar peach-house— but many who have failed somehow to fulfil all the requirements and obey the traditional regulations that necessarily precede such a visit. Thus one can only imagine what the peach-house is like. Perhaps this is not difficult, for there is little reason to suppose that the peach-house is much different from those hothouses with which one is already familiar.

Only it must be remembered that built on to the old gardener's peach-house is a fine cool potting shed.

Let us then imagine this dual erection! Let us snub our noses on the flat glass panes of this hothouse—so that we can almost smell the mellow warmth within: and then let us peer through the door of the potting shed and savour the sweet shade within, the earthen cool that lies over this cobwebbed granary of old, loved implements.

The hothouse is founded on a short wall of red brick. From this wall the glass sides ascend vertically—then slope off to meet at the apex of a triangular roof. Each wood window frame is painted white: but occasionally round iron pillars intervene, and these are washed blue-green, the faded garden blue of old sheds and weathered stable doors. At each end of the hothouse roof there rise the tall white flagpoles, and between them, crowning the length of the rooftop like a dragon's ruff, there rides a scalloped iron decoration. Forgotten dabs of whitewash obscure some of the upper glass panes; the bleached droppings of birds streak others; and these two films, together with the dusty webs of longdead spiders, veil the clarity of the glass roof, so that the blue of the sky can never be seen from within, and so that looking up through the peach leaves one feels that the sky itself is perpetually, whitely misted. This is an added quietude, for because of the veil life in the peach-house can never be disturbed by the movements of clouds and the darting shadows of high birds.

The old gardener's bed stood between the twisted trunks of two of the largest peach trees. The floor—his bedroom floor, you might say—was a red brick path moistened coolly with dark mosses. Heavy leaves clustered above his pillow: a ripe yellow peach bloomed where his bedside lamp might have been. And for a bedhead he had the nests of fat iron hothouse pipes. Beneath these he stored his books on the cultivation of peaches. The gardener's books, his thoughts and his solitude were his only companions: now for many years. No one ever entered the great empty garden and no one, therefore, visited the peach-house. The old gardener lived quite alone. He lived in the peach-house in the winter, and in the summer he rested in the cool of the adjoining potting shed. Such were his material contacts, winter, summer, winter, summer—the peach-house and the potting shed.

It is hard to say which is the more delightful—the peach-house or the potting shed. Finally, of course, their delight is complementary—for they are a dual erection and depend upon one another in a spirit of contrast serviced to the mood. Only together can they be finally appreciated. Yet separately they still retain many intrinsic charms. That ripe fragrance of the warm peach-house, the luxuriance of growing things: and then the cool reaches of the shaded potting shed, breathing so drily the calm companionship of death.

How cool it is in the potting shed! The hinges creak with dust, the door drags on a few dried bulbs that lie about the floor. Then—long before your eyes, alert with sunlight, can accustom themselves to these softer shadows—the odours rise up around you. The potting shed smells rarely of old earth and dried wood. To stand in the potting shed is like standing beneath a mushroom. The odours are damp, yet the potting shed is remarkably dry. Gradually your eyes descry this dryness. Over by the window, filmed with dust, stands the gardener's table. Flower-pots, cakes of earth, bulbs, nails, strands of raffia, a vice and an old basket stand choked with the dust of crumbled earth. A scythe hangs from a huge nail. The ceiling corners seem lost in shadow: but really these shadows are huge black cobwebs that lean over into the shed, so thick, so immobile that they have walled out the square corners and reshaped the whole shed. Somewhere deep in these webs lie the shrunk carcasses of old spiders. But in no way are these macabre. They are indeed the satisfied, comfortable remnants of a slow life lived in the spacious corners: in this potting shed even the spiders are benevolent. Here there is an air of contented desolation, of things that have never once been used, that could be used again, but never will be.

Up on the moonlit roof the old gardener clung to his flagpole and peered at the moon. The moon hung low over a clump of black elms. Cloudshapes came riding from nowhere into the far circle of light seeming to hand back from the moon itself, as a distant sailing ship seems to hang back on its own speed—until the dreadful moment when at last those clouds smoked sluggishly over the white bright kernel of the light. As he watched the movement of the clouds, the gardener shivered. A ragged hunger came eating into his serenity. The black elms grew blacker as the noiseless shadows from so high above crept across the garden. Then moonlight silvered the scene afresh. But still the gardener shivered. The moon appeared to upset him just as much as the clouds had. He glanced down at his feet, at his boots balanced precariously on the iron apex of the roof. The moonlight bathed his boots in its ancient light. The gardener frowned, shook his head a little uncertainly, loosened his collar, poked a finger round his earhole, peered anxiously again at the moon. Possibly he wished to free himself from some disturbing emotion; perhaps with these gestures he wished, somehow, to let new air into his body, which must have been choked by the presence of so much disquiet. Nevertheless, each ruse was unsuccessful. He peered again at the moon. And then, quite quietly ... a little tune began to drift from his lips. He could hardly project it through his moustache, between his old gums with their few blackened teeth. But sing he did, whistling a little, in a shrill broken pitch, every moment straining the song out louder, until finally he was whining at the height of his voice—a song from somewhere years away in a forgotten life that someone like him had once lived.

"Poor Jenny is a-weeping,
a-weeping,
a-weeping. . . ."

It was not as though the gardener lost his reason during these attacks. On the contrary, he knew exactly how the attacks felt, how they contrasted with his real serenity of the peach-house-potting-shed. He knew them so well that they were in no way unreal to him. He recognized that they were impulses as real as the even tenor they disturbed. But, granted that, why did these attacks arise? For what reason did they molest his sanctuary? The gardener used to mumble over his watering-can as he speculated on this problem. He picked at the wax in his ear and he shuffled his boots on the moss, looking down at them anxiously to see if they were still there. But they always were. And as he stared down at them—it sometimes seemed to him that those boots, perhaps, were the real phenomenon. For they were always there. They were constant. They were his beautiful, ceaseless boots. They stepped forward in search, yet remained the same in themselves. Their leather grew worn, certainly; but so did his own skin. That was another thing—a simple material process. His dear, constant boots! They were precisely how he had imagined life would have been in the peach-house-potting-shed.

The gardener had striven hard to obtain his appointment. Many years ago some forgotten twist of youthful events had in a flash cleared his adolescent mind, and he had seen most definitely how his life should be shaped. From that time he had followed impeccably this impulse, shaping accordingly every facet of his conduct, persevering through the most rigorous examinations, complying with every whim of the Estate Office to which he had become apprenticed. This had been difficult, but perhaps not so difficult for the gardener, with his youthful resolution, as for one who might have approached office from more settled environments and more formed years.

Thus, after the long disciplinary apprenticeship, the gardener had been granted his appointment! Thenceforth he had to live along with the peaches and the porous earth. Beautifully isolated, his life would be devoted to the cultivation of the peaches in whose warmth he lived. The Estate Office provided him with all the latest literature and information. The old gardener cultivated the fruit actively and then, through his books, he learnt the latest processes and ideas: and at nights, when the moon shone in through the dark leaves, with the fragrance of the sleeping fruit all round him, comforted by those great warm pipes, eased by the presence of the soil—the old gardener lay alone and mused upon his cultivations. It was a life of contemplation and labour in surroundings of beauty and comfort, a life whose clean equilibrium should never have been rocked. And yet . . . the attacks!

The attacks were inexplicable. They were irregular. They varied in occasion and in intensity. The old gardener could find nothing at all consistent in them—except perhaps their symptom. This could best be described as a great uneasiness, a hunger of the spirit.

Of the spirit? The gardener could not even be quite sure of that: sometimes he felt intuitively that his attacks were really part of a vague animal yearning—with no particular organic signal. For months the gardener might muse contentedly among his fruit, isolated, warm, occupied: then abruptly into this month-long sanctuary would steal the importunate fevers. The old gardener would be off his bed and out on the roof within a few hours!

Moonlit vigils at the flagpole were not his only excursions. There had been a summer's afternoon, for instance, when he had decided to cut sticks in the cool of the potting shed. It was a slow afternoon. A square of hot sunlight shimmered at the doorway, making the shadowed interior seem all the cooler. You could almost see the heat in a bright line of light that cut through the darkness from a crack in the doorway. Through a small cobwebbed window the gardener could see the top leaves of a high beech: they never fluttered. They stood silver green against a dark blue sky and they never moved, not by the whisper of a breath of wind. There was nothing outside but the dull, intolerable heat. The gardener passed his hand thankfully over the cool grey wood of a sickle handle.

But even as his hand began to enjoy the cool wood, a feeling of doubt tapped the back of his head. Instantly he looked round the shed to reassure himself. The earth, the coolness, the mossed bricks on the floor. As in the urgent moment just before a calamity, his mind surveyed in a long second the compact months of certainty and contemplation behind him. Yes, all had been well! And should now be well! But doubt began to spread its terrible umbrella over his uncertain brain. Then, with the doubt, came desire. He desired more than his own will to leave the shadow and walk in the sunlight. Not for the sunlight's sake: but just because he felt he must stand outside, at a certain place outside, just between the window and the door, so that his back would almost touched the outside wall. If he did that, he felt that something would happen.

The gardener wrestled with this uncertainty for several hours: then, with a shiver of defeat, he walked slowly out into the sun. He stood exactly where he had imagined he would stand. The sun sweated into his old clothes: the heat thumped at his heart. He stood and waited, peering as far as he could out into the garden, shadowing his eyes and watching for something he could not place. The wax melted in his ears, the hours passed, he lolled sweating on to the wall behind him. Still he waited and watched. Until the gnats came out with the dusk and the black waves of the garden's great trees rose up and drenched the sinking sun. And nothing happened! He shrugged off his uneasiness and shumbled off to the hothouse.

Sometimes he did not recognize the attack until it had already begun. Sometimes he only realized his restive behaviour in the very middle of an attack! One day, when the hothouse was fresh, when he was watering the warm peaches with a cool spray from his wet eel of a garden hose—one day like this, he caught sight of an ant on the moss just by the hothouse door. Without thinking he followed the ant out of the door and along the path to its nest. His eyes followed the ant until it eventually disappeared into its hive of earth crumbs. Then he knelt down and settled himself to watch the little ants. His old head nodded with emotion as he saw the insects darting earnestly from one task to another, pausing to caress a colleague with a flick of the antenna, bustling, elbowing, rearing up suddenly with alert mandibles circling the shocked air. The old gardener watched on and he began to remember things. His mind travelled into the nest, through the sightless labyrinths, until he arrived at the base of the nest: and things he had once known came creeping back . . . that down there in the dark might be mushrooms, that in their subterranean gardens the ants might have laid down upon a compost of their own preparation the spores of a minute and delicious fungus, that with his blind eyes and his seven senses an old ant-gardener might have been watching over the pinprick globular vegetation he tended deep down in that beloved darkness. Thinking thus, the old gardener woke to find himself envying the ant-gardener! He felt that the ant-gardener was more fortunate than he! Why? Why? The gardener rose wildly to his feet. He shook his head from side to side. He, the cultivator of peaches, had been watching *ants*! He had interrupted his contemplations to spend an hour watching the ants! It was ridiculous! With horror he ran back to the hothouse—to find the hose abandoned on the floor and the precious hothouse flooded.

Now the gardener was restive again. But this time his excitement seemed to have a cause. At least, it had seized him at precisely the same time—coincidentally perhaps?—as a revolutionary occurrence in the garden.

The attack coincided precisely with the arrival of the gentleman in the garden.

One day, with no word from the Estate Office, with absolutely no warning of any kind, the great iron gates at the end of the avenue of beeches had opened, a gentleman had stepped in, and the gates had clanged shut. Afterwards there had been vague movements behind the gate. Possibly officers of the Estate Office were making fast the locks and chains. Then—nothing but the gentleman! He stood for a second of uncertainty in the path, looking from one side to the other; then he walked quickly through a gap in the rhododendron and disappeared from view.

This had happened as many as twenty-nine days before. The gentleman had never reappeared. The gardener had seen him enter, in broad daylight, with his own eyes. He had not, of course, recognized any particular of the gentleman's appearance: the whole affair had taken place too far away. Only this the gardener knew—that a gentleman had entered the garden and that he must still be somewhere inside it. For egress was impossible. No one could scale the high wall; and, had the gates once been reopened during the night, the gardener would never have slept through such an unusual clanging of the gates. No, there was a gentleman in the garden undoubtedly. And from the moment of that gentleman's appearance, the gardener's heart had been overcome with a terrible excitement quite disproportionate to the event.

Of course, there had been really no reason to expect notice of any kind from the Estate Office. The Estate Office had never communicated with the gardener since his first appointment. The garden had always remained quite empty. Books had been left outside the gate, certainly, but otherwise—no sign at all from the Estate Office that the gardener's conduct was ever questioned, or even considered.

There are times when one expects something to happen, something unknown, but as real and important as the measure of expectancy that warns the heart. Then—something does happen! But whether it really is the event one expected, or whether it is some other event which the waiting heart, in its anguish, easily welcomes—that is a matter of which one can never be sure. Something of this nature occurred within the gardener. Although his new excitement raged higher than ever before, nevertheless he felt a certain fulfilment of his hunger. Or perhaps what he felt was a premonition of fulfilment, the certainty of achievement that calms but does not slacken the motors of ambition. Now the gardener spent his days between the flagpole and the windows of the peach-house. The necessity of his culture could not be abandoned: yet, even in the breathless security of the still air that hung among the hothouse leaves, his thoughts flew out of the window towards the garden. Hour upon hour he peered out, each pulsing artery alert for a glimpse of the hidden gentleman. Perhaps the gentleman would suddenly walk out from that copse of pollarded box-trees! Or, barefaced as you like, he might come running round the corner of the thick privet wall that buttressed from the shrubbery at the end of the peach-house path! Perhaps, perhaps even at this very moment he might be standing just behind the privet wall, so that his shoulder just matched the sharp vertical of the wall's corner, with not a hairsbreadth to spare—yet remaining quite unseen! That was a terrible thought! The gardener pursed up his gums to repress his growing emotion as he thought of this terrible possibility. His brain whirling, he began to create such a presence behind the privet wall that before long he was certain that the gentleman stood there—and dropping his watering-can he darted roughly up the path and swung round the corner.

But there was no one there. For a long moment he stood with arms outstretched as the empty reality slowly smothered his hope. Then a tear watered his red underlid, and he walked slowly back to the peach-house.

The next morning an unpredictable affair took place. The gardener received a communication from the Estate Office!

It was a letter, enclosed in a plain white envelope, in no way ostentatious, with no crest, unsealed! It lay, tremendously innocent, right on the top of a pile of new books that must have been delivered during the night.

The gardener was overcome with mixed terrors and hopes. He kept the letter all day without opening it. He placed it on the whitewashed trestle in the hothouse, and throughout the day he kept watch on it. Then, as evening fell, he opened it. The rending of the paper tore sharply through the hothouse quiet. Then silence again as the gardener read what words were written. High up in the glass dome, among the topmost peach leaves, a large blue-bottle buzzed heavily.

To the Peach Cultivator:
  Sir,
The office wishes to inform you that the garden is now occupied by a gentleman.

It is requested that you should in no way hinder this gentleman, nor, in fact, show yourself to him. The gentleman has requisitioned absolute solitude. In this respect you will appreciate that any disturbance of this trust will create great difficulties between ourselves and the new tenant. If possible—and we hope that you will make every effort to assure this possibility—the gentleman should remain quite ignorant of your presence. Naturally, we were compelled to inform him of your position: but the gentleman considered that he could perhaps tactfully forget this.

With good wishes for the future success of your labours, which **we** *follow with the greatest interest.*
                              Secretary to the Estate Office.

The gardener read and re-read the letter, trying vainly to discover some possible loophole in what was, to him, a sentence rather than a communication. He repeated each word till he could recite the whole script. Anguish gripped his heart. The blood beat against his temples. He fingered his collar wildly: and where one blue-bottle had buzzed, now the silence shook with an infinite buzzing inside his own ears. Striding wildly up and down the brick path, he tore at the wax in his buzzing ears.

Every footstep in the hothouse echoes dully around the panes and up to the roof. There is noise—but the leaves never move. They do not move because they are wholly concerned with their own growth. The leaves, the branches, the peaches are growing fast in the heat. Theirs is a waxen stillness, yet they move. In the breathless air there is the sense of wetness, of water clustered behind each leaf, of the dripping of tropical forests, of rich earth swelling black round the waterous roots, of climbing saps and the wet, incessant hum of growth. . . . But you can see nothing move! That is the terrible thing!

So in this muffled, urgent atmosphere the gardener wept and shivered as the old hunger came back, striding to and fro, brandishing the letter, bruising the quiet mosses, straining hard at the brink of his reason—until suddenly out of the corner of his eye he saw a figure come flying up the path to the hothouse!

It was the gentleman! His coat-tails flapped wildly behind him as he came running and gesticulating towards the glass hothouse! But the wind of his hurry had wound his cloak over his head—his features were hidden! The frantic windmill of his arms showed an urgent need for help. His arms were stretched out at full length, waving wildly towards the hothouse, appearing from afar to embrace it and pull it towards him in each great circling gesture.

The gardener sobbed his welcome and stumbled for the door. But as he reached for the handle, his arm caught in a crook of one of the pear-tree's branches. Somehow, this arm became locked in the grip of the tree. He tugged at the elbow's socket with his free hand. Then that free hand, too, became entangled in a growth of leaves that hung down from over his head. Pinioned by both arms, he arched his chest fiercely forward, now shouting at the top of his voice. His anguish shrieked up to the topmost leaves. His old eyes rolled white above their red lids. His feet kicked madly at the moss. Then the welt of one boot got wedged between two bricks, which seemed to have thrust themselves up from the ground like the shell pincers of a clam. . . .

Just as this happened, the gentleman ran up against the door. The cloak now wound inextricably round his head. He tore at it with his hands, but nothing would undo the cloak. So, sightless and muffled, the gentleman began to fling himself repeatedly at the door, battering himself against it like a huge moth blinded to everything but its mad, preposterous urgency. . . .

And the gardener's shouting had turned into words:

> "Poor Jenny is a-weeping,
> a-weeping,
> a-weeping."

We villagers scaled the wall next morning. I had been at my telescope and seen that something was wrong. We found the two of them—half-dead. The gentleman was lying battered and bleeding on the path outside the door. And, inside, the gardener sagged purple, nearly throttled by the green creature of his own culture.

We released him. And there, in the early dawn, we led him out to where the gentleman lay. It was quite beautiful to see the great tenderness with which they fell into one another's arms. There were no caresses—just a silent, thankful embrace.

Yes, it was only through the agency of others that the need for others was fulfilled in that embrace. Only through the agency of us, the others.

THE WHITE HOUSE

By Wrey Gardiner

THE big house in the quiet road that was not much more than a country lane shone dead white in the sun on that fine day. They would let him go out for a walk surely, and it turned out as he expected. He found himself ambling along by the hedges looking at the tall sunflowers and the magnificent magnolia in full flower in the shelter of the brick wall of the doctor's house. But he wanted to get away from these immediate surroundings that he knew too well.

There was only one of two ways. Up the road to the little village on the top of the hill or down the road to the duck pond. This was a day for the duck pond, especially as he was alone.

It wasn't very far, just beyond a clump of elms where the lane turned and you came to it, a little sheet of water like a miniature lake with pieces of duck-weed covering parts of it like the edges of a jig-saw puzzle or the coastline of a map. And two or three ducks followed each other towards the stranger who often fed them. They looked up at him with a hard, queer knowing gaze that he returned as from one friend to another.

He was always fascinated by the flat mirror-like surface of the water. Leaning over and looking into it he saw things that took him away to another country quite different to this green quiet one. There were bells in the air, and long solemn processions of people and crowded dusty streets. There were tall grey houses with dark entrances full of cats and old women knitting. Then there were gardens full of children playing, and fine buildings at the end of avenues of trees and massive sculptured figures bearing worlds on their light fingers with the ease of art. And all the birds were tame. At this point something seemed to grip his nervous system in a vice of steel, and the vision swirled away and faded and only the ducks were looking up at him with their little beady eyes, hoping.

He walked on then, farther down the lane to where the trees were very thick. There was one special tree, a tall poplar, that he loved particularly. When the wind blew the spidery branches seemed to part and he saw a woman sitting behind them high up in the middle of the tree. Sometimes she was his wife, sometimes a woman he had loved more than his wife, sometimes it was a face he did not know at all, looking at him with a queer sideways glance of recognition that made him turn his head away as though he had seen someone he did not want to meet. When he looked again there was nothing but the shimmering glaze of the green-gold leaves turning and rustling in the wind.

It was time to go back to the big white house where there were so many people he did not know or want to know.

After tea there would be the usual walk up to the village, but he would not be alone this time. There would be the hunch-back who would talk interminably about sermons and the love of God, and the epileptic who followed a few paces behind. The hunch-back knew all the right doors to knock on where he would be given a penny or even perhaps sixpence.

But there was a bookshop kept by a little old man with a grey beard, piercing eyes and thick corduroy trousers. He left the hunch-back and the epileptic sitting together on a bench in the entrance and went in by himself. This was perhaps his best hour, for to the bookseller, who never seemed to sell any books, he could talk as to an equal.

The little room was filled with books from floor to ceiling, most of them in eighteenth-century bindings, books which nobody in the village would ever have thought of buying, and which the little man in the worn corduroys probably would not have cared to sell. Apart from the eighteenth century, he could talk with knowledge on the French symbolists. When they got to discussing Verlaine's adventures in Soho the epileptic began drumming his feet on the bench and the hunch-back groaned deeply into his long beard. The hour was up and he would have to return from this real world the mind back to the insane routine of the big white house.

As he walked with his two companions, now angry at being kept waiting for an hour without even the recompense of a single penny, down the straight main road out of the village, his mind remained still wandering through the streets of Paris, along the *quais*, from bookshop to bookshop, under the trees, in the squares in the rain and the warm sunshine, at a café table reading. Anger rose up in him and drowned the vision. Why shouldn't he go back to this normal, pleasant, intelligent life? Why should he be kept here among these ignorant boobs slavishly following their idiotic routine? He would speak to the doctor very severely about it. There was no reason at all why he should not take the train back to Paris, back to his wife, back to the old life.

When they got back to the hated white house which he was quite determined to leave for ever and got into his own room, the doctor came in almost at once, although he could not remember asking for him. The man's cold blue eyes fixed on his always made him look away, say what he did not mean to say. There was another, a much younger man with large eyes behind horn-rimmed glasses who was sympathetic but who talked too much, much too much.

Today there were a lot of people in the room and he was already beginning to forget his anger. The doctor was gentler in his manner than usual. He seemed to have something important to say. "We have had a communication from the Red Cross about your wife and daughter in France. I am afraid it is bad news. They both died three months ago. The food situation in their district was particularly acute."

"The food situation," he said. "But in France there are a hundred different kinds of cheese. It is impossible to"—his lips just formed the words—"starve." He looked out of the window which was barred, and a memory came to him of a busy office in London, something to do with refugees, then more work, too much work, then nothing, nothing but these green trees, the duck pond and the queer, haunting smile of the unknown woman in the shimmering poplar down the road.

WHO KNOCKS AT THE DOOR?

By Olive Schreiner

I LAY upon my couch. Outside for days heavy snow had fallen, and the long trails of the roses that grew over the balcony were weighted with balls of frozen snow, and the wind blew them hither and thither. They tapped upon the window panes and against the woodwork of the balcony.

I had grown weary of looking at that dreary world outside; and I rose and drew the curtains across the windows and lit the light at the head of my couch, and lay down again to read the evening newspaper.

It was the old, old story, such as one read every night: Death and destruction; "heavy losses of the enemy"—always that; and then the long straight list of names, which one followed holding onself tight, lest one among them should stab one to the very heart; then columns of hatred and abuse; then statements which men in calm hours would never make, or balanced men listen to; omissions and suppressions, till, amid it all, the mind groped like a small animal under a pile of decaying mould seeking to find the way to one ray of light; one judged what might be truth only by what was left out, and the reality by what was denied. It was an old, old story; one read it every day. There was nothing new in it.

I was going to drop the newspaper on to the floor, and try to turn my thoughts to other matters, and then my eye caught sight of a paragraph, in very small type, at the left-hand corner on the inside page. It was printed in type so fine and the paragraph was so short that many reading might not notice it, and if they did, might not trouble to decipher it. Yet, it was something new; it seemed to have crept into the corner of the paper by chance. Having read it once, one read it over, and then again. It set one's thoughts travelling far.

Holding the paper in my hands, I think I must have fallen fast asleep, for I thought I found myself in a great forest. On every side the stems of the trees towered up above me like the aisles of some vast cathedral, and high above my head the wind struck their mighty branches together. I wrapped my mantle tight about my head and struggled on in the darkness: there was no path, and the dead branches cracked beneath my feet. It seemed to be one of those primeval forests, such as sheltered the forbears of our peoples—Suevi and Alamanni, Goth and Visigoth, Frank and Saxon, Lombard and Burgundian, before we spread ourselves out over Europe from the shores of the Atlantic and the Bay of Biscay to Gothland, from the wet Tin Islands of the North Sea to the blue waters of the Mediterranean; who followed Ruric into the frozen steppes of the north, and Theodoric into Italy; and drank Sicilian wines with our Northmen leaders under the slopes of Mount Etna.

As I wandered in that impenetrable darkness, at last it seemed to me as though, from far off, I saw a gleam of light, and it almost seemed to me I heard distant sounds which were not those of the forest and the storm. I struggled onward, and, at last, I came to a place where through the darkness, under the over-arching trees, I could see looming a mighty building; light streamed from its windows of many-coloured glass, and from within came sounds of song and music, and loud laughter and shouts, as of those who applaud and rejoice.

I crept close up to the building, and pressed my face against a pane in a small window and looked in. It was a wonderful scene that met my eyes. Within was a vast hall built of richly carved woods, and the pillars that supported it were shaped in every lovely form, and sprang upwards into the groined roof, from which hung thousands of glittering lights; and along the walls golden torches were flaming; and beneath stood works of art, and scattered about the Hall were large tables, covered with glittering crystal and gold and silver vessels; and upon the tables were loaded all of rich and rare of viands and wines that the earth produces.

Around the tables sat men and women clad in gorgeous robes; some had golden crowns on their heads and sceptres in their hands, and others paid court to them; and the women wore jewels of gold set heavily with precious stones, till they seemed weighted with them.

And I saw that from table to table they passed the rare viands and wines, exchanging them with one another; and men and women sang and danced now before this table and then before that, and the feasters showered gold and jewels upon them; and I saw men take ornaments from their own breasts and pass them on to men at other tables. And I noticed that though there were differences between those who sat at the different tables, yet they were all really of one garb and one appearance. And I said to myself: "Surely this is some vast banqueting house, where a great kindred are holding high festival together." And I thought: "Surely never since earth was earth has so much of richness, of rarity, been gathered together in one spot." And I marvelled when I thought of the labour which had brought all these things together, where once only the trees of the forest stood.

And then, as I looked, I noticed that all the men wore daggers fastened at their sides: and as I watched, I thought I saw that though their lips were smiling sometimes their brows lowered; and I thought that some cast looks of envy as the viands passed from table to table; and it even seemed to me some whispered behind their hands as they glanced at one another: and though dance and song and feasting went on, the feeling came to me that perhaps all was not so well with that great company.

And then I hardly seemed to know what happened, but at a table at the far end some drew their daggers and a man and woman fell dead upon the floor. Then from other tables others arose and stabbed at one another, and flung one another to the earth; and more and more arose, till from end to end of that great Hall blood flowed and men fell wounded and dying to the ground. And the tables were overturned; and the rare viands and the rich wines and glittering crystals and costly ornaments and rare works of art fell scattered and broken on the ground. And I saw that, in their mad rage, men seized broken fragments from the floor and hurled them at one another, till the glass in every door and window was shattered and the very walls were indented. And I saw women, who, with wild, hoarse voices, called on the men to stab and kill yet more; and some passed on to the men fragments to hurl at one another, though they themselves fell often buried beneath the heaps of killed and wounded.

And I, looking on through the shattered window, wrung my hands and cried: "Stop it! Stop it! Can you not see, you are destroying all?" But it might have been two small leaves in the forest trees overhead clapping themselves together, for any sound the feeble words made in that vast tumult.

And in their madness I saw men drag down the great glittering lights that hung from the centre of the Hall, and fling the fragments at one another; and tear down the lighted torches that were fastened to the walls, and strike one another with them. And as the lights fell down on that seething mass that covered the floor, they set fire to the garments of the fallen, and smoke began to rise. And outside the window where I stood came the stench of burning human flesh.

And I was silent with horror; for surely never since man was man upon the earth was there such a great and horrible destruction in any Hall where a great human kindred were gathered together.

And then, as I stood gazing in, it almost seemed to me, though I could not tell surely, that, from the far end of the Hall, where the great shattered doorway stood, I heard—three, slow, clear, distinct knocks! I listened; and then again I heard the sounds, and this time I knew I was not mistaken—slow, clear, distinct! And as I looked across that fallen mass of ruin, it seemed to me, I saw, through a broken pane in the great shattered doorway at the far end, a human face looking in! The smoke came in between it and me; but I know I saw it.

And as I gazed, the flames began to creep up the walls of the Hall, and up the carved pillars, towards the roof itself.

And I wrapped my mantle tight about my head, and turned away into the darkness and the night. For my heart was *wae* for the great desolation I had seen—that men with their own hands should tear down that which with so much toil they had reared, and should consume that which with so much labour they had gathered, and that so much of the rare and beautiful should be no more! I sorrowed me over that great, brave company which had wrought so much. It might be, I knew well, that those whose knock I had heard might enter in, and take possession of that great Banquet House, and might even rebuild it in a nobler and fairer form: might build it so wide that not only one kindred but all kindreds might gather in it; and that the wine which they drank might give no madness, and the weapons be no more found at the sides of those who banqueted.

But for me, I was sore sorrowful over the destruction of that great kindred, and I wept as I stumbled onwards in the dark.

And the trees of that primeval forest, as they knocked their vast branches together over my head, cried: "*Mad!*—MAD!—M A D!"

I woke: I was still lying stretched on the couch with the electric light burning at my head: the paper I had held up in my hand had fallen down on my breast. Outside the wild wind that had raged had grown silent, and the rose branches no longer tapped on the woodwork. I listened to the silence.

Then again I took up the evening paper and re-read the small paragraph at the left-hand corner on the inside page. And one's thoughts travelled far into the future.

THE FANCIFUL

AN AIR-RAID SEEN FROM ABOVE

By Stella Benson

THE moonlight lay like cream upon the pavement when the witch and Harold her broomstick left the Higgins' doorstep. London was a still Switzerland in silver and star-grey, unblotted by people. There was a hint of pale green about the moonlight, and the lamps with their dim light downcast were like daffodils in faery fields.

The witch mounted. Harold, who was every inch a thoroughbred and very highly strung, trembled beneath her, but not with fear. They reached Piccadilly Circus with supernatural speed, and flashed across it. The sound of people singing desultorily while taking shelter in the Tube floated up to them. Here the witch said "Yoop" to Harold, and he reared and shot upwards, narrowly missing the statue of One In A Bus-catching Attitude, which marks the middle of the Circus.

As soon as the witch had out-distanced the noise of expectant London, she heard quite distinctly the approach of London's guests. They came with a chorus of many notes, all deep and dangerous.

There were a few clouds wandering about among the stars, and to one of these the witch and her faithful Harold repaired. A cloud gives quite reasonable support to magic people, and most witches and wizards have discovered the delight of paddling knee-deep about those quicksilver continents. They wander along shining and changing valleys under a most ardent sky; they climb the purple thunderclouds, or launch the first snowflake of a blizzard; they spring from pink stepping-stone to pink stepping-stone of clouds each no bigger than a baby's hand, across great sunsets. Often when in London I am battling with a barrage of rain, or falling over unseen strangers into gutters during fogs, I think happily of the sunlit roof of cloud above my head, and of the witches and wizards, lying on their backs with their coats off, among cloud-meadows in a glory of perfect summer and sun.

The witch, with one soothing hand on the bristling mane of her Harold, lay on her front on the cloud she had chosen, and looked down through a little hole in it. It was practically the only cloud present that would have afforded reasonable cover; the others were mere wisps of sky-weed floating in the moon-light.

There was a greater chorus of aeroplanes below her now; the whole sky was ringing with it. The witch could hear a deep bass-voiced machine, a baritone, a quavering tenor, and—thin and sharp as a pin—a little treble sound that made Harold rear and struggle to be free.

"Another witch," said the witch. "I was wondering why the Huns hadn't got their magic organized by now." She mounted her Harold and slipped off the cloud.

The guns were shouting now, and the shells wailed and burst not so very far below them, but Harold trembled no longer. More quickly than a falling star he swooped, and in a second the alien witch was in sight, an unwieldy figure whose broomstick sounded rather broken-winded, probably owing to the long-distance flight and to the fourteen stone of Teutonic magic on its back. There was a wicked-looking apparatus attached to the collar of the German broom-stick, obviously designed to squirt unpleasant enchantments downward. This contrivance was apparently giving some trouble, for the German was so busy attending to it that at first she did not see or hear the approach of Harold and his rider. She was aroused to her danger by a heavy chunk of magic which struck and nearly unseated her. In a second, however, she was ready with a parrying enchantment, and the fight began. The two broomsticks reared and circled round each other, and over and under each other. From their riders' finger-tips magic of the most explosive kind crackled, and incantations of such potency were exchanged that, I am told, the tiles and chimney-pots of the streets below suffered a good deal. Round and round and over and under whirled the broomsticks, till the very spaces went mad, and London seemed to rush down nightmare slopes into a stormy sky, while its lights swung from pole to pole and were entangled with the stars.

Both broomsticks were by now so uproariously excited that neither witch was able to aim her magic missiles very carefully, and, indeed, it was not long before Harold passed entirely beyond control. After bucking violently once or twice, he gave a wild high cry that was like the wind howling through the fierce forest past of his race, and fell upon the other broomstick, fixing his bristles into its throat. The shock of the collision was too much for both witches. Our witch—if I may call her so—was shot over Harold's head, and landed on the ample breast of her adversary, who, in consequence, lost her balance. They fell together into space.

"Oh, lost, lost . . ." cried our witch, and thoughts rushed through her mind of green safe places, and old safe years, and the little hut in a pale bluebell wood, where she was born. She had time to remember the blue ground, dimpled and starred with sunlight, and the way the bees pulled over the bluebells, and swung on them to the tune of cuckoos in a May mist; she had time to think of the green globe ghosts of the bluebells that haunted the wood after the spring was dead. Bluebells and being young were in all her thoughts, and it was some time before she noticed how slowly she and her enemy were falling.

For they were locked together. And the enemy witch's cloak, an orthodox witch cloak except for its colour, which with German field-grey instead of red, was spread out like a parachute, and was supporting them upon their peaceful and almost affectionate descent.

For all I know they might have alighted gently in the Strand, and the authorities might by now be regretting the capture of a most embarrassing and unaccountable prisoner. But something intervened. The cloud, like a sheep suffering from the lack of other sheep to follow, had not yet quitted the scene. The witches' battle had tended upward, and it had ended several hundred feet above the level of the cloud, which was apparently sinking. The downward course of the combatants' fall was therefore arrested, and they found themselves still interlocked, prostrate and embedded, with their eyes and mouths full of woolly wisps of cloud.

Our witch was the first to recover herself. She stood up and brushed herself, remarking: "By Jove, that parachute cloak of yours is a great dodge. I wish I'd thought of it. I always keep my full-dress togs put away, like the ass that I am. A stitch or two, and a few lengths of whalebone would have done the trick."

The German was an older woman, and less adaptable to the strange chances of War. She was silent for a few minutes, seated in the small crater made in the cloud by her fall. She was not exactly ugly. She had the sort of face about which one could not help feeling that one could have done it better oneself, or at least that one could have taken more trouble. It seemed moulded—even kneaded—carelessly, in very soft material. Beneath her open cloak her dress was of the ordinary German *Reform-Kleid* type, and her figure had the rather jelloid appearance of those who affect this style. Her regulation witch's hat was by now, probably, in the Serpentine, and her round head was therefore disclosed, with two stout sand-coloured plaits pursuing each other round it.

The witches faced each other for some seconds. A long way away they could hear the spitting and crackling sound of the two broomsticks fighting. Looking up, they could see the combatants, like black comets in collision. Our witch, who had good sight, saw that the enemy broomstick was uppermost, and that the writhing Harold was being shaken like a mouse. Their bristles were interlocked. One twig floated down between the witches, and our witch recognized it as coming from her poor Harold's mane. As, for this purpose, she brought her eyes to her immediate surroundings, it seemed to her suddenly that the sky was growing larger, and then she realized that this was because their refuge was growing smaller. The edges of the cloud were dissolving. She saw at last her peril and her disadvantage. If Harold should be killed or disabled she could never reach the earth again, except by means of a fatal fall of several thousand feet. The enemy witch, with her ingenious cloak contrivance strapped securely about her, stood a reasonable chance of escape. But our witch was an amateur in War, she was without support, forlornly dressed in her faithful blue serge three-year-old, and her little squirrel tippet.

Magic, as you know, has limitations. Fire is, of course, a plaything in magic hands. Water has its docile moments, the earth herself may be tampered with, and an incantation may call man or any of his possessions to attention. But space is too great a thing, space is the inconceivable Hand, holding aloft this fragile delusion that is our world. There is no power that can mock at space, there is no enchantment that is not lost between us and the moon, and all magic people know—and tremble to know—that in a breath, between one second and another, that Hand may close, and the shell of time first crack and then be crushed, and magic be one with nothingness and death and all other delusions. This is why magic, which treats the other elements as its servants, bows before space, and has to call such a purely independent contrivance as a broomstick to its help in the matter of air-travel.

The witches faced each other on their little unstable sanctuary in the kingdom of space. Our witch felt secretly sick, and at the same time she tore fear from her mind, and knew that death was but an imperfectly kept secret, and that not an evil one. After all, we have condemned it unheard.

Both witches could talk a magic tongue, and make themselves mutually understood. Neither knew the other's natural tongue. But when our witch noticed several large ferocious tears rolling down her opponent's cheeks, she was able, by means of magic, to say: "Great Scott, my good person, what are you crying for?"

"I am not crying," replied the German witch. "I would not allow one tear of mine to fall upon and water one possible grain of wheat in this accursed country of yours. Certainly I am not crying."

"Accursed country?" echoed the astounded English witch. "How d'you mean—accursed? This is England, you know. England hasn't done anything accursed. Aren't you muddling it up with Germany?"

"England is the World Enemy," said the German, evidently pleased to meet someone to whom this information was fresh. "Throughout the ages she has been the Robber State, crushing the weaker nations, adding to her own wealth by treachery, and now forcing this war of aggression upon her peace-loving neighbours."

Our witch laughed. She was forgetting her danger. "This is really rather funny," she said. "Do you know what's happened? You've been reading the *Daily Mail* and misunderstanding it. The whole of that quotation applied to Germany, not England. It's Germany that's being naughty. You made a mistake, but never mind, I won't repeat it."

The German took no notice of this. The past three years had made her an adept in taking no notice.

"And now," she added, "after all these weary months of hoping, and long-distance broomstick practice, and of parachute practice, and of conflict with narrow officialdom, I have come—and this is the result. I am separated from my broomstick, which has all the germ-bombs hanging from its collar—the germs are those of dissension and riot—I am marooned upon an English cloud, with no enemy at my mercy but a paltry and treacherous non-combatant——"

"At your mercy," breathed our witch, remembering. She looked up. The broomsticks were closer now, and through the breathless air, amidst the dream-like firing of the guns below, she could hear the difficult gasping of the hard-pressed Harold, still fighting bravely but with hardly a twig on his head.

The tide of space was coming in. The edge of the cloud was barely six inches from her hand. Our witch's mind overflowed with the thought of invasions and

H

the coming in of tides. It seemed that all her life she had been living on a narrowing shore. She remembered all her dawns as precarious footholds of peace on a threatened rock, and all her evenings as golden sands sloping down into encroaching sleep. She realized Everything was a little hopeless garrison against the army of Nothing.

She clutched a pinch of cloud nervously, and it broke off in her hand. She recalled her senses with a devastating effort.

"Do you mean to say," she said, after a moment, "that poor dear Germany really believes that she is right and we are wrong? I suppose, when you come to think of it, a man-eating tiger feels the same way. It fights with a high heart, and a hot reproach, just as we do——"

"We are Crusaders," said the German. "Crusaders at War with Evil."

"Why, how funny—so are we," said our witch. "But then how very peculiar that two Crusaders should apparently be fighting each other. Where then is the Evil? In No Man's Land?"

"We are fighting," recited the German glibly, "because England is the World Enemy. Throughout the ages she has been the Rob——"

There was a violent explosion quite close to them, and the cloud reeled and shook. About a foot of the German end of it broke off and was dissolved.

"We're within range of our guns," said our witch, looking down. "This cloud must be sinking."

"It will never sink enough to save you," said the German, trying to conceal the nervousness with which she rearranged her rigid-looking cloak round her. She seemed to be sinking herself to a certain extent; perhaps the warmth of her emotions was melting the cloud beneath her. Certainly she now sat, apparently squat as an idol, her figure submerged in cloud to the waist.

The English witch looked down, singing a little to keep up her *morale*. London looked exactly like the maps you buy for sixpence from sad-looking gentlemen in the Strand, only it was sown with a thin crop of lights, and was chiefly designed in grey and darker grey, and the Tubes did not show so indecently. With surprising clearness the rhythmic whispering of the trains and the scanty traffic could be heard, and once even the shrill characteristic voice of an ambulance. Somehow, space did not seem disturbed by these sounds; its quietness pressed upon the listeners' minds like a heavy dream, and there was no real believing in anything but space. Our witch felt she could have smudged London off the face of space with her finger, and the thought of seven million lives involved in the fate of that sliding chart carried no conviction to her. She forced into her mind the realization of humanity, and of little lives lived in little rooms.

"As one Crusader to another," she said, "do you find it does much good in the war against Evil to drop bombs on people in their homes? After all, every baby is good in bed, and even soldiers when on leave are anti-militarist."

"It always does good to exterminate vermin in their lair," said the German, trying restlessly to raise herself more to the level of her lighter companion, who was still perched on the surface of the cloud. "It is at home that Evil is originated, it is at home that English women conceive and bear a new generation of enemies of the Right, it is at home that English children are bred up in their marauding ways. It is on the home, the vital place of Evil, that the scourge should fall."

"Oh, but surely not," said our witch eagerly. "It is at home that people are kindly and think what they will have for supper, and bathe their babies. Men come home when they are hurt or hungry, and women when they are lonely or tired. Nobody is taught anything stupid or international at home. You can bring death to a home, but never a righteous scourge. Nobody feels scourged or instructed by a bomb in their parlour, they just feel dead, and dead without a reason."

The cloud was very small now. The filmy edges of it were faintly rising and falling like the seaweed frill of a rock in the sea. The witch kept her eyes on her opponent's face, because to look anywhere else gave her a white feeling in her head.

"Crusades of the high explosive kind," she said, "can work only on battle-fields. Indeed, even on battle-fields—ah, what are we about, what are we about? We are neither of us killing Evil, we are killing youth. . . ."

"I know, I know," wept the German witch. "My wizard fell at Vimy Ridge. . . ."

"You are talking magic at last," said our witch. "Dear witch, why don't you go home and ask how it can be a good plan for one Crusader against Evil to blow up another? How can two people be righteously scourging each other at the same time? It is like the old problem of two serpents eating each other, starting at the tail. There must be some misunderstanding somewhere. Or else some real Evil somewhere."

"There is," said the German, recovering herself. "England is Evil. England is the World Enemy. Throughout the ages she has been the Robber State, crushing——"

But she had little luck. Once more she was interrupted by an explosion, a much louder one, directly above them. Our witch hardly heard the noise; she seemed suddenly to have found the climax of her life, and the climax was pain. There was pain and a feeling of terrible change all over her, smothering her, and a super-pain in her shoulder. After a second or two as long as death, she realized dimly that she was all tensely strung to an attitude, like a marionette. Her hands were up trying to shield her head, her chin was pressed down to her drawn-up knees. Her blue serge shoulder was extraordinarily wet and im-movable, She looked along the cloud. Her enemy was not there. There was a round hole in the cloud, and as she leaned painfully towards it, she could see a few of the lights of London, and something falling spasmodically towards them.

The cloud had been shaken to its foundations by the two explosions, and the German witch, who had been seated perhaps on a seam in the material, or at any rate on one of the less stable parts of the fabric, had fallen through. Her parachute cloak, in passing through the hole in the cloud, had been turned inside out above her head, and rendered useless. Over and about her falling figure her broomstick darted helplessly, uttering curious sad cries, like a sea-gull's.

Even as the English witch watched her enemy's disaster, the larger part of the cloud, weakened by all the shock and movement, broke away with a hissing sound. The witch's feet hung now over space, she dared not move; she had difficulty in steadying herself with her unwounded arm, for her hand could find only a quicksand of dissolving cloud to lean on. She had no thoughts left but thoughts of danger and of pain.

But Harold the Broomstick came back. The witch heard a rustling sound close to her, and it startled her more than all the noise of the guns, which had come, as it seemed, from the forgotten other side of eternity. The rough head of Harold appeared over the cloud's edge, and insinuated itself pathetically under her arm. Very carefully and very painfully the witch reached a kneeling position, damaging her refuge with every movement in spite of her care. She gasped with pain, and Harold tried to look very strong and hopeful to comfort her. He straightened his back, and she crawled into the saddle. The tremor of their launching split the cloud into several parts, which disintegrated. There was no more foot-hold on it; the tide had come up and submerged it.

Harold the Broomstick was crippled, he stumbled as he flew, sometimes he dropped a score of feet, and span. He did stunts by mistake.

They had not strength enough between them to get home. They made a forced landing in the silver loneliness of Kensington Gardens. It was a fortunate place, for there is much magic there. Wherever there are children who pretend, there grows a little magic in the air, and therefore the wind of Kensington Gardens thrills with enchantment, and the Round Pond, full of much pretence of great Armadas, crossed and re-crossed with the abiding wakes of ships full of treasure and romance, is a blessed lake to magic people.

The witch bathed Harold, her broomstick, in the Round Pond. He evidently felt its healing quality at once, for after the first minute of immersion, he swam about exultantly, and shook drops full of moonlight out of his mane.

The bugles sounded All-clear in many keys all round the ear's horizon; their sound matched the waning moonlight.

The witch bathed her shoulder, and then she found her way to a little quiet place she knew of, where no park-keeper ever looks, a place where secret and ungardened daffodils grow in springtime, a place where all the mice and birds play unafraid, because no cat can find the way thither. You can see the Serpentine from that place, and the bronze shadows under its bridge, but no houses, and no railways, and no signs of London.

Here the witch made a little fire, and leaned three sticks together over it; she lighted the fire with her finger-tip and hung over it the little patent folding cauldron, which she always carried on a chatelaine swinging from her belt. And she made a charm of daisy-heads, and spring-smelling grasses, and the roots of unappreciated weeds, and the mosses that cover the tiny faery cliffs of the Serpentine. Over the mixture she shook out the contents of one of her little paper packets of magic. All this she boiled over her fire for many hours, sitting beside it in the silver darkness, with her knees drawn up and her hands clasped in front of them. The trees sprang up into the moonlight like dark fountains from the pools of their own shadows. Little shreds of cloud flowed wonderfully across the sky. There was no sound except the sound of the water, like an uncertain player upon a little instrument. The charm was still unfinished when the dawn passed over London, and the sun came up, the seed of another day, sown in a rich red soil. The trees of the Gardens remembered their daylight shadows again, and forgot their mystery. The water-birds, after examining their shoulder-blades with minute care for some moments, launched themselves upon a lake of diamonds. There seemed a veil of mist and bird-song over the world. The sudden song of the birds was like finding the hearing of one's heart restored, after long deafness.

The witch anointed her shoulder with the charm, after having first made a drop of potion out of the bubbles in it. This potion she drank, and was healed of her wound and her weariness, and of all desires except a desire to sleep with her face among the daffodils. She was the most beautifully alone person in the world that morning; nobody could have found her. A thin string of very blue smoke went up from her faint fire and was tangled among the boughs of a flowering tree, but the coarse eye of a park-keeper could never have seen it. She had escaped from the net of the cruel hours; for her the stained world was washed clean; for her all horror held its breath; for her there was absolute spring, and an innocent sun, and the shadows of daffodils upon closed eyes. . . .

THE OPEN WINDOW

H. H. Munro ("Saki")

"My aunt will be down presently, Mr. Nuttel," said a very self-possessed young lady of fifteen; "in the meantime you must try and put up with me."

Framton Nuttel endeavoured to say the correct something which should duly flatter the niece of the moment without unduly discounting the aunt that was to come. Privately he doubted more than ever whether these formal visits on a succession of total strangers would do much towards helping the nerve cure which he was supposed to be undergoing.

"I know how it will be," his sister had said when he was preparing to migrate to this rural retreat; "you will bury yourself down there and not speak to a living soul, and your nerves will be worse than ever from moping. I shall just give you letters of introduction to all the people I know there. Some of them, as far as I can remember, were quite nice."

Framton wondered whether Mrs. Sappleton, the lady to whom he was presenting one of the letters of introduction, came into the nice division.

"Do you know many of the people round here?" asked the niece, when she judged that they had had sufficient silent communion.

"Hardly a soul," said Framton. "My sister was staying here, at the rectory, you know, some four years ago, and she gave me letters of introduction to some of the people here."

He made the last statement in a tone of distinct regret.

"Then you know practically nothing about my aunt?" pursued the self-possessed young lady.

"Only her name and address," admitted the caller. He was wondering whether Mrs. Sappleton was in the married or widowed state. An undefinable something about the room seemed to suggest masculine habitation.

"Her great tragedy happened just three years ago," said the child; "that would be since your sister's time."

"Her tragedy?" asked Framton; somehow in this restful country spot tragedies seemed out of place.

"You may wonder why we keep that window wide open on an October afternoon," said the niece, indicating a large french window that opened on to a lawn.

"It is quite warm for the time of the year," said Framton; "but has that window got anything to do with the tragedy?"

"Out through that window, three years ago to a day, her husband and her two young brothers went off for their day's shooting. They never came back. In crossing the moor to their favourite snipe-shooting ground they were all three engulfed in a treacherous piece of bog. It had been that dreadful wet summer, you know, and places that were safe in other years gave way suddenly without warning. Their bodies were never recovered. That was the dreadful part of it." Here the child's voice lost its self-possessed note and became falteringly human. "Poor aunt always thinks that they will come back some day, they and the little brown spaniel that was lost with them, and walk in at that window just as they used to do. That is why the window is kept open every evening till it is quite dusk. Poor dear aunt, she has often told me how they went out, her husband with his white waterproof coat over his arm, and Ronnie, her youngest brother, singing 'Bertie, why do you bound?' as he always did to tease her, because she said it got on her nerves. Do you know, sometimes on still, quiet evenings like this, I almost get a creepy feeling that they will all walk in through that window——"

She broke off with a little shudder. It was a relief to Framton when the aunt bustled into the room with a whirl of apologies for being late in making her appearance.

"I hope Vera has been amusing you?" she said.

"She has been very interesting," said Framton.

"I hope you don't mind the open window," said Mrs. Sappleton briskly; "my husband and brothers will be home directly from shooting, and they always come in this way. They've been out for snipe in the marshes today, so they'll make a fine mess over my poor carpets. So like you men-folk, isn't it?"

She rattled on cheerfully about the shooting and the scarcity of birds, and the prospects for duck in the winter. To Framton it was all purely horrible. He made a desperate but only partially successful effort to turn the talk on to a less ghastly topic; he was conscious that his hostess was giving him only a fragment of her attention, and her eyes were constantly straying past him to the open window and the lawn beyond. It was certainly an unfortunate coincidence that he should have paid his visit on this tragic anniversary.

"The doctors agree in ordering me complete rest, an absence of mental excitement, and avoidance of anything in the nature of violent physical exercise," announced Framton, who laboured under the tolerably widespread delusion that total strangers and chance acquaintances are hungry for the least detail of one's ailments and infirmities, their cause and cure. "On the matter of diet they are not so much in agreement," he continued.

"No?" said Mrs. Sappleton, in a voice which only replaced a yawn at the last moment. Then she suddenly brightened into alert attention—but not to what Framton was saying.

"Here they are at last!" she cried. "Just in time for tea, and don't they look as if they were muddy up to the eyes!"

Framton shivered slightly and turned towards the niece with a look intended to convey sympathetic comprehension. The child was staring out through the open window with dazed horror in her eyes. In a chill shock of nameless fear Framton swung round in his seat and looked in the same direction.

In the deepening twilight three figures were walking across the lawn towards the window; they all carried guns under their arms, and one of them was additionally burdened with a white coat hung over his shoulders. A tired brown spaniel kept close at their heels. Noiselessly they neared the house, and then a hoarse young voice chanted out of the dusk : "I said, Bertie, why do you bound?"

Framton grabbed wildly at his stick and hat; the hall-door, the gravel-drive, and the front gate were dimly-noted stages in his headlong retreat. A cyclist coming along the road had to run into the hedge to avoid an imminent collision.

"Here we are, my dear," said the bearer of the white mackintosh, coming in through the window; "fairly muddy, but most of it's dry. Who was that who bolted out as we came up?"

"A most extraordinary man, a Mr. Nuttel," said Mrs. Sappleton; "could only talk about his illnesses, and dashed off without a word of good-bye or apology when you arrived. One would think he had seen a ghost."

"I expect it was the spaniel," said the niece calmly; "he told me he had a horror of dogs. He was once hunted into a cemetery somewhere on the banks of the Ganges by a pack of pariah dogs, and had to spend the night in a newly dug grave with the creatures snarling and grinning and foaming just above him. Enough to make anyone lose their nerve."

Romance at short notice was her speciality.

THE BELL OF SAINT EUSCHEMON

By Richard Garnett

THE town of Epinal, in Lorraine, possessed in the Middle Ages a peal of three bells, respectively dedicated to St. Eulogius, St. Eucherius, and St. Euschemon, whose tintinnabulation was found to be an effectual safeguard against all thunderstorms. Let the heavens be ever so murky, it was merely requisite to set the bells ringing, and no lightning flashed and no thunder peal broke over the town, nor was the neighbouring country within hearing of them ravaged by hail or flood.

One day the three saints, Eulogius, Eucherius and Euschemon, were sitting together, exceedingly well content with themselves and everything around them, as indeed they had every right to be, supposing that they were in Paradise. We say supposing, not being for our own part entirely able to reconcile this locality with the presence of certain cans and flagons, which had been fuller than they were.

"What a happy reflection for a Saint," said Eulogius, who was rapidly passing from the mellow stage of good fellowship to the maudlin, "that even after his celestial assumption he is permitted to continue a source of blessing and benefit to his fellow-creatures as yet dwelling in the shade of mortality! The thought of the services of my bell, in averting lightning and inundation from the good people of Epinal, fills me with indescribable beatitude."

"*Your* bell!" interposed Eucherius, whose path had lain through the mellow to the quarrelsome. "*Your* bell, quotha! You had as good clink this cannakin" (suiting the action to the word) "as your bell. It's my bell that does the business."

"I think you might put in a word for *my* bell," interposed Euschemon, a little squinting saint, very merry and friendly when not put out, as on the present occasion.

"Your bell!" retorted the big saints, with incredible disdain; and, forgetting their own altercation, they fell so fiercely on their little brother that he ran away, stopping his ears with his hands, and vowing vengeance.

A short time after this fracas, a personage of venerable appearance presented himself at Epinal, and applied for the post of sacristan and bell-ringer, at that time vacant. Though he squinted, his appearance was far from disagreeable, and he obtained the appointment without difficulty. His deportment in it was in all respects edifying; or if he evinced some little remissness in the service of Saints Eulogius and Eucherius, this was more than compensated by his devotion to the hitherto somewhat slighted Saint Euschemon. It was, indeed, observed that candles, garlands, and other offerings made at the shrines of the two senior saints were found to be transferred in an unaccountable and mystical manner to the junior, which induced experienced persons to remark that a miracle was certainly brewing. Nothing, however, occurred until, one hot summer afternoon, the indications of a storm became so threatening that the sacristan was directed to ring the bells. Scarcely had he begun than the sky became clear, but instead of the usual rich volume of sound the townsmen heard with astonishment a solitary tinkle, sounding quite ridiculous and unsatisfactory in comparison. St. Euschemon's bell was ringing by itself.

In a trice priests and laymen swarmed to the belfry, and indignantly demanded of the sacristan what he meant.

"To enlighten you," he responded. "To teach you to give honour where honour is due. To unmask those canonized impostors."

And he called their attention to the fact that the clappers of the bells of Eulogius and Eucherius were so fastened up that they could not emit a sound, while that of Euschemon vibrated freely.

"Ye see," he continued, "that these sound not at all, yet is the tempest stayed. Is it not thence manifest that the virtue resides solely in the bell of the blessed Euschemon?"

The argument seemed conclusive to the majority, but those of the clergy who ministered at the altars of Eulogius and Eucherius stoutly resisted, maintaining that no just decision could be arrived at until Euschemon's bell was subjected to the others. Their view eventually prevailed, to the great dismay of Euschemon, who, although firmly convinced of the virtue of his own bell, did not in his heart disbelieve in the bells of his brethren. Imagine his relief and amazed joy when, upon his bell being silenced, the storm, for the first time in the memory of the oldest inhabitant, broke with full fury over Epinal, and, for all the frantic pealing of the other two bells, raged with unspeakable fierceness until his own was brought into requisition, when, as if by enchantment, the rain ceased, the thunder-clouds dispersed, and the sun broke out gloriously from the blue sky.

"Carry him in procession!" shouted the crowd.

"Amen, brethren; here I am," rejoined Euschemon, stepping briskly into the midst of the troop.

"And why in the name of Zernebock should we carry *you*?" demanded some, while others ran off to lug forth the image, the object of their devotion.

"Why, verily," Euschemon began, and stopped short. How, indeed, was he to prove to them that he *was* Euschemon? His personal resemblance to his effigy, the work of a sculptor of the idealistic school, was in no respect remarkable; and he felt, alas! that he could no more work a miracle than you or I. In the sight of the multitude he was only an elderly sexton with a cast in his eye, with nothing but his office to keep him out of the workhouse. A further and more awkward question arose, how on earth was he to get back to Paradise? The ordinary method was not available, for he had already been dead for several centuries; and no other presented itself to his imagination.

Muttering apologies, and glad to be overlooked, Euschemon shrank into a corner, but slightly comforted by the honours his image was receiving at the hands of the good people of Epinal. As time wore on he became pensive and restless, and nothing pleased him so well as to ascend to the belfry on moonlight nights, scribbling disparagement on the bells of Eulogius and Eucherius, which had ceased to be rung, and patting and caressing his own, which now did duty for all three. With alarm he noticed one night an incipient crack, which threatened to become a serious flaw.

"If this goes on," said a voice behind him, "I shall get a holiday."

Euschemon turned round, and with indescribable dismay perceived a gigantic demon, negligently resting his hand on the top of the bell, and looking as if it would cost him nothing to pitch it and Euschemon together to the other side of the town.

"Avaunt, fiend," he stammered, with as much dignity as he could muster, "or, at least, remove thy unhallowed paw from my bell."

"Come, Eusky," replied the friend, with profane familiarity, "don't be a fool. You are not *really* such an ass as to imagine that your virtue has anything to do with the virtue of this bell?"

"Whose virtue, then?" demanded Euschemon.

"Why truly," said the demon, "mine! When this bell was cast I was imprisoned in it by a potent enchanter, and so long as I am in it no storm can come within sound of its ringing. I am not allowed to quit it except by night, and then no further than an arm's length: this, however, I take the liberty of measuring by my own arm, which happens to be a long one. This must continue, as I learn, until I receive a kiss from some bishop of distinguished sanctity. Thou hast done some bishoping in thy time, peradventure?"

Euschemon energetically protested that he had been on earth but a simple laic, which was, indeed, the fact, and was also the reason why Eulogius and Eucherius despised him, but which, though he did not think it needful to tell the demon, he found a singular relief under present circumstances.

"Well," continued the fiend, "I wish he may turn up shortly, for I am half deaf already with the banging and booming of this infernal clapper, which seems to have grown much worse of late; and the blessings and the crossings and the aspersions which I have to go through are most repugnant to my tastes, and unsuitable to my position in society. Bye-bye, Eusky; come up tomorrow night." And the fiend slipped back into the bell, and instantly became invisible.

The humiliation of poor Euschemon on learning that he was indebted for his credit to the devil is easier to imagine than to describe. He did not, however, fail at the rendezvous next night, and found the demon sitting outside the bell in a most affable frame of mind. It did not take long for the devil and the saint to become very good friends, both wanting company, and the former being apparently as much amused by the latter's simplicity as the latter was charmed by the former's knowingness. Euschemon learned numbers of things of which he had not had the faintest notion. The demon taught him how to play cards (just invented by the Saracens), and iniated him into divers "arts, though unimagined, yet to be", such as smoking tobacco, making a book on the Derby, and inditing queer stories for Society journals. He drew the most profane but irresistibly funny caricatures of Eulogius and Eucherius, and the rest of the host of heaven. He had been one of the demons who tempted St. Anthony, and retailed anecdotes of that eremite which Euschemon had never heard mentioned in Paradise. He was versed in all scandal respecting saints in general, and Euschemon found with astonishment how much about his own order was known downstairs. On the whole he had never enjoyed himself so much in his life; he became proficient in all manner of minor devilries, and was ceasing to trouble himself about his bell or his ecclesiastical duties, when an untoward incident interrupted his felicity.

It chanced that the Bishop of Metz, in whose diocese Epinal was situated, finding himself during a visitation journey within a short distance of the town, determined to put up there for the night. He did not arrive until nightfall, but word of his intention having been sent forward by a messenger the authorities, civil and ecclesiastical, were ready to receive him. When, escorted in state, he had arrived at the house prepared for his reception, the Mayor ventured to express a hope that everything had been satisfactory to his Lordship.

"Everything," said the bishop emphatically. "I did, indeed, seem to remark one little omission, which no doubt may be easily accounted for."

"What was that, my Lord?"

"It hath," said the bishop, "usually been the practice to receive a bishop with the ringing of bells. It is a laudable custom, conducive to the purification of the air and the discomfiture on the prince of the powers thereof. I caught no sound of chimes on the present occasion, yet I am sensible that my hearing is not what it was."

The civil and ecclesiastical authorities looked at each other. "That graceless knave of a sacristan!" said the Mayor.

"He hath, indeed, of late strangely neglected his charge," said a priest.

"Poor man, I doubt his wits are touched," charitably added another.

"What!" exclaimed the bishop, who was very active, very fussy, and a great stickler for discipline. "This important church, so renowned for its three miraculous bells, confided to the tender mercies of an imbecile rogue who may burn it down any night! I will look to it myself without losing a minute."

And in spite of all remonstrances, off he started. The keys were brought, the doors flung open, the body of the church thoroughly examined, but neither in nave, choir, or chancel could the slightest trace of the sacristan be found.

"Perhaps he is in the belfry," suggested a chorister.

"We'll see," responded the bishop, and bustling nimbly up the ladder, he emerged into the open belfry in full moonlight.

Heavens! What sight met his eye! The sacristan and the devil sitting *vis-à-vis* close by the miraculous bell, with a smoking can of hot spiced wine between them, finishing a close game of cribbage.

"Seven," declared Euschemon.

"And eight are fifteen," retorted the demon, marking two.

"Twenty-three and paid," cried Euschemon, marking in his turn.

"And seven is thirty."

"Ace, thirty-one, and I'm up."

"It *is* up with you, my friend," shouted the bishop, bringing his crook down smartly on Euschemon's shoulders.

"Deuce!" said the devil, and vanished into his bell.

When poor Euschemon had been bound and gagged, which did not take very long, the bishop briefly addressed the assembly. He said that the accounts of the bell which had reached his ears had already excited his apprehensions. He had greatly feared that all could not be right, and now his anxieties were but too well justified. He trusted there was not a man before him who would not suffer his flocks and his crops to be destroyed by tempest fifty times over rather than purchase their safety by unhallowed means. What had been done had doubtless been done in ignorance, and could be made good by a mulct to the episcopal treasury. The amount of this he would carefully consider, and the people of Epinal might rest assured that it should not be too light to entitle them to the benefit of a full absolution. The bell must go to his cathedral city, there to be examined and reported on by the exorcists and inquisitors. Meanwhile, he would himself institute a slight preliminary scrutiny.

The bell was accordingly unhung, tilted up, and inspected by the combined beams of the moonlight and torchlight. Very slight examination served to place the soundness of the bishop's opinion beyond dispute. On the lip of the bell were engraven characters unknown to everyone else, but which seemed to affect the prelate with singular consternation.

"I hope," he exclaimed, "that none of you know anything about these characters! I earnestly trust that none can read a single one of them. If I thought anybody could I would burn him as soon as look at him!"

The bystanders hastened to assure him that not one of them had the slightest conception of the meaning of the letters, which had never been observed before.

"I rejoice to hear it," said the bishop. "It will be an evil day for the church when these letters are understood."

And next morning he departed, carrying off the bell, with the invisible fiend inside it; the cards, which were regarded as a book of magic; and the luckless Euschemon, who shortly found himself in total darkness, the inmate of a dismal dungeon.

It was some time before Euschemon became sensible of the presence of any partner in his captivity, by reason of the trotting of the rats. At length, however, a deep sigh struck upon his ear.

"Who art thou?" he exclaimed.

"An unfortunate prisoner," was the answer.

"What is the occasion of thy imprisonment?"

"Oh, a mere trifle. A ridiculous suspicion of sacrificing a child to Beelzebub. One of the little disagreeables that must occasionally occur in our profession."

"*Our* profession!" exclaimed Euschemon.

"Art thou not a sorcerer?" demanded the voice.

"No," replied Euschemon, "I am a saint."

The warlock received Euschemon's statement with much incredulity, but becoming eventually convinced of its truth——

"I congratulate thee," he said. "The devil has manifestly taken a fancy to thee, and he never forgets his own. It is true that the bishop is a great favourite with him also. But we will hope for the best. Thou hast never practised riding a broomstick? No? 'Tis pity; thou mayest have to mount one at a moment's notice."

This consolation had scarcely been administered ere the bolts flew back, the hinges grated, the door opened, and gaolers bearing torches informed the sorcerer that the bishop desired his presence.

He found the bishop in his study, which was nearly choked up by Euschemon's bell. The prelate received him with the greatest affability, and expressed a sincere hope that the very particular arrangements he had enjoined for the comfort of his distinguished prisoner had been faithfully carried out by his subordinates. The sorcerer, as much a man of the world as the bishop, thanked his Lordship, and protested that he had been perfectly comfortable.

"I have need of thy art," said the bishop, coming to business. "I am exceedingly bothered—flabbergasted were not too strong an expression—by this confounded bell. All my best exorcists have been trying all they know with it, to no purpose. They might as well have tried to exorcise my mitre from my head by any other charm than the offer of a better one. Magic is plainly the only remedy, and if thou canst disenchant it, I will give thee thy freedom."

"It will be a tough business," observed the sorcerer, surveying the bell with the eye of a connoisseur. "It will require fumigations."

"Yes," said the bishop, "and suffumigations."

"Aloes and mastic," advised the sorcerer.

"Aye," assented the bishop, "and red sanders."

"We must call in Primeumaton," said the warlock.

"Clearly," said the bishop, "and Amioram."

"Triangles," said the sorcerer.

"Pentacles," said the bishop.

"In the hour of Methon," said the sorcerer.

"I should have thought Tafrac," suggested the bishop, "but I defer to your better judgment."

"I can have the blood of a goat?" queried the wizard.

"Yes," said the bishop, "and of a monkey also."

"Does your Lordship think that one might venture to go so far as a little unweaned child?"

"If absolutely necessary," said the bishop.

"I am delighted to find such liberality of sentiment on your Lordship's part," said the sorcerer. "Your Lordship is evidently of the profession."

"These are things which stuck by me when I was an inquisitor," explained the bishop, with some little embarrassment.

Ere long all arrangements were made. It would be impossible to enumerate half the crosses, circles, pentagrams, naked swords, cross-bones, chafing-dishes, and vials of incense which the sorcerer found to be necessary. The child was fortunately deemed superfluous. Euschemon was brought up from his dungeon, and, his teeth chattering with fright and cold, set beside his bell to hold a candle to the devil. The incantations commenced, and speedily gave evidence of their efficacy. The bell trembled, swayed, split open, and a female figure of transcendent loveliness attired in the costume of Eve stepped forth and extended her lips towards the bishop. What could the bishop do but salute them? With a roar of triumph the demon resumed his proper shape. The bishop swooned. The apartment was filled with the fumes of sulphur. The devil soared majestically out of the window, carrying the sorcerer under one arm and Euschemon under the other.

It is commonly believed that the devil good-naturedly dropped Euschemon back again into Paradise, or wheresoever he might have come from. It is even added that he fell between Eulogius and Eucherius, who had been arguing all the time respecting the merits of their bells, and resumed his share in the discussion as if nothing had happened. Some maintain, indeed, that the devil, chancing to be in want of a chaplain, offered the situation to Euschemon, by whom it was accepted. But how to reconcile this assertion with the undoubted fact that the duties of the post in question are at present ably discharged by the Bishop of Metz, in truth we see not. One thing is certain: thou wilt not find Euschemon's name in the calendar, courteous reader.

The mulct to be imposed upon the parish of Epinal was never exacted. The bell, ruptured beyond repair by the demon's violent exit, was taken back and deposited in the museum of the town. The bells of Eulogius and Eucherius were rung freely on occasion; but Epinal has not since enjoyed any greater immunity from storms than the contiguous districts. One day an aged traveller, who had spent many years in Heathenesse and in whom some discerned a remarkable resemblance to the sorcerer, noticed the bell, and asked permission to examine it. He soon discovered the inscription, recognized the mysterious characters as Greek, read them without the least difficulty:

Μήχινει Καμαρίναν ἀχινητος γὰρ ἀμεινων—and favoured the townsmen with this free but substantially accurate translation:

· CAN'T YOU LET WELL ALONE?

THE STORY OF A PANIC

By E. M. Forster

I

EUSTACE'S career—if career it can be called—certainly dates from that afternoon in the chestnut woods above Ravello. I confess at once that I am a plain, simple man, with no pretensions to literary style. Still, I do flatter myself that I can tell a story without exaggerating, and I have, therefore, decided to give an unbiassed account of the extraordinary events of eight years ago.

Ravello is a delightful place with a delightful little hotel in which we met some charming people. There were the two Miss Robinsons, who had been there for six weeks with Eustace, their nephew, a boy of about fourteen. Mr. Sandbach had also been there some time. He had held a curacy in the north of England, which he had been compelled to resign on account of ill-health, and while he was recuperating at Ravello he had taken in hand Eustace's education—which was then sadly deficient—and was endeavouring to fit him for one of our great public schools. Then there was Mr. Leyland, a would-be artist, and, finally, there was the nice landlady, Signora Scafetti, and the nice English-speaking waiter, Emmanuele—though at the time of which I am speaking Emmanuele was away, visiting a sick father.

To this little circle, I, my wife, and my two daughters made, I venture to think, a not unwelcome addition. But though I liked most of the company well enough, there were two of them to whom I did not take at all. They were the artist, Leyland, and the Miss Robinsons' nephew, Eustace.

Leyland was simply conceited and odious, and, as those qualities will be amply illustrated in my narrative, I need not enlarge upon them here. But Eustace was something besides: he was indescribably repellent.

I am fond of boys as a rule, and was quite disposed to be friendly. I and my daughters offered to take him out. "No, walking was such a fag." Then I asked him to come and bathe. "No, he could not swim."

"Every English boy should be able to swim," I said, "I will teach you myself."

"There, Eustace dear," said Miss Robinson; "here is a chance for you."

But he said he was afraid of the water!—a boy afraid!—and, of course, I said no more.

I would not have minded so much if he had been a really studious boy, but he neither played hard nor worked hard. His favourite occupations were lounging on the terrace in an easy chair and loafing along the high road, with his feet shuffling up the dust and his shoulders stooping forward. Naturally enough, his features were pale, his chest contracted, and his muscles undeveloped. His aunts thought him delicate; what he really needed was discipline.

That memorable day we all arranged to go for a picnic up in the chestnut woods—all, that is, except Janet, who stopped behind to finish her water-colour of the cathedral—not a very successful attempt, I am afraid.

I wander off into these irrelevant details, because in my mind I cannot separate them from an account of the day; and it is the same with the conversation during the picnic: all is imprinted on my brain together. After a couple of hours' ascent, we left the donkeys that had carried the Miss Robinsons and my wife, and all proceeded on foot to the head of the valley—Vallone Fontana Caroso is its proper name, I find.

I have visited a good deal of fine scenery before and since, but have found little that has pleased me more. The valley ended in a vast hollow, shaped like a cup, into which radiated ravines from the precipitous hills around. Both the valley and the ravines and the ribs of hill that divided the ravines were covered with leafy chestnut, so that the general appearance was that of a many-fingered green hand, palm upwards, which was clutching convulsively to keep us in its grasp. Far down the valley we could see Ravello and the sea, but that was the only sign of another world.

"Oh, what a perfectly lovely place," said my daughter Rose. "What a picture it would make!"

"Yes," said Mr. Sandbach. "Many a famous European gallery would be proud to have a landscape a tithe as beautiful as this upon its walls."

"On the contrary," said Leyland, "it would make a very poor picture. Indeed, it is not paintable at all."

"And why is that?" said Rose, with far more deference than he deserved.

"Look, in the first place," he replied, "how intolerably straight against the sky is the line of the hill. It would need breaking up and diversifying. And where we are standing the whole thing is out of perspective. Besides, all the colouring is monotonous and crude."

"I do not know anything about pictures," I put in, "and I do not pretend to know: but I know what is beautiful when I see it, and I am thoroughly content with this."

"Indeed, who could help being contented!" said the elder Miss Robinson; and Mr. Sandbach said the same.

"Ah!" said Leyland, "you all confuse the artistic view of Nature with the photographic."

Poor Rose had brought her camera with her, so I thought this positively rude. I did not wish any unpleasantness; so I merely turned away and assisted my wife and Miss Mary Robinson to put out the lunch—not a very nice lunch.

"Eustace dear," said his aunt, "come and help us here."

He was in a particularly bad temper that morning. He had, as usual, not wanted to come, and his aunts had nearly allowed him to stop at the hotel to vex Janet. But I, with their permission, spoke to him rather sharply on the subject of exercise; and the result was that he had come, but was even more taciturn and moody than usual.

Obedience was not his strong point. He invariably questioned every command, and only executed it grumbling. I should always insist on prompt and cheerful obedience, if I had a son.

"I'm—coming—Aunt—Mary," he at last replied, and dawdled to cut a piece of wood to make a whistle, taking care not to arrive till we had finished.

"Well, well, sir!" said I, "you stroll in at the end and profit by our labours." He sighed, for he could not endure being chaffed. Miss Mary, very unwisely, insisted on giving him the wing of the chicken, in spite of all my attempts to prevent her. I remember that I had a moment's vexation when I thought that, instead of enjoying the sun, and the air, and the woods, we were all engaged in wrangling over the diet of a spoilt boy.

But, after lunch, he was a little less in evidence. He withdrew to a tree trunk, and began to loosen the bark from his whistle. I was thankful to see him employed, for once in a way. We reclined, and took a *dolce far niente*.

Those sweet chestnuts of the South are puny striplings compared with our robust Northerners. But they clothed the contours of the hills and valleys in a most pleasing way, their veil being only broken by two clearings, in one of which we were sitting.

And because these few trees were cut down, Leyland burst into a petty indictment of the proprietor.

"All the poetry is going from Nature," he cried, "her lakes and marshes are drained, her seas banked up, her forests cut down. Everywhere we see the vulgarity of desolation spreading."

I have had some experience of estates, and answered that cutting was very necessary for the health of the larger trees. Besides, it was unreasonable to expect the proprietor to derive no income from his lands.

"If you take the commercial side of landscape, you may feel pleasure in the owner's activity. But to me the mere thought that a tree is convertible into cash is disgusting."

"I see no reason," I observed politely, "to despise the gifts of Nature because they are of value."

It did not stop him. "It is no matter," he went on, "we are all hopelessly steeped in vulgarity. I do not except myself. It is through us, and to our shame, that the Nereids have left the waters and the Oreads the mountains, that the woods no longer give shelter to Pan."

"Pan!" cried Mr. Sandbach, his mellow voice filling the valley as if it had been a great green church, "Pan is dead. That is why the woods do not shelter him." And he began to tell the striking story of the mariners who were sailing near the coast at the time of the birth of Christ, and three times heard a loud voice saying: "The great God Pan is dead."

"Yes. The great God Pan is dead," said Leyland. And he abandoned himself to that mock misery in which artistic people are so fond of indulging. His cigar went out, and he had to ask me for a match.

"How very interesting," said Rose. "I do wish I knew some ancient history."

"It is not worth your notice," said Mr. Sandbach. "Eh, Eustace?"

Eustace was finishing his whistle. He looked up, with the irritable frown in which his aunts allowed him to indulge, and made no reply.

The conversation turned to various topics and then died out. It was a cloudless afternoon in May, and the pale green of the young chestnut leaves made a pretty contrast with the dark blue of the sky. We were all sitting at the edge of the small clearing for the sake of the view, and the shade of the chestnut saplings behind us was manifestly insufficient. All sounds died away—at least that is my account: Miss Robinson says that the clamour of the birds was the first sign of uneasiness that she discerned. All sounds died away, except that, far in the distance, I could hear two boughs of a great chestnut grinding together as the tree swayed. The grinds grew shorter and shorter, and finally that sound stopped also. As I looked over the green fingers of the valley, everything was absolutely motionless and still; and that feeling of suspense which one so often experiences when Nature is in repose, began to steal over me.

Suddenly, we were all electrified by the excruciating noise of Eustace's whistle. I never heard any instrument give forth so ear-splitting and discordant a sound.

"Eustace dear," said Miss Mary Robinson, "you might have thought of your poor Aunt Julia's head."

Leyland, who had apparently been asleep, sat up.

"It is astonishing how blind a boy is to anything that is elevating or beautiful," he observed. "I should not have thought he could have found the wherewithal out here to spoil our pleasure like this."

Then the terrible silence fell upon us again. I was now standing up and watching a catspaw of wind that was running down one of the ridges opposite, turning the light green to dark as it travelled. A fanciful feeling of foreboding came over me; so I turned away, to find to my amazement that all the others were also on their feet, watching it too.

It is not possible to describe coherently what happened next: but I, for one, am not ashamed to confess that, though the fair blue sky was above me, and the green spring woods beneath me, and the kindest of friends around me, yet I became terribly frightened, more frightened than I ever wish to become again, frightened in a way I never have known either before or after. And in the eyes of the others, too, I saw blank, expressionless fear, while their mouths strove in vain to speak and their hands to gesticulate. Yet, all around us were prosperity, beauty, and peace, and all was motionless, save the catspaw of wind, now travelling up the ridge on which we stood.

Who moved first has never been settled. It is enough to say that in one second we were tearing away along the hill-side. Leyland was in front, then Mr. Sandbach, then my wife. But I only saw for a brief moment; for I ran across the little clearing and through the woods and over the undergrowth and the rocks and down the dry torrent beds into the valley below. The sky might have been black as I ran, and the trees short grass, and the hill-side a level road; for I saw nothing and heard nothing and felt nothing, since all the channels of sense and reason were blocked. It was not the spiritual fear that one has known at other times, but brutal overmastering physical fear, stopping up the ears, and dropping clouds before the eyes, and filling the mouth with foul tastes. And it was no ordinary humiliation that survived; for I had been afraid, not as a man, but as a beast.

II

I cannot describe our finish any better than our start; for our fear passed away as it had come, without cause. Suddenly I was able to see, and hear, and cough, and clear my mouth. Looking back, I saw that the others were stopping, too; and, in a short time, we were all together, though it was long before we could speak, and longer before we dared to.

No one was seriously injured. My poor wife had sprained her ankle, Leyland had torn one of his nails on a tree trunk, and I myself had scraped and damaged my ear. I never noticed it till I had stopped.

We were all silent, searching one another's faces. Suddenly, Miss Mary Robinson gave a terrible shriek. "Oh, merciful heavens! Where is Eustace?" And then she would have fallen if Mr. Sandbach had not caught her.

"We must go back, we must go back at once," said my Rose, who was quite the most collected of the party. "But I hope—I feel he is safe."

Such was the cowardice of Leyland, that he objected. But, finding himself in a minority, and being afraid of being left alone, he gave in. Rose and I supported my poor wife, Mr. Sandbach and Miss Robinson helped Miss Mary, and we returned slowly and silently, taking forty minutes to ascend the path that we had descended in ten.

Our conversation was naturally disjointed, as no one wished to offer an opinion on what had happened. Rose was the most talkative: she startled us all by saying that she had very nearly stopped where she was.

"Do you mean to say that you weren't—that you didn't feel compelled to go?" said Mr. Sandbach.

"Oh, of course, I did feel frightened"—she was the first to use the word—"but I somehow felt that if I could stop on it would be quite different, that I shouldn't be frightened at all, so to speak." Rose never did express herself clearly: still, it is greatly to her credit that she, the youngest of us, should have held on so long at that terrible time.

"I should have stopped, I do believe," she continued, "if I had not seen mamma go."

Rose's experience comforted us a little about Eustace. But a feeling of terrible foreboding was on us all, as we painfully climbed the chestnut-covered slopes and neared the little clearing. When we reached it our tongues broke loose. There, at the farther side, were the remains of our lunch, and close to them, lying motionless on his back, was Eustace.

With some presence of mind I at once cried out: "Hey, you young monkey! Jump up!" But he made no reply, nor did he answer when his poor aunts spoke to him. And, to my unspeakable horror, I saw one of those green lizards dart out from under his shirt-cuff as we approached.

We stood watching him as he lay there so silently, and my ears began to tingle in expectation of the outbursts of lamentations and tears.

Miss Mary fell on her knees beside him and touched his hand, which was convulsively entwined in the long grass.

As she did so he opened his eyes and smiled.

I have often seen that peculiar smile since, both on the possessor's face and on the photographs of him that are beginning to get into the illustrated papers. But, till then, Eustace had always worn a peevish, discontented frown; and we were all unused to this disquieting smile, which always seemed to be without adequate reason.

His aunts showered kisses on him, which he did not reciprocate, and then there was an awkward pause. Eustace seemed so natural and undisturbed; yet, if he had not had astonishing experiences himself, he ought to have been all the more astonished at our extraordinary behaviour. My wife, with ready tact, endeavoured to behave as if nothing had happened.

"Well, Mr. Eustace," she said, sitting down as she spoke, to ease her foot, "how have you been amusing yourself since we have been away?"

"Thank you, Mrs. Tytler, I have been very happy."

"And where have you been?"

"Here."

"And lying down all the time, you idle boy?"

"No, not all the time."

"What were you doing before?"

"Oh; standing or sitting."

"Stood and sat doing nothing! Don't you know the poem 'Satan finds some mischief still for——' "

"Oh, my dear madam, hush! hush!" Mr. Sandbach's voice broke in; and my wife, naturally mortified by the interruption, said no more and moved away. I was surprised to see Rose immediately take her place, and, with more freedom than she generally displayed, run her fingers through the boy's tousled hair.

"Eustace! Eustace!" she said, hurriedly, "tell me everything—every single thing."

Slowly he sat up—till then he had lain on his back.

"Oh, Rose . . ." he whispered, and, my curiosity being aroused, I moved nearer to hear what he was going to say. As I did so I caught sight of some goats' footmarks in the moist earth beneath the trees.

"Apparently you have had a visit from some goats," I observed. "I had no idea they fed up here."

Eustace laboriously got on to his feet and came to see; and when he saw the footmarks he lay down and rolled on them, as a dog rolls in dirt.

After that there was a grave silence, broken at length by the solemn speech of Mr. Sandbach.

"My dear friends," he said, "it is best to confess the truth bravely. I know that what I am going to say now, is what you are all now feeling. The Evil One has been very near us in bodily form. Time may yet discover some injury that he has wrought among us. But, at present, for myself at all events, I wish to offer up thanks for a merciful deliverance."

With that he knelt down, and as the others knelt, I knelt too, though I do not believe in the Devil being allowed to assail us in visible form, as I told Mr. Sandbach afterwards. Eustace came, too, and knelt quietly enough between his aunts after they had beckoned to him. But when it was over he at once got up, and began hunting for something.

"Why! Someone has cut my whistle in two," he said. (I had seen Leyland with an open knife in his hand—a superstitious act which I could hardly approve.)

"Well, it doesn't matter," he continued.

"And why doesn't it matter?" said Mr. Sandbach, who has ever since tried to entrap Eustace into an account of that mysterious hour.

"Because I don't want it any more."

"Why?"

At that he smiled; and, as no one seemed to have anything more to say, I set off as fast as I could through the wood, and hauled up a donkey to carry my poor wife home. Nothing occurred in my absence, except that Rose had again asked Eustace to tell her what had happened; and he, this time, had turned away his head, and had not answered her a single word.

As soon as I returned, we all set off. Eustace walked with difficulty, almost with pain, so that, when we reached the other donkeys, his aunts wished him to mount one of them and ride all the way home. I make it a rule never to interfere between relatives, but I put my foot down at this. As it turned out, I was perfectly right, for the healthy exercise, I suppose, began to thaw Eustace's sluggish blood and loosen his stiffened muscles. He stepped out manfully, for the first time in his life, holding his head up and taking deep draughts of air into his chest. I observed with satisfaction to Miss Mary Robinson, that Eustace was at last taking some pride in his personal appearance.

Mr. Sandbach sighed, and said that Eustace must be carefully watched, for we none of us understood him yet. Miss Mary Robinson being very much—over-much, I think—guided by him, sighed, too.

"Come, come, Miss Robinson," I said, "there's nothing wrong with Eustace. Our experiences are mysterious, not his. He was astonished at our sudden departure, that's why he was so strange when we returned. He's right enough —improved, if anything."

"And is the worship of athletics, the cult of insensate activity, to be counted as an improvement?" put in Leyland, fixing a large, sorrowful eye on Eustace, who had stopped to scramble on to a rock to pick some cyclamen. "The passionate desire to rend from Nature the few beauties that have been still left her —that is to be counted as an improvement, too?"

It is mere waste of time to reply to such remarks, especially when they come from an unsuccessful artist, suffering from a damaged finger. I changed the conversation by asking what we should say at the hotel. After some discussion it was agreed that we should say nothing, either there or in our letters home. Importunate truth-telling, which brings only bewilderment and discomfort to the hearers, is, in my opinion, a mistake; and, after a long discussion, I managed to make Mr. Sandbach acquiesce in my view.

Eustace did not share in our conversation. He was racing about like a real boy, in the wood to the right. A strange feeling of shame prevented us from openly mentioning our fright to him. Indeed, it seemed almost reasonable

to conclude that it had made but little impression on him. So it disconcerted us when he bounded back with an armful of flowering acanthus, calling out:
"Do you suppose Gennaro'll be there when we get back?"

Gennaro was the stop-gap waiter, a clumsy, impertinent fisher-lad, who had been had up from Minori in the absence of the nice English-speaking Emmanuele. It was to him that we owed our scrappy lunch; and I could not conceive why Eustace desired to see him, unless it was to make mock with him of our behaviour.

"Yes, of course he will be there," said Miss Robinson. "Why do you ask, dear?"

"Oh, I thought I'd like to see him."

"And why?" snapped Mr. Sandbach.

"Because, because I do, I do; because, because I do." He danced away into the darkening wood to the rhythm of his words.

"This is very extraordinary," said Mr. Sandbach. "Did he like Gennaro before?"

"Gennaro has only been here two days," said Rose, "and I know that they haven't spoken to each other a dozen times."

Each time Eustace returned from the wood his spirits were higher. Once he came whooping down on us as a wild Indian, and another time he made believe to be a dog. The last time he came back with a poor dazed hare, too frightened to move, sitting on his arm. He was getting too uproarious, I thought; and we were all glad to leave the wood, and start upon the steep staircase path that leads down into Ravello. It was late and turning dark; and we made all the speed we could, Eustace scurrying in front of us like a goat.

Just where the staircase path debouches on the white high road the next extraordinary incident of this extraordinary day occurred. Three old women were standing by the wayside. They, like ourselves, had come down from the woods, and they were resting their heavy bundles of fuel on the low parapet of the road. Eustace stopped in front of them, and, after a moment's deliberation, stepped forward and—kissed the left-hand one on the cheek!

"My good fellow," exclaimed Mr. Sandbach, "are you quite crazy?"

Eustace said nothing, but offered the old woman some of his flowers, and then hurried on. I looked back; and the old woman's companions seemed as much astonished at the proceeding as we were. But she herself had put the flowers in her bosom, and was murmuring blessings.

This salutation of the old lady was the first example of Eustace's strange behaviour, and we were both surprised and alarmed. It was useless talking to him, for he either made silly replies, or else bounded away without replying at all.

He made no reference on the way home to Gennaro, and I hoped that that was forgotten. But, when we came to the Piazza, in front of the cathedral, he screamed out: "Gennaro! Gennaro!" at the top of his voice, and began running up the little alley that led to the hotel. Sure enough, there was Gennaro at the end of it, with his arms and legs sticking out of the nice little English-speaking waiter's dress suit, and a dirty fisherman's cap on his head—for, as the poor landlady truly said, however much she superintended his toilette, he always managed to introduce something incongruous into it before he had done.

Eustace sprang to meet him, and leapt right up into his arms, and put his own arms round his neck. And this in the presence, not only of us, but also of the landlady, the chambermaid, the facchino, and of two American ladies who were coming for a few days' visit to the little hotel.

I always make a point of behaving pleasantly to Italians, however little they may deserve it; but this habit of promiscuous intimacy was perfectly intolerable, and could only lead to familiarity and mortification for all. Taking Miss Robinson aside, I asked her permission to speak seriously to Eustace on the subject of intercourse with social inferiors. She granted it; but I determined to wait till the absurd boy had calmed down a little from the excitement of the day. Meanwhile, Gennaro, instead of attending to the wants of the two new ladies, carried Eustace into the house, as if it was the most natural thing in the world.

"Ho capito," I heard him say as he passed me. "Ho capito" is the Italian for "I have understood"; but, as Eustace had not spoken to him, I could not see the force of the remark. It served to increase our bewilderment, and, by the time we sat down at the dinner-table, our imaginations and our tongues were alike exhausted.

I omit from this account the various comments that were made, as few of them seem worthy of being recorded. But, for three or four hours, seven of us were pouring forth our bewilderment in a stream of appropriate and inappropriate exclamations. Some traced a connection between our behaviour in the afternoon and the behaviour of Eustace now. Others saw no connection at all. Mr. Sandbach still held to the possibility of infernal influences, and also said that he ought to have a doctor. Leyland only saw the development of "that unspeakable Philistine, the boy". Rose maintained, to my surprise, that everything was excusable; while I began to see that the young gentleman wanted a sound thrashing. The poor Miss Robinsons swayed helplessly about between these diverse opinions; inclining now to careful supervision, now to acquiescence, now to corporal chastisement, now to Eno's Fruit Salt.

Dinner passed off fairly well, though Eustace was terribly fidgety, Gennaro as usual dropping the knives and spoons, and jawking and clearing his throat. He only knew a few words of English, and we were all reduced to Italian for making known our wants. Eustace, who had picked up a little somehow, asked for some oranges. To my annoyance, Gennaro, in his answer, made use of the second person singular—a form only used when addressing those who are both intimates and equals. Eustace had brought it on himself; but an impertinence of this kind was an affront to us all, and I was determined to speak, and to speak at once.

When I heard him clearing the table, I went in, and, summoning up my Italian, or rather Neapolitan—the Southern dialects are execrable—I said: "Gennaro! I heard you address Signor Eustace with 'Tu'."

"It is true."

"You are not right. You must use 'Lei' or 'Voi'—more polite forms. And remember that, though Signor Eustace is sometimes silly and foolish—this afternoon, for example—yet you must always behave respectfully to him; for he is a young English gentleman, and you are a poor Italian fisher-boy."

I know that speech sounds terribly snobbish, but in Italian one can say things that one would never dream of saying in English. Besides, it is no good speaking delicately to persons of that class. Unless you put things plainly, they take a vicious pleasure in misunderstanding you.

An honest English fisherman would have landed me one in the eye in a minute for such a remark, but the wretched downtrodden Italians have no pride. Gennaro only sighed, and said: "It is true."

"Quite so," I said, and turned to go. To my indignation I heard him add: "But sometimes it is not important."

"What do you mean?" I shouted.

He came close up to me with horrid gesticulating fingers.

"Signor Tytler, I wish to say this. If Eustazio asks me to call him 'Voi', I will call him 'Voi'. Otherwise, no."

With that he seized up a tray of dinner-things and fled from the room with them; and I heard two more wine-glasses go on the courtyard floor.

I was now fairly angry, and strode out to interview Eustace. But he had gone to bed, and the landlady, to whom I also wished to speak, was engaged.

After more vague wonderings, obscurely expressed owing to the presence of Janet and the two American ladies, we all went to bed, too, after a harassing and most extraordinary day.

III

But the day was nothing to the night.

I suppose I had slept for about four hours, when I woke suddenly, thinking I heard a noise in the garden. And, immediately, before my eyes were open, cold, terrible fear seized me—not fear of something that was happening, like the fear in the wood, but fear of something that might happen.

Our room was on the first floor, looking out on to the garden—or terrace, it was rather: a wedge-shaped block of ground covered with roses and vines, and intersected with little asphalt paths. It was bounded on the small side by the house; round the two long sides ran a wall, only three feet above the terrace level, but with a good twenty feet drop over it into the olive yards, for the ground fell very precipitously away.

Trembling all over, I stole to the window. There, pattering up and down the asphalt paths, was something white. I was too much alarmed to see clearly; and in the uncertain light of the stars the thing took all manner of curious shapes. Now it was a great dog, now an enormous white bat, now a mass of quickly travelling cloud. It would bounce like a ball, or take short flights like a bird, or glide slowly like a wraith. It gave no sound—save the pattering sound of what, after all, must be human feet. And, at last, the obvious explanation forced itself upon my disordered mind; and I realized that Eustace had got out of bed, and that we were in for something more.

I hastily dressed myself and went down into the dining-room which opened upon the terrace. The door was already unfastened. My terror had almost entirely passed away, but for quite five minutes I struggled with a curious cowardly feeling, which bade me not interfere with the poor strange boy, but leave him to his ghostly patterings and merely watch him from the window, to see he took no harm.

But better impulses prevailed and, opening the door, I called out:

"Eustace! What on earth are you doing? Come in at once."

He stopped his antics and said: "I hate my bedroom. I could not stop in it, it is too small."

"Come! come! I'm tired of affectation. You've never complained of it before."

"Besides, I can't see anything—no flowers, no leaves, no sky: only a stone wall." The outlook of Eustace's room certainly was limited; but, as I told him, he had never complained of it before.

"Eustace, you talk like a child. Come in! Prompt obedience, if you please."

He did not move.

"Very well: I shall carry you in by force," I added, and made a few steps towards him. But I was soon convinced of the futility of pursuing a boy through a tangle of asphalt paths, and went in instead, to call Mr. Sandbach and Leyland to my aid.

When I returned with them he was worse than ever. He would not even answer us when we spoke, but began singing and chattering to himself in a most alarming way.

"It's a case for the doctor now," said Mr. Sandbach, gravely tapping his forehead.

He had stopped his running and was singing, first low, then loud—singing five-finger exercises, scales, hymn tunes, scraps of Wagner—anything that came into his head. His voice—a very untuneful voice—grew stronger and stronger, and he ended with a tremendous shout which boomed like a gun among the mountains, and awoke everyone who was still sleeping in the hotel. My poor wife and the two girls appeared at their respective windows, and the American ladies were heard violently ringing their bell.

"Eustace," we all cried, "stop! Stop, dear boy, and come into the house."

He shook his head and started off again—talking this time. Never have I listened to such an extraordinary speech. At any other time it would have been ludicrous, for here was a boy, with no sense of beauty and a puerile command of words, attempting to tackle themes which the greatest poets have found almost beyond their power. Eustace Robinson, aged fourteen, was standing in his nightshirt saluting, praising, and blessing, the great forces and manifestations of Nature.

He spoke first of night and the stars and planets above his head, of the swarms of fire-flies below him, of the invisible sea below the fire-flies, of the great rocks covered with anemones and shells that were slumbering in the invisible sea. He spoke of the rivers and waterfalls, of the ripening bunches of grapes, of the smoking cone of Vesuvius and the hidden fire-channels that made the smoke, of the myriads of lizards who were lying curled up in the crannies of the sultry earth, of the showers of white rose-leaves that were tangled in his hair. And then he spoke of the rain and the wind by which all things are changed, of the air through which all things live, and of the woods in which all things can be hidden.

Of course, it was all absurdly high-faluting: yet I could have kicked Leyland for audibly observing that it was "a diabolical caricature of all that was most holy and beautiful in life".

"And then"—Eustace was going on in the pitiable conversational doggerel which was his only mode of expression—"and then there are men, but I can't make them out so well." He knelt down by the parapet, and rested his head on his arms.

"Now's the time," whispered Leyland. I hate stealth, but we darted forward and endeavoured to catch hold of him from behind. He was away in a twinkling, but turned round at once to look at us. As far as I could see in the starlight he was crying. Leyland rushed at him again, and we tried to corner him among the asphalt paths, but without the slightest approach to success.

We returned, breathless and discomfited, leaving him to his madness in the farther corner of the terrace. But my Rose had an inspiration.

"Papa," she called from the window, "if you get Gennaro, he might be able to catch him for you."

I had no wish to ask a favour of Gennaro, but as the landlady had by now appeared on the scene I begged her to summon him from the charcoal-bin in which he slept, and make him try what he could do.

She soon returned, and was shortly followed by Gennaro, attired in a dress coat, without either waistcoat, shirt, or vest, and a ragged pair of what had been trousers, cut short above the knees for purposes of wading. The landlady, who had quite picked up English ways, rebuked him for the incongruous and even indecent appearance which he presented.

"I have a coat and I have trousers. What more do you desire?"

"Never mind, Signora Scafetti," I put in. "As there are no ladies here, it is not of the slightest consequence." Then, turning to Gennaro, I said: "The aunts of Signor Eustace wish you to fetch him into the house."

He did not answer.

"Do you hear me? He is not well. I order you to fetch him into the house."

"Fetch! Fetch!" said Signora Scafetti, and shook him roughly by the arm. "Eustazio is well where he is."

"Fetch! Fetch!" Signora Scafetti screamed, and let loose a flood of Italian, most of which, I am glad to say, I could not follow. I glanced up nervously at the girls' window, but they hardly knew as much as I do, and I am thankful to say that none of us caught one word of Gennaro's answer.

The two yelled and shouted at each other for quite ten minutes, at the end of which Gennaro rushed back to his charcoal-bin and Signora Scafetti burst into tears, as well she might, for she greatly valued her English guests.

"He says," she sobbed, "that Signor Eustace is well where he is, and that he will not fetch him. I can do no more."

But I could, for, in my stupid British way, I have got some insight into the Italian character. I followed Mr. Gennaro to his place of repose, and found him wriggling down on to a dirty sack.

"I wish you to fetch Signor Eustace to me," I began.

He hurled at me an unintelligible reply.

"If you fetch him, I will give you this." And out of my pocket I took a new ten-lira note.

This time he did not answer.

"This note is equal to ten lire in silver," I continued, for I knew that the poor-class Italian is unable to conceive of a single large sum.

"I know it."

"That is, two hundred soldi."

"I do not desire them. Eustazio is my friend."

I put the note into my pocket.

"Besides, you would not give it me."

"I am an Englishman. The English always do what they promise."

"That is true." It is astonishing how the most dishonest of nations trust us. Indeed, they often trust us more than we trust one another. Gennaro knelt up on his sack. It was too dark to see his face, but I could feel his warm garlicky breath coming out in gasps, and I knew that the eternal avarice of the South had laid hold upon him.

"I could not fetch Eustazio to the house. He might die there."

"You need not do that," I replied patiently. "You need only bring him to me; and I will stand outside in the garden." And to this, as if it were something quite different, the pitiable youth consented.

"But give me first the ten lire."

"No." For I knew the kind of person with whom I had to deal. Once faithless, always faithless.

We returned to the terrace, and Gennaro, without a single word, pattered off towards the pattering that could be heard at the remoter end. Mr. Sandbach, Leyland, and myself moved away a little from the house, and stood in the shadow of the white climbing roses, practically invisible.

We heard "Eustazio" called, followed by absurd cries of pleasure from the poor boy. The pattering ceased, and we heard them talking. Their voices got nearer, and presently I could discern them through the creepers, the grotesque figure of the young man, and the slim little white-robed boy. Gennaro had his arm round Eustace's neck, and Eustace was talking away in his fluent, slip-shod Italian.

"I understand almost everything," I heard him say. "The trees, hills, stars, water, I can see all. But isn't it odd! I can't make out men a bit. Do you know what I mean?"

"Ho capito," said Gennaro gravely, and took his arm off Eustace's shoulder. But I made the new note crackle in my pocket; and he heard it. He stuck his hand out with a jerk; and the unsuspecting Eustace gripped it in his own.

"It is odd!" Eustace went on—they were quite close now—"it almost seems as if—as if——"

I darted out and caught hold of his arm and Leyland got hold of the other arm, and Mr. Sandbach hung on to his feet. He gave shrill, heart-piercing screams; and the white roses, which were falling early that year, descended in showers on him as we dragged him into the house.

As soon as we entered the house he stopped shrieking; but floods of tears silently burst forth, and spread over his upturned face.

"Not to my room," he pleaded. "It is so small."

His infinitely dolorous look filled me with strange pity, but what could I do? Besides, his window was the only one that had bars to it.

"Never mind, dear boy," said kind Mr. Sandbach. "I will bear you company till the morning."

At this his convulsive struggles began again.

"Oh, please, not that. Anything but that. I will promise to lie still and not to cry more than I can help, if I am left alone."

So we laid him on the bed, and drew the sheets over him, and left him sobbing bitterly, and saying: "I nearly saw everything, and now I can see nothing at all."

We informed the Miss Robinsons of all that had happened, and returned to the dining-room, where we found Signora Scafetti and Gennaro whispering together. Mr. Sandbach got pen and paper, and began writing to the English doctor at Naples. I at once drew out the note and flung it down on the table to Gennaro.

"Here is your pay," I said sternly, for I was thinking of the Thirty Pieces of Silver.

"Thank you very much, sir," said Gennaro, and grabbed it.

He was going off, when Leyland, whose interest and indifference were always equally misplaced, asked him what Eustace had meant by saying "he could not make out men a bit".

"I cannot say. Signor Eustazio" (I was glad to observe a little deference at last) "has a subtle brain. He understands many things."

"But I heard you say you understood," Leyland persisted.

"I understand, but I cannot explain. I am a poor Italian fisher-lad. Yet, listen: I will try." I saw to my alarm that his manner was changing, and tried to stop him. But he sat down on the edge of the table and started off, with some absolutely incoherent remarks.

"It is sad," he observed at last. "What has happened is very sad. But what can I do? I am poor. It is not I."

I turned away in contempt. Leyland went on asking questions. He wanted to know who it was that Eustace had in his mind when he spoke.

"That is easy to say," Gennaro gravely answered. "It is you, it is I. It is all in this house, and many outside it. If he wishes for mirth, we discomfort him. If he asks to be alone, we disturb him. He longed for a friend, and found none for fifteen years. Then he found me, and the first night I—I who have been in the woods and understood things too—betray him to you, and send him in to die. But what could I do?"

"Gently gently," said I.

"Oh, assuredly he will die. He will lie in the small room all night, and in the morning he will be dead. That I know for certain."

"There, that will do," said Mr. Sandbach. "I shall be sitting with him."

"Filomena Giusti sat all night with Caterina, but Caterina was dead in the morning. They would not let her out, though I begged, and prayed, and cursed, and beat the door, and climbed the wall. They were ignorant fools, and thought I wished to carry her away. And in the morning she was dead."

"What is all this?" I asked Signora Scafetti.

"All kinds of stories will get about," she replied, "and he, least of anyone, has reason to repeat them."

"And I am alive now," he went on, "because I had neither parents nor relatives, nor friends, so that, when the first night came I could run through the woods, and climb the rocks, and plunge into the water until I had accomplished my desire!"

We heard a cry from Eustace's room—a faint but steady sound, like the sound of wind in a distant wood heard by one standing in tranquillity.

"That," said Gennaro, "was the last noise of Caterina. I was hanging on to her window then, and it blew out past me."

And, lifting up his hand, in which my ten-lira note was safely packed, he solemnly cursed Mr. Sandbach, and Leyland, and myself, and Fate because Eustace was dying in the upstairs room. Such is the working of the Southern mind; and I verily believe that he would not have moved even then, had not Leyland, that unspeakable idiot, upset the lamp with his elbow. It was a patent self-extinguishing lamp, bought by Signora Scafetti, at my special request, to replace the dangerous thing that she was using. The result was, that it went out; and the mere physical change from light to darkness had more power over the ignorant animal nature of Gennaro than the most obvious dictates of logic and reason.

I felt, rather than saw, that he had left the room and shouted out to Mr. Sandbach: "Have you got the key of Eustace's room in your pocket?" But Mr. Sandbach and Leyland were both on the floor, having mistaken each other for Gennaro, and some more precious time was wasted in finding a match. Mr. Sandbach had only just time to say that he had left the key in the door, in case the Miss Robinsons wished to pay Eustace a visit, when we heard a noise on the stairs, and there was Gennaro, carrying Eustace down.

We rushed out and blocked up the passage, and they lost heart and retreated to the upper landing.

"Now they are caught," cried Signora Scafetti. "There is no other way out."

We were cautiously ascending the staircase, when there was a terrific scream from my wife's room, followed by a heavy thud on the asphalt path. They had leapt out of her window.

I reached the terrace just in time to see Eustace jumping over the parapet of the garden wall. This time I knew for certain he would be killed. But he alighted in an olive tree, looking like a great white moth, and from the tree he slid on to the earth. And as soon as his bare feet touched the clods of earth he uttered a strange loud cry, such as I should not have thought the human voice could have produced, and disappeared among the trees below.

"He has understood and he is saved," cried Gennaro, who was still sitting on the asphalt path. "Now, instead of dying he will live!"

"And you, instead of keeping the ten lire, will give them up," I retorted, for at this theatrical remark I could contain myself no longer.

"The ten lire are mine," he hissed back, in a scarcely audible voice. He clasped his hand over his breast to protect his ill-gotten gains, and, as he did so, he swayed forward and fell upon his face on the path. He had not broken any limbs, and a leap like that would never have killed an Englishman, for the drop was not great. But those miserable Italians have no stamina. Something had gone wrong inside him, and he was dead.

The morning was still far off, but the morning breeze had begun, and more rose leaves fell on us as we carried him in. Signora Scafetti burst into screams at the sight of the dead body, and, far down the valley towards the sea, there still resounded the shouts and the laughter of the escaping boy.

THE QUAINT

"OH, WHISTLE, AND I'LL COME TO YOU, MY LAD"

By M. R. James

"I SUPPOSE you will be getting away pretty soon, now Full term is over, Professor," said a person not in the story to the Professor of Ontography, soon after they had sat down next to each other at a feast in the hospitable hall of St. James's College.

The Professor was young, neat, and precise in speech.

"Yes," he said; "my friends have been making me take up golf this term, and I mean to go to the East Coast—in point of fact, to Burnstow (I dare say you know it) for a week or ten days, to improve my game. I hope to get off tomorrow."

"Oh, Parkins," said his neighbour on the other side, "if you are going to Burnstow I wish you would look at the site of the Templars' preceptory, and let me know if you think it would be any good to have a dig there in the summer."

It was, as you might suppose, a person of antiquarian pursuits who said this, but, since he merely appears in this prologue, there is no need to give his entitlements.

"Certainly," said Parkins, the Professor; "if you will describe to me whereabouts the site is I will do my best to give you an idea of the lie of the land when I get back; or I could write to you about it, if you would tell me where you are likely to be."

"Don't trouble to do that, thanks. It's only that I'm thinking of taking my family in that direction in the Long, and it occurred to me that, as very few of the English preceptories have ever been properly planned, I might have an opportunity of doing something useful on off days."

The Professor rather sniffed at the idea that planning out a preceptory could be described as useful. His neighbour continued:

"The site—I doubt if there is anything showing above ground—must be down quite close to the beach now. The sea has encroached tremendously, as you know, all along that bit of coast. I should think, from the map, that it must be about three-quarters of a mile from the Globe Inn, at the north end of the town. Where are you going to stay?"

"Well, *at* the Globe Inn, as a matter of fact," said Parkins; "I have engaged a room there. I couldn't get in anywhere else; most of the lodging-houses are shut up in winter, it seems; and, as it is, they tell me that the only room of any size I can have is really a double-bedded one, and that they haven't a corner in which to store the other bed, and so on. But I must have a fairly large room for I am taking some books down, and mean to do a bit of work; and though I don't quite fancy having an empty bed—not to speak of two—in what I may call for the time being my study, I suppose I can manage to rough it for the short time I shall be there."

"Do you call having an extra bed in your room roughing it, Parkins?" said a bluff person opposite. "Look here, I shall come down and occupy it for a bit; it'll be company for you."

The Professor quivered, but managed to laugh in a courteous manner.

"By all means, Rogers; there's nothing I should like better. But I'm afraid you would find it rather dull; you don't play golf, do you?"

"No, thank Heaven!" said rude Mr. Rogers.

"Well, you see, when I'm not writing I shall most likely be out on the links, and that, as I say, would be rather dull for you, I'm afraid."

"Oh, I don't know! There's certain to be somebody I know in the place; but, of course, if you don't want me, speak the word, Parkins; I shan't be offended. Truth, as you always tell us, is never offensive."

Parkins was, indeed, scrupulously polite and strictly truthful. It is to be feared that Mr. Rogers sometimes practised upon his knowledge of these characteristics. In Parkins's breast there was a conflict now raging, which for a moment or two did not allow him to answer. That interval being over, he said:

"Well, if you want the exact truth, Rogers, I was considering whether the room I speak of would really be large enough to accommodate us both comfortably; and also whether (mind, I shouldn't have said this if you hadn't pressed me) you would not constitute something in the nature of a hindrance to my work."

Rogers laughed loudly.

"Well done, Parkins!" he said. "It's all right. I promise not to interrupt your work; don't you disturb yourself about that. No, I won't come if you don't want me; but I thought I should do so nicely to keep the ghosts off." Here he might have been seen to wink and to nudge his next neighbour. Parkins might also have been seen to become pink. "I beg pardon, Parkins," Rogers continued; "I oughtn't to have said that. I forgot you didn't like levity on these topics."

"Well," Parkins said, "as you have mentioned the matter, I freely own that I do *not* like careless talk about what you call ghosts. A man in my position," he went on, raising his voice a little, "cannot, I find, be too careful about appearing to sanction the current beliefs on such subjects. As you know, Rogers, or as you ought to know—for I think I have never concealed my views——"

"No, you certainly have not, old man," put in Rogers *sotto voce*.

"——I hold that any semblance, any appearance of concession to the view that such things might exist is equivalent to a renunciation of all that I told most sacred. But I'm afraid I have not succeeded in securing your attention."

"Your *undivided* attention, was what Dr. Blimber actually *said*,"* Rogers interrupted, with every appearance of an earnest desire for accuracy. "But I beg your pardon, Parkins: I'm stopping you."

"No, not at all," said Parkins. "I don't remember Blimber; perhaps he was before my time. But I needn't go on. I'm sure you know what I mean."

"Yes, yes," said Rogers, rather hastily, "just so. We'll go into it fully at Burnstow, or somewhere."

In repeating the above dialogue I have tried to give the impression which it made on me, that Parkins was something of an old woman—rather hen-like, perhaps, in his little ways; totally destitute, alas! of the sense of humour, but at the same time dauntless and sincere in his convictions, and a man deserving of the greatest respect. Whether or not the reader has gathered so much, that was the character which Parkins had.

On the following day Parkins did, as he had hoped, succeed in getting away from his college, and in arriving at Burnstow. He was made welcome at the Globe Inn, was safely installed in the large double-bedded room of which we have heard, and was able, before retiring to rest, to arrange his materials for work in apple-pie order upon a commodious table which occupied the outer end of the room, and was surrounded on three sides by windows looking out seaward; that is to say, the central window looked straight out to sea, and those on the left and right commanded prospects along the shore to the north and south respectively. On the south you saw the village of Burnstow. On the north no houses were to be seen, but only the beach and the low cliff backing it.

---

* Mr. Rogers was wrong, vide *Dombey and Son*, chapter xii.

Immediately in front was a strip—not considerable—of rough grass, dotted with old anchors, capstans, and so forth; then a broad path; then the beach. Whatever may have been the original distance between the Globe Inn and the sea, not more than sixty yards now separated them.

The rest of the population of the inn was, of course, a golfing one, and included few elements that call for a special description. The most conspicuous figure was, perhaps, that of an *ancien militaire*, secretary of a London club, and possessed of a voice of incredible strength, and of views of a pronouncedly Protestant type. These were apt to find utterance after his attendance upon the ministrations of the Vicar, an estimable man with inclinations towards a picturesque ritual, which he gallantly kept down as far as he could out of deference to East Anglian tradition.

Professor Parkins, one of whose principal characteristics was pluck, spent the greater part of the day following his arrival at Burnstow in what he had called improving his game, in company with this Colonel Wilson: and during the afternoon—whether the process of improvement were to blame or not, I am not sure—the Colonel's demeanour assumed a colouring so lurid that even Parkins jibbed at the thought of walking home with him from the links. He determined, after a short and furtive look at that bristling moustache and those incarnadined features, that it would be wiser to allow the influence of tea and tobacco to do what they could with the Colonel before the dinner hour should render a meeting inevitable.

"I might walk home tonight along the beach," he reflected, "yes, and take a look—there will be light enough for that—at the ruins of which Disney was talking. I don't exactly know where they are, by the way; but I expect I can hardly help stumbling on them."

This he accomplished, I may say, in the most literal sense, for, in picking his way from the links to the shingle beach, his foot caught partly in a gorse-root and partly in a biggish stone, and over he went. When he got up and surveyed his surroundings, he found himself in a patch of somewhat broken ground, covered with small depressions and mounds. These latter, when he came to examine them, proved to be simply masses of flints embedded in mortar and grown over with turf. He must, he quite rightly concluded, be on the site of the preceptory he had promised to look at. It seemed not unlikely to reward the spade of the explorer; enough of the foundations was probably left at no great depth to throw a good deal of light on the general plan. He remembered vaguely that the Templars, to whom this site had belonged, were in the habit of building round churches, and he thought a particular series of the humps or mounds near him did appear to be arranged in something of a circular form. Few people can resist the temptation to try a little amateur research in a department quite outside their own, if only for the satisfaction of showing how successful they would have been had they only taken it up seriously. Our Professor, however, if he felt something of this mean desire, was also truly anxious to oblige Mr. Disney. So he paced with care the circular area he had noticed, and wrote down its rough dimensions in his pocket-book. Then he proceeded to examine an oblong eminence which lay east of the centre of the circle, and seemed to his thinking likely to be the base of a platform or altar. At one end of it, the northern, a patch of the turf was gone—removed by some boy or other creature *ferae naturae*. "It might," he thought, "be as well to probe the soil here for evidence of masonry," and he took out his knife and began scraping away the earth. And now followed another little discovery: a portion of soil fell inward as he scraped, and disclosed a small cavity. He lighted one match after another to help him to see of what nature the hole was, but the wind was too strong for them all. By tapping and scratching the sides with his knife, however, he was able to make out that it must be an artificial hole in masonry. It was rectangular, and the sides, top, and bottom, if not actually plastered, were smooth and regular. Of course it was empty. No! As he withdrew the knife he heard a metallic clink, and when he introduced his hand it met with a cylindrical object lying on the floor of the hole. Naturally enough, he picked it up, and when he brought it into the light, now fast fading, he could see that it, too, was of man's making—a metal tube about four inches long, and evidently of some considerable age.

By the time Parkins had made sure that there was nothing else in this odd receptacle, it was too late and too dark for him to think of undertaking any further search. What he had done had proved so unexpectedly interesting that he determined to sacrifice a little more of the daylight on the morrow to archaeology. The object which he now had safe in his pocket was bound to be of some slight value at least, he felt sure.

Bleak and solemn was the view on which he took a last look before starting homeward. A faint yellow light in the west showed the links, on which a few figures moving towards the club-house were still visible, the squat martello tower, the lights of Aldsey village, the pale ribbon of sands intersected at intervals by black wooden groynes, the dim and murmuring sea. The wind was bitter from the north, but was at his back when he set out for the "Globe". He quickly rattled and clashed through the shingle and gained the sand, upon which but for the groynes which had to be got over every few yards, the going was both good and quiet. One last look behind, to measure the distance he had made since leaving the ruined Templars' church, showed him a prospect of company on his walk, in the shape of a rather indistinct personage, who seemed to be making great efforts to catch up with him, but made little, if any, progress. I mean that there was an appearance of running about his movements, but that the distance between him and Parkins did not seem materially to lessen. So, at least, Parkins thought, and decided that he almost certainly did not know him, and that it would be absurd to wait until he came up. For all that, company, he began to think, would really be very welcome on that lonely shore, if only you could choose your companion. In his unenlightened days he had read of meetings in such places which even now would hardly bear thinking of. He went on thinking of them, however, until he reached home, and particularly of one which catches most people's fancy at some time of their childhood. "Now I saw in my dream that Christian had gone but a very little way when he saw a foul fiend coming over the field to meet him." "What should I do now," he thought, "if I looked back and caught sight of a black figure sharply defined against the yellow sky, and saw that it had horns and wings? I wonder whether I should stand or run for it. Luckily, the gentleman behind is not of that kind, and he seems to be about as far off now as when I saw him first. Well, at this rate he won't get his dinner as soon as I shall; and, dear me!—it's within a quarter of an hour of the time now. I must run!"

Parkins had, in fact, very little time for dressing. When he met the Colonel at dinner, Peace—or as much of her as that gentleman could manage—reigned once more in the military bosom; nor was she put to flight in the hours of bridge that followed dinner, for Parkins was a more than respectable player. When, therefore, he retired towards twelve o'clock, he felt that he had spent his evening in quite a satisfactory way, and that, even for so long as a fortnight or three weeks, life at the "Globe" would be supportable under similar conditions— "especially", thought he, "if I go on improving my game."

As he went along the passages he met the boots of the "Globe", who stopped and said:

"Bet your pardon, sir, but as I was a-brushing your coat just now there was somethink fell out of the pocket. I put it on your chest of drawers, sir, in your room, sir—a piece of a pipe or something of that, sir. Thank you, sir. You'll find it on your chest of drawers, sir—yes, sir. Good night, sir."

The speech served to remind Parkins of his little discovery of that afternoon.

It was with some considerable curiosity that he turned it over by the light of his candles. It was of bronze, he now saw, and was shaped very much after the manner of the modern dog-whistle; in fact it was—yes, certainly it was—actually no more nor less than a whistle. He put it to his lips, but it was quite full of a fine, caked-up sand or earth, which would not yield to knocking, but must be loosened with a knife. Tidy as ever in his habits, Parkins cleared out the earth on to a piece of paper, and took the latter to the window to empty it out. The night was clear and bright, as he saw when he had opened the casement, and he stopped for an instant to look at the sea and note a belated wanderer stationed on the shore in front of the inn. Then he shut the window, a little surprised at the late hours people kept at Burnstow, and took his whistle to the light again. Why, surely there were marks on it, and not merely marks, but letters! A very little rubbing rendered the deeply-cut inscription quite legible, but the Professor had to confess, after some earnest thought, that the meaning of it was as obscure to him as the writing on the wall to Belshazzar. There were legends both on the front and on the back of the whistle. The one read thus:

FLA
FUR   BIS
FLE

The other:

卐   QUIS EST ISTE QUI VENIT   卐

"I ought to be able to make it out," he thought; "but I suppose I am a little rusty in my Latin. When I come to think of it I don't believe I even know the word for a whistle. The long one does seem simple enough. It ought to mean 'Who is this who is coming?' Well, the best way to find out is evidently to whistle for him."

He blew tentatively and stopped suddenly, startled and yet pleased at the note he had elicited. It had a quality of infinite distance in it, and, soft as it was, he somehow felt it must be audible for miles round. It was a sound, too, that seemed to have the power (which many scents possess) of forming pictures in the brain. He saw quite clearly for a moment a vision of a wide, dark expanse at night, with a fresh wind blowing, and in the midst a lonely figure, how employed he could not tell. Perhaps he would have seen more had not the picture been broken by the sudden surge of a gust of wind against his casement, so sudden that it made him look up, just in time to see the white glint of a sea-bird's wing somewhere outside the dark panes.

The sound of the whistle had so fascinated him that he could not help trying it once more, this time more boldly. The note was little, if at all, louder than before, and repetition broke the illusion—no picture followed, as he had half hoped it might. "But what is this? Goodness! What force the wind can get up in a few minutes! What a tremendous gust! There! I knew that window-fastening was no use! Ah! I thought so—both candles out. It's enough to tear the room to pieces."

The first thing was to get the window shut. While you might count twenty, Parkins was struggling with the small casement, and felt almost as if he were pushing back a sturdy burglar, so strong was the pressure. It slackened all at once, and the window banged to and latched itself. Now to relight the candles and see what damage, if any, had been done. No, nothing seemed amiss; no glass even was broken in the casement. But the noise had evidently roused at least one member of the household: the Colonel was to be heard stumping in his stockinged-feet on the floor above, and growling.

Quickly as it had risen, the wind did not fall at once. On it went, moaning and rushing past the house, at times rising to a cry so desolate that, as Parkins disinterestedly said, it might have made fanciful people feel quite uncomfortable; even the unimaginative, he thought after a quarter of an hour, might be happier without it.

Whether it was the wind, or the excitement of golf, or of the researches in the preceptory that kept Parkins awake, he was not sure. Awake he remained, in any case, long enough to fancy (as I am afraid I often do myself under such conditions) that he was the victim of all manner of fatal disorders: he would lie counting the beats of his heart, convinced that it was going to stop work every moment, and would entertain grave suspicions of his lungs, brain, liver, etc.—suspicions which he was sure would be dispelled by the return of daylight, but which, until then, refused to be put aside. He found a little vicarious comfort in the idea that someone else was in the same boat. A near neighbour (in the darkness it was not easy to tell his direction) was tossing and rustling in his bed, too.

The next stage was that Parkins shut his eyes and determined to give sleep every chance. Here again over-excitement asserted itself in another form—that of making pictures. *Experto crede*, pictures do come to the closed eyes of one trying to sleep, and are often so little to his taste that he must open his eyes and disperse them.

Parkins's experience on this occasion was a very distressing one. He found that the picture which presented itself to him was continuous. When he opened his eyes, of course, it went; but when he shut them once more it framed itself afresh, and acted itself out again, neither quicker nor slower than before. What he saw was this:

A long stretch of shore—shingle edged by sand, and intersected at short intervals with black groynes running down to the water—a scene, in fact, so like that of his afternoon's walk that, in the absence of any landmark, it could not be distinguished therefrom. The light was obscure, conveying an impression of gathering storm, late winter evening, and slight cold rain. On this bleak stage at first no actor was visible. Then, in the distance, a bobbing black object appeared; a moment more, and it was a man running, jumping, clambering over the groynes, and every few seconds looking eagerly back. The nearer he came the more obvious it was that he was not only anxious, but even terribly frightened, though his face was not to be distinguished. He was, moreover, almost at the end of his strength. On he came; each successive obstacle seemed to cause him more difficulty than the last. "Will he get over this next one?" thought Parkins; "it seems a little higher than the others." Yes; half climbing, half throwing himself, he did get over, and fell all in a heap on the other side (the side nearest to the spectator). There, as if really unable to get up again, he remained crouching under the groyne, looking up in an attitude of painful anxiety.

So far no cause whatever for the fear of the runner had been shown; but now here began to be seen, far up the shore, a little flicker of something light coloured moving to and fro with great swiftness and irregularity. Rapidly growing larger, it, too, declared itself as a figure in pale, fluttering draperies, ill-defined. There was something about its motion which made Parkins very unwilling to see it at close quarters. It would stop, raise arms, bow itself towards the sand, then run stooping across the beach to the water-edge and back again; and then, rising upright, once more continue its course forward at a speed that was startling and terrifying. The moment came when the pursuer was hovering about from left to right only a few yards beyond the groyne where the runner lay in hiding. After two or three ineffectual castings hither and thither it came to a stop, stood upright, with arms raised high, and then darted straight forward towards the groyne.

It was at this point that Parkins always failed in his resolution to keep his eyes shut. With many misgivings as to incipient failure of eyesight, over-worked brain, excessive smoking, and so on, he finally resigned himself to light his candle, get out a book and pass the night waking, rather than be tormented by this persistent panorama, which he saw clearly enough could only be a morbid reflection of his walk and his thoughts on that very day.

The scraping of match on box and the glare of light must have startled some creatures of the night—rats or what not—which he heard scurry across the floor from the side of his bed with much rustling. Dear, dear! the match is out! Fool that it is! But the second one burnt better, and a candle and book were duly procured, over which Parkins pored till sleep of a wholesome kind came upon him, and that in no long space. For about the first time in his orderly and prudent life he forgot to blow out the candle, and when he was called next morning at eight there was still a flicker in the socket and a sad mess of guttered grease on the top of the little table.

After breakfast he was in his room, putting the finishing touches to his golfing costume—fortune had again allotted the Colonel to him for a partner—when one of the maids came in.

"Oh, if you please," she said, "would you like any extra blankets on your bed, sir?"

"Ah! thank you," said Parkins. "Yes, I think I should like one. It seems likely to turn rather colder."

In a very short time the maid was back with the blanket.

"Which bed should I put it on, sir?" she asked.

"What? Why, that one—the one I slept in last night," he said, pointing to it.

"Oh yes! I beg your pardon, sir, but you seemed to have tried both of 'em; leastways, we had to make 'em both up this morning."

"Really? How very absurd!" said Parkins. "I certainly never touched the other, except to lay some things on it. Did it actually seem to have been slept in?"

"Oh yes, sir!" said the maid. "Why, all the things was crumpled and throwed about all ways, if you'll excuse me, sir—quite as if anyone 'adn't passed but a very poor night, sir."

"Dear me," said Parkins. "Well, I may have disordered it more than I thought when I unpacked my things. I'm very sorry to have given you the extra trouble, I'm sure. I expect a friend of mine soon, by the way—a gentleman from Cambridge—to come and occupy it for a night or two. That will be all right, I suppose, won't it?"

"Oh yes, to be sure, sir. Thank you, sir. It's no trouble, I'm sure," said the maid, and departed to giggle with her colleagues.

Parkins set forth with a stern determination to improve his game.

I am glad to be able to report that he succeeded so far in this enterprize that the Colonel, who had been rather repining at the prospect of a second day's play in his company, became quite chatty as the morning advanced; and his voice boomed out over the flats, as certain also of our own minor poets have said, "like some great bourdon in a minster tower".

"Extraordinary wind that we had last night," he said. "In my old home we should have said someone had been whistling for it."

"Should you, indeed!" said Parkins. "Is there a superstition of that kind still current in your part of the country?"

"I don't know about superstition," said the Colonel. "They believe in it all over Denmark and Norway, as well as on the Yorkshire coast; and my experience is, mind you, that there's generally something at the bottom of what these country-folk hold to, and have held to, for generations. But it's your drive," (or whatever it might have been: the golfing reader will have to imagine appropriate digressions at the proper intervals).

When conversation was resumed, Parkins said, with a slight hesitancy:

"Apropos of what you were saying just now, Colonel, I think I ought to tell you that my own views on such subjects are very strong. I am, in fact, a convinced disbeliever in what is called the 'supernatural'."

"What!" said the Colonel. "Do you mean to tell me you don't believe in second sight, or ghosts, or anything of that kind?"

"In nothing whatever of that kind," returned Parkins firmly.

"Well," said the Colonel, "but it appears to me at that rate, sir, that you must be little better than a Sadducee."

Parkins was on the point of answering that, in his opinion, the Sadducees were the most sensible persons he had ever read of in the Old Testament; but feeling some doubt as to whether much mention of them was to be found in that work, he preferred to laugh the accusation off.

"Perhaps I am," he said: "but—— Here, give me my cleek, boy! Excuse me one moment, Colonel." A short interval. "Now, as to whistling for the wind, let me give you my theory about it. The laws which govern winds are really not at all perfectly known—to fisher-folk and such, of course, not known at all. A man or woman of eccentric habits, perhaps, or a stranger, is seen repeatedly on the beach at some unusual hour, and is heard whistling. Soon afterwards a violent wind rises; a man who could read the sky perfectly or who possessed a barometer could have foretold that it would. The simple people of a fishing village have no barometers, and only a few rough rules for prophesying weather. What more natural than that the eccentric personage I postulated should be regarded as having raised the wind, or that he or she should clutch eagerly at the reputation of being able to do so? Now, take last night's wind: as it happens, I myself was whistling. I blew a whistle twice, and the wind seemed to come absolutely in answer to my call. If anyone had seen me . . ."

The audience had been a little restive under this harangue, and Parkins had, I fear, fallen somewhat into the tone of a lecturer; but at the last sentence the Colonel stopped.

"Whistling, were you," he said. "And what sort of whistle did you use? Play this stroke first." Interval.

"About that whistle you were asking, Colonel. It's rather a curious one. I have it in my—— No; I see I've left it in my room. As a matter of fact, I found it yesterday."

And then Parkins narrated the manner of his discovery of the whistle, upon hearing which the Colonel grunted, and opined that, in Parkins's place, he should himself be careful about using a thing that had belonged to a set of Papists, of whom, speaking generally, it might be affirmed that you never knew what they might not have been up to. From this topic he diverged to the enormities of the Vicar, who had given notice on the previous Sunday that Friday would be the Feast of St. Thomas the Apostle, and that there would be service at eleven o'clock in the church. This and other similar proceedings constituted in the Colonel's view a strong presumption that the Vicar was a concealed Papist, if not a Jesuit; and Parkins, who could not very readily follow the Colonel in this region, did not disagree with him. In fact, they got on so well together in the morning that there was no talk on either side of their separating after lunch.

Both continued to play well during the afternoon, or, at least, well enough to make them forget everything else until the light began to fail them. Not until then did Parkins remember that he had meant to do some more investigating at the preceptory; but it was of no great importance, he reflected. One day was as good as another; he might as well go home with the Colonel.

As they turned the corner of the house, the Colonel was almost knocked down by a boy who rushed into him at the very top of his speed, and then, instead of running away, remained hanging on to him and panting. The first words of the warrior were naturally those of reproof and objurgation, but he very quickly discerned that the boy was almost speechless with fright. Inquiries were useless at first. When the boy got his breath he began to howl, and still clung to the Colonel's legs. He was at last detached, but continued to howl.

"What in the world *is* the matter with you? What have you been up to? What have you seen?" said the two men.

"Ow, I seen it wive at me out of the winder," wailed the boy, "and I don't like it."

"What window?" said the irritated Colonel. "Come, pull yourself together, my boy."

"The front winder it was, at the 'otel," said the boy.

At this point Parkins was in favour of sending the boy home, but the Colonel refused; he wanted to get to the bottom of it, he said; it was most dangerous to give a boy such a fright as this one had had, and if it turned out that people had been playing jokes, they should suffer for it in some way. And by a series of questions he made out this story: the boy had been playing about on the grass in front of the "Globe" with some others; then they had gone home to their teas, and he was just going, when he happened to look at up the front window and see it a-wiving at him. *It* seemed to be a figure of some sort, in white as far as he knew—couldn't see its face; but it wived at him, and it warn't a right thing —not to say not a right person. Was there a light in the room? No, he didn't think to look if there was a light. Which was the window? Was it the top one or the second one? The seckind one it was—the big winder what got two little uns at the sides.

"Very well, my boy," said the Colonel, after a few more questions. "You run away home now. I expect it was some person trying to give you a start. Another time, like a brave English boy, you just throw a stone—well, no, not that exactly, but you go and speak to the waiter, or to Mr. Simpson, the landlord, and—yes—and say that I advised you to do so."

The boy's face expressed some of the doubt he felt as to the likelihood of Mr. Simpson's lending a favourable ear to his complaint; but the Colonel did not appear to perceive this, and went on:

"And here's a sixpence—no, I see it's a shilling—and you be off home, and don't think any more about it."

The youth hurried off with agitated thanks, and the Colonel and Parkins went round to the front of the "Globe" and reconnoitred. There was only one window answering to the description they had been hearing.

"Well, that's curious," said Parkins; "it's evidently my window the lad was talking about. Will you come up for a moment, Colonel Wilson? We ought to be able to see if anyone has been taking liberties in my room."

They were soon in the passage, and Parkins made as if to open the door. Then he stopped and felt in his pockets.

"This is more serious than I thought," was his next remark. "I remember now that before I started this morning I locked the door. It is locked now, and, what is more, here is the key." And he held it up. "Now," he went on, "if the servants are in the habit of going into one's room during the day when one is away, I can only say that—well, that I don't approve of it at all." Conscious of a somewhat weak climax, he busied himself in opening the door (which was, indeed, locked) and in lighting candles. "No," he said, "nothing seems disturbed."

"Except your bed," put in the Colonel.

"Excuse me, that isn't my bed," said Parkins. "I don't use that one. But it does look as if someone had been playing tricks with it."

It certainly did: the clothes were bundled up and twisted together in a most tortuous confusion. Parkins pondered.

"That must be it," he said at last. "I disordered the clothes last night in unpacking, and they haven't made it since. Perhaps they came in to make it, and that boy saw them through the window; and then they were called away and locked the door after them. Yes, I think that must be it."

"Well, ring and ask," said the Colonel, and this appealed to Parkins as practical.

The maid appeared, and, to make a long story short, deposed that she had made the bed in the morning when the gentleman was in the room, and hadn't been there since. No, she hadn't no other key. Mr. Simpson, he kep' the keys; he'd be able to tell the gentleman if anyone had been up.

This was a puzzle. Investigation showed that nothing of value had been taken, and Parkins remembered the disposition of the small objects on tables and so forth well enough to be pretty sure that no pranks had been played with them. Mr. and Mrs. Simpson furthermore agreed that neither of them had given the duplicate key of the room to any person whatever during the day. Nor could Parkins, fair-minded man as he was, detect anything in the demeanour of master, mistress, or maid that indicated guilt. He was much more inclined to think that the boy had been imposing on the Colonel.

The latter was unwontedly silent and pensive at dinner and throughout the evening. When he bade good night to Parkins, he murmured in a gruff undertone:

"You know where I am if you want me during the night."

"Why, yes, thank you Colonel Wilson, I think I do: but there isn't much prospect of my disturbing you, I hope. By the way," he added, "did I show you that old whistle I spoke of? I think not. Well, here it is."

The Colonel turned it over gingerly in the light of the candle.

"Can you make anything of the inscription?" asked Parkins, as he took it back.

"No, not in this light. What do you mean to do with it?"

"Oh, well, when I get back to Cambridge I shall submit it to some of the archaeologists there, and see what they think of it; and, very likely, if they consider it worth having, I may present it to one of the museums."

" 'M !" said the Colonel. "Well, you may be right. All I know is that, if it were mine, I should chuck it straight into the sea. It's no use talking, I'm well aware, but I expect that with you it's a case of live and learn. I hope so, I'm sure, and I wish you a good night."

He turned away, leaving Parkins in fact to speak at the bottom of the stair, and soon each was in his own bedroom.

By some unfortunate accident there were neither blinds nor curtains to the windows of the Professor's room. The previous night he had thought little of this, but tonight there seemed every prospect of a bright moon rising to shine directly on his bed, and probably wake him later on. When he noticed this he was a good deal annoyed, but, with an ingenuity which I can only envy, he succeeded in rigging up, with the help of a railway rug, some safety-pins, and a stick and umbrella, a screen which, if it only held together, would completely keep the moonlight off his bed. And shortly afterwards he was comfortably in that bed. When he had read a somewhat solid work long enough to produce a decided wish for sleep, he cast a drowsy glance round the room, blew out the candle, and fell back upon the pillow.

He must have slept soundly for an hour or more, when a sudden clatter shook him up in a most unwelcome manner. In a moment he realized what had happened: his carefully-constructed screen had given way, and a very bright frosty moon was shining directly on his face. This was highly annoying. Could he possibly get up and reconstruct the screen? or could he manage to sleep if he did not?

For some minutes he lay and pondered over the possibilities; then he turned over sharply, and with his eyes open, lay breathlessly listening. There had been a movement, he was sure, in the empty bed on the opposite side of the room. Tomorrow he would have it moved, for there must be rats or something playing about in it. It was quiet now. No! the commotion began again. There was a rustling and shaking: surely more than any rat would cause.

I can figure to myself something of the Professor's bewilderment and horror, for I had in a dream thirty years back seen the same thing happen; but the reader will hardly, perhaps, imagine how dreadful it was to him to see a figure suddenly sit up in what he had known was an empty bed. He was out of his own bed in one bound, and made a dash towards the window, where lay his only weapon, the stick with which he had propped his screen. This was, as it turned out, the worst thing he could have done, because the personage in the empty bed, with a sudden smooth motion, slipped from the bed and took up a position, with outspread arms, between the two beds, and in front of the door. Parkins watched it in a horrid perplexity. Somehow, the idea of getting past it and escaping through the door was intolerable to him; he could not have borne —he didn't know why—to touch it; and as for its touching him, he would sooner dash himself through the window than have that happen. It stood for the moment in a band of dark shadow, and he had not seen what its face was like. Now it began to move, in a stooping posture, and all at once the spectator realized, with some horror and some relief, that it must be blind, for it seemed to feel about it with its muffled arms in a groping and random fashion. Turning half-away from him, it became suddenly conscious of the bed he had just left, and darted towards it, and bent over and felt the pillows in a way which made Parkins shudder as he had never in his life thought it possible. In a very few moments it seemed to know that the bed was empty, and then, moving forward into the area of light and facing the window, it showed for the first time what manner of thing it was.

Parkins, who very much dislikes being questioned about it, did once describe something of it in my hearing, and I gathered that what he chiefly remembers about it is a horrible, an intensely horrible, face *of crumpled linen*. What expression he read upon it he could not, or would not, tell, but that the fear of it went nigh to maddening him is certain.

But he was not at leisure to watch it for long. With formidable quickness it moved into the middle of the room, and, as it groped and waved, one corner of its draperies swept across Parkins's face. He could not—though he knew how perilous a sound was—he could not keep back a cry of disgust, and this gave the searcher an instant clue. It leapt towards him upon the instant, and the next moment he was half-way through the window backwards, uttering cry upon cry at the utmost pitch of his voice, and the linen face was thrust close into his own. At this, almost the last possible second, deliverance came, as you will have guessed: the Colonel burst the door open, and was just in time to see the dreadful group at the window. When he reached the figures, only one was left. Parkins sank forward into the room in a faint, and before him on the floor lay a tumbled heap of bed-clothes.

Colonel Wilson asked no questions, but busied himself in keeping everyone else out of the room and in getting Parkins back to his bed; and himself, wrapped in a rug, occupied the other bed for the rest of the night. Early on the next day, Rogers arrived, more welcome than he could have been a day before, and the three of them held a very long consultation in the Professor's room. At the end of it the Colonel left the hotel door carrying a small object between his finger and thumb, which he cast as far into the sea as a very brawny arm could send it. Later on, the smoke of a burning ascended from the back premises of the "Globe".

Exactly what explanation was patched up for the staff and visitors at the hotel I must confess I do not recollect. The Professor was somehow cleared of the ready suspicion of delirium tremens, and the hotel of the reputation of a troubled house.

There is not much question as to what would have happened to Parkins if the Colonel had not intervened when he did. He would either have fallen out of the window or else lost his wits. But it is not so evident what more the creature that came in answer to the whistle could have done than frighten. There seemed to be absolutely nothing material about it save the bed-clothes on which it had made itself a body. The Colonel, who remembered a not very dissimilar occurrence in India, was of opinion that if Parkins had closed with it it could really have done very little, and that its one power was that of frightening. The whole thing, he said, served to confirm his opinion of the Church of Rome.

There is really nothing more to tell, but, as you may imagine, the Professor's views on certain points are less clear cut than they used to be. His nerves, too, have suffered: he cannot even now see a surplice hanging on a door quite unmoved, and the spectacle of a scarecrow in a field late on a winter afternoon has cost him more than one sleepless night.

NO ROOM

By T. F. Powys

THERE could be no doubt about it, that those who said, "thik grave ground do belong to Mr. Truggin," were nearer to the truth of the matter, at least in the local idea, than the few austere ones who would still call the Tadnol churchyard "God's Acre".

" 'Tain't no acre at all," Mr. Truggin had once said, in contradiction of the grander notion. " 'Tis only two of they roods and three small poles."

No one in Tadnol, not even Farmer Spenke's father, whose memory went back until it was near washed by the waters of the flood, had ever remembered any other sexton than Mr. Truggin.

Mr. Truggin, who was by no means wizened or ghoulish, but an old man of spirit whose cheeks were like Pride's pippins, trimmed the graves all the year round, with the same thought and care that a popular grocer bestows upon his shop windows at Christmas time.

And, indeed, Mr. Truggin by such care and tending, aided by the natural grace and friendliness of the place, gave to this final home such a comforting and pleasant look—outside at least—that no one, not even those who knew their days were numbered, could fail to think cheerfully and happily of the brown soil below, and the white snowdrops above, in Mr. Truggin's garden. If anyone had a welcome anywhere, they found it there. Nowhere else the air blew so feelingly, and no tree's shade in the summer was so heavy with love as the great yew's, and no moss flowered so finely in February as the moss that grew upon the churchyard wall.

If anyone in Tadnol wished to do anything from whence real happiness was sure to follow, "to die" was the word; and next, "to be buried by Truggin".

As was proper and right, no person who understood such an important mystery as well as Mr. Truggin did, could take a lenient view of any interference in the arrangement of those grassy mounds. And when Mr. Dibben, from Weyminster, with the long face and longer trousers of a curate at St. Luke'st came to do a month's duty at Tadnol, and told Mr. Truggin disrespectfully tha, dead bodies ought to be planted in rows like broad beans, the sexton sniffed with disapproval.

"At Weyminster," said Mr. Dibben, "they are all lined up like soldiers."

"They town ways bain't ours," Mr. Truggin replied.

"For folk do like to bide where they be known. They dead," said the **sexton**, warming to his subject, "be as particular as we. 'Twouldn't do for Miss Jarrett to be put next to wold Burt, who did fall into river twenty times before 'e drowned 'isself in en."

Mr. Dibben looked at the grave mounds, and took from his pocket the chart of the churchyard, and held it out for Mr. Truggin to see.

" 'Tis a pretty picture," remarked the sexton, smiling.

"If they had been buried decently," said Mr. Dibben sternly, "there wouldn't be all this overcrowding."

"Oh, there be room for woon more," said Mr. Truggin.

The next week old Barker died.

A few days before he was forced to take to his bed, old Barker had shown a proper interest in the churchyard, which was highly pleasing to Mr. Truggin, who always liked people to be glad to come there. "For what be there to hurt 'ee," he would say. "An' for a half-crown extra I'd trim up thee's graveside as fine as a Christmas cracker, and who else be so safe an' well, or so well-cared for as they happy dead!"

Old Barker had looked about him with the exact interest of one who is going to hire a new house. He noticed the birds. " 'Tis all nice," he said, looking about with approval, "an' they little birds in yew tree be twittering."

"All volk, birds and t'others, be happy here," said Truggin, with the same superior gesture that the mayor of a town might give to a prospective builder of new and bright-coloured residential villas.

"Perhaps," inquired Mr. Barker, in the mild voice of one who asks a favour, "thee will let I in next to Aunt Jane; she did give I a penny when I were a young boy. . . ."

Mr. Truggin began to dig Barker's grave with all the satisfaction that a good workman shows when about his duties.

The idea of generous Aunt Jane pleased his imagination, but even if he had seen two bony fingers holding another penny, he wouldn't have touched it, because, of course, it was meant for her nephew Jimmy Barker, aged eighty.

But when Mr. Dibben came to the churchyard and watched the proceedings, Mr. Truggin grew more and more nervous. Any others who had ever come to look had shown a proper and earthy interest, and a shudder at any dark stains that might be seen on the side of the grave, but Mr. Dibben watched from a different outlook altogether—a spiritual one.

The day was mild and it rained a little, and old Mr. Truggin, who kept his coat on as he worked, soon found himself unpleasantly warm.

Had he been alone he would never have done so foolish a thing as to take his coat off when he was hot and sweating; but what with Mr. Dibben watching him, and making unseemly remarks about the vileness of life and the glories of heaven—that were by no means the kind of subjects that Mr. Truggin was used to, or liked—Truggin clutched off his coat and cast it from him.

Mr. Dibben was beginning to speak in tones of exaltation about the grand awakening as Truggin carefully scraped the last shovelful of earth out of the grave. He patted the sides in a friendly manner.

"Wold Barker's bed be made," he said, and climbed out of the grave.

When Mr. Truggin returned to his cottage he so far forgot himself as to say, " 'Twon't do for they dead folk to hear no more of what parson do tell of, or they'll soon start a-swearing."

"What did Mr. Dibben say?" inquired the sexton's lady.

"Nothing but insults to the dead," replied Mr. Truggin. The sexton shivered.

"You bain't caught no cold, 'ave 'ee?" asked Mrs. Truggin.

"Most like I have," replied Mr. Truggin crossly. . . .

The spring winds gathered together that night, and shook the trees and threw to the ground many a little twig that was already decorated with spots of green.

And splashes of rain driven through his roof by the gale fell upon Mr. Truggin, who lay ill.

" 'Tis a poor house, this be," said the sexton, awaking about midnight from the heavy stupor that he had fallen into, and wiping the rain from his face. "An' 'tis well I do know of a better."

Mr. Truggin sat up in bed.

"Wold Barker bain't buried yet," he said aloud, "and Mr. Dibben do say there bain't no more room in Truggin's garden."

The sexton looked at his wife; she slept soundly with her grey hair buried in the pillow.

Mr. Truggin smiled.

He crept from the bed and dressed slowly, shaking his head from side to side and smiling to himself as he put on each garment.

"A good dry housen where God Almighty be landlord and do keep roof in repair be best for I," he muttered; "an 'tis right for Sexton Truggin to have the last house that be vacant."

He softly closed the cottage door and went out into the night.

" 'Tain't stealing," he said, "and I'll tell wold Barker's aunt who I be."

The church clock struck twelve. Dim clouds hurried quickly over the sky when Mr. Truggin reached the churchyard, and the moon peeped out between them as though to ask the dying sexton what he did there.

" 'Tis a pretty thing to see, a housen of woon's own making," murmured Mr. Truggin, looking with pride at the open grave.

He stood for a moment to take a last look at the green mounds that he had tended for so long, and then, letting himself down into the grave, he lay contentedly at the bottom.

His stupor returned; he became unconscious. But after an hour or two he awoke and, turning his head a little, he remarked to the side of the grave:

"No, no, Aunt Jane, don't 'ee go handing I no money. I bain't thee's relation; I be Sexton Truggin."

He remained contentedly conscious for the few moments that he was dying.

"No room," he whispered, "no more room."

ALTARWISE BY OWL-LIGHT

By Pamela Hansford Johnson

THE house lying midway between the villages of Shrove and Tuesday stood on a high ridge rank with dandelion and Old Man's Beard, with nettle and dock-leaves long enough to drown a tramp. But no tramps ever came to lie in the ditch below, for the house was too dreary a sleeping companion and the trees that seethed across the blind upper windows went about their dancing in too heart-breaking a fashion to bring ease to the traveller sheltering in their shadow.

The way from Shrove to Tuesday was long and silent, yet no country walkers ever took their long legs up to the door of the house or knocked for a glass of water on the kitchen panes, for it was well known that the Cantrips gave no entry to visitors.

In the top room, under the winged gables, old Simon Cantrip lay in bed. He was very ill. The whiskers had grown like tangleweed over his cheeks and into his ears and he smelled evilly, for neither Miss Fanny Cantrip nor Miss Morganlefay Cantrip cared to go about the business of washing him. They knew that he must die soon because, apart from his long illness, they had for months past been giving him sweet poison in his jar of night-syrup.

Miss Fanny walked with her sister in the garden. The grass was slimy with recent rain. Miss Fannny wore yellow galoshes to protect her feet from the damp. She herself was very dry; her skin was flaky, her hair brittle with years.

Miss Morganlefay was younger. She was tall and thin; in her black dress she looked like an ebony pole, unribboned with maytime, planted by a madman in the earth. She pointed to the window of the top room.

"When father dies," she said, "for many years after we shall see him leaning over the sill, like the little green ghost of Petrouchka." Miss Morganlefay was the artistic one. She had visited the ballet and the opera.

Impatiently, Miss Fanny pinched her arm. "Stuff," she said, "stuff and nonsense. Petrouchka would be out of place in an English tragedy."

Her sister shrugged. "Have it your own way. You never had any imagination."

They paced together down the tangled paths. Miss Fanny knocked a spider-web to streamers with her stick. Miss Morganlefay stamped her foot smartly upon the late tenant as he tried to trundle away across the stones.

Though the sisters could hear old Simon crying for company, they took no notice. He cried like that every day. It was cruel, he said, that they should keep him shut up all alone with no one to talk to. This annoyed Miss Fanny. He should know by now that she was too busy about the house to bother with callers, even if callers came. Once he had asked if she would not write to one or two of his old friends, asking them if they would come and smoke a pipe in his room, talk to him freely as in the days when he was a nimble-witted young man, even though he was now too weak to speak to them at great length in return, but to this request Fanny thought it needless to reply. She had just laughed at him, drawn the curtains, for punishment, against the sunshine that gave him some small pleasure, and left him to himself from noon till suppertime.

Miss Morganlefay tickled the white frill at her breast. With thumb and forefinger she drew down the wrinkles from her cheeks. Miss Fanny watched her. "You're ageing," she said.

Her sister smiled. Nipping out a white hair from Fanny's temples, she dropped it on a dark leaf for all the world of slug and spider to see and deride.

The breeze had dropped. The sky soured yellowish along the western ridge. Tonight there would be more rain. Miss Fanny held out her hand. A big drop fell on to the palm of it, trembled, and ran along the lifeline. Taking off her scarf she draped it around her head, crossing the ends under her chin and throwing them back over her shoulders. Miss Morganlefay laughed. She was not scared by the weathers.

The sisters went into the house. Beneath the bay window in the parlour tea was laid. They sat down. Miss Fanny flicked a fly off the butter and cut away, with her knife, the pastures his little feet had trod. Through the ceiling they could hear the thumping of the old man's stick on the floor. They smiled at each other. He could wait for his slop of bread and milk. They did the work while he lay idle upstairs. It was only right that the living should be considered before the dead.

Miss Fanny liked her tea weak, with three lumps of sugar. Miss Morganlefay liked her tea strong with neither milk nor sugar, but a half-moon of lemon floating in it.

Mr. Simon Cantrip licked his lips because they were so dry, then spat out the disagreeable hairs that he had raked up with his tongue. It grew dark. He was very thirsty and very hungry. The headlamps of a passing car swept their rods of light across the ceiling. The old man wished there was something else for him to do. The days were so long. Already he had counted, times beyond number, the dead fruit on the wallpaper, the knobs along the bedrail, the stripes on the valance of the dressing-table. He had worked the edge of the sheet into a hundred little pleats, he had sucked up the pillow-case around his head into a dozen little wet mountains, and he had bitten nine of his fingernails to the quick. He was saving the tenth for tomorrow, so that he should wake knowing there was still something left undone.

He said the alphabet right through, forwards, backwards and missing out alternate letters. He said the Lord's Prayer both ways, too. He had already counted up to one hundred, but he could not remember what figures came after that and he was too tired to go back to the beginning. So now there was nothing for him to do but think, and he disliked thinking because it made him more unhappy.

Consider, he said to himself, the lilies of my field; how they grew. Fanny was a spiky child, quick as lightning with her hands but slow with her heart. Morganlefay was neither quick of hand nor heart, but she was the clever one.

He remembered the days, just before his illness, when he had taken her to town to the ballet and the opera. He refused to take Fanny because she would not wear a frock that had no sleeves in it, nor go out into the night unhatted. But Morganlefay, in her corner of the stage box, had looked quite handsome. She had worn a black dress with shining beads in flowers on her breast and in fringes over the tops of her arms. She had put white powder on her face and had fastened the hard knot of her hair with a shining comb. She would not talk of the dancers nor of the men and women who sang so beautifully, and she would not lift her hands to applaud; but for all that you could see that she was seeing, tell that she was hearing. She might have been a soft woman had a young man loved her.

Mr. Simon Cantrip sighed deeply. He knew that she and her sister were poisoning him. However foolish they thought him, he could still detect the queerness in the syrup. It was only the dark bottle that he had not seen; he wondered whether Miss Fanny kept it in her reticule or Miss Morganlefay in the pocket of her sewing apron. He wondered. But he was too old to guess, and, anyway, he did not care. To save himself he might make a Deed of Gift, transferring to his daughters all that he had, thereby saving them a great deal of trouble and risk. He might, but why should he? He did not want to live, for he was tired and lonely, and one of the few pleasures left to him was speculating how long the poison would take to work. Perhaps it was working now, slowly and painlessly, in which case Miss Fanny and Miss Morganlefay were good women and kind.

Starting out of his headaching thoughts, he banged again on the floor. He was terribly, terribly thirsty! They should give him his milk, they should, they should!

A traveller making his way from Shrove to Tuesday, climbed up the ridge, pushed his way through the webbed brown daisies that obscured the path, and knocked on the door of the half-way house just as the rain fell heavily.

Miss Fanny cleared away the tea-things. Miss Morganlefay took out her fancy-work and started on the intricate shading of a threaded petal.

Old Simon, hearing the noise, trembled with glee. "All right, old chap," he called, hoping that his feeble voice would, by some magic chance, carry to the garden. "They may not let you in now, but you'll be in the house before midnight. You'll be in, all right." He drew the bed-clothes to his chin. He was happy. He knew who the fellow was.

Miss Fanny and Miss Morganlefay did not. Had they known they might not have sent him away.

The traveller, hearing no response to his knocking, no sound of footsteps along the hall-way, went back down the path once more. He had an errand in Tuesday. He would see to that first and then return. The rain drenched down. It fell on every face in the open country except his own.

The sisters shuttered the night out. Sitting down on either side of the open hearth, they spoke of pleasant things. Miss Fanny was knitting a tea-cosy in red and yellow wool. She had clean forgotten to take bread and milk to Simon, and Miss Morganlefay could not be bothered to remind her.

"The days draw in," said Miss Fanny; "it is quite dark by five."

"I wish I were rich," said Miss Morganlefay. "I would buy a gramophone and play on it the music I heard at the opera."

"If I were rich," said her sister, "I would change paper into gold and keep it in a big safe."

"We will both be rich some day."

"Some day soon," agreed Miss Fanny, with satisfaction.

Miss Morganlefay rolled her brooch of black opals round and round between her fingers. "I hate poor people." She smelt the sweat of their rags. "Faugh!" she said, and crossed the room to open the windows a little at the top. Miss Fanny shivered with cold. Taking up a shawl, she arranged it on her shoulders. "It must be cold in the draughty, jerry-built houses at Tuesday," she said.

"There's a sick baby there," said Miss Morganlefay, "a baby of poor people."

"Yes," said Miss Fanny, "Mrs. Holly's baby. Poor little thing! How I hope it gets well and does not die!" She was so concerned that she dropped two great red stitches.

Let us consider Miss Fanny Cantrip as she goes about the kitchen preparing supper for old Simon. The rustle of her dress is dry on the stones. She changes silk for serge as the autumn comes on, for she feels the cold.

She stirs a mess of porridge in the pan over the fire. She has burned it a little round the edges, but she does not worry about that. She will scrape the black part underneath.

On the wall is a list, neatly painted in black on white wood, of sundry household necessities, with a little hole next to each. Into the holes opposite "Butter", "Eggs", "Rice" and "Flour" Miss Fanny drives four little red pegs, so that she may forget nothing tomorrow when she goes in a dog-cart to Shrove.

She makes the syrup; blackcurrant it is, with hot water added and one drop of colourless liquid from the green bottle. She ladles out the porridge, slops it with milk, and sticks a spoon like a flag into the top of it. Simon has to be fed like a child, though no child would eat so dirtily. Morganlefay feeds him. It is her share of the work.

The rain drives inward through the open window, spattering the piled crockery on the draining-board.

The traveller, did Miss Fanny know it, is nearly at Tuesday. He will spend an hour or so there.

Miss Fanny thinks of pleasant matters, of the money she will save when old Simon goes, of the fine satin dress she will buy for best, thick enough to last a lifetime. She remembers the day when she would not put on evening dress. Because of that the old man refused to take her to the opera; which was what she wanted, for she felt she could not bear to sit side by side in public with handsome Morganlefay, knowing that she would be robbed by her sister's dark dazzle of the last light she possessed. Yet all had gone well. No young men had come to bear Morganlefay to their proud houses, to lead her up the satisfying aisle, and she had aged and withered even as Fanny had aged and withered until there was no distinguishing ray between the two of them.

Miss Fanny pours the hot syrup into a jar and sets it with the porridge on a tray. She slips the bottle into her reticule. She wears a large black silk purse hanging from her waist by a leather strap like a dog's lead. Now she is ready to go upstairs to the old man.

Let us consider Miss Morganlefay Cantrip as she veins a green leaf with golden thread. Later she is to feed the old man. That is her job. Fanny's is to get his meal and set it on the tray.

Miss Morganlefay is intent on her embroidery. Her nose seems to follow the yellow serpent as it pricks its way along from vein to stem. Her nose is small and sharp with a pink dot at the tip of it. She pauses for a moment to spread her skirts more graciously about her feet because she cannot bear that even the eunuch shadows should see her at a disadvantage, and when her skirts are rucked up a little above her ankles, she is at a disadvantage, indeed, for then it can be seen that her stockings are clumsily knitted to keep out the cold. It is only in her legs that she feels the weathers; she is prone to rheumatism.

She bites the silk with her teeth, wincing a little at the unpleasant tingle of the thread on the nerve. She chooses a fresh colour, turning her attention to the tobacco heart of a rose.

She has waited long for the old man to die, for when he does so she will be rich, and a young man, blind to the meaningless mask of age, will ask her hand in marriage. She will live in a proud house, lit by shaded sun in the daytime and by candleglow at night, and she will buy such rich salves for her face that the wrinkles will disappear of themselves, unsmoothed by a finger and thumb.

Miss Morganlefay thinks she will go to the ballet and to the opera. She will hear the fat Norse gods shouting their way to Valhalla, she will see the little green ghost of Petrouchka wagging over the side of his box. But then, she says to herself, perhaps Fanny is right; there is no place for Petrouchka in an English tragedy.

In the oak-tree outside the window sits an owl. He hoots his woe at the rain. His feathers are damp; the water has so clotted the plumy fringes of his great gold eyes that he must blink and blink to keep his vision sharp to the sneaking mouse.

Miss Morganlefay, hearing his cry, holds her hands to the flames for joy that she is so warm while he is so cold. Mr. Simon Cantrip is hooting like an owl for his supper, but she cannot hear that. The ceilings are too thick.

Miss Fanny comes in with the tray. "Better get it over," she says. Now they are ready to go upstairs to the old man.

Consider Mr. Simon Cantrip as he lies upstairs sucking a strangely-furred acid-drop. As he leaned out of bed just now to bang upon the floor he found the sweet lying on the carpet. Miss Fanny eats acid-drops. It must have fallen from her pocket. The tablet is fresh and sour upon the tongue, and Simon is appeased. He can wait a little longer for his supper. Nevertheless, he moans his hunger aloud; he does not want his daughters to think him more occupied than usual, for that might make them hasten upstairs to see what was happening, and Mr. Simon, for the first time in several years, desires solitude.

He has a fine plan in his head. He will serve Miss Fanny and Miss Morganlefay even as they have served him, and he will do it with a cunning for which neither of them would give him credit. He knows now where the small bottle is hidden. It is in Miss Fanny's reticule. It could not be in Miss Morganlefay's needlework pocket because she would be too afraid that it might come unstoppered and spoil her silks.

In a vase on the mantelshelf are three peacock's feathers. The old man cannot see them now because it is black in the room save for a thin patterning of rainy light on the wall, but he knows that their shining circles are obliterated by dust and that along the quivering antennae a spider crawls. Mr. Simon sometimes fancies that he can see in the dark; but then the pictures form, not beyond his eyes but behind his forehead, far, far back in his head.

He will work as cunningly as the spider. Before Miss Morganlefay has time to light the two bedhead candles he will have pickpocketed Miss Fanny and taken death away from her. And then what will he do? He will be very ill; oh, very ill! And they shall stay up all night to watch him die. He will die,

of course; he would not for the world disappoint his daughters, but before that happens he will play a little joke upon them.
Mr. Simon Cantrip hears his four-legged supper coming up the stairs.

Mr. Simon moaned like the owl in the oak-tree.
"What's the matter with you?" asked Miss Fanny. Miss Morganlefay, hurrying to the bedside, fumbled for matches with which to light the candle, but could find none, because the old man had hidden them under the sheet.

He cried out with a great noise. Setting the tray on top of the chest of drawers, Miss Fanny came to his side. Her sister went about the room, groping for light.

The rain hit the window-panes, shivered with the force of its impact, and dribbled like mercury down the glass.

Mr. Simon clutched Miss Fanny. With one hand he plucked at her breasts and her skirt as if for comfort. With the other he nibbled at the clasp of her reticule, and all the while he howled like a man gone mad. Miss Fanny's heart was beating. He must be in a bad way. In less than an hour he would, with any luck, be gone. In less than an hour she and Miss Morganlefay would be rich, with money for minting and money for young men.

"What's the matter with you?" she repeated, hardly able to speak for the trembling of her lips.

Mr. Simon smiled in the dark. He had found the little bottle and had hidden it with the matches beneath the sheet. Now he thought he had better put the matchbox back on the table for Miss Morganlefay to find. He was so pleased that he almost forgot to howl.

Meanwhile, the traveller was on his way back from Tuesday. Now he was only a mile or so from the half-way house.

The candles were lit. The raindrops on the window flashed with sudden gold. The old man, peering beady-eyed over the blankets, was now a little worried. Though he had, by his cleverness, captured death, he did not know how to use it. Miss Fanny set the tray on a chair by the bed. The old man saw the wicked syrup, and he wanted to laugh. He was sad again, however, when he saw the porridge, for it had caught the fire round the edges and the burnt state always made him retch. Usually they forced him to eat it whether he wanted to or not, but tonight he would resist them. Childishly he turned his head away. A rainy tear ran down into his whiskers. Miss Fanny lightly slapped him on the cheek.

"What's the matter with you?"
He did not answer.
"Let me try," said Miss Morganlefay; "I can do more with him than you can." She shook him.

Mr. Simon remembered to moan. "I am very weak," he said, glancing slyly from one to the other to see if they believed him. "I think that I am dying."

Miss Fanny tried to make him sit up so that he could eat his porridge, but he pushed her from him and he crouched even lower in his bed. He was saying the Lord's Prayer to himself, saying it the right way round, too, for he needed help. Something must happen to show him what he should do. Miss Morganlefay held the syrup to his lips. He drank it greedily, trying not to smile at their stupidity. They imagined that he didn't know!

After that he seemed very ill indeed, weeping like a child, complaining of an ache he could not define, even vomiting a little over his flannel nightshirt.

The traveller was less than half a mile from the half-way house. The rain fell on every face in the open country except his own. He had performed his errand in Tuesday and was a little sad for poor Mrs. Holly.

Mr. Simon Cantrip pretended to sleep. Miss Fanny Cantrip, creeping to her sister's side, whispered: "We'd better sit up with him. It should be soon now, and we shall have to tell the doctor about his peaceful end."

Miss Morganlefay nodded. She agreed. Sitting down one on either side of the bed, they watched the old man. The room was quiet. The ticking of the clock was very loud and very slow. The owl hooted for loneliness in the drenched oak-tree. Mr. Simon answered each call with a small, distressful cry of his own. The sisters bent their heads to hear, for they were sure that it could not be long now.

Miss Morganlefay said she was cold. "We may have to sit here all night," she said fretfully.

"Wrap yourself in the eiderdown," said Miss Fanny. They were silent for a long while.

The traveller had arrived before his time. Patiently he watched the house until his hour should come. Had either of the sisters glanced out of the window they would have seen his face uplifted to their own.

Miss Morganlefay, peevish with weariness, asked if Miss Fanny would not go down to the kitchen and boil up some of the black-currant syrup to ease the long waiting.

Mr. Simon, hearing her, crimped his toes with excitement.

Miss Fanny thought it a good idea. She saw no reason why a whole household should be made uncomfortable just because an old man was dying.

As she went about the kitchen she did not hear the traveller rapping his knuckles on the pane, nor did she see his face pressed against the glass. She filled two tumblers with the syrup, sipped a little from her own to see that it was strong enough, and returned to the top room.

She set the glasses on the old man's tray. The owl was noisier than ever in the tree. Miss Morganlefay rose and came round the bed to take her glass, but before she could do so the old man had shot out an arm and pushed the lattice window ajar. The rain doused in on a wing of wind, and out went the candles. Then there was high confusion. Miss Fanny shrieked with irritation, Miss Morganlefay blundered back to look for the matches, but as the old man had knocked them on to the floor she had a long search.

Miss Fanny blamed the wretched fastenings of the window.

Miss Morganlefay blamed the wicked weather. On all fours she raked along the carpet.

Mr. Simon Cantrip sat up in the dark. He was as strong as a lion, nimble-witted as the boy he used to be. In his hand was the stolen death bottle. Quickly he emptied its contents into the two glasses, trying to gauge an equal share for each. Then, nipping the bottle under the pillow, he lay back, to give as pretty an imitation of an old man sleeping as one would wish to see.

Miss Morganlefay lit the candles and put out the dark. Securely she latched the window. She smiled at Miss Fanny and Miss Fanny smiled back. Together they drank their glassfuls of steaming syrup and, because one was thinking of young men and the other of minted gold, they noticed nothing strange in the taste of it.

Mr. Simon was very tired. His prank had been a great effort to him, and now he wanted to sleep in good earnest.

The rain ceased. In the oak-tree the draggled owl closed his eyes.

The traveller knocked at the door. Shaking themselves as from a long sleep, Miss Fanny and Miss Morganlefay rose up. Hand in hand, like little children, they went downstairs and lifted the bars.

He came in. Thinking him only a friend of the old man's, they knew him and were not afraid, for they could not guess the joke that had been played upon them. Miss Fanny would have offered their guest dry clothes, but saw that he had no need for them, being unharmed by the weathers. She felt a strange expectancy. The traveller touched her cheek and she fell to the ground. Miss Morganlefay looked on. Curiously she tickled the frill at her throat. Then she fingered her flesh, wondering that her heart should rise suddenly like the tassel of a fountain into her mouth. The traveller, because she was younger than Miss Fanny, smoothed her breast as a lover should, and she fell to the ground.

He went on his way upstairs to the old man.

The little mouse squeaked his coming, hopping before him silk-footed from step to step. He came to the top room. For a moment he wondered if he were too early, but the clock ticked an answer.

The old man had no need to cry "Come in," for the door yielded to the finger of the traveller's shadow. The clock struck. With a sudden whirring of steel it ran to a stop. The pendulum shivered and stood still.

The traveller crossed the floor till he came to the bedside. He smiled down at the old man and the old man smiled back. They understood each other too well to worry about making conversation.

Unlatching itself, the window swung inward, bringing the grassy night air with it. A few drops tinkled from the eaves. As the moon mounted the sky, the bedhead candles flickered and went out.

The traveller leaned over the counterpane.

He and Mr. Cantrip shook hands.

And in the years after, if the old man, like the little green ghost of Petrouchka, ever leaned over the sill to see the weathers blowing to beauty the weeds in his dead garden, there was no one there to see him. But it is probable that he never did; he would have realized, with Miss Morganlefay, that Petrouchka has no place in an English tragedy.

WINTER

By Walter de la Mare

"All the other gifts appertinent to man, as the malice of this age shapes them, are not worth a gooseberry. . . ."

ANY event in this world—any human being for that matter—that seems to wear even the faintest cast or warp of strangeness, is apt to leave a disproportionately sharp impression on one's senses. So at least it appears to me. The experience lives on secretly in the memory, and you can never tell what trivial reminder may not at some pregnant moment bring it back—bring it back as fresh and living and green as ever. That, at any rate, is my experience.

Life's mere ordinary day-by-day—its thoughts, talk, doings—wither and die away out of the mind like leaves from a tree. Year after year a similar crop recurs: and that goes, too. It is mere debris; it perishes. But these other anomalies survive, even through the cold of age—forsaken nests, everlasting clumps of mistletoe.

Not that they either are necessarily of any use. For all we know they may be no less alien and parasitic than those flat and spotted fungi that rise in a night on time-soiled birch trees. But such is their power to haunt us. Why else, indeed, should the recollection of that few moments' confrontation with one who, I suppose, must have been some sort of a "fellow-creature" remain so sharp and vivid?

There was nothing much unusual in the circumstances. I must have so met, faced, passed by, thousands of human beings: many of them in almost as unfrequented places. Without effort I can recall not one. But this one! At the first unexpected premonitory gloom of Winter; at sight of any desolate stretch of snow; at sound at dusk of the pebble-like tattling of a robin; at call, too, of a certain kind of dream I have—any such reminder instantly catches me up, transports me back. The old peculiar disquietude possesses me. I am once more an unhappy refugee. It is a distasteful experience.

But such things are difficult to describe—to share. Date, year, are, at any rate, of no account; if only for the reason that what impresses us most in life is independent of time. One can in memory, indeed, live over again events in one's life even twenty years or more gone by, with the same fever of shame, anxiety, unrest. Mere time is nothing.

Nor is now the actual motive of my journey of any consequence. At the moment I was in no particular trouble. No burden lay on my mind—nothing, I mean, heavier than that of being the kind of self one is—a fret common enough in these late days. And though my immediate surroundings were unfamiliar, they were not unusual or unwelcome, since, like others who would not profess to be morbid, I can never pass unvisited either a church of any age or its yard.

Even if I have but a few minutes to spare, I cannot resist hastening in to ponder awhile on its old glass and brasses, its stones, shrines, and monuments. Sir Tompkins This, Lord Mount Everest That—one reads with a curious amusement the ingenuous bygones of their blood and state. I have sometimes laughed out. And queer the echo sounds in a barrel roof. And perhaps an old skimpy verger looks at you, round a pillar. Like a bat.

In sober fact this human pomposity of ours shows a little more amiably against any protracted background of time—even a mere two centuries of it. There is an almost saturnine vanity in the sepulchral—'scutcheons, pedigrees, polished alabaster cherubin and what not. You see it there—like a scarcely legible scribbling on the wall. Well, on this occasion it was not any such sacred interior I was exploring, but a mere half-acre of gravestones huddling under their tower, in the bare glare of a winter's day.

It was an afternoon in January. For hours I had been trudging against a bitter winter wind awhirl with snow. Fatigue had set in—that leaden fatigue when the body seems to have shrunken; while yet the bones keep up a kind of galvanic action like the limbs of a machine. Thought itself—that capricious deposit—had ceased for the time being. I was like the half-dried mummy of a man, pressing on with bent head along an all but obliterated track.

Then, as if at a signal, I looked up; to find that the snow had ceased to fall, that only a few last, and as if forgotten, flakes, were still floating earthwards to their rest in the pallid light of the declining sun.

With this breaking of the clouds a profounder silence had fallen upon the dome-shaped summit of the hill on which I stood. And at its point of vantage I came to a standstill awhile, surveying beneath me under the blueing vacancy of the sky, amidst the white-sheeted fields, a squat church tower, its gargoyles stooping open-mouthed—scarcely less open-mouthed than the frosted bells within. The low mounded wall that encircled the place was but just perceptible, humped with its snow. Its yews stood like gigantic umbrellas clotted with swansdown; its cypresses like torches, fringed, crested, and tufted with ash.

No sound broke the frozen hush as I entered the lych-gate; not a figure of man or beast moved across that far-stretching savanna of new-fallen snow. You could have detected the passage of a fly. Dazzling light and gem-clear coloured shadow played in hollow and ripple. I was treading a virgin wilderness, but one long since settled and densely colonized.

In surroundings like these—in any vast vacant quiet—the senses play uncommonly queer tricks with their possessor. The very air, cold and ethereal and soon to be darkened, seemed to be astir with sounds and shapes on the edge of complete revelation. Such are our fancies. A curious insecure felicity took possession of me. Yet on the face of it the welcome of a winter churchyard is cold enough; and the fare scanty!

The graves were old: many of them recorded only with what nefarious pertinacity time labours and the rain gnaws. Others, befrosted growths, had now patterned over, and their tale was done. But for the rest—some had texts: "I am a Worm, and no Man"; "In Rama was there a Voice heard: Lamentation and Weeping"; "He knoweth the Way that I take." And a few still bore their bits of doggerel:

> Stranger, a light I pray!
> Not that I pine for day:
> Only one beam of light—
> To show me Night!

That struck me as a naive appeal to a visitor not as yet in search of a roof "for when the slow dark hours begin", and almost blinded for the time being by the dazzle of the sunlight striking down on these abodes around him!

I smiled to myself and went on. Dusk, as a matter of fact, is my mind's natural illumination. How many of us, I wonder, "think" in anything worthy of being called a noon-day of consciousness? Not many: it's all in a mirk, without arrangement or prescience. And as for dreaming—well, here were sleepers enough. I loafed on—cold and vacant.

A few paces farther I came to a stand again, before a large oval stone, encircled with a blunt loop of marble myrtle leaves, embellishing the words:

> "He shall give His angels charge over thee,
> To keep thee in all thy ways."

This stone was clasped by two grotesque marble hands, as if he who held it knelt even now behind it in hiding. Facing north, its lower surface was thickly swathed with snow. I scraped it off with my hands:

> I was afraid,
> Death stilled my fears:
> In sorrow I went,
> Death dried my tears:
> Solitary too,
> Death came. And I
> Shall no more want
> For company.

So, so: the cold alone was nipping raw, and I confess its neighbour's philosophy pleased me better: i.e., it's better to be anything animate than a dead lion; even though that lion be a Corporal Pym:

> This quiet mound beneath
> Lies Corporal Pym,
> He had no fear of death;
> Nor death of him.

Or even if the anything animate be nothing better than a Logge:

> Here lies Thomas Logge   —   a Rascally Dogge;
> A poor useless creature   —   by choice as by nature;
> Who never served God   —   for kindness or Rod;
> Who, for pleasure or penny, —   never did any
> Work in his life   —   but to marry a Wife,
>   And live aye in strife:
> And all this he says   —   at the end of his days
>   Lest some fine canting pen
>   Should be at him again.

Canting pens had had small opportunity in this hill-side acre; and the gentry of the surrounding parts, like those of most parts, had preferred to lie inside under cover—where no doubt Mr. Jacob Todd had prepared for many of them a faster and less starry lodging:

> Here be the ashes of Jacob Todd,
> Sexton now in the land of Nod.
> Digging he lived, and digging died,
> Pick, mattock, spade, and nought beside.
> Here oft at evening he would sit
> Tired with his toil, and proud of it;
> Watching the pretty Robins flit.
> Now slumbers he as deep as they
> He bedded for ye Judgement Day.

Mr. Todd's successor, it seemed, had entrusted him with a little protegée who for a few years—not quite nine—had been known as Alice Cass:

> My mother bore me:
> My father rejoiced in me:
> The good priest blest me:
> All people loved me:
> But Death coveted me:
> And free'd this body
> of its youthful soul.

For youthful company she had another Alice. A much smaller parcel of bones this—though in sheer date upwards of eighty years her senior:

> Here lyeth our infant, Alice Rodd:
> She were so small
> Scarce aught at all,
> But a mere breath of Sweetness sent from God.
>
> Sore we did weepe; our heartes on sorrow set.
> Till on our knees
> God sent us ease:
> And now we weepe no more than we forget.

Tudor roses had been carved around the edge of her stone—vigorously and delicately, too, for a rustic mason. Every petal held its frozen store. I wandered on, restlessly enough, now that my journey was almost at an end, stooping to read at random; here an old broken wooden cross leaning crookedly over its one legible word "Beloved"; here the great, flat, seventeenth-century vault of Abraham Devoyage, "who was of France, and now, please God, is of Paradise"; and not far distant from him some Spanish exile, though what had brought such a wayfarer to these outlandish parts, heaven alone could tell:

> Laid in this English ground
> A Spaniard slumbers sound.
> Well might the tender weep
> To think how he doth sleep—
> Strangers on either hand—
> So far from his own land.
> O! when the last Trump blow,
> May Christ ordain that so
> This friendless one arise
> Under his native skies.
> How bleak to wake, how dread a doom,
> To cry his sins so far from home!

And then Ann Poverty's stone a pace or two beyond him:

> Stranger here lies
> Ann Poverty;
> Such was her name
> And such was she.
> May Jesu pity
> Poverty.

A meagre memorial and a rather shrill appeal somehow in that vacancy. Indeed, I must confess that this snowy waste, these magpie stones, the zebra-like effect of the thin snow-stripings on the dark tower beneath a leaden winter sky suggested an influence curiously pagan in effect. Church sentiments were far more alien in this scene of nature than beneath a roof. And after all, Nature—if She she be—teaches us mortals, I suppose, little but endurance, patience, despair, or fear. That she can be entrancing proves nought.

On the contrary, the rarer kinds of natural loveliness—enormous forests of flowering chestnuts, their league-long broken chasms a-roar with cataracts and foaming with wild flowers; precipitous green steeps—quartz, samphire, cormorant—plunging a thousand fathoms into dark gulfs of emerald ocean—such memories hint far rather at the inhuman divinities. This place, too, was scarcely one that happy souls would choose to haunt. And yet, here was I . . . in a Christian burial-ground.

But then, of course, one's condition of spirit and body must be taken into account. I was exhausted, and my mind like a vacant house with the door open—so vacant by now that I found I had read over and over the first two or three lines of Asrafel (or was it Israfel?) Holt's blackened inscription without understanding a single word; and then, suddenly, two dark eyes in a long cadaverous face pierced out at me as if from the very fabric of his stone:

> Here is buried a Miser:
> Had he been wiser,
> He would not have gone bare
> Where Heaven's garmented are.
> He'd have spent him a penny
> To buy a Wax Taper;
> And of Water a sprinkle
> To quiet a poor Sleeper.
> He'd have cried on his soul,
> "O my Soul, moth and rust!——
> What treasure shall profit thee
> When thou art dust?"
> "Mene, Tekel, Upharsin!"
> God grant, in those Scales,
> His Mercy avail us
> When all Earth's else fails!

". . . Departed this life, May the First 1700": two long centuries dead, seraphic Israfel! Was time nothing to him, too?

"Now withered is the Garland on the . . ." the fragment of old rhyme chased its tail awhile in the back of my mind, and then was gone.

And I must be going. Winter twilight is brief. Frost was already glittering along the crisping surface of the snow. A crescent moon showed silvery in the sun's last red. I made her a distant obeisance. But the rather dismal sound of the money I rattled in my pocket served only to scare the day's last robin off. She—she paid me no heed.

Here was the same old unanswerable question confronting the traveller. "I have no Tongue," cried one from his corner, "and Ye no Ears." And this, even though nearby lay Isaac Meek, who in certain features seems easily to have made up for these deficiencies:

> Hook-nosed was I; loose-lipped. Greed fixed its gaze
> In my young eyes ere they knew brass from gold.
> Doomed to the blazing market-place my days
> A sweating chafferer of the bought, and sold.
> Frowned on and spat at, flattered and decried,
> One only thing man asked of me—my price.
> I lived, detested; and forsaken, died,
> Scorned by the Virtuous and the jest of Vice.
> And now behold, you Christians, my true worth!
> Step close: I have inherited the Earth.

I turned to go—wearied a little even of the unwearying. Epitaphs in any case are only "marginal" reading. There is rarely anything unusual or original in such sentiments as theirs. Up to that moment (apart from the increasing cold) this episode—this experience—had been merely that of a visitor ordinarily curious, vulgarly intrusive, perhaps, and one accustomed to potter about among the antiquated and forgotten.

No: what followed came without premonition or warning. I had been stooping, for the last time, my body now dwarfed by the proximity of the dark stone tower. I had been reading all that there was to be read about yet another forgotten stranger; and so rapidly had the now north-east wind curdled the air that I had been compelled to scrape off the rime from the lettering with numb finger-tips. I had stooped (I say) to read:

> O passer-by, beware!
> Is the day fair?——
> Yet unto evening shall the day spin on
> And soon thy sun be gone;
> Then darkness come,
> And this, a narrow home.
> Not that I bid thee fear:
> Only, when thou at last lie here,
> Bethink thee, there shall surely be
> Thyself for company.

And with its last word a peculiar heat coursed through my body. Consciousness seemed suddenly to concentrate itself (like the tentacles of an anemone closing over a morsel of strange food), and I realized that I was no longer alone. But—and of this I am certain—there was no symptom of positive fear in the experience. Intense awareness, a peculiar physical ominous absorption, possibly foreboding; but no actual fear.

I say this because what impressed me most in the figure that I now saw standing amid that sheet of whiteness—three or four grave-mounds distant on these sparse northern skirts of the churchyard—what struck me instantly was the conviction that to him I myself was truly such an object. Not exactly of fear; but of unconcealed horror. It is not, perhaps, a pleasing thing to have to record. My appearance there—dark clothes, dark hair, wearied eyes, ageing face, a skin maybe somewhat cadaverous at that moment with fasting and the cold—all this (just what my body and self looked like, I mean) cannot have been much more repellant than that of scores and scores of men of my class and means and kind.

I was merely, that is, like one of the "Elder Ladies or Children" who were bidden (by Mr. Nash's Rules of the Pump Room in Bath in 1709) be contented "with a second bench . . . as being past, or not come to, Perfection."

None the less, there was no doubt of it. The fixed open gaze answering mine suggested that of a child confronted with a fascinating but repulsive reptile. Yet so strangely and arrestingly beautiful was that face, beautiful with the strangeness, I mean, of the dream-like, with its almost colourless eyes and honey-coloured skin, that unless the experience of it had been thus sharply impressed, no human being could have noticed the emotion depicted upon its features.

There was not the faintest faltering in the steady eyes—fixed, too, as if this crystal graveyard air were a dense medium for a sight unused to it. And so intent on them was I myself that, though I noticed the slight trembling of the hand that held what (on reflection) appeared to resemble the forked twig which "diviners" of waters use in their mysteries, I can give no account of this stranger's dress except that it was richly yet dimly coloured.

As I say, my own dark shape was now standing under the frowning stone-work of the tower. With an effort one of its gargoyles could have split heaven's dews upon my head, had not those dews been frozen. And the voice that fell on my ear (as if from within rather than from without) echoed cold and solemnly against its parti-coloured stone :

"Which is the way?"

Realizing more sharply with every tardy moment that this being, in human likeness, was not of my kind, nor of my reality; standing there in the cold and snow, winter nightfall now beginning to lour above the sterile landscape; I could merely shake a shivering head.

"Which is yours?" said the tranquil and high, yet gentle, voice.

"There!" I cried, pointing out with my finger the pent-roofed gate on to the human road. The astonishment and dread in the strange face seemed to deepen as I looked.

"But I would gladly . . ." I began, turning an instant towards the gloomy snow clouds that were again gathering in the north—"I would gladly . . ." But the sentence remained unfinished, for when I once more brought my eyes back to this confronter, he was gone.

I agree I was very tired; and never have I seen a more sepulchral twilight than that which now overspread this desolate descent of hill. Yet strange though it may appear, I knew then and know now this confrontation was no illusion of the senses. There are hours in life, I suppose, when we are weaker than we know; when a kind of stagnancy spreads over the mind and heart that is merely a masking of what is gathering beneath the surface. Whether or not, as I stood looking back for an instant before pushing through the worn lych-gate, an emotion of fear, remorse, misery—I know not—swept over me. My eyes seemed to lose for that moment their power to see aright. The whole scene was distorted, awry.

THE EERIE

THE FAMILIAR

By J. Sheridan Le Fanu

I WAS a young man at the time, and intimately acquainted with some of the actors in this strange tale; the impression which its incidents made on me, therefore, were deep and lasting. I shall now endeavour, with precision, to relate them all, combining, of course, in the narrative, whatever I have learned from various sources, tending, however imperfectly, to illuminate the darkness which involves its progress and termination.

Somewhere about the year 1794, the youngest brother of a certain baronet, whom I shall call Sir James Barton, returned to Dublin. He had served in the navy with some distinction, having commanded one of His Majesty's frigates during the greater part of the American war. Captain Barton was apparently some two or three-and-forty years of age. He was an intelligent and agreeable companion when he pleased it, though generally reserved, and occasionally even moody.

In society, however, he deported himself as a man of the world, and a gentleman. He had not contracted any of the noisy brusqueness sometimes acquired at sea; on the contrary, his manners were remarkably easy, quiet, and even polished. He was in person about the middle size, and somewhat strongly formed—his countenance was marked with the lines of thought, and on the whole wore an expression of gravity and melancholy. Being, however, as I have said, a man of perfect breeding, as well as of good family and in affluent circumstances, he had, of course, ready access to the best society of Dublin without the necessity of any other credentials.

In his personal habits, Captain Barton was unexpensive. He occupied lodgings in one of the then fashionable streets in the south side of the town—kept but one horse and one servant—and though a reputed free-thinker, yet lived an orderly and moral life—indulging neither in gambling, drinking, nor any other vicious pursuit—living very much to himself, without forming intimacies, or choosing any companions, and appearing to mix in gay society rather for the sake of its bustle and distraction, than for any opportunities it offered of interchanging thought or feeling with its votaries.

Barton was, therefore, pronounced a saving, prudent, unsocial sort of fellow, who bid fair to maintain his celibacy alike against stratagem and assault, and was likely to live to a good old age, die rich, and leave his money to a hospital.

It was now apparent, however, that the nature of Captain Barton's plans had been totally misconceived. A young lady, whom I shall call Miss Montague, was at this time introduced into the gay world by her aunt, the Dowager Lady L——. Miss Montague was decidedly pretty and accomplished, and having some natural cleverness and a great deal of gaiety, became for a while a reigning toast.

Her popularity, however, gained her for a time nothing more than that unsubstantial admiration which, however pleasant as an incense to vanity, is by no means necessary antecedent to matrimony—for, unhappily for the young lady in question, it was an understood thing that, beyond her personal attractions, she had no kind of earthly provision. Such being the state of affairs, it will readily be believed that no little surprise was consequent upon the appearance of Captain Barton as the avowed lover of the penniless Miss Montague.

His suit prospered, as might have been expected, and in a short time it was communicated by old Lady L—— to each of her hundred-and-fifty particular friends in succession, that Captain Barton had actually tendered proposals of marriage, with her approbation, to her niece, Miss Montague, who had, moreover, accepted the offer of his hand, conditionally upon the consent of her father, who was then upon his homeward voyage from India, and expected in two or three weeks at the furthest.

About this consent there could be no doubt—the delay, therefore, was one merely of form—they were looked upon as absolutely engaged, and Lady L——, with a rigour of old-fashioned decorum with which her niece would, no doubt, gladly have dispensed, withdrew her thenceforward from all further participation in the gaieties of the town.

Captain Barton was a constant visitor as well as a frequent guest at the house, and was permitted all the privileges of intimacy which a betrothed suitor is usually accorded. Such was the relation of the parties, when the mysterious circumstances which darken this narrative first began to unfold themselves.

Lady L—— resided in a handsome mansion at the north side of Dublin, and Captain Barton's lodgings, as we have already said, were situated at the south. The distance intervening was considerable, and it was Captain Barton's habit generally to walk home without an attendant, as often as he passed the evening with the old lady and her fair charge.

His shortest way in such nocturnal walks lay, for a considerable space, through a line of street which had as yet merely been laid out, and little more than the foundations of the houses constructed.

One night, shortly after his engagement with Miss Montague was commenced, he happened to remain unusually late, in the company with her and Lady L——. The conversation had turned upon the evidences of revelation, which he had disputed with the callous scepticism of a confirmed infidel. What were called "French principles" had, in those days, found their way a good deal into fashionable society, especially that portion of it which professed allegiance to Whiggism, and neither the old lady nor her charge were so perfectly free from the taint as to look upon Captain Barton's views as any serious objection to the proposed union.

The discussion had degenerated into one upon the supernatural and the marvellous, in which he had pursued precisely the same line of argument and ridicule. In all this it is but truth to state, Captain Barton was guilty of no affectation—the doctrines upon which he insisted were, in reality, but too truly basis of his own fixed belief, if so it might be called; and perhaps not the least strange of the many strange circumstances connected with my narrative was the fact that the subject of the fearful influences I am about to describe was himself, from the deliberate conviction of years, an utter disbeliever in what are usually termed prenatural agencies.

It was considerably past midnight when Captain Barton took his leave and set out upon his solitary walk homeward. He had now reached the lonely road, with its unfinished dwarf walls tracing the foundations of the projected row of houses on either side—the moon was shining mistily, and its imperfect light made the road he trod but additionally dreary—that utter silence which has in it something indefinably exciting reigned there and made the sound of his steps, which alone broke it, unnaturally loud and distinct.

He had proceeded thus some way, when he heard, on a sudden, other footfalls pattering at a measured pace, and, as it seemed, about two score steps behind him.

The suspicion of being dogged is at all times unpleasant: it is, however, especially so in a spot so lonely; and this suspicion became so strong in the mind of Captain Barton, that he abruptly turned about to confront his pursuer, but though there was quite sufficient moonlight to disclose any object upon the road he had traversed, no form of any kind was visible there.

The steps he had heard could not have been the reverberation of his own, for he stamped his foot upon the ground, and walked briskly up and down, in the vain attempt to awake an echo; though by no means a fanciful person, therefore, he was at last fain to charge to sounds upon his imagination, and treat them as an illusion. Thus satisfying himself, he resumed his walk, and before he had proceeded a dozen paces the mysterious footfall was again audible from behind, and this time, as if with the special design of showing that the sounds were not the responses of an echo, the steps sometimes slackened nearly to a halt, and sometimes hurried for six or eight strides to a run, and again abated to a walk.

Captain Barton, as before, turned suddenly round, and with the same result —no object was visible above the deserted level of the road. He walked back over the same ground, determined that, whatever might have been the cause of the sound which had disconcerted him, it should not escape his search—the endeavour, however, was unrewarded.

In spite of all his scepticism he felt something like a superstititious fear stealing fast upon him, and with these unwonted and uncomfortable sensations he once more turned and pursued his way. There was no repetition of these haunting sounds until he had reached the point which he had last stopped to retrace his steps—here they resumed—and with sudden starts of running which threatened to bring the unseen pursuer up to the alarmed pedestrian.

Captain Barton arrested his course as formerly—the unaccountable nature of the occurrence filled him with vague and disagreeable sensations—and yielding to the excitement that was gaining upon him, he shouted sternly: "Who goes there?" The sound of one's own voice thus exerted, in utter solitude, and followed by total silence, has in it something unpleasantly dismaying, and he felt a degree of nervousness which, perhaps, from no cause he had ever known before.

To the very end of this solitary street the steps pursued him—and it required a strong effort of stubborn pride on his part to resist the impulse that prompted him every moment to run for safety at the top of his speed. It was not until he had reached his lodgings, and safe by his own fireside, that he felt sufficiently reassured to rearrange and reconsider in his own mind the occurrences which had so discomposed him. So little a matter, after all, is sufficient to upset the prise of scepticism and vindicate the old simple laws of nature within us.

Captain Barton was next morning sitting at a late breakfast, reflecting upon the incidents of the previous night, with more of inquisitiveness than awe, so speedily do gloomy impressions upon the fancy disappear under the cheerful influence of day, when a letter just delivered by the postman was placed upon the table before him.

There was nothing remarkable in the address of this missive, except that it was written in a hand which he did not know—perhaps it was disguised—for the tall, narrow characters were sloped backward; and with the self-inflicted suspense which we often see practised in such cases he puzzled over the inscription for a full minute before he broke the seal. When he did so he read the following words, written in the same hand:

Mr. Barton, late captain of the 'Dolphin' is warned of DANGER. He will do wisely to avoid —— Street (here the locality of his last night's adventure was named)—if he walks there as usual he will meet with something unlucky—let him take warning, once for all, for he had reason to dread.

THE WATCHER.

Captain Barton read and re-read this strange effusion; in every light and in every direction he turned it over and over; he examined the paper on which it was written, and scrutinized the handwriting once more. Defeated here, he turned to the seal; it was nothing but a patch of wax, upon which the accidental impression of a thumb was imperfectly visible.

There was not the slightest mark, or clue of any kind, to lead him to even a guess as to its possible origin. The writer's object seemed a friendly one, and yet he subscribed himself as one whom he had "reason to dread". Altogether, the letter, its author, and its real purpose were to him an inexplicable puzzle, and one, moreover, unpleasantly suggestive, in his mind, of other associations connected with his last night's adventure.

In obedience to some feeling—perhaps of pride—Captain Barton did not communicate, even to his intended bride, the occurrences which I have just detailed. Trifling as they might appear, they had in reality most disagreeably affected his imagination, and he cared not to disclose, even to the young lady in question, what she might possibly look upon as evidence of weakness. The letter might very well be but a hoax, and the mysterious footfall but a delusion or a trick. But although he affected to treat the whole affair as unworthy of a thought, it yet haunted him pertinaciously, tormenting him with perplexing doubts and depressing him with undefined apprehensions. Certain it is that for a considerable time afterwards he carefully avoided the street indicated in the letter as the scene of danger.

It was not until a week after the receipt of the letter which I have transcribed that anything further occurred to remind Captain Barton of its contents, or to counteract the gradual disappearance from his mind of the disagreeable impressions then received.

He was returning one night, after the interval I have stated, from the theatre, which was then situated in Crow Street, and having there seen Miss Montague and Lady L—— into their carriage he loitered for some time with two or three acquaintances.

With these, however, he parted close to the college, and pursued his way alone. It was now fully one o'clock, and the streets were quite deserted. During the whole of his walk with the companions from whom he had just parted, he had been at times painfully aware of the sound of steps, as it seemed, dogging them on their way.

Once or twice he had looked back, in the uneasy anticipation that he was again about to experience the same mysterious annoyances which had so disconcerted him a week before, and earnestly hoping that he might see some form to account naturally for the sounds. But the street was deserted—no one was visible.

Proceeding now quite alone upon his homeward way he grew really nervous and uncomfortable, as he became sensible, with increased distinctness, of the well-known and now absolutely dreaded sounds.

By the side of the dead wall which bounded the college park, the sounds followed, recommencing almost simultaneously with his own steps. The same unequal pace—sometimes slow, sometimes for a score yards or so, quickened almost to a run—was audible from behind him. Again and again he turned; quickly and stealthily he glanced over his shoulder—almost at every half-dozen steps; but no one was visible.

The irritation of this intangible and unseen pursuit became gradually all but intolerable; and when at last he reached his home his nerves were strung to such a pitch of excitement that he could not rest, and did not attempt even to lie down until after the daylight had broken.

He was awakened by a knock at his chamber-door, and his servant, entering, handed him several letters which had just been received by the penny post. One among them instantly arrested his attention—a single glance at the direction aroused him thoroughly. He at once recognized its character, and read as follows:

You may as well think, Captain Barton, to escape from your own shadow as from me; do what you may, I will see you as often as I please, and you shall see me, for I do not want to hide myself, as you fancy. Do not let it trouble your rest, Captain Barton; for, with a good conscience, what need you fear from the eye of
THE WATCHER.

It is scarcely necessary to dwell upon the feelings that accompanied a perusal of this strange communication. Captain Barton was observed to be unusually absent and out of spirits for several days afterwards. . . . But no one divined the cause.

Whatever he might think as to the phantom steps which followed him, there could be no possible illusion about the letters he had received; and, to say the least, their immediate sequence upon the mysterious sounds which had haunted him was an odd coincidence.

The whole circumstance was, in his own mind, vaguely and instinctively connected with certain passages in his past life, which of all others he hated to remember.

It happened, however, that in addition to his own approaching nuptials, Captain Barton had just then—fortunately, perhaps, for himself—some business of an engrossing kind connected with the adjustment of a large and long-litigated claim upon certain properties.

The hurry and excitement of business had its natural effect in gradually dispelling the gloom which had for a time occasionally oppressed him, and in a little while his spirits had entirely recovered their accustomed tone.

During all this time, however, he was, now and then, dismayed by indistinct and half-heard repetitions of the same annoyance, and that in lonely places, in the daytime as well as after nightfall. These renewals of the strange impressions from which he had suffered so much were, however, desultory and faint, insomuch that often he really could not, to his own satisfaction, distinguish between them and the mere suggestions of an excited imagination.

One evening he walked down to the House of Commons with a Member, an acquaintance of his and mine. This was one of the few occasions upon which I have been in company with Captain Barton. As we walked down together, I observed that he became absent and silent, and to a degree that seemed to argue the pressure of some urgent and absorbing anxiety.

I afterwards learned that during the whole of our walk he had heard the well-known footsteps tracking him as we proceeded.

This, however, was the last time he suffered from this phase of the persecution, of which he was already the anxious victim. A new and a very different one was about to be presented.

Of the new series of impressions which were afterwards gradually to work out his destiny, I that evening witnessed the first; and but for its relation to the train of events which followed, the incident would scarcely have been now remembered by me.

As we were walking in at the passage from College Green, a man, of whom I remember only that he was short in stature, looked like a foreigner, and wore a kind of fur travelling-cap, walked very rapidly, and, as if under fierce excitement, directly towards us, muttering to himself fast and vehemently the while.

This odd-looking person walked straight toward Barton, who was foremost of the three, and halted, regarding him for a moment or two with a look of maniacal menace and fury; and then turning about as abruptly he walked before us at the same agitated pace and disappeared at a side passage. I do distinctly remember being a good deal shocked at the countenance and bearing of this man, which indeed irresistibly impressed me with an undefined sense of danger, such as I have never felt before or since from the presence of anything human; but these sensations were, on my part, far from amounting to anything disconcerting as to flurry or excite me—I had seen only a singularly evil countenance, agitated, as it seemed, with the excitement of madness.

I was absolutely astonished, however, at the effect of this apparition upon Captain Barton. I knew him to be a man of proud courage and coolness in real danger—a circumstance which made his conduct upon this occasion the more conspicuously odd. He recoiled a step or two as the stranger advanced, and clutched my arm in silence, with what seemed to be a spasm of agony or terror! And then, as the figure disappeared, shoving me roughly back, he followed it for a few paces, stopped in great disorder, and sat down upon a form. I never beheld a countenance more ghastly and haggard.

"For God's sake, Barton, what is the matter?" said ——, our companion, really alarmed at his appearance. "You're not hurt, are you? Or unwell? What is it?"

"What did he say?—I did not hear it—what was it?" asked Barton, wholly disinclining the question.

"Nonsense," said ——, greatly surprised, "who cares what the fellow said? You are unwell, Barton, decidedly unwell; let me call a coach."

"Unwell! No, not unwell," he said, evidently making an effort to recover his self-possession; "but, to say the truth, I am fatigued—a little over-worked—and perhaps over-anxious. You know I have been in Chancery, and the winding-up of a suit is always a nervous affair. I have felt uncomfortable all this evening; but I am better now. Come, come—shall we go on?"

"No, no. Take my advice, Barton, and go home; you really do need rest; you are looking quite ill. I really do insist on your allowing me to see you home," replied his friend.

I seconded ——'s advice, the more readily as it was obvious that Barton was not himself disinclining to be persuaded. He left us, declining our offered escort. I was not sufficiently intimate with —— to discuss the scene we had both just witnessed. I was, however, convinced from his manner in the few commonplace comments and regrets we exchanged, that he was just as little satisfied as I with the extempore plea of illness with which he had accounted for the strange exhibition, and that we were both agreed in suspecting some lurking mystery in the matter.

I called next day at Barton's lodgings to inquire for him, and learned from the servant that he had not left his room since his return the night before; but that he was not seriously indisposed, and hoped to be out in a few days. That evening he sent for Dr. R——, then in large and fashionable practice in Dublin, and their interview was, it is said, an odd one.

He entered into a detail of his own symptoms in an abstracted and desultory way, which seemed to argue a strange want of interest in his own cure, and, at all events, make it manifest that there was some topic engaging his mind of more engrossing importance than his present ailment. He complained of occasional palpitations and headache.

Dr. R—— asked him, among other questions, whether there was any irritating circumstance or anxiety then occupying his thoughts. This he denied quickly and almost peevishly; and the physician thereupon declared his opinion that there was nothing amiss except slight derangement of the digestion, for which he accordingly wrote a prescription, and was about to withdraw when Captain Barton, with the air of a man who recollects a topic which had nearly escaped him, recalled him.

"I beg your pardon, Doctor, but I really almost forgot: will you permit me to ask you two or three medical questions—rather odd ones, perhaps, but a wager depends upon their solution; you will, I hope, excuse my unreasonableness?"

The physician readily undertook to satisfy the inquirer.

Barton seemed to have some difficulty about opening the proposed interrogatories, for he was silent for a minute, then walked to his bookcase and returned as he had gone; at last he sat down, and said:

"You'll think them very childish questions, but I can't recover my wager without a decision; so I must put them. I want to know first about lock-jaw. If a man actually has had that complaint, and appears to have died of it—so much so that a physician of average skill pronounces him actually dead—may he, after all, recover?"

The physician smiled, and shook his head.

"But—but a blunder may be made," resumed Barton. "Suppose an ignorant pretender to medical skill; may he be so deceived by any stage of the complaint, as to mistake what is only part of the progress of the disease, for death itself?"

"No one who had ever seen death," answered he, "could mistake it in a case of lock-jaw."

Barton mused for a few minutes. "I am going to ask you a question, perhaps still more childish; but first, tell me, are the regulations of foreign hospitals, such as that of Naples, very lax and bungling? May not all kinds of blunders and slips occur in their entries of names, and so forth?"

Dr. R—— professed his incompetence to answer that query.

"Well then, Doctor, here is the last of my questions. You will, probably, laugh at it; but it must out, nevertheless. Is there any disease, in all the range of human maladies, which would have the effect of perceptibly contracting the stature and the whole frame—causing the man to shrink in all his proportions, and yet to preserve his exact resemblance to himself in every particular—with the one exception, his height and bulk; any disease mark—no matter how rare —how little believed in, generally—which could possibly result in producing such an effect?"

The physician replied with a smile, and a very decided negative.

"Tell me, then," said Barton, abruptly, "if a man be in reasonable fear of assault from a lunatic who is at large, can he not procure a warrant for his arrest and detention?"

"Really, that is more a lawyer's question than one in my way," replied Dr. R——; "but I believe, on applying to a magistrate, such a course would be directed."

The physician then took his leave; but, just as he reached the hall door, remembered that he had left his cane upstairs and returned. His reappearance was awkward, for a piece of paper, which he recognized as his own prescription, was slowly burning upon the fire, and Barton sitting close by with an expression of settled gloom and dismay.

Dr. R—— had too much tact to observe what presented itself; but he had seen quite enough to assure him that the mind, and not the body, of Captain Barton was in reality the seat of suffering.

A few days afterwards the following advertisement appeared in the Dublin newspapers:

If Sylvester Yelland, formerly a foremast man on board His Majesty's frigate, *Dolphin*, or his nearest of kin, will apply to Mr. Hubert Smith, attorney, at his office Dame Street, he or they may hear of something greatly to his or their advantage. Admission may be had at any hour up to twelve o'clock at night, should parties desire to avoid observation; and the strictest secrecy, as to all communications intended to be confidential, shall be honourably observed.

The *Dolphin*, as I have mentioned, was the vessel which Captain Barton had commanded; and this circumstance, connected with the extraordinary exertions made by the circulation of handbills, etc., as well as by repeated advertisements to secure for this strange notice the utmost possible publicity, suggested to Dr. R—— the idea that Captain Barton's extreme uneasiness was somehow connected with the individual to whom the advertisement was addressed, and he himself the author of it.

This, however, it is needless to add, was no more than a conjecture, No information, whatsoever, as to the real purpose of the advertisement was divulged by the agent, nor yet any hint as to who his employer might be.

Captain Barton, although he had latterly begun to earn for himself the character of an hypochondriac, was yet very far from deserving it. Though by no means lively, he had yet, naturally, what are termed "even spirits", and was not subject to undue depressions.

He soon, therefore, began to return to his former habits; and one of the earliest symptoms of this healthier tone of spirits was his appearing at a grand dinner of the Freemasons, of which worthy fraternity he was himself a brother.

Barton, who had been at first gloomy and abstracted, drank much more freely than was his wont—possibly with the purpose of dispelling his own secret anxieties—and under the influence of good wine and pleasant company, became gradually (unlike himself) talkative, and even noisy.

It was under this unwonted excitement that he left his companions at about half-past ten o'clock; and as conviviality is a strong incentive to gallantry, it occurred to him to proceed forthwith to Lady L——'s, and pass the remainder of the evening with her and his destined bride.

Accordingly, he was soon at —— Street and chatting gaily with the ladies. It is not to be supposed that Captain Barton had exceeded the limits which propriety prescribes to good fellowship—he had merely taken enough wine to raise his spirits, without, however, in the least degree unsteadying his mind or affecting his manners.

With this undue elevation of spirits had supervened an entire oblivion or contempt of those undefined apprehensions which had for so long weighed upon his mind, and to a certain extent estranged him from society; but as the night wore away and his artificial gaiety began to flag, these painful feelings gradually intruded themselves again, and he grew abstracted and anxious as heretofore.

He took his leave at length, with an unpleasant foreboding of some coming mischief, and with a mind haunted with a thousand mysterious apprehensions, such as, even while he acutely felt their pressure, he, nevertheless, inwardly strove or affected to contemn.

It was this proud defiance of what he regarded as his own weakness which prompted him upon the present occasion to that course which brought about the adventure I am now about to relate.

Captain Barton might have easily called a coach, but he was conscious that his strong affliction to do so proceeded from no cause other than what he desperately persisted in representing to himself to be his own superstitious tremors.

He might also have returned home by a route different from that against which he had been warned by his mysterious correspondent; but, for the same reason he dismissed this idea also, and with a dogged and half-desperate resolution to force matters to a crisis of some kind, if there were any reality in the causes of his former suffering, and if not, satisfactorily to bring their delusiveness to the proof, he determined to follow precisely the course which he had trodden upon the night so painfully memorable in his own mind as that on which his strange persecution commenced. Though, sooth to say, the pilot who, for the first time, steers his vessel under the muzzles of a hostile battery, never felt his resolution more severely tasked than did Captain Barton, as he breathlessly pursued his solitary path—a path which, in spite of every effort of scepticism and reason, he felt to be infested by some (as respected him) malignant being.

He pursued his way steadily and rapidly, scarcely breathing from intensity of suspense; he, however, was troubled by no renewal of the dreaded footsteps, and was beginning to feel a return of confidence as, more than three fourths of the way being accomplished with impunity, he approached the long line of twinkling oil lamps which indicated the frequented street.

This feeling of self-congratulation was, however, momentary. The report of a musket at some hundred yards behind him, and the whistle of a bullet close to his head, disagreeably and startlingly dispelled it. His first impulse was to retrace his steps in pursuit of the assassin; but the road on either side was, as we have said, embarrassed by the foundations of a street, beyond which extended waste fields, full of rubbish and neglected lime and brick kilns, and all now as utterly silent as though no sound had ever disturbed their dark and unsightly solitude. The futility of, single-handed, attempting, under such circumstances, a search for the murderer, was apparent; especially as no sound, either of retreating steps or any other kind, was audible to direct his pursuit.

With the tumultuous sensations of one whose life has just been exposed to a murderous attempt, and whose escape has been the narrowest possible, Captain Barton turned again; and without, however, quickening his pace actually to a run, hurriedly pursued his way.

He had turned, as I have said, after a pause of a few seconds, and had just commenced his rapid retreat, when on a sudden he met the well-remembered little man in the fur cap. The encounter was but momentary. The figure was walking at the same exaggerated pace, and with the same strange air of menace as before; and as it passed him he thought he heard it say, in a furious whisper: "Still alive, still alive!"

The state of Captain Barton's spirits began now to work a corresponding alteration in his health and looks, and to such a degree that it was impossible that the change should escape general remark.

For some reasons known but to himself he took no steps whatever to bring the attempt upon his life, which he had so narrowly escaped, under the notice of the authorities; on the contrary, he kept it jealously to himself; and it was not for many weeks after the occurrence that he mentioned it, and then in strict confidence, to a gentleman, whom the torments of his mind at last compelled him to consult.

In spite of his blue devils, however, poor Barton, having no satisfactory reason to render to the public for any undue remissness in the attentions exacted by the relation existing between himself and Miss Montague, was obliged to exert himself, and present to the world a confident and cheerful bearing.

The true source of his sufferings, and every circumstance connected with him, he guarded with a reserve so jealous that it seemed dictated by at least a suspicion that the origin of his strange persecution was known to himself, and that it was of a nature which, upon his own account, he could not, or dared not, disclose.

The mind thus turned upon itself, and constantly occupied with a haunting anxiety which it dared not reveal or confide to any human breast, became daily more excited, and, of course, more vividly impressible, by a system of attack which operated through the nervous system; and in this state he was destined to sustain, with increasing frequency, the stealthy visitations of that apparition which from the first had seemed to possess so terrible a hold upon his imagination.

It was about this time that Captain Barton called upon the then celebrated preacher, Dr. ——, with whom he had a slight acquaintance, and an extraordinary conversation ensued.

The divine was seated in his chambers in college, surrounded with works upon his favourite pursuit, and deep in theology, when Barton was announced.

There was something at once embarrassed and excited in his manner, which, along with his wan and haggard countenance, impressed the student with the unpleasant consciousness that his visitor must have recently suffered terribly indeed to account for an alteration so striking—almost shocking.

After the usual interchange of polite greeting, and a few commonplace remarks, Captain Barton, who obviously perceived the surprise which his visit had excited, and which Doctor —— was unable wholly to conceal, interrupted a brief pause by remarking:

"This is a strange call, Doctor ——, perhaps scarcely warranted by an acquaintance so slight as mine with you. I should not under ordinary circumstances have ventured to disturb you; but my visit is neither an idle nor impertinent intrusion. I am sure you will not so account it, when I tell you how afflicted I am."

Doctor —— interrupted him with assurances such as good breeding suggested, and Barton resumed.

"I am come to task your patience by asking your advice. When I say your patience, I might, indeed, say more; I might have said your humanity—your compassion; for I have been, and am, a great sufferer."

"My dear sir," replied the churchman, "it will, indeed, afford me infinite gratification if I can give you comfort in any distress of mind! But—you know——"

"I know what you would say," resumed Barton, quickly; "I am an unbeliever, and, therefore, incapable of deriving help from religion; but don't take that for granted. At least you must not assume that, however unsettled my convictions may be, I do not feel a deep—a very deep—interest in the subject. Circumstances have lately forced it upon my attention in such a way as to compel me to review the whole question in a more candid and teachable spirit, I believe, than I ever studied it in before."

"Your difficulties, I take it for granted, refer to the evidences of revelation," suggested the clergyman.

"Why—no—not altogether; in fact, I am ashamed to say I have not considered even my objections sufficiently to state them connectedly; but—but there is one subject on which I feel a peculiar interest."

He paused again, and Dr. —— pressed him to proceed.

"The fact is," said Barton, "whatever may be my uncertainty as to the authenticity of what we are taught to call revelation, of one fact I am deeply and horribly convinced, that there does exist beyond this spiritual world—a system whose workings are generally in mercy hidden from us—a system which may be, and which is sometimes, partially and terribly revealed. I am sure—I know," continued Barton, with increasing excitement, "that there is a God—a dreadful God—and that retribution follows guilt, in ways the most mysterious and stupendous—by agencies the most inexplicable and terrific; there is a spiritual system—great God, how I have been convinced!—a system malignant, and implacable, and omnipotent, under whose persecutions I am, and have been, suffering the torments of the damned! Yes, sir—yes—the fires and frenzy of hell!"

As Barton spoke his agitation became so vehement that the Divine was shocked, and even alarmed. The wild and excited rapidity with which he spoke, and, above all, the indefinable horror that stamped his features, afforded a contrast to his ordinary cool and unimpassioned self-possession, striking and painful in the last degree.

"My dear sir," said Dr. ——, after a brief pause, "I fear you have been very unhappy, indeed; but I venture to predict that the depression under which you labour will be found to originate in purely physical causes, and that with a change of air, and the aid of a few tonics, your spirits will return and the tone of your mind be once more cheerful and tranquil as heretofore. There was, after all, more truth than we are quite willing to admit in the classic theories which assigned the undue predominance of any one affection of the mind to the undue action or torpidity of any one or other of our bodily organs. Believe me, that a little attention to diet, exercise, and the other essentials of health, under competent direction, will make you as much yourself as you can wish."

"Dr. ——," said Barton, with something like a shudder, "I cannot delude myself with such a hope. I have no hope to cling to but one, and that is, that by some other spiritual agency more potent than that which tortures me, it may be combated, and I delivered. If this may not be, I am lost—now and for ever lost."

"But, Captain Barton, you must remember," urged his companion, "that others have suffered as you have done, and——"

"No, no, no," interrupted he, with irritability; "no, sir, I am not a credulous —far from a superstitious man. I have been, perhaps, too much the reverse—too sceptical, too slow of belief; but unless I were one whom no amount of evidence could convince unless I were to contemn the repeated, the perpetual evidence of my own senses, I am now—now at last constrained to believe—I have no escape from the conviction—the overwhelming certainty—that I am haunted and dogged, go where I may, by—by a DEMON!"

There was a prenatural energy of horror in Barton's face, as, with its damp and death-like lineaments turned towards his companion, thus he delivered himself.

"God help you, my poor friend," said Dr. ——, much shocked. "God help you; for, indeed, you are a sufferer, however your sufferings may have been caused."

"Ay, ay, God help me," echoed Barton, sternly; "but will He help me—will He help me?"

"Pray to Him—pray in an humble and trusting spirit," said he.

"Pray, pray," echoed he again; "I can't pray—I could as easily move a mountain by an effort of my will. I have not belief enough to pray; there is something within me that will not pray. You prescribe impossibilities—literal impossibilities."

"You will not find it so, if you will but try," said Dr. ——.

"Try! I have tried, and the attempt only fills me with confusion; and, sometimes, terror: I have tried in vain and more than in vain. The awful, unutterable idea of eternity and infinity oppresses and maddens my brain whenever my mind approaches the contemplation of the Creator: I recoil from the effort, scared. I tell you, Dr. ——, if I am to be saved, it must be by other means. The idea of an eternal Creator is to me intolerable—my mind cannot support it."

"Say, then, my dear sir," urged he, "say how you would have me serve you: what you would learn of me—what I can do or say to relieve you?"

"Listen to me first," replied Captain Barton, with a subdued air, and an effort to suppress his excitement, "listen to me while I detail the circumstances of the persecution under which my life has become all but intolerable—a persecution which has made me fear death and the world beyond the grave as much as I have grown to hate existence."

Barton then proceeded to relate the circumstances which I have already detailed, and then continued:

"This has now become habitual—an unaccustomed thing. I do not mean the actual seeing him in the flesh—thank God, that at least is not permitted daily. Thank God, from the ineffable horrors of that visitation I have been mercifully allowed intervals of repose, though none of security; but from the consciousness that a malignant spirit is following and watching me wherever I go, I have never, for a single instant, a temporary respite. I am pursued with blasphemies, cries of despair and appalling hatred. I hear those dreadful sounds called after me as I turn the corners of the streets; they come in the night-time, while I sit in my chamber alone; they haunt me everywhere, charging me with hideous crimes, and—Great God!—threatening me with coming vegeance and eternal misery. Hush! do you hear that?" he cried, with a horrible smile of triumph; "there—there, will that convince you?"

The clergyman felt a chill of horror steal over him, while, during the wail of a sudden gust of wind he heard, or fancied he heard, the half-articulate sounds of rage and derision mingling in the sough.

"Well, what do you think of that?" at length Barton cried, drawing a long breath through his teeth.

"I heard the wind," said Dr. ——. "What should I think of it—what is there remarkable about it?"

"The prince of the powers of the air," muttered Barton, with a shudder.

"Tut, tut! my dear sir," said the student, with an effort to reassure himself; for although it was broad daylight there was, nevertheless, something disagreeably contagious in the nervous excitement under which his visitor so miserably suffered. "You must not give way to these wild fancies; you must resist these impulses of the imagination."

"Ay, ay; 'resist the devil and he will flee from thee'," said Barton, in the same tone; "but how resist him? Ay, there it is—there is the rub. What—what am I to do? What can I do?"

"My dear sir, this is fancy," said the man of folios; "you are your own tormentor."

"No, no, sir—fancy has no part in it," answered Barton, somewhat sternly. "Fancy! Was it that made you, as well as me, hear, but this moment, those accents of hell? Fancy, indeed! No, no."

"But you have seen this person frequently," said the ecclesiastic; "why have you not accosted or secured him? Is it not a little precipitate, to say no more, to assume, as you have done, the existence of a preternatural agency; when, after all, everything may be easily accountable, if only proper means were taken to sift the matter."

There are circumstances connected with this—this appearance," said Barton, "which it is needless to disclose, but which to me are proofs of its horrible nature. I know that the being that follows me is not human—I say I know this; I could prove it to your own conviction." He paused for a minute, and then added: "And as to accosting it, I dare not, I could not; when I see it I am powerless; I stand in the gaze of death, in the triumphant presence of infernal power and malignity. My strength, and faculties, and memory, all forsake me. O God, I fear, sir, you know not what you speak of. Mercy, mercy; heaven have pity on me!"

He leaned his elbow on the table and passed his hand across his eyes, as if to exclude some image of horror, muttering the last words of the sentence he had just concluded again and again.

"Dr. ——," he said, abruptly raising himself, and looking full upon the clergyman with an imploring eye, "I know you will do for me whatever may be done. You know now fully the circumstances and the nature of my affliction. I tell you I cannot help myself; I cannot help to escape; I am utterly passive. I conjure you, then, to weigh my case well, and if anything may be done for me by vicarious supplication—by the intercession of the good—or by any aid or influence whatsoever, I implore of you, I adjure you in the name of the Most High, give me the benefit of that influence—deliver me from the body of this death. Strive for me, pity me; I know you will; you cannot refuse this; it is the purpose and object of my visit. Send me away with some hope—however little—some faint hope of ultimate deliverance, and I will nerve myself to endure, from hour to hour, the hideous dream into which my existence has been transformed."

Dr. —— assured him that all he could do was to pray earnestly for him, and that so much he would not fail to do. They parted with a hurried and melancholy valediction. Barton hastened to the carriage that awaited him at the door, drew down the blinds, and drove away, while Dr. —— returned to his chamber, to ruminate at leisure upon the strange interview which had just interrupted his studies.

It was not to be expected that Captain Barton's changed and eccentric habits should long escape remark and discussion. Various were the theories suggested to account for it. Some attributed the alteration to the pressure of secret pecuniary embarrassments; others to a repugnance to fulfil an engagement into which he was presumed to have too precipitately entered; and others, again, to the supposed incipiency of mental disease, which latter, indeed, was the most plausible, as well as the most generally received, of the hypotheses circulated in the gossip of the day.

From the very commencement of this change, at first so gradual in its advances, Miss Montague had, of course, been aware of it. The intimacy involved in their peculiar relation, as well as the near interest which it inspired, afforded, in her case, a like opportunity and motive for the successful exercise of that keen and penetrating observation peculiar to her sex.

His visits became, at length, so interrupted, and his manner, while they lasted, so abstracted, strange and agitated, that Lady L——, after hinting her anxiety and her suspicions more than once, at length distinctly stated her anxiety, and pressed for an explanation.

The explanation was given, and although its nature at first relieved the worst solicitudes of the old lady and her niece, yet the circumstances which attended it, and the really dreadful consequences which it obviously indicated, as regarded the spirits, and indeed the reason of the now wretched man who made the strange declaration, were enough, upon little reflection, to fill their minds with perturbation and alarm.

General Montague, the young lady's father, at length arrived. He had himself slightly known Barton some ten or twelve years previously and, being aware of his fortune and connections, was disposed to regard him as an exceptional and indeed a most desirable match for his daughter. He laughed at the story of Barton's supernatural visitations, and lost no time in calling upon his intended son-in-law.

"My dear Barton," he continued, gaily, after a little conversation, "my sister tells me that you are a victim to blue devils in quite a new and original shape."

Barton changed countenance, and sighed profoundly.

"Come, come; I protest this will never do," continued the General; "you are more like a man on his way to the gallows than to the altar. These devils have made——"

Barton made an effort to change the conversation.

"No, no, it won't do," said the visitor, laughing; "I am resolved to say what I have to say upon this magnificent mock mystery of yours. You must not be angry, but really it is too bad to see you at your time of life absolutely frightened into good behaviour, like a naughty child by a bugaboo, and as far as I can learn a very contemptible one. Seriously, I have been a good deal annoyed at what they tell me; but at the same time thoroughly convinced that there is nothing in the matter that may not be cleared up, with a little attention and management, within a week at furthest."

"Ah, General, you do not know——" he began.

"Yes, but I do know quite enough to warrant my confidence," interrupted the soldier; "don't I know that all your annoyance proceeds from the occasional appearance of a certain little man in a cap and greatcoat, with a red vest and a bad face, who follows you about, and pops upon you at corners of lanes, and throws you into ague fits. Now, my dear fellow, I'll make it my business to catch this mischievous little mountebank, and either beat him to a jelly with my own hands, or have him whipped through the town, at the cat's tail, before a month passes."

"If you knew what I knew," said Barton, with gloomy agitation, "you would speak very differently. Don't imagine that I am so weak as to assume, without proof the most overwhelming, the conclusion to which I have been forced—the proofs are here, locked up here." As he spoke he tapped upon his breast, and with an anxious sigh continued to walk up and down the room.

"Well, well, Barton," said his visitor, "I'll wager a rump and a dozen I collar the ghost, and convince even you before many days are over."

He was running on in the same strain when he was suddenly arrested, and not a little shocked, by observing Barton, who had approached the window, stagger slowly back, like one who had received a stunning blow; his arm extended towards the street—his face and his very lips white as ashes—while he muttered: "There—by heaven!—there—there!"

General Montague started mechanically to his feet, and from the window of the drawing-room saw a figure corresponding, as well as his hurry would permit him to discern, with the description of the person whose appearance so persistently disturbed the repose of his friend.

The figure was just turning from the rails of the area upon which it had been leaning, and, without waiting to see more, the old gentleman snatched his cane and hat, and rushed down the stairs and into the street, in the furious hope of securing the person, and punishing the audacity of the mysterious stranger.

He looked round him, but in vain, for any trace of the person he had himself distinctly seen. He ran breathlessly to the nearest corner, expecting to see from thence the retiring figure, but no such form was visible. Back and forward, from crossing to crossing, he ran, at fault, and it was not until the curious gaze and laughing countenances of the passers-by reminded him of the absurdity of his pursuit, that he checked his hurried pace, lowered his walking-cane from the menacing altitude which he had mechanically given it, adjusted his hat, and walked composedly back again, inwardly vexed and flurried. He found Barton pale and trembling in every joint; they both remained silent, though under emotions very different. At last Barton whispered, : "You saw it?"

"It—him—someone—you mean—to be sure I did," replied Montague, testily. "But where is the good or the harm of seeing him? The fellow runs like a lamplighter. I wanted to catch him, but he had stolen away before I could reach the hall door. However, it is no great matter; next time, I dare say, I'll do better; and, egad, if I once come within reach of him, I'll introduce his shoulders to the weight of my cane."

Notwithstanding General Montague's undertakings and exhortations, however, Barton continued to suffer from the selfsame unexplained cause; go how, when, or where he would, he was still constantly dogged or confronted by the being who had established over him so horrible an influence.

Nowhere and at no time was he secure against the odious appearance which haunted him with such diabolical perseverance.

His depression, misery, and excitement became more settled and alarming every day, and the mental agonies that ceaselessly preyed upon him began, at last, so sensibly to affect his health that Lady L—— and General Montague succeeded without, indeed, much difficulty in persuading him to try a short tour on the Continent, in the hope that an entire change of scene would, at all events, have the effect of breaking through the influences of local association, which the more sceptical of his friends assumed to be by no means inoperative in suggesting and perpetuating what they conceived to be a mere form of nervous illusion.

General Montague, indeed, was persuaded that the figure which haunted his intended son-in-law was by no means the creation of his imagination, but on the contrary, a substantial form of flesh and blood, animated by a resolution, perhaps with some murderous object in perspective, to watch and follow the unfortunate gentleman.

Even this hypotheses was not a very pleasant one; that it was plain that if Barton could ever be convinced that there was nothing preternatural in the phenomenon which he had hitherto regarded in that light, the affair would lose all its terrors in his eyes, and wholly cease to exercise upon his health and spirits the baleful influence which it had hitherto done. He therefore reasoned that if the annoyance were actually escaped by mere locomotion and change of scene, it obviously could not have originated in any supernatural agency.

Yielding to their persuasions, Barton left Dublin for England accompanied by General Montague. They posted rapidly to London, and thence to Dover, whence they took the packet with a fair wind for Calais. The General's confidence in the result of the expedition on Barton's spirits had risen day by day since their departure from the shores of Ireland; for to the inexpressible relief and delight of the latter, he had not since then so much as even once fancied a repetition of those impressions which had, when at home, drawn him gradually down to the very depths of despair.

This exemption from what he had begun to regard as the inevitable condition of his existence, and the sense of security which began to pervade his mind, were inexpressibly delightful; and in the exultation of what he considered his deliverance, he indulged in a thousand happy anticipations for a future into which so lately he had hardly dared to look; and, in so short, both he and his companion secretly congratulated themselves upon the termination of that persecution which had been to its immediate victim a source of such unspeakable agony.

It was a beautiful day, and a crowd of idlers stood upon the jetty to receive the packet and enjoy the bustle of the new arrivals. Montague walked a few paces in advance of his friend, and as he made his way through the crowd a little man touched his arm and said to him, in a broad provincial *patois*:

"Monsieur is walking too fast; he will lose his sick comrade in the throng, for, by my faith, the poor gentleman seems to be fainting."

Montague turned quickly, and observed that Barton did, indeed, look deadly pale. He hastened to his side.

"My dear fellow, are you ill?" he asked anxiously.

The question was unheeded, and twice repeated, ere Barton stammered:

"I saw him—by ——, I saw him!"

"Him!—the wretch—who—where now?—where is he?" cried Montague, looking around him.

"I saw him—but he is gone," repeated Barton, faintly.

"But where—where? For God's sake speak," urged Montague, vehemently.

"It is but this moment—here," said he.

"But what did he look like—what had he on—what did he wear—quick, quick," urged his excited companion, ready to dart among the crowd and collar the delinquent on the spot.

"He touched your arm—he spoke to you—he pointed to me. God be merciful to me, there is no escape," said Barton, in the low, subdued tones of despair.

Montague had already bustled away in all the flurry of mingled hope and rage; but though the singular personnel of the stranger who had accosted him was vividly impressed upon his recollection, he failed to discover among the crowd even the slightest resemblance to him.

After a fruitless search, in which he enlisted the services of several of the bystanders, who aided all the more zealously as they believed he had been robbed, he at length, out of breath and baffled, gave over the attempt.

"Ah, my friend, it won't do," said Barton, with the faint voice and bewildered, ghastly look of one who had been stunned by some mortal shock; "there is no use contending; whatever it is, the dreadful association between me and it is now established—I shall never escape—never!"

"Nonsense, nonsense, my dear Barton; don't talk so," said Montague, with something at once of irritation and dismay; "you must not, I say; we'll jockey the scoundrel yet; never mind, I say—never mind."

It was, however, but labour lost to endeavour henceforward to inspire Barton with one ray of hope; he became desponding.

This intangible and, as it seemed, utterly inadequate influence was fast destroying his energies of intellect, character, and health. His first object was now to return to Ireland, there, as he believed, and now almost hoped, speedily to die.

To Ireland accordingly he came, and one of the first faces he saw upon the thore was again that of his implacable and dreaded attendant. Barton seemed as last to have lost not only all enjoyment and every hope in existence, but all independence of will besides. He now submitted himself passively to the management of the friends most nearly interested in his welfare.

With the apathy of entire despair he implicitly assented to whatever measures they suggested and advised; and as a last resource it was determined to remove him to a house of Lady L——'s, in the neighbourhood of Clontarf, where, with the advice of his medical attendant, who persisted in his opinion that the whole train of consequences resulted merely from some nervous derangement, it was resolved that he was to confine himself strictly to the house, and make use only of those apartments who commanded a view of an enclosed yard, the gates of which were to be kept jealously locked.

Those precautions would certainly secure him against the casual appearance of any living form that his excited imagination might possibly confound with the spectre which, as it was contended, his fancy recognized in every figure that bore even a distant or general resemblance to the peculiarities with which his fancy had at first invested it.

A month or six weeks of absolute seclusion under these conditions, it was hoped might, by interrupting the series of these terrible impressions, gradually dispel the predisposing apprehensions, and the associations which had confirmed the supposed disease, and rendered recovery hopeless.

Cheerful society and that of his friends was to be constantly supplied, and on the whole, very sanguine expectations were indulged in, that under the treatment thus detailed, the obstinate hypochondria of the patient might at length give way.

Accompanied, therefore, by Lady L——, General Montague and his daughter—his own affianced bride—poor Barton—himself never daring to cherish a hope of his ultimate emancipation from the horrors under which his life was literally wasting away—took possession of the apartments, whose situation protected him against the intrusions from which he shrank with such unutterable terror.

After a little time a steady persistence in this system began to manifest its results in a very marked though gradual improvement, alike in the health and spirits of the invalid. Not, indeed, that anything at all approaching complete recovery was yet discernible. On the contrary, to those who had not seen him since the commencement of his strange sufferings, such an alteration would have been apparent as might well have shocked them.

The improvement, however, such as it was, was welcomed with gratitude and delight, especially by the young lady, whom her attachment to him, as well as her now singularly painful position, consequent upon his protracted illness, rendered an object scarcely one degree less to be commiserated than himself.

A week passed—a fortnight—a month—and yet there had been no recurrence of the hated visitation. The treatment had, so far forth, been followed by complete success. The chain of associations was broken. The constant pressure upon the overtasked spirits had been removed, and, under these comparatively favourable circumstances, the sense of social community with the world about him, and something of human interest, of not of enjoyment, began to reanimate him.

It was about this time that Lady L——, who, like most old ladies of the day, was deep in family receipts, and a great pretender to medical science, dispatched her own maid to the kitchen garden with a list of herbs, which were there to be carefully culled and brought back to her housekeeper for the purpose stated. The handmaiden, however, returned with her task scarce half-completed, and a good deal flurried and alarmed. Her mode of accounting for her precipitate retreat and evident agitation was odd and, to the old lady, startling.

It appeared that she had repaired to the kitchen garden, pursuant to her mistress' directions, and had there begun to make the specified election among the rank and neglected herbs which crowded one corner of the enclosure; and while engaged in this pleasant labour she carelessly sang a fragment of an old song, as she said, "to keep herself company". She was, however, interrupted by an ill-natured laugh; and, looking up, she saw through the old thorn hedge which surrounded the garden a singularly ill-looking little man, whose countenance wore the stamp of menace and malignity, standing close to her at the other side of the hawthorn screen.

She described herself as utterly unable to move or speak, while he charged her with a message for Captain Barton, the substance of which she distinctly remembered to have been to the effect that he, Captain Barton, must come abroad as usual, to show himself to his friends out of doors, or else prepare for a visit in his own chamber.

On concluding this brief message the stranger had, with a threatening air, got down in the outer ditch and, seizing the hawthorn stems in his hands, seemed on the point of climbing through the fence—a feat which might have been accomplished without much difficulty.

Without, of course, awaiting this result, the girl—throwing down her treasures of thyme and rosemary—had turned and run, with the swiftness of terror, to the house. Lady L—— commanded her, on pain of instant dismissal, to observe an absolute silence respecting all that passed of the incident which related to Captain Barton; and, at the same time, directed instant search to be made for her men in the garden and the fields adjacent. This measure, however, was as usual unsuccessful, and, filled with indefinable misgivings, Lady L—— communicated the incident to her brother. The story, however, until long afterwards, went no further, and, of course, it was jealously guarded from Barton, who continued to amend though slowly.

Barton now began to walk occasionally in the courtyard which I have mentioned, and which, being enclosed by a high wall, commanded no view beyond its own extent. Here he, therefore, considered himself perfectly secure: and, but for a careless violation of orders by one of the grooms, he might have enjoyed, at least for some time longer, his much-prized immunity. Opening upon the public road, this yard was entered by a wooden gate, with a wicket in it, and was further defended by an iron gate upon the outside. Strict orders had been given to keep both carefully locked; but, in spite of these, it happened that one day, as Barton was slowly pacing this narrow enclosure in his accustomed walk, and reaching the farther extremity was turning to retrace his steps, he saw the boarded wicket ajar, and the face of his tormentor immovably looking at him through the iron bars. For a few seconds he stood riveted to the earth—breathless and bloodless—in the fascination of that dreaded gaze, and then fell helplessly insensible upon the pavement.

There he was found a few minutes afterwards, and conveyed to his room—the apartment which he was never afterwards to leave alive. Henceforward, a marked and unaccountable change was observable in the tone of his mind. Captain Barton was now no longer the excited and despairing man he had been before; a strange alteration had passed upon him—an unearthly tranquillity reigned in his mind—it was the anticipated stillness of the grave.

"Montague, my friend, this struggle is nearly ended now," he said, tranquilly, but with a look of fixed and fearful awe. "I have, at last, some comfort from the world of spirits from which my punishment has come. I now know that my sufferings will soon be over."

Montague pressed him to speak on.

"Yes," said he, in a softened voice, "my punishment is nearly ended. From sorrow, perhaps, I shall never, in time or eternity, escape; but my agony is almost over. Comfort has been revealed to me, and what remains of my allotted struggle I will bear with submission—even with hope."

"I am glad to hear you speak so tranquilly, my dear Barton," said Montague; "peace and cheer of mind are all you need to make you what you were."

"No, no—I never can be that," said he mournfully. "I am no longer fit for life. I am soon to die. I am to see him but once again, and then all is ended."

"He said so, then?" suggested Montague.

"He? No, no; good tidings could scarcely come through him; and these were good and welcome; and they came so solemnly and sweetly—with unutterable love and melancholy, such as I could not—without saying more than is needful, or fitting, of other long past scenes and persons—fully explain to you." As Barton said this he shed tears.

"Come, come," said Montague, mistaking the source of his emotions, "you must not give way. What is it, after all, but a pack of dreams and nonsense; or, at worst, the practices of a scheming rascal that enjoys his power of playing upon your nerves, and loves to exert it—a sneaking vagabond that owes you a grudge, and pays it off this way, not daring to try a more manly one."

"A grudge, indeed, he owes me—you say rightly," said Barton, with a sudden shudder; "a grudge as you call it. Oh, my God! when the justice of Heaven permits the Evil one to carry out a scheme of vengeance—when its execution is committed to the lost and terrible victim of sin, who owes his own ruin to the man, the very man, whom he is commissioned to pursue—then, indeed, the torments and terrors of hell are anticipated on earth. But heaven has dealt mercifully with me—hope has opened to me at last; and if death could come without the dreadful sight I am doomed to see, I would gladly close my eyes this moment upon the world. But though death is welcome, I shrink with an agony you cannot understand—an actual frenzy of terror—from the last encounter with that—that DEMON, who has drawn me thus to the verge of the chasm, and who is himself to plunge me down. I am to see him again—once more—but under circumstnaces unutterably more terrific than ever."

As Barton thus spoke he trembled so violently that Montague was really alarmed at the extremity of his sudden agitation, and hastened to lead him back to the topic which had before seemed to exert so tranquillizing an effect upon his mind.

"It was not a dream," he said, after a time; "I was in a different state—I felt differently and strangely; and yet it was all as real, as clear and vivid as what I now see and hear—it was a reality."

"And what did you see and hear?" urged his companion.

"When I wakened from the swoon I fell into on seeing him," said Barton, continuing as if he had not heard the question, "it was slowly, very slowly—I was lying by the margin of a broad lake, with misty hills all round, and a soft, melancholy, rose-coloured light illuminated it all. It was unusually sad and lonely, and yet more beautiful than any earthly scene. My head was leaning on the lap of a girl, and she was singing a song that told, I know not how—whether by words or harmonies—of all my life—all that is past, and all that is still to come; and with the song the old feelings that I thought had perished within me came back, and tears flowed from my eyes—partly for the song and its mysterious beauty, and partly for the unearthly sweetness of her voice; and yet I knew the voice—oh! how well; and I was spellbound as I listened and looked at the solitary scene, without stirring, almost without breathing—and, alas! alas! without turning my eyes towards the face that I knew was near me, so sweetly powerful was the enchantment that held me. And so, slowly, the song and scene grew fainter, and fainter, to my senses, till all was dark and still again. And then I awoke to this world, as you saw, comforted, for I knew that I was forgiven much." Barton wept again long and bitterly.

From this time, as we have said, the prevailing tone of his mind was one of profound and tranquil melancholy. This, however, was not without its interruptions. He was thoroughly impressed with the conviction that he was to experience another and final visitation, transcending in horror all he had before experienced. From this anticipated and unknown agony he often shrank in such paroxysms of abject terror and distraction, as filled the whole household with dismay and superstititious panic. Even those among them who affected to discredit the theory of preternatural agency, were often in their secret souls visited during the silence of night with qualms and apprehensions, which they would not have readily confessed; and none of them attempted to dissuade Barton from the resolution on which he now systematically acted, of shutting himself up in his own apartment. The window-blinds of this room were kept jealously down, and his own man was seldom out of his presence, day or night, his bed being placed in the same chamber.

This man was an attached and respectable servant; and his duties, in addition to those ordinarily imposed upon valets, but which Barton's independent habits generally dispensed with, were to attend carefully to the simple precautions by means of which his master hoped to exclude the dreaded intrusion of the "Watcher". And, in addition to attending to those arrangements, which amounted merely to guarding against the possibility of his master's being, through any unscreened window or open door, exposed to the dreaded influence, the valet was never to suffer him to be alone—total solitude, even for a minute, had become to him now almost as intolerable as the idea of going abroad into the public ways—it was an instinctive anticipation of what was coming.

It is needless to say, that under these circumstances no steps were taken toward the fulfiment of that engagement into which he had entered. There was quite disparity enough in point of years, and indeed of habits, between the young lady and Captain Barton to have precluded anything like very vehement or romantic attachment on her part. Though grieved and anxious, therefore, she was very far from being heartbroken.

Miss Montague, however, devoted much of her time to the patient but fruitless attempt to cheer the unhappy invalid. She read to him and conversed with him; but it was apparent that whatever exertions he made, the endeavour to escape from the one ever waking fear that preyed upon him was utterly and miserably unavailing.

Young ladies are much given to the cultivation of pets; and among those who shared the favour of Miss Montague was a fine old owl, which the gardener, who caught him napping among the ivy of a ruined stable, had dutifully presented to that young lady.

The caprice which regulates such preferences was manifested in the extravagant favour with which the grim and ill-favoured bird was at once distinguished by his mistress; and, trifling as this whimsical circumstance may seem, I am forced to mention it, inasmuch as it is connected, oddly enough, with the concluding scene of the story.

Barton, so far from sharing in this liking for the new favourite, regarded it from the first with an antipathy as violent as it was utterly unaccountable. Its very vicinity was unsupportable to him. He seemed to hate and dread it with a vehemence absolutely laughable, and which, to those who have never witnessed the exhibition of antipathies of this kind, would seem all but incredible.

With these few words of preliminary explanation, I shall proceed to state the particulars of the last scene in this strange series of incidents. It was almost two o'clock one winter's night, and Barton was, as usual at that hour, in his bed; the servant we have mentioned occupied a smaller bed in the same room, and a light was burning. The man was on a sudden aroused by his master, who said:

"I can't get it out of my head that accursed bird has got out somehow, and is lurking in some corner of the room. I have been dreaming about him. Get up, Smith, and look about; search for him. Such hateful dreams!"

The servant rose and examined the chamber, and while engaged in so doing he heard the well-known sound, more like a long-drawn gasp than a hiss, with which these birds from their secret haunts affright the quiet of the night.

This ghostly indication of its proximity—for the sound proceeded from the passage upon which Barton's chamber door opened—determined the search of the servant, who, opening the door, proceeded a step or two forward for the purpose of driving the bird away. He had, however, hardly entered the lobby, when the door behind him slowly swung to under the impulse, as it seemed, of some gentle current of air; but as immediately over the door there was a kind of window, intended in the daytime to aid in lighting the passage, and through which at present the rays of the candle were issuing, the valet could see quite enough for his purpose.

As he advanced he heard his master—who, lying in a well-curtained bed, had not, as it seemed, perceived his exit from the room—call him by name, and direct him to place the candle on the table by his bed. The servant, who was now some way in the long passage, and not liking to raise his voice for the purpose of replying, lest he should startle the sleeping inmates of the house, began to walk hurriedly and softly back again, when, to his amazement, he heard a voice in the interior of the chamber answering calmly, and actually saw, through the window which overtopped the door, that the light was slowly shifting, as if carried across the room in answer to his master's call. Palsied by a feeling akin to terror, yet not intermingled with curiosity, he stood breathless and listening at the threshold, unable to summon resolution to push open the door and enter. Then came a rustling of the curtains, and a sound like that of one who in a low voice hushes a child to rest, in the midst of which he heard Barton say, in a tone of stifled horror: "Oh, God—oh, my God!" and repeat the same exclamation several times. Then ensued a silence, which again was broken by the same soothing sound; and at last there burst forth, in one swelling peal, a yell of agony so appalling and hideous that, under some impulse of ungovernable horror, the man rushed to the door, and with his whole strength strove to force it open. Whether it was that, in his agitation, he had himself but imperfectly turned the handle, or that the door was really secured upon the inside, he failed to effect an entrance; and as he tugged and pushed, yell after yell rang louder and wilder through the chamber, accompanied all the while by the same hushed sounds. Actually freezing with terror, and scarce knowing what he did, the man turned and ran down the passage, wringing his hands in the extremity of horror and irresolution. At the stair-head he was encountered by General Montague, scared and eager, and just as they met the fearful sounds had ceased.

"What is it? Who—where is your master?" said Montague, with the incoherence of extreme agitation. "Has anything—for God's sake is anything wrong?"

"Lord have mercy on us, it's all over," said the man, staring wildly towards his master's chamber. "He's dead, sir, I'm sure he's dead."

Without waiting for enquiry or explanation, Montague, closely followed by the servant, hurried to the chamber door, turned the handle, and pushed it open. As the door yielded to his pressure the ill-omened bird of which the servant had been in search, uttering its spectral warning, started suddenly from the far side of the bed, and flying through the doorway close over their heads, and extinguishing, in its passage, the candle which Montague carried, crashed through the skylight that overlooked the lobby and sailed away into the darkness of the outer space.

"There it is, God bless us," whispered the man, after a breathless pause.

"Curse that bird," muttered the General, startled by the suddenness of the apparition, and unable to conceal his discomposure.

"The candle is moved," said the man, after another breathless pause, pointing to the candle that still burned in the room; "see, they put it by the bed."

"Draw the curtains, fellow, and don't stand gaping there," whispered Montague, sternly.

The man hesitated.

"Hold this, then," said Montague, impatiently thrusting the candlestick into the servant's hand, and himself advancing to the bedside, he drew the curtains apart. The light of the candle, which was still burning at the bedside, fell upon a figure huddled together, and half upright, at the head of the bed. It seemed as though it had slunk back as far as the solid panelling would allow, and the hands were still clutched in the bed-clothes.

"Barton, Barton, Barton!" cried the General, with a strange mixture of awe and vehemence. He took the candle, and held it so that it shone full upon the face. The features were fixed, stern, and white; the jaw was fallen; and the sightless eyes, still open, gazed fixedly towards the front of the bed. "God Almighty! He's dead," muttered the General, as he looked upon this fearful spectacle. They both continued to gaze upon it in silence for a minute or more. "And cold, too," whispered Montague, withdrawing his hand from that of the dead man.

"And see, see—may I never have life, sir," added the man, after another pause, with a shudder, "but there was something else on that bed with him. Look there—look there—see that, sir."

As the man thus spoke, he pointed to a deep indenture, as if caused by a heavy pressure, near the foot of the bed.

Montague was silent.

"Come, sir, come away, for God's sake," whispered the man, drawing close up to him, and holding fast by his arm, while he glanced fearfully round; "what good can be done here now—come away, for God's sake!"

At this moment they heard the steps of more than one approaching, and Montague, hastily desiring the servant to arrest their progress, endeavoured to loose the rigid grip with which the fingers of the dead man were clutched in the bed-clothes, and drew, as well as he was able, the awful figure into a reclining posture; then closing the curtains carefully upon it, he hastened himself to meet those persons that were approaching.

It is needless to follow the personages so slightly connected with this narrative into the events of their after-life; it is enough to say, that no clue to the solution of these mysterious occurrences was ever after discovered; and so long an interval having now passed since the event which I have just described concluded this strange history, it is scarcely to be expected that time can throw any new lights upon its dark and inexplicable outline. Until the secrets of the earth shall be no longer hidden, therefore, these transactions must remain shrouded in their original obscurity.

The only occurrence in Captain Barton's former life to which reference was ever made, as having any possible connection with the sufferings with which his existence closed, and which he himself seemed to regard as working out a retribution for some grievous sin of his past life, was a circumstance which not for several years after his death was brought to light. The nature of the disclosure was painful to his relatives, and discreditable to his memory.

It appeared that some six years before Captain Barton's final return to Dublin, he had formed, in the town of Plymouth, a guilty attachment, the object of which was the daughter of one of the ship's crew under his command. The father had visited the frailty of his unhappy child with extreme harshness, and even brutality, and it was said that she had died heartbroken. Presuming upon Barton's implication in her guilt, this man had conducted himself towards him with marked insolence; and Barton retaliated this, and what he resented was still more exasperated bitterness—his treatment of the unfortunate girl—by a systematic exercise of those terrible and arbitrary severities which the regulations of the navy placed at the command of those who are responsible for its discipline. The man had at length made his escape, while the vessel was in port at Naples, but died, as it was said, in an hospital in that town, of the wounds inflicted in one of his recent and sanguinary punishments.

Whether these circumstances in reality bear, or not, upon the occurrences of Barton's after-life, it is, of course, impossible to say. It seems, however, more than probable that they were at least, in his own mind, closely associated with them. But however the truth may be as to the origin and motives of this mysterious persecution, there can be no doubt that, with respect to the agencies by which it was accomplished, absolute and impenetrable mystery is like to prevail until the day of doom.

MR. HOPKINS AND GALATEA

By James Laver

THE sea was bluer than that which washes the barnacles on the pier at Margate, the sand more golden than that which stretches to the horizon at Southend, the bathing-tents more brilliant in colour, the white tops of the waves more fantastically curled; and they—the bathers—though clothed in human shape (with the slight addition of gay costumes adapted for sun-bathing), were not of the same flesh as the crowds thronging the promenades, esplanades, sea-view terraces and cast-iron piers of our popular English resorts. No! Their figures had an elegance, their wraps and parasols a *chic*, their smiles an *insouciance* which proclaimed them to the world: creatures with backs unbent by ill-paid toil, with souls unseared by monetary cares, whom but to see was to love, and whose perfect clothes were given to them, as by an over-ruling Providence, not for what they did but for what they were.

Proud of their distinction, they lolled carelessly but gracefully in wicker-chairs beside bright green tables on which stood their untouched glasses; or posed delicately at the edge of the waves, or gathered in groups, the pattern of which suggested a studied negligence. They smiled strange non-committal smiles and seemed to speak, but did not; for between them and the vulgar world there hung some invisible curtain, as if a transparent barrier of plate-glass isolated their perfection.

But not completely, for as one watched a strange, uncouth figure emerged from behind a rock, moving stealthily among the unconscious bathers. So a satyr, save that the newcomer was milder and not so hairy. He was, indeed, a quiet little man with a ragged moustache and pince-nez, which gave to his watery blue eyes a pale metallic glitter.

He advanced on tiptoe among the unconscious bathers, skirted the table on which stood the coloured cocktails and, reaching the group in the corner beside the bathing-tent, stretched upwards, his hands emerging scraggily from his frayed cuffs, and placed upon the head of the tallest of the ladies a bright green india-rubber cap. Then he retired as gingerly as he had come, leaving the aristocratic figures as undisturbed by his departure as they had been by his presence.

"Now, Mr. Simpson," he said, rather sharply, "we have another window to do before ten o'clock."

Mr. Simpson, a fair-haired young man with an elegant figure clad in a black coat and striped trousers, ceased making eyes at the pretty blonde behind the scent counter and followed Mr. Hopkins, for such was the little man's name, into a kind of Gothic chamber, where a wedding was in progress, at least, it shortly would be, for at present the bridesmaids wore only a calico wrap round their middles and exposed their wax bosoms shamelessly to the public gaze.

The whole business bored Mr. Simpson extremely. He would have liked to dress the windows himself, but Mr. Hopkins never gave him a chance. All he was required to do was to stand by with a packet of pins and watch the older man slipping the dresses over the heads of the mannequins. A pin-cushion could do his job, he told himself bitterly; but a time would come. . . . Not that Hopkins was a bad sort of chap, but dry and uncommunicative to a degree, and he secretly resented the presence of this young man, destined one day to replace him.

With his quiet, self-effacing ways it had taken him twenty years to reach his present position in the great departmental store. Gradually the dressing of the wax figures in the windows had become more and more completely his province; but a new and energetic young man had succeeded the old Managing Director, and Mr. Hopkins was aware that he did not stand quite so high in the opinion of his chiefs as he once did. There had been so many changes in window-dressing since the War. All these golden women, black women, women half an inch thick—how he hated them! He liked the ones that looked real, with pink cheeks and flaxen hair, hair which grew out of their scalps and was not merely painted on, like some of the new figures recently brought over from Paris.

He had done his best to keep up with the times. He understood all about colour schemes and he could still dress a window to the satisfaction of his employers; only they had given him this young man "to help him". He needed no help, except, perhaps, one of the girls from the counter to hand him the dresses.

"The bridesmaids' bouquets, Mr. Simpson," he said, and Mr. Simpson obediently brought them. He was sent away again to bring two yards of broad blue ribbon and as he passed the scent counter paused for a moment to exchange a word with the pretty blonde.

"What's he like this morning?" she asked.
"Oh, grumpy as usual. I could dress those windows so much better myself."
"I am sure you could," said her admiring eyes.
"I must go now. See you tonight at the entrance?"
"Rather."

Mr. Simpson hurried on to the ribbon department.

. . . . .

The "staff door" of the big shop was down an unfrequented side street, unfrequented, that is, during the hours when customers were to be seen in the shop; but at six o'clock every evening it became suddenly animated. The shop-girls came through the grimy door laughing and chattering with all the gaiety of children released from school. Friends linked arms and hurried away to catch their buses, or stood about waiting for late-comers. Young men bade cheerful "Good nights" to their fellows: Mr. Simpson awaited his friend from the scent counter.

When she appeared he raised his hat, for they still treated one another with a certain ceremony. He proposed that they should walk a little way before catching their bus.

"Well, just a little way."
"Good night, Mr. Hopkins!" said the young man.
"Good night."

Mr. Hopkins was alone. He never waited about when his work was over. A peculiar square bowler hat on his head, his thin body wrapped in an overcoat with a velvet collar carefully brushed, he passed on, glancing neither to the right hand nor to the left. At the top of the street was a bus stop and he waited patiently for his bus. The first was full, and he waited for the second. When it came he found a seat inside. He did not smoke. When the conductor came he held out twopence without a word. His ticket punched, he placed it carefully in the cuff of his coat. A girl came and sat down beside him, but he did not turn his head.

At Hammersmith he climbed down from the bus and walked rapidly to the small house which he shared with his unmarried sister, and let himself in with his latchkey. His sister, a thin, grey woman three years older than himself, was setting the table for supper.

Neither of the pair was very talkative. After the preliminary greetings they fell silent. Had he been busy, she asked, after a pause. Yes, very busy. Then silence again while Mr. Hopkins dropped two lumps of sugar into his cup and stirred it methodically. Mr. Hopkins had always been quiet.

In his veins the Puritan blood of his ancestors had been thinned by a process of gradual refinement until it had lost all positive qualities and served only to restrain him from any kind of excess. In the same way the Old Testament fervour of the name Obadiah which his parents had given him had dwindled in his signature to a non-committal O. He read very little, his sister even less. In the long winter evenings they played draughts. They went to the pictures about once a year. Sometimes a few quiet friends dropped in for a chat, but very seldom. They went to bed early so that Mr. Hopkins should be fresh for the morrow. Neither had ever shown any inclination to marry. The store where he worked had always prided itself on the prettiness and smartness of its assistants, but Mr. Hopkins had worked among them for twenty years unmoved. His sister prided herself in secret that he had never "walked out" with anyone. If Mr. Hopkins thought about women at all, it was of the wax women in the windows of the shop, whose rigid limbs it was his business to clothe anew whenever the display was changed. He knew them all, as it were, personally, and during the years he had spent dressing the windows he had followed the course of their brief and melancholy lives. He remembered, as quite a young man, dressing the very first wax mannequins his employers had ever purchased. Their hair was piled high above their foreheads, their cheeks were shiny and very red, their eyes glassy, their busts enormous. Mr. Hopkins's entire knowledge of the changes which have occurred in the female figure during the last twenty years was derived from his acquaintance with dummies. Before the War the wax bosoms descended from the wax necks at an angle of forty-five degrees, then fell sharply inwards to the tiny waists. When the first mannequins of the new style had arrived, Mr. Hopkins had been mildly shocked at the frankness of the moulded wax breasts, to which the line of the chest fell steeply. It had seemed to him not quite nice, this insistence on the actual female form, but he had quickly taken it for granted, and now moved among them—even before he had slipped on their gowns—as unconcernedly as he moved among the living assistants in the shop. It was only these new-fangled dummies with the coloured concave faces that distressed him.

Half unconsciously he had been saddened by the way in which the older dummies had been discarded. As more fashionable figures arrived, the full-bosomed ladies who had once been the pride of the shop were relegated to side windows, where they served to display corsets or kitchen pinafores. Two, he knew, had been sawn in half and sold to a hairdresser. He still saw their somewhat chipped and melted faces gazing at him pathetically whenever he passed the shop.

In the morning he was up early and reached the scene of his labours two minutes before the time. He was always a little early, and during his whole career had only been late once, owing to an impenetrable fog. Now that he occupied an advanced position he felt it his duty to set a good example. That young fellow Simpson, for instance, was nearly always a minute or so late. Young men were like that nowadays.

Mr. Hopkins, having deposited his hat and coat in the Staff Cloakroom, went to the cellar in which packing and unpacking was done. He had been informed the day before of the arrival from Paris of several new wax figures. He found the workmen busily prising open a crate.

"Gently," he said; "gently! You broke one last time."

"That's all right, Mr. Hopkins," said the foreman; "we'll be careful."

The case, when the lid was lifted, seemed to contain nothing but tissue paper. There had evidently been some mistake.

"Nothing here but paper, sir," said the workman, throwing it out by handfuls.

"Let me see," said Mr. Hopkins.

He bent over the case and felt among the crackling tissue and had almost convinced himself that there was nothing in the thing at all when his hand touched something solid. He pulled the paper aside and saw, within a foot of his own, a human face, a woman's face of an extraordinary beauty. Sanity returned to him almost immediately. Of course, it was only a dummy; for an instant he had actually imagined it to be real. Some obscure instinct prevented him from touching the head, from pulling it out of its packing and showing it, bodiless as it was, to the workmen. It was as if he wished to keep some dream for a moment or two longer.

"There's one dummy in the box, anyway," he said, abruptly. "Put it together and send it up to the shop."

He was busy for the next hour or two arranging a window of stockings and had almost forgotten the new mannequin and the curious effect it had had on him—that calm face peering up among the white tissue paper. He wondered where young Simpson had got to. He ought to have been at his orders. There was still a window to be dressed; he must see to it.

The window in question was at the other end of the long façade of the shop, and it was generally used to display lingerie. Mr. Hopkins sometimes wondered who bought such things and how they managed to keep warm when they wore them. Both he and his sister believed in wool.

He slid back the panel which gave access to the window and was astonished to see young Simpson giving the final adjustment to a frilly diaphanous garment of lace and green silk which he had just placed on—could it be? Yes!—the new mannequin. The beautiful, melancholy face was turned towards him and seemed to reproach him with leaving her in the hands of this young man.

Mr. Hopkins's thin voice shook with a strange fury as he cried: "Leave her alone! Don't touch her!"

The young man turned in astonishment.

"I'm sorry, Mr. Hopkins," he stammered, astonished at the other's vehemence. "I was just making a preliminary arrangement till you came."

"I will dress her myself," said Mr. Hopkins, and realized that he had twice called the wax figure "her"—a thing he had certainly never done before. Wax figures, even the most expensive, had always been "it" to him. Somehow, this one was different.

"I shan't need you," he said, not unkindly, to his assistant. "I will finish dressing this window myself."

The young man paused at the scent counter to exchange a few words with Marjorie. She looked radiant this morning, he thought, in the glow of the pink lights, surrounded by huge jars of bath salts, impossibly expensive bottles of perfume, silver-handled brushes—all the trimmings of luxury. If only he could get a rise he would ask her to marry him.

"How's the old man today?"

"You know," he said, cautiously glancing round to see that no one was listening, "I think he's going loopy. He jumped down my throat this morning because I touched one of his precious figures. They might be alive, he's so careful of them."

They both giggled. Alive, indeed! The young man at least knew what live flesh was, how warm, how soft to the touch; but for that, he must wait. He saw the floor-walker approaching and walked rapidly away.

* * * * *

Over supper, Mr. Hopkins was so silent, even for him, that his sister began to think he was sickening for something. He admitted feeling tired and announced that he was going early to bed. She watched him go with a troubled face. Something certainly had put him out. That young assistant, probably. Her brother had hinted more than once that he was getting too big for his boots.

Alone, in his own small room, Mr. Hopkins could not sleep. The beautiful and pathetic face which he had seen with such dramatic suddenness in the morning, which he had watched half furtively while he was dressing the window, floated before him now. The very indifference which had always obscured his relationships with real women lent this phantom an added reality. There was in his consciousness so small a chasm to be bridged over; the barrier between dreaming and reality was very thin. It was easy for him to lend to the modelled wax cheeks a glow of youth which stirred his blood strangely.

The strange quality, the seductive vividness which had crept into his thoughts distressed him. Fevered by turning from one side to the other, with the calm, imagined face always before him, he wondered for a moment if he were going mad. It was as if some long-frozen river had melted at last and was now rushing onward, sweeping away in its path the accumulated habits of a lifetime. The obsession seemed ridiculous, even to him; he could not possibly tell anyone else about it; his sister, for instance, or young Simpson . . . Impossible! It would pass, no doubt, and with that thought, he slept.

* * * * *

Next morning Mr. Hopkins arrived at the store even earlier than usual, but he did not go immediately to the side door where the clock-machine was. Instead, he walked round to the front of the shop to the end window where the lingerie was displayed. There she was, the new arrival, and his heart beat more quickly as he looked at the long, smooth limbs emerging from the scanty underclothes which he himself had adjusted with so much care. Mr. Hopkins, forgetting his dignity, almost flattened his nose against the window, conscious as he did so that he was taking the very worst course possible, if he hoped to lay the ghost that had troubled him. How fatal his action had been he did not realize until that night when the vision returned to him again, and not only the face of the wax woman that haunted him so strangely, but the whole body. He began to think of her as if she were really his—he hardly knew what; his wife sounded too ridiculous and he was unable to envisage any other relationship. His inherited Puritanism, demure as it was, was yet strong enough to introduce a new emotion into his already feverish condition of mind. He began to be ashamed for her, and to be sorry that she was compelled to show herself to the public in such scanty attire. It was indecent. He would change it tomorrow.

He carried out his resolution. To the astonishment of young Simpson, he began to undo the work he had done so carefully but a short time before. Simpson even ventured a mild protest, but Mr. Hopkins cut him short. It was he, after all, who was responsible for dressing the windows. The new mannequin, he had decided, should have the very best clothes he could give her. He moved her to another window and clothed her tenderly in a beautiful evening gown of white chiffon and having done so he could not restrain himself from going out into the street to see the effect.

How beautiful she was! How completely she eclipsed all the other mannequins in the window! But Mr. Hopkins hardly considered that the other mannequins had never come to life in his imagination. Only this one seemed to live and to smile back at him with infinite melancholy from the other side of the plate-glass window.

His assistant met him as he returned to the shop and was astonished at the fixed look in his eyes and by the lock of hair which hung damply over his forehead. Mr. Hopkins had always been so neat in his appearance. Timidly, the young man reminded him that there was another window to dress—a whole assortment of new jumpers to be displayed as soon as possible. Mr. Hopkins did not seem to understand at first and even when he did so, his air was still absent.

"Go and get on with it," he said; "I'll leave that window to you."

Simpson hurried away before he could change his mind, and Mr. Hopkins went out into the street again for yet another look at his beloved. He did not admit it to himself, but that was what she had undoubtedly become.

The progress of Mr. Hopkins's emotions was, indeed, very similar to an ordinary infatuation. How many men have loved a graven image on the other side of some invisible but impossible barrier, have worshipped a body they could never touch and desired lips they could never kiss! But Mr. Hopkins could touch the body which had begun to fill his dreams, could clothe and unclothe it, could live with it in an intimacy impossible to less fortunate lovers. The strange thing was that the feel of the hard, dummy figure did not dispel his dream. He lacked the memory of real embraces to keep him sane, and there could be no doubt that he was rapidly approaching the line which divides sanity from madness.

The wax image was never out of his thoughts. As the days passed he left the dressing of the windows more and more to his assistant, but confused and bothered the young man by insisting on introducing his beloved figure into the midst of every successful *ensemble*. The climax came when he decided, without warning, to despoil the bride of her white veil and long dress of cream satin, and to adorn his favourite with them. It needed a whole day's hard work, but was accomplished at last, and Mr. Hopkins went home that evening tired but happy.

His sister's fear that something was wrong had now deepened to a genuine anxiety. His behaviour was certainly most peculiar. After supper he had always been willing, his feet in carpet slippers, to sit quietly on one side of the fire till bedtime, while she sat on the other side knitting. Then, one evening, a month or six weeks after the arrival of the mannequin which had so altered and illuminated his life—although his sister knew nothing of that, for he kept the whole affair a jealous secret—he announced that he was going out "to take a breath of air".

"But it's late, Obadiah, almost bedtime."

"Not yet," he said, almost guiltily, and began to put on his boots.

"Would you like me to come with you? I have not been out today."

Mr. Hopkins's courage failed him.

"All right," he said, but a strange, hunted look came into his eyes.

It took her nearly half an hour to get ready while Mr. Hopkins stood dejectedly in the tiny hall lit only by a dim gas-jet in a coloured lantern hung from the ceiling. The bamboo hatstand, with inset coloured tiles, had a small mirror in its middle panel. Mr. Hopkins gazed into it. He could only see a fraction of his face—the mirror was so narrow—but his eyes gleamed at him strangely, wild and a little bloodshot. He waited in a state of exasperated impatience. There was no object in his walk now, but anything was better than waiting there with his hat on under the melancholy hall light. At last she was ready, and they went out, closing the door carefully behind them.

The curious, pathetic couple walked to Hammersmith Broadway and back again, Mr. Hopkins silent and morose; his sister wondering what was the meaning of the unusual jaunt. That night she could hear him in the next room, tossing and turning, without sleep. Should she send for the doctor? Obadiah would be very angry, but he might see that she had acted for the best.

Next day he left all the work to young Simpson and spent the greater part of his time on the pavement. He did not dare to spend too long in front of one window, so he walked rapidly from one end of the long façade to another, pausing each time as he came opposite his beloved—the Bride, all in white. As he stopped for the fifth time, he became aware of two eyes watching him over the wooden screen that divided the window from the shop. Questioning eyes ! Suspicious eyes ! Young Simpson's, of course. That young man, indeed, had begun not only to suspect but to hope that Mr. Hopkins was mad. After all, he had had some experience by this time in dressing windows and if Mr. Hopkins should be dismissed . . . The vision of Marjorie floated before him. She would make an enchanting bride. Just like the one in the window. And there old Hopkins was again gazing at the white figure, a peculiar smile on his lips and a strand of mouse-coloured hair hanging into his eyes.

It was no wonder that Mr. Hopkins looked distraught, for he could sleep very little—two or three hours at most, and then he was troubled by nightmares full of vague terror such as he had not experienced since childhood. At last a night came when he could bear it no longer. He awoke with his whole body bathed in perspiration. The blind was flapping with a menacing persistence and the light from a street lamp opposite came through the side of the curtains as they blew open and cast shapes of horror on the wall. He threw off the bed-clothes and started up, shivering a little as his bare legs emerged from the fetid warmth of the bed. Tremblingly, he struck a match and looked at the alarm clock. It was half-past three. The match burned his fingers and went out. He crept to the door of his room and opened it, straining his ear to catch the sound of his sister's breathing in the next room. She snored, and Mr. Hopkins thanked God for it, for she was snoring now.

With clumsy haste he groped for his trousers, placed with the braces still attached to them over the end of the iron bedstead. He found his socks on the rail below and put them on. Without troubling to put on his day-shirt he knotted a handkerchief round his neck and adjusted his coat and waistcoat over it. His boots were in the back kitchen standing on the boiler, where he always left them, ready to be cleaned in the morning.

With terror tugging at his heart, he crept in his stockinged feet past his sister's door and lowered himself with infinite caution on to the creaking stairs. Instinct prompted him to tread as close as possible to the banisters, for there the stairs creaked less. His one thought was to get out of the house without waking its other occupant; to escape into the streets, to be free, free as he never was in the daytime. Straight ahead of him he could see the pale gleam of the fanlight, with the enamelled iron letters reversed : "1ᙓ". The last stair gave out a creak which seemed to Mr. Hopkins's disordered imagination loud enough to wake not only his sister, but the whole street. He listened. If she appeared at the top of the stairs he would say he didn't feel well and had come down to the kitchen for a drink of water. But the bathroom was on the first floor ! He could have gone to that. She would think it very strange that he had taken the trouble to dress. But she had evidently heard nothing.

In the kitchen he put on his boots, the desire for escape still strong upon him, and with greater care than ever, for he now made more noise, he groped his way to the front door. He knocked his shoulder against a picture—the large steel engraving after Landseer, in an Oxford frame. For a moment it swung perilously sideways, but did not fall.

The door reached, he opened it gently, inserted his key in the lock and turned it so that the door should make no sound in closing. There was a sharp click, and Mr. Hopkins was safe on the pavement.

It occurred to him at once that he had forgotten his hat. Never mind; he would go without it. Too dangerous to turn back. Go? But where? He never troubled to ask himself, but set off at a brisk trot in the direction of the Broadway, where he could take a bus. . . . But, of course, he couldn't! All the buses had stopped long ago. No matter! He would walk.

He strode forward with a quick springy step very different from the nervous slouch of ordinary habit. A policeman looked at him suspiciously for he made a strange figure, without his hat and with the handkerchief knotted round his throat; but Mr. Hopkins was so obviously inoffensive that he was allowed to pass. It must have been at least a mile and a half to the scene of his daily work, but he had lost all consciousness of time and all consciousness of his surroundings until he stood once more before the windows of the store. The lights were now out and only a neighbouring lamp-post shed a ghostly gleam through the plate glass and lighted on the dim white figure which had assumed so fantastic a place in Mr. Hopkins's thoughts, sleeping or waking.

He hardly knew now whether he was asleep or not, for so did the vision come to him in his dreams, standing like a spectre amid the shadows and smiling a melancholy far-away smile. As in his dreams, he strove to draw nearer, to see more plainly, but some invisible barrier held him back, some shadow extinguished the pale radiance of the face. A burly form, indeed, had come between Mr. Hopkins and the street-lamp, and a gruff voice growled:

"Come along, now! Move on! Move on!"

The policeman was on the point of making an arrest, for the face which Mr. Hopkins turned towards him was guilty and confused. So distorted was it by terror and some emotion which the policeman could not understand that he started back and, seeing the strange little figure walking rapidly away, he watched it out of sight without pursuing.

The way home seemed as unreasonably long as the outward journey had seemed short. In his hurry Mr. Hopkins had not put on one of his socks properly and there was a ridge of wool underneath his right heel. The excitement which had driven him out had now evaporated, and exaltation, fear and all other emotions had been replaced by a blank misery heightened, as he walked, by a return of his habitual timidity and self-consciousness, for the streets were almost light and not so empty as they had been when he set out. He reached his own door in such a state of exhaustion that he had hardly strength to mount the steps, and his hand trembled so violently that it took him several minutes to insert the key in the lock.

Once inside the door he made a final effort, took off his boots in the kitchen, went upstairs in his stockinged feet, too dazed to care whether his sister awoke or not, and fell, rather than lay, upon his bed. He had just strength enough left to pull the clothes over him before falling into a profound sleep, which, for once, was unhaunted by any dreams. The clock on his mantelpiece stood at half-past five.

. . . . .

The change in Mr. Hopkins's appearance began to be remarked by all the shop assistants. Even the manager noticed it and wondered if the little man had taken to drink. Mr. Hopkins had always been so careful in his dress and so correct in saluting the manager when he met him in the shop that the latter's astonishment was all the greater when Mr. Hopkins passed him without any sign of recognition, staring straight ahead as if (as the manager remarked to himself) the old chap were really seeing things.

Back in his private office the manager touched the bell.

"Ask Mr. Hopkins to step this way."

But when Mr. Hopkins stood before him, he wondered if he had been mistaken. For this was the unassuming employee he had known for so long. The wild gleam had gone from his eyes. They merely looked sunken and almost extinct. His voice was quite normal, except that it sounded infinitely weary.

"You asked to see me, sir?"

"Yes, Hopkins. I have been noticing that you don't seem too well lately,"

"Oh, there's nothing wrong with me, sir. I haven't been sleeping very well, that's all."

"You seem to me to be a bit run down, and I was going to propose that you should take a fortnight's holiday at the firm's expense and see if you can't pull up a bit."

"That's very kind of you, sir, but——"

"That's settled, then," broke in the manager with the air of closing the discussion. "You can be off from tomorrow. Young Simpson can dress the windows while you are away."

The manager had begun to rummage among the papers on his desk. Mr. Hopkins sighed and turned heavily away. A holiday! What did he want with a holiday? He decided not to tell his sister anything about it and to avoid leaving London at all costs. The mere thought of being separated from the object of his infatuation sent the blood to his ears. He would not be able to come to the store during working hours—the manager would think that too peculiar—but he would come when the shop was closed.

When work was over he handed his keys to young Simpson and told him that he should be away for a fortnight. Perhaps he had been told already; there was a look of triumph on the fellow's face which Mr. Hopkins did not like at all. He had a free hand at last and he meant to make use of it. He little knew that an eye would be watching him.

Mr. Hopkins got off his bus at Hammersmith and began to take the familiar route to his home. He had hardly gone a hundred yards, however, when he felt suddenly faint. It was as if a black curtain rose before his eyes—a wall of blackness as tall as himself shut him in on every side. He could not see where he was going, lurched heavily and collapsed in a crumpled heap on the pavement. He was dimly concious of being helped up and of the little crowd which had already collected round him.

"He's drunk!" said a passing navvy.

"Do you feel better now?" said a man in a spotted tie, bending over him.

"Yes," said Mr. Hopkins. "Take me home." He gave his address, reflecting as he did so that the manager was right after all, and that he did need a holiday.

He was taken home and put to bed, and there he stayed for a week, in blessed oblivion, the weight which had been pressing on his mind completely lifted.

It was the doctor who reminded him of it and brought back his obsession with crushing force. He had passed the store that very morning, he said, and had noticed that all the windows had been re-dressed.

"They seem to be getting along all right without you," he said, jocularly; "there's no need for you to worry."

As soon as he had gone, Mr. Hopkins fell back on his pillow and groaned. "No need to worry!" The vision of young Simpson re-arranging the windows drove him frantic. The thought that at that moment he might have his hands on . . . If Mr. Hopkins had been able to express what he felt, to give a name to his fear and horror, he might have saved his sanity; but the emotions which shook him were so completely irrational that rational argument was no match for them. Mr. Hopkins was possessed by one passion, round which all his thoughts and feelings were inextricably twined. It was as if all his actions were dictated to him by something outside himself, something more powerful and more cunning than he could ever be, unprompted and undriven. As soon as he heard the front door close and the doctor's car drive away, he slipped out of bed. Supporting himself by the bedposts, for he still felt very weak, he stood, listening, wondering if his sister would come upstairs to discuss the doctor's visit. He heard her moving pans in the kitchen and, reassured, went to the bedroom cupboard and took out his clothes. He dressed quickly but carefully, for he had no desire to create remark in the streets by the absence of hat or collar. It seemed to him almost impossible that he should be able to slip out of the house without being noticed, but, moving as quietly as he could, he reached the street unhindered. He felt breathless and exhausted already, and it was with infinite difficulty that he reached the bus stop. It was about five o'clock in the evening and the shop would be open until six. The purpose at the back of his mind, although it was not yet clearly formulated, was to ask to see the manager and demand to be taken back.

In such a condition as that of Mr. Hopkins, consciousness is very intermittent. It is like the revolving light of a lighthouse, painfully bright for an instant and then extinguished for what seems a long period. Mr. Hopkins remembered leaving his house, remembered seeing his face reflected dimly in the window of the bus, and the next thing he knew was that he was walking up the steps to the manager's office, situated on the first floor. He walked in without knocking.

Straight in front of him, poised, as it seemed, over the mahogany wall of the desk, was a bald head, framed by oiled wisps of black hair, for the manager was still comparatively young. A sudden despair invaded Mr. Hopkins's heart. The head seemed to him a face, blank, uncomprehending, a face to which he had to explain—what? What could he explain? That he wanted to be taken back? The manner of the request would be enough to make refusal certain. Then the manager looked up and said:

"Hello, Hopkins! Whatever are you doing here?"

. . . .

Down in the shop the news of Mr. Hopkins's return had spread rapidly. Young Simpson had seen him striding upstairs like a man in a dream, without a single glance of recognition to right or left. Mr. Hopkins's wild appearance frightened him, but it was with an obscure feeling of triumph that he hurried to the perfume counter to spread the news.

"He's gone up to see the manager."

"What for? Doesn't he like the way you've dressed the windows?"

"I don't care," said the young man, defiantly. "The manager told me yesterday I was managing very well."

"Well, perhaps he's got something on his mind."

. . . .

Mr. Hopkins left the manager's office with a sense of hopeless outrage. He was very weak, and on the verge of tears. He leaned for a moment over the iron balustrade, for the first floor, as well as the floors above it, was open in the middle so that a huge well stretched up from the street level to the roof in the centre of the store. Mr. Hopkins mopped his forehead.

"So he thinks I need a long rest," he muttered. "Has been thinking for some time of putting me on my pension. 'New blood, Mr. Hopkins! We must move with the times.' Every consideration for my long service! For my long . . ."

A dozen yards from where Mr. Hopkins was standing stood a group of dummy figures half covered with a dust-sheet. They had probably been brought up from below for a corset display or something of the kind. An awful anxiety tugged at Mr. Hopkins's heart and, bent almost double, he ran towards them. With an angry gesture he plucked away the sheet and stood, frozen for a moment, gazing into the calm eyes he had come to love so well. So she, She, was to be banished from the windows and used to advertise corsets on the first floor! The corset was already clasped round her middle and Mr. Hopkins's excited fingers tore themselves on the fastenings as he tried to undo them. He heard shouts and saw people running towards him. They would think him mad, but he was past caring what they thought.

Hearing the noise, young Simpson turned and looked up and Marjorie came from behind the counter and stood beside him. He put his arm, half-unconsciously, round her waist.

Mr. Hopkins had the dummy figure in his arms. He was leaning against the balustrade and his lips moved as if he were making a speech. Then, before anyone could stop him, he had climbed on to the railing and, in another instant, crashed downwards, still holding the figure tightly to him as though he would never let it go.

The noise of his fall brought a crowd of assistants running to see, but the shop-walkers sent the girls back to their counters. Mr. Hopkins lay in a huddled heap, a thin stream of blood flowing from his head. Around him lay the unrecognizable fragments of the wax image.

. . . . . .

"It was positively eerie," said young Simpson. "When I ran up his lips were still moving and he was staring at something just above his head. And—you'll laugh at me—but I thought I saw something . . ."

"Something?"

"Yes! Like a puff of smoke from a cigarette. I don't know . . . It wasn't like that, either. It was like a veil floating in the air, as if someone was wearing it. A bridal veil."

"Mr. Simpson," said one of the assistants, hurrying up, "the manager wants to speak to you."

Simpson came back in ten minutes, his eyes shining.

"He's given me the job," he said, "and, talking of bridal veils . . ."

THE DIARY OF WILLIAM CARPENTER

By John Atkins

IT was nearly three years ago that I bought Park Farm.

My wife and I had been looking unsuccessfully for several months for a not too small house in the country. Therefore, when I found that Park Farm was going for next to nothing, and furnished at that, I didn't hesitate.

My wife was staying with relatives in Somerset at the time. I wrote to her, rather guiltily, of my marvellous "find". I am afraid I was so guilty about signing the contract so hastily that I tried to cover things up with wordy explanations of how we could have repairs done if necessary; of what a wonderful thing it would be for Pauline to be brought up in a big house with a big garden so that she would never suffer from any form of claustrophobia; of my high hopes for a book just going to press, the royalties of which would more than cover our outlay; and so on.

Instead of answering by letter as I had expected, she came down to see me, although she was supposed to stay in Somerset for at least another week. We looked over the house together, and she could find nothing in its favour. I was quite nonplussed, and still am, why she behaved like that, for there was very little to complain about. The state of repair was much better than I had expected; it lacked one or two modern conveniences, such as a good range and central heating, but nothing that could not have been installed. Yet she said she didn't like it. I kept asking her why, and she kept putting me off. She didn't know what her objections were herself, but naturally couldn't admit it. But I had rashly settled everything with the agent, and there wasn't much we could do about it. At last Joan said she would give the place a trial if we furnished the whole place anew.

I was amazed. At first, I said, you grumble about the expense of possible repairs, then you go to the other extreme and suggest a complete refurnishing! And there was nothing wrong with the furniture. It was old and old-fashioned, but extremely comfortable and well made. However, it was senseless to make an issue of it, and we went up to town and looked over the stores.

We bought the furniture, had a man down from London to value what was there already, and found a buyer. Then we had a couple of hectic days while armchairs and bedsteads crossed each other almost on the doorstep, one lot going out, the other in. Joan went away again while this happened, but I stayed on to supervise. During the change-over I came across a lot of books, letters and papers in a cupboard in the sitting-room. There was nothing outstanding there, none of the books worth keeping, and the letters (which, I must admit, I read) were family and business ones, and just as boring as usual. But one thing did interest me, and I kept it.

It was a blue exercise book. On the first page was written, in capitals, "The Diary of William Carpenter."

· · · ·

May 14th
Found a place at last! And after all the disappointments I've had, a damned good one at that. Park Farm, it's called. The house is just about all I've been looking for—country house style, all right, but not too big: four bedrooms, storeroom, nursery (I'll clear that out and use it as a study), dining-room, lounge, kitchen, scullery, a smaller drawing-room and cellars. Farm doesn't exist—thank God! Now I shall really be able to settle down and live the kind of life I've longed for over the past twenty years. Country walks in the morning—a nap in the afternoon, or a potter round the garden if it's fine—and the evening with my stamps upstairs. Once a week to town to see Cutler and some of the others.

Best of all, the house has a story attached to it! The Estate Agent behaved like all the others—showed me all kinds of junk I didn't want, and I was getting more and more fed up. But when he ran through the cards he missed one. I'm always on the look-out for that sort of thing—they keep them back for themselves or their friends when there's a bargain going. So I insisted on seeing it. I got the surprise of my life—he said it was a white elephant, no one would touch it. There had been a murder there five years ago, and the place had a bad name. It was going dirt cheap—£2 10s. a week, furnished! I said I didn't care what happened there—it could be a massacre for all I cared, but if it was what I wanted I'd take it. The agent said people got nervous, but I said I didn't believe in all this bunk about spirits returning and murderers coming back to the scene of the crime. He said I needn't worry about that—he'd been hanged a long time ago. Apparently it was an amateur affair—the man had a row with his wife and did her in. Not a very exciting murder—certainly not an unusual one.

The beauty of it is, everything is ready for me to move in. A village woman has cleaned it out once a week, and it looked like any other house when I went there, except that it had far more style to it than most. Of course, it seemed empty—you can always tell when a house hasn't been lived in for some time, but I'll soon put that right. Hope to move in at the end of the week.

May 17th
First day at Park Farm. Hardly had time to look round yet. All kinds of annoying little things to see to—engaging an old man to look after the garden and an old girl to cook and "do" for me. She strikes me as being a bit of an old fool, but I don't suppose there's much else to be had. I offered her a room so that she could live and sleep in. She looked at me as though I'd made an immoral suggestion, and then she said, very abruptly: "No, thank you—not for a million pounds!" Of course, it's this silly superstition about a murder. I suppose country people have always been a lot less enlightened than town-dwellers. Just imagine being superstitious about murders in London! Why, half the population would have to evacuate.

I indulged in a bit of swank when I got here. Why not? I've worked pretty hard to get it. If I'd chucked my money around when I was younger the way chaps like McCartney and Page did I'd still be where they are—catching the 8.37 every morning and living in a cramped little shack in Barnes. I stopped the car at the gates, paid the driver, and *walked* up the drive to the front door. It's a very pleasant drive, semi-circular, sweeping up to the porch and round again to gates the other side. (These look as though they've been shut for half a century. The drive that side is covered with weeds. I'll have them taken up and the gates opened—I don't see why only one lot of gates should be used.) Between the porch and the railings is a very fine lawn—I must say Parkin, the old gardener, has kept the grounds in excellent order, except for the half of the drive.

Mrs. Dane, the old girl I've already mentioned, met me at the porch. She seems a most unpleasant person—just grunted and took my bag. But I will say she did an excellent lunch for me.

May 18th
Spent today getting used to the place. Had some men in clearing the nursery. Must say the previous occupants seem to have been very fond of their kid. It was a little boy, one of the men told me—about nine when the affair happened. No end of junk there—a rocking-horse, meccano sets, toy trains, soldiers, a whole farmyard, games of every description, lots of children's picture books. Must have cost them a hell of a lot. Sometimes used to think I'd have liked a kid, but when I saw all this I realized I wouldn't be here now if I had.

Spent quite a time in the garden with old Parkin. He's a grand old chap—real countryman, full of country lore. Told me the names of several birds and plants, all of which I've forgotten. (How do they remember them all? Still, I'd like to see old Parkin in a City office—he'd have a fit.) Think I'm going to get on well with him—not like old Dane. Every time I see her I'm reminded that a murderer occupied the house before me. I wonder why it is. It's not that I'm nervous—why should I be? I've nothing on *my* conscience—but I'm sure it's all she thinks of. Parkin isn't like that. He's only concerned with the garden. It means everything to him.

May 20th
The local bigwigs are beginning to call on me. Today it was the parson, Mr. Lambert. He's a small, frail man of about fifty, and smokes a pipe to look tough. Still, he didn't come preaching God at me, and as long as he keeps off that and expecting me to go to church, he's welcome. He stayed half an hour, and told me quite a lot about the Ruskins (the people before me).

Everyone was shocked and dumbfounded, he said, when they heard what had happened. Everyone thought them a well-suited pair, and the boy was always very happy, which, says Lambert, is usually a sign of domestic harmony (he ought to know—he's got five). He laid great stress on the fact that they had all been regular churchgoers (these parsons will think that churchgoing means virtue !). Apparently there had been nothing in the nature of a standing quarrel between them—the whole thing had flared up quite suddenly when Ruskin discovered, or thought he discovered, that the kid wasn't his ! Lambert says the case was never properly cleared up at the trial. Both Mrs. Ruskin and the supposed father were dead, and anyway, it had nothing to do with R's guilt. That was obvious enough. Mrs. Dane had come down in the morning (she slept in then, which isn't very complimentary to me !) and found Mrs. R. lying at the foot of the stairs. R. was in the small drawing-room (where I am now) with his head in his hands. Apparently they had had an argument on the landing and he had knocked her downstairs, and she broke her neck. Dane had slept all through it (you can see she sleeps like a log just by one look at her). L. had been the first to see them after Dane, because she had run straight to him (he doesn't live a hundred yards away). He insisted on showing me exactly where everything had happened—the landing, the foot of the stairs where Mrs. R. fell, and the chair where R. was still sitting when he arrived. He even pointed out what he called a "dark stain" on the carpet, supposed to be caused by blood from a wound in Mrs. R.'s head, but I'm damned if I could see it. Then he started like all the rest—wasn't I nervous? I said, what's there to be nervous of? I'm not superstitious. He mumbled something about a "presence". I laughed, and said: Show me your "presence", let me touch it and hear it speak, then I'll believe you. Of course, he had no answer to that—they never have, these dreamers. Thank God I'm a man of the world !

Heard from Saunders today. Says the auction raised £1,853 12s. Not bad !

May 22nd

Like yesterday, today was very quiet. Unless I get to know people soon I'll be feeling lonely. Old Lambert's not such a bad old stick, but I'm a bit chary of parsons—their side of the contract is usually that you should go to church. I miss all the old faces—Cutler especially—but I bet they envy me. Anyway, I'll be seeing them tomorrow.

What seems so strange is the silence of the place. It's like the grave. I spent a couple of hours in my study, busy with my stamps, and apart from an occasional sparrow or starling by the window I didn't hear a sound. Then I found I couldn't concentrate, it was *too quiet* ! I suppose I'm so used to working in the midst of noise it will take some time to accommodate myself to a new environment. But everything will work out all right in time. Meanwhile, I'm making some serious mistakes. Tonight I found a 10 *reales* Brazilian (1913) among my Nicaraguan collection ! I hope to God I haven't made any more mistakes like that. It would take hours to check up.

May 23rd

A wonderful day with a rotten ending. Went to town, met Cutler and the others, and we all had a grand lunch at Mattini's. Cutler's fund of jokes is as extensive as ever, and I'm afraid none of us were quite sober by the time we left. I'm afraid I'll never get this life out of my system. Good company, good food, good wine—what more can there be to a good life?

Then I come home and find a letter from Mildred. She's coming tomorrow —not even time to put her off for a few days. I had half hoped she would take this opportunity to stay away and live with her mother for good, but no— she's too dense. Or perhaps she likes annoying me—she must know I can't get any more pleasure from her company, and I'm damned sure she gets none from mine. But she must claim her "rights", whatever the consequences.

May 24th
This is the worst day I've had here. Just as I was getting used to the place M. has to butt in. Now I know she had only come to make me uncomfortable—to haunt me, you might say. She hadn't even a smile for me when she arrived. You would have thought she could have manufactured one, even if it meant nothing. I showed her round the place, but she didn't say a word. After dinner I started to go up to my study, but she said in her semi-hysterical way: "*Surely* we can spend the first evening in our new home together!" That's just like her, the supreme egoist. The *first* evening, after I've been here a week. We sat in the drawing-room all the evening, and hardly said a word.

May 25th
I went for a long walk in the morning and spent the afternoon in the garden talking to old Parkin. He told me he had found sixty-three birds' nests in the orchard and garden and on the house this Spring! Sixty-three!
The same thing happened again this evening as yesterday. I was just going upstairs again when M. started nagging. "William, you *might* stay with me—this house is so big and lonely, and it gives me the creeps when I'm all alone." I was just going to stand out, but decided not to. I've had all this before. If you dare to say anything there's a row, and it doesn't matter how it all ends, you feel irritable for the rest of the evening. So no stamps again.
We sat opposite each other for a full hour. She was knitting something or other, and I read the newspaper at least three times. Then I had an idea. It sounds cunning, but you have to be cunning with this type.
I told her about the murder. I made a real story about it. I didn't say anything about the kid—that would have spoilt it. I said it very chattily, just as though I wanted to make a conversation. *I just said the couple who lived here before us didn't get on very well together, and one day they quarrelled and he threw her downstairs.* She didn't say a word, but I watched her very closely. It went home all right. She became stiffer than ever, and her mouth closed tight and thin. A few minutes later she asked me to make some coffee. For the first time in my life I enjoyed making coffee. I'm glad now that Mrs. Dane goes home after dinner. It gives me a chance to get away from M., even if only for a few moments. But unless I'm very much mistaken we won't be together much longer. It won't take me long to work on her nerves. They never were very strong.

May 26th
My birthday, and what a birthday! Fifty-four years old. With M. here I feel sixty-four, without her it would have been more like forty-four, with a grand visit to town and a binge with the boys.
I've given up any idea of spending the evening alone now. I'm going to turn last night's experiment into a full-scale attack. I developed it this evening. I said something like this: "Fancy a murder being committed in this house! It sort of puts you on the *qui vive*, doesn't it? You seem to be listening all the time, listening for something—but what? Funny, I've never considered myself a nervous man, and I'm certainly not superstitious, yet I always seem to have one ear cocked for something. Always something! I wonder what it could be?" And so on, and so on, a nice little monologue, aimed right at the heart of her nerves. She didn't like it, and tried to change the subject. "Do you think there are any nice people round here we could get friendly with?" she said. "That would help destroy the loneliness." "Why, of course," I said, "you must see Mr. Lambert, the parson. I'll ask him round tomorrow evening."
Oh yes, Mr. Lambert will be a very useful person to me!

May 27th

Lambert has come and gone. A most successful evening. L. did his stuff (all unknowingly) and after he had gone there was a first-class row. His description of the murder was lurid and detailed. He really enjoys telling the story. He wanted to show M. the historic spots, but she said she'd rather not. He loves the word "murder", too, and uses it far more than is necessary. He spits it off his tongue as though it were a shade too unpleasant for the palate. I'm sure M. thought I'd coached him beforehand.

After he had gone she came up to me and said: "William, you're trying to drive me out!" Of course, I was amazed. I said: "What on earth do you mean? You're raving!" That set her off. She said I was cruel to her; why couldn't we be happy like we used to be; if I thought I could frighten her by these methods I was mistaken; and so on.

I was going to answer, but thought how useless it would be, so I went straight up to bed. I give her another ten days.

May 28th

I didn't mention the murder tonight. There's no need to. She's scared. I sat and read for a bit, then put the paper aside and stared at her. She knew I was staring at her, but she couldn't face me. How stiff, old, ugly, dull, lifeless and useless she looked. Her face was an unpleasant grey—the grey of fear! I couldn't help thinking of the girl I had married. Oh yes, I made mistakes. She was a shrew from the start, and she always loathed my friends—not for themselves but because she looked on them as rivals. But at least she lived, she had some flesh on her, and she knew how to laugh.

May 29th

Changed my tactics today. In the morning I 'phoned Cutler to say I wouldn't be coming up tomorrow as previously arranged.

In the evening I insisted on going upstairs. She began to argue but I brushed it aside. I said it was just waste of time to sit downstairs all the evening doing nothing. She saw my mind was made up, and didn't say any more.

Of course, I couldn't do any work. I lay in my chair and tried to keep my mind a blank, but it was impossible. I kept thinking of the Ruskins. I even imagined I knew what Ruskin himself looked like. A mild little man with grey hair round the sides of his skull, and big, sad eyes. I suddenly realized how much I owed to him. Without him and his murder my position would be intolerable. As it is I find it wearing enough—it is impossible to live like this without feeling the strain. I must confess I sometimes stop whatever I'm doing and thinking, and wonder what the noise was I had just heard—nothing supernatural, of course, just ordinary noises you hear in any house, but which normally you don't register consciously. But without Ruskin my problem would be insoluble.

May 30th

I had a funny experience tonight. On my way upstairs I had the impression that Ruskin was at my side. It was especially strong on the landing. Purely imagination, of course, but not the kind of imagination I either like or am addicted to. But if the situation is doing this to me, God knows what it is doing to her.

June 2nd

After a couple of quiet nights two rather significant things happened this evening. The first sounds childish, but it is symptomatic of the state I'm in. When I got upstairs I found I'd left my pipe and pouch in the dining-room. I started to go down for it, but when I had nearly got to the landing I stopped.

The presentiment that Ruskin was there was very strong. I even thought I saw some kind of *shape* there—no form or outline, just a darker patch of shadow. Of course, it was nonsense, but it shook me. After all, I felt, a murder had actually been committed there. Not a particularly pleasant thought to have in a dark lonely house. And the feeling that Ruskin was there made it worse, for when all is said and done, R. was a murderer. However mild he appeared to me in my imagination he must have been a pretty objectionable sort of fellow. Anyhow, I went back and did without my pipe and baccy. It sounds damned silly, writing this now, but that's what happened.

About half an hour later (just after nine o'clock, to be exact) I heard a scream. If my nerves had really been on edge I'd have been frightened, but instead I felt a tide of happiness sweep over me. I knew what that scream was, I had been waiting for it, expecting it, for several nights. It was Mildred. Some little thing had happened—an owl had hooted, a mouse had scuttled across the floor, or the branch of a tree had brushed the window-pane—and her blood had gone cold. I hoped it had happened on her way upstairs, for recently she had been going to bed very early. I just sat where I was, waiting for developments.

I couldn't stand it for long. The house seemed like an empty shell. One moment it had seemed full of some kind of life—I don't know how to express it—perhaps what L. calls "presences", though something far more subtle than anything he could imagine. Then a scream, and silence—I even felt as though the air currents had suddenly congealed and the atmosphere itself was suspended.

I felt I had to see M. It seemed impossible to me that anything could live in this house—I was even surprised to find myself still breathing and capable o feeling. I became overwhelmed with the thought that I had gone too far, that the shriek I had heard had been something more than a shriek of fear. It seemed to have a finality about it—it was like the last howl of a broken valve. I jumped up and tore downstairs. As I ran my terror grew, and by the time I got to the landing I felt I was being jostled by a thousand enemies. Or rather, they were harassing me, but never actually touching me. I hunched my shoulders and jumped down the rest of the stairs, three at a time. I had the absurd fear that myriads of hands were clutching at the back of my neck.

I burst into the drawing-room and stopped dead. I will never forget what I saw, as, indeed, I will never forget the whole of this terrible evening. M. lay on the floor before the fireplace, stiff as a wooden doll. Only her mouth was moving, and that was twitching and gibbering in a frenzy. Her eyes were bulging and staring—not at me, it seemed, but through me. I even looked behind, but could see nothing but the wall and the half-open door. I suddenly felt swamped with pity. I had been guilty of the worst possible cruelty, I had been treating her worse than Ruskin had treated his wife (yes, the comparison occurred to me even then!). Mildred was not to blame for what she was. As I looked at her then I found myself wondering how that poor broken thing could ever have aroused me to the cold, knife-like fury I had known against her.

And now I am exhausted. How honest should a diary be? To be of any value completely honest, I suppose. I hope I shall have the strength to leave what I have written untouched. And now I require more strength to write what I still have to say. I picked her up, comforted her, and took her to bed. And all the time I filled her ears with the most cowardly lies—I said I loved her, yes, still loved her, I was ashamed of my behaviour, I stood naked in front of her and hurled accusations at myself. All she could say was: "Something touched me—something took hold of my arm on the landing." She kept repeating it, over and over again. So there *is* something—but what?

Now I am a bit cooler I can ask myself what really happened. Do I pity her? Yes, I pity her with all my heart, that poor, tortured fellow creature with whom I have slept and lived for so long. But do I love her? No, it is impossible; quite impossible, any more. And what is this hold that an empty house has clamped upon our nerves? I planned an attack upon hers, but mine were to go free. And now mine are as much victims as hers. What is this mystery?

June 3rd

Before God, I swear I meant nothing. No, more than that, it wasn't me. It was someone else—or something else—but not me. Everything has crashed, I have only my diary left, and the world must read it. I feel I am in a sea, I am being beaten and tossed by waves, and there is nothing to cling to. All of me is here, my rottenness, my absurd foolishness, but there is something no one will find here, and that is a murderer. No one could write that lightly, and to me it is as though it were scratched in my own agonized flesh. I must put it down. All of it. Then God will decide. Men will come and accuse me, I know what is going to happen, but before God I am clean. And if there are any just men I am clean before them. And it would be as impossible for me to write a lie now as to sleep in my bed.

God knows, there is something foul and horrible in me. After all my confessions of yesterday, my realization that I had sinned and my determination to make amends, I woke up this morning as though I had been dreaming. I had had a nightmare in which I had been beaten to my knees and forced to say something in which I did not believe. All my old hatred of her reappeared, stronger, if anything, than before. I felt she had played a trick on me, had compelled me to say just those things she wanted me to say. All day long I avoided her, and my anger grew blacker and more intense. I knew I would have to get rid of her, pity alone could not provide the basis for a partnership. She was like an evil presence that brooded at table and haunted the dark corners. She implored me not to go upstairs, but I wouldn't be won over. She clung to my arms, but I threw her off. I said more of what I thought of her in those few minutes than ever before. I told her she was a parasite—not on my wealth, she could have all of that—but on my peace of mind. She sucked away my peace and happiness, and clothed herself in a shoddy righteousness pieced together out of jealousy and spite. I left her crying.

Then the idea came to me. It was an evil idea, I know, a stupid, underhand, inhuman idea, *but not a murderous one*. She had to go and she had to be driven. I waited for her to come to bed. I would meet her on the landing, I would loom out of the darkness of the corner and lay my hand on her arm. I sat in my room with the door open, listening for the sound of her step on the stair. I heard it a hundred times, and each time I was wrong. I knew who it was, it was Ruskin. Oh yes, Ruskin was there, urging me on, trying to persuade me to do more than simply approach her and touch her. I felt myself struggling to retain my sanity. The whole atmosphere was stuffed with evil.

Then I heard her. Silently I crept downstairs, and huddled in the corner of the landing. Slowly she came up—I saw her holding her hand out in front, as though to ward off evil spirits. By the dim light of the lamp in the hall below I could see the terror stamped on her face. And she had reason to be terrified, for Ruskin was there, beckoning her on irresistibly and crouching by my side, whispering instructions.

Then I was no longer myself. I mean that literally. I stepped out to meet her. I suddenly felt my arm raised—I did not raise it, I had no control over it— and it struck her a blow in the chest. She disappeared backwards, and I heard her crashing downstairs. It was my arm, it was my body, but it wasn't *me*! I was possessed. I swear that before God. I know who possessed my body. I even vaguely remember watching myself (or him) strike her. One moment I stood firm; the next I was trembling, because he had left me and I was myself again.

There is no more. I feel dry and lifeless now. Everything is clear and positive to me. The machinery of justice will move, there will be a prosecution,

I have little doubt of what will happen to me. No one will understand, no one will even be capable of belief. The only men who understand this type of experience are the victims themselves. Cutler will think I'm mad. The world decides on its own insanities.

It is horrible now in my intensely lucid state of mind to think back on what followed. How I ran down the stairs, picked up her lifeless body (for I knew then it was lifeless), tried to coax it back, actually kissed her face, rubbed her hands, whispered to her, spoke her name, and then shouted—but who knows what I shouted? I can even see objectively, and without the distortion of horror that disturbed me then, the pool of her blood by the side of her head. I held her head in my hands, but there was no cut, not even an abrasion; certainly no blood. Mrs. Ruskin had supplied her own blood. Hadn't Lambert told me so?

Now I can do nothing but wait. I know, at least, that something irrevocable has happened. Her snapped body lies outside, and if Ruskin were to walk in here and now I, for all my lucidity, would not see him.

That's how William Carpenter's diary ends.

Then I made a discovery. It is my habit to write in my notebooks all over the place, with little respect for order or continuity. I don't know how many others share this peculiarity with me, but I am not so egoistic as to suppose that I am unique in this respect. At any rate, when I had finished reading what is printed above, I started turning the remaining pages, half hoping that I would find something else that might tell me more about this unhappy couple. And there, on the very next page, I found this!

Last entry
I, Mildred Ann Carpenter, have witnessed the death of my husband, William George Carpenter. I witnessed it without compassion, with a cold objectivity similar to that with which he witnessed my supposed death. I do not desire to overlay it with heroics.

I do not know how long I stayed in the hallway, stunned and near to the death I had half hoped for. Apart from a bruised arm I felt none the worse for his attack. I walked into the drawing-room, not expecting to find him there.

He sat with his head lying on his arms, asleep! He was in a deep sleep, for when I spoke to him he only stirred but did not raise his head. Then I shook his arm. He slowly raised his head, then looked up at me. For a moment he seemed to struggle with himself for recognition. Then he humped up and almost immediately fell to the floor. Unlike him, I made completely sure that he *was* dead, and not simply unconscious.

William George Carpenter, you wished to kill me. Your courage was not equal to your cunning. It was a good idea to start a diary which would explain how a dead man had killed your wife. It was also remarkably well acted for a man of your meagre talents. But its overriding virtue lay in the fact that it allowed me to kill you in a perfectly legal manner.

.   .   .   .   .

Anyone want a house, rent free?

THE GREETING

By Sir Osbert Sitwell

FROM outside the long, large windows fires could be seen flickering in many wide grates, while the comforting sense, more than smell, of warm food oozed out of the whole house, subduing the sharper scent of frosty air. The dining-room table, she noticed as she passed by, was laid for three persons, and decorated with four small silver vases, from which a few very rigid flowers drew themselves up into the light of the windows. The sideboard showed beyond, bearing various drab meats and some pieces of plate, its cold glitter tempered by the flames with patches of warm orange.

As soon as Nurse Gooch was shown into the drawing-room, almost, indeed, before she had shaken hands or remarked how nice it was to see a fire, they went in to luncheon. But seated before this white expanse, these three people could not succeed in materializing any conversation, that, as talk should, drawing its strength from the group but stronger than any individual member of it, would continue almost automatically, reproducing itself or taking on a fresh form from time to time. In the same way in which spiritualists claim that the presence of one sceptic at a seance is sufficient to prevent any manifestation, however hoped for and credited by the majority, here it was difficult for the talk to glow or prosper, when one of this small party was continually exerting her will to the utmost in order to produce a lasting and uncomfortable silence. The stagnant quiet of the room was seldom broken, then, except by the rather horse-like stepping of the footmen, or by the thin, stringy voice of the invalid projected through the mute air in querulous inquiry. And, in the very act of speaking herself, both by the purpose and calculated tone of her question, she enforced a silence on the others. Colonel Tonge tried to make conversation to the new-comer, placed between him and his sick wife, but his abrupt, pompous little sentences soon withered, frozen on the air by his wife's disapproval. Mrs. Tonge, however, as we have said, permitted herself to ask a question occasionally—a question which, though it appeared innocent, was designed to convey to her new nurse the impression that she was an injured, ill-used woman. "When, Humphrey," she would ask, "do you intend to put electric light into the house? I have asked you to do it for so many years now. I am sure I should sleep better, and should not be such a worry to you or to nurse." Or: "What about that summer-house, Humphrey? Will it be ready for me in the spring? If I am still with you, I intend going there every day when the weather is warmer. Perhaps I shall find a little peace there in the woods. But I fear it hasn't been touched yet." To these questions the Colonel returned smooth, soothing answers, but ones which did not commit him in any way; but these, rather than conciliating the invalid, seemed only to vex her the more. But at this early period, before she understood her nurse, before she knew that anything she said would soon be pardoned, she did not actually as yet accuse her husband of doing all in his power to make and keep her ill, but was content to let this accusation remain implicate in her questions, and in the sound of her voice. Still, Nurse Gooch felt instinctively that Mrs. Tonge did not want to hurt her, that she was not in reality ill-natured, but that this calculated putting-out of the social fire was the outcome of a thousand little injuries inflicted by an imagination warped by constant illness and want of sleep. But whether it was due to the atmosphere created by this friction between husband and wife, or to something in the surroundings—in the house itself—she did most certainly, at this first moment of her arrival, experience an uneasy feeling, a slight repulsion from the Grove, which passed as soon as she became better acquainted with it.

Tonge's Grove, a square house, lies like a box thrown down among hanging woods and open commons—a charming residence in many ways. Like a doll's house it seems, each room giving the correct proportion to the rather under life-size figures it displays. A curiously inappropriate setting, certainly, for any drama, the protagonists of which must find themselves cramped in their action by the wealth of detail imposed. The very comfort and well-being of the place would give a grotesque air to any but an accustomed or trivial event. For here, long habit appears so much more important than the occasion or fact it originally enshrined, inanimate objects so much more actual, more active, than human beings, that it is upon the house, and not upon its owners, that our attention is first focused. It is this superfluity of things, combined with a rigorous pruning of reality, that gives a certain significance to any fact of life should it be strong enough to enter these gates, yet remain quick. For reality, which is usually unpleasant, seldom touches lives such as these except at birth, of which, fortunately, we are all ignorant, or at death, a latent, lurking fear (an ogre at the end of every passage), but one which it is our very human convention to ignore.

The Grove is not really a small house; the rooms in it are large and numerous, but, like a square toy thrown in among garden-beds and stables, crinoline-shaped lime trees and red-walled angular orchards, among, in fact, all the long-settled paraphernalia annexed to a prosperous, well-ordered way of life, it was endowed with a perfection such as at first to make it seem miniature, like some exquisite model seen through a glass case.

Certainly there is beauty about an estate of this kind: that tamed country sentiment, so English in quality, clings to it, till even the bird song that trickles down through the dripping blue shadows thrown by tall trees seems arranged, punctual and correct as the mechanical chirping of one of those clockwork birds that lifts enamelled wings out of a square black box; and even the cuckoo, who makes so ominous a sound from the cool green fortifications of wood or hedgerow, here changes his note till it rings hollow and pure as a church bell. No sense of mystery broods in the green and open spaces bathed in yellow summer sunlight; here are no caves, grottos, or tumbling torrents; everything is near, shallow as the clear, slightly running streams that border the wood; yet surely such beauty is, in a way, more fantastic than any of Leonardo's piled-up rocks or those worlds of ogres and giants to which we are carried off by some of the primitive painters.

In the winter it is that all these country places are seen in their best, their most typical, phase. Stout built for cold weather, these houses take on a new quality, upstanding among hoarfrost, glowing warmly through the crisp, grey air. The first impression of the Grove would be, we think, a childlike memory of potting-shed smells, full of the scents of hidden growth; an odour of bulbs, stoves, rich fibrous mould, and bass, mingles with the sharp aromatic smell of the bonfire that crackles outside. On the walls of the shed the bass is hung up like so many beards of old men—ritual beards, like those of Pharaoh or Egyptian priest, which, perhaps, the gardener will don for the great occasions of his year. This one he would put on for the opening of the first spring flower, coming up glazed and shrill, its petals folded as if in prayer, out of the cold brown earth, beneath the laced shadows woven by the bare branches of the trees; this he will wear for the brazen trumpet-like blowing of the tulip tree; while that one he reserves for the virginal unfolding of the magnolia, or the gathering up of petals let drop by the last rose. But the gardener himself soon dispels these tender imaginings, as you see his burly form bent over various cruel tasks—the trapping of the soft mole, or in aiming at the fawn-coloured fluffy arcs of the rabbits, as they crouch in their green cradles, their ears well back, nibbling the tender white shoots that he has so carefully nurtured.

Outside the shed, in many glass frames, large violets, ranging in tone from a deep purple through magenta to an almost brick-red, their petals scintillating damply, glisten like crystallized fruit seen through a glass window, sweet but unapproachable. The ground of the kitchen garden is hard and shiny, starched with frost; trees, shrubs, and the very grass are stiff and brittle, sweeping down under the slight wind with a shrill, steely wound. But the orchard walls still glow as if stained with the juice of the ripe fruits that press against them in summer and autumn, red, purple, and bloomy, while the house beyond shows warmly through the trees whose topmost twigs pattern themselves about it, like cobwebs against the sky; soft it is, as if cut from red velvet. Out of its doors and windows sounds the monotonous, dry-throated rattle of pet dogs, setting up a comfortable yet irritating competition with the noises of stable and farmyard, where rosy-faced men bustle about, lumbering in heavy boots; or, leaning to one side, the right arm lifted and at an angle, blow loudly and whistle, as they polish still more the varnished horses, their breathing lingering on after them in the sharp air like dragon's breath. Through the windows of the house each fireplace shows up, while the red flowers blaze in it, or die down to a yellow flicker, fighting ineffectually against the thin silver rapiers of the winter sun. But more than all these things would you notice here the bitter cackle of a green parrot, falling through the drawn-out air with a horrid clatter, tumbling all lesser sounds down like a pack of cards. Certainly that menacing silly sound of a parrot's laughter would be your most abiding memory.

On such a noon as this it was that Nurse Gooch had first driven up to the Grove; so that, even if her first impression was a rather uneasy one, she had at any rate seen it wearing its most pleasant, most comfortable, aspect; for at night the character of every house changes—and this one alters more than most. The smiling comfort of the surroundings is lost, fades out into utter blackness, and a curious sub-flavour, unnoticed in the day, manifests itself. There are places and moments when the assumptions, the lean conventions on which our lives are based, become transparent, while, for an instant, the world we have made rocks with them. It is, for example, usually assumed that there are no such creatures as sea serpents, yet there are certain places in Europe, on our own placid coasts even, of such marvellous formation that we feel, suddenly, that the existence of these monsters is a certainty—that it would surprise us less to see a vast beast, such as those painted by Piero di Cosimo, with flame-forked tongue, gigantic head, and long writhing body, coming up out of the fathomless green depths, than to see a passing country cart, a clergyman, or anything to which our experience has accustomed us. There are moments, too, when death, which, as we have said, it is usually our custom to hide away in a dusty corner of our minds, peeps round at us, grimacing—and we realize it as one of the universal and most awful conditions upon which we are permitted to take up life. So it was with the Grove, when darkness coffined it round. The dwarf perfection which we have attempted to describe, would gradually disappear; for the very dimensions of the house seemed to alter as the rooms became swollen with darkness, full of inexplicable sound. Dead people walk here with more certain step than the living, their existence seems more substantial, their breathing more audible. The boarding of the floor yields under an invisible step, as if some strange memory stirs in it, and the panelling of the walls, the very furniture, make themselves heard with a hard, wooden creaking, which is magnified in these rooms now grown to the new proportions with which night endows them. And, in the darkness outside, everything moves, stirs, rustles.

It was therefore not to be wondered at that the Grove should have acquired the reputation of being haunted, though really, the unhappy restless air that pervaded it at night may have been due more to its long association with a family of sad, unfortunate temperament—amounting in certain cases to something worse—than to the actual walking presence of any ghost. For ever since the present house was built, late in the seventeenth century, it had been in the possession of the Tonges and, until recently, until in fact the present owner had inherited the estate, there had been a long history connected with it of brooding melancholy, that must have been nearly allied to madness.

But Colonel Tonge, as we have seen, presented an ordinary enough character, with nerves unaffected, betraying no sign of hereditary disorder. Among the properties we have described—house, lawn, garden, farm, and stables—this not altogether unattractive figure emerges, strutting like a bantam. A proud little man, with a fairly distinguished military career, fond of hunting and shooting, he was much engaged in the business of an estate, the extent and importance of which he was apt to magnify in his own mind. In addition to these interests, he was involved in the affairs of every district committee, and, as became him in his dual capacity of squire and military man, was much to the fore in all these local philanthropic schemes which had for their object the welfare of the ex-soldier, or the helping of widow and children.

Yet in spite of this inherited make-up of country gentleman and the acquired one of soldier, there was about the Colonel, on closer acquaintance, some quality that removed him ever so little from the usual specimen of his class, just as there was something about the Grove that differentiated it from the run of English country houses. In what, then, did this difference consist? Partly, perhaps, in the stress that he laid upon the importance of his belongings, and therefore of himself; but more, surely, in the extraordinary calm that marked his demeanour—a quiet unruffled calm, not quite in accord with his bristling appearance and apparent character. One never saw him lose his temper, never even about trivialities, such as is the way of most military commanders; yet this restraint did not seem to arise so much from good nature, as from the fear of losing his self-control even for a moment—suggesting that he was suppressing some instinct or emotion which must be very strong within him, if it was necessary continually to exert such an iron self-discipline. This contrast between nature and manner showed itself, too, in the difference between his uneasy, wandering eyes and the tightly drawn mouth. But if Nurse Gooch had, with more than her normal sensitiveness, felt at first that there was a rather queer atmosphere about the house, she had at any rate detected nothing unusual in the look or manner of this amiable, rather pompous, little man and, indeed, the only person who appreciated thoroughly these various subtle distinctions was Mrs. Tonge. This poor lady had married her first cousin, and appeared to have inherited or acquired his, as well as her own, share of the peculiarly nervous temperament of this family. Thin, tall, and of that ash-grey colour which betokens constant sleeplessness, her rather sweet expression, while it was in direct contradiction to her restless, irritable soul, was the only remnant of a former prettiness. For, when first she married, she had been a good-looking, high-spirited girl, but had suddenly, swiftly, sunk into this state of perpetual and somewhat nagging melancholy. She was in reality a stupid woman, but her frayed nerves bestowed upon her an understanding of, and insight into, the unpleasant side of life that were alarming in the sureness of their judgment, and must have made of her a trying companion. She added to these heightened perceptions a sense of grievance, aggravated by an absolute lack of any interest or occupation, and by the fact that she was childless. She complained constantly, her chief lament being that there were only three creatures in the world that cared for her, two dogs—a Pomeranian and a Pekinese—and her beloved green parrot! Often she would add a remark to the effect that her husband would like—was, in fact, only waiting for—Polly to die. His triumph would then, apparently, be complete. And it must truthfully be said that the only thing which ever seemed to disturb the Colonel's calm was the idiot laughter which the parrot would let fall through the darkened air of the sick woman's room. But though the slightest noise at any other time would strain Mrs. Tonge's taut nerves almost to breaking point, she appeared actually to enjoy her bird's head-splitting mirth; while the parrot, in return, seemed to acknowledge some bond of affection between his mistress and himself, for, were she more than usually ill, he would be ever so quiet, not venturing to exercise his marked mimetic gifts, even repressing his habitual laughter.

This love for her parrot and her pet dogs, together with a certain trust in, more than affection for, her young nurse—a trust which developed as the months passed—were all the assets of which Mrs. Tonge was conscious in this life. For the rest she was lonely and frightened . . . very frightened. Her whole existence was spent in a continual state of fear—one of the worst symptoms, though quite a common one, of neurasthenia; she was afraid of her neighbours, her husband, her house, terrified by everything and everybody alike. But, while frightened of everything, she was as consistently opposed to any plan for the alleviation of these imagined terrors.

Afraid, though seemingly without reason, of her husband, she was yet never able to refrain from making the fullest use of any opportunity to irritate, hurt, or annoy him. But he was very patient with her. She would taunt him with things big and little; she would attack him about his self-importance, or goad him before the nurse about his fondness for giving good advice to others, in a manner that must have made him feel the sting of truth. She would even accuse him of wishing to be rid of her—a poor invalid and one who was in his way—an accusation which, however, she could never really have believed for a moment. She would tell him that he had a cruel soul, and in her sick mind seemed to have fashioned a grotesque, caricatured little image of her husband, which, to her, had at last come to be the reality—an image, unlike yet in a way recognizable, of a queer, patient, cruel, rather wolf-like creature, hiding his true self beneath the usual qualities attached to the various very ordinary interests and pursuits in which his life was spent.

In spite of this extraordinary conception of him, Mrs. Tonge was always calling for her husband. Her plaintive voice echoing through the square, lofty rooms would be answered by his gruff, military tones so often that one of the parrot's most ingenious tricks was a perfect rendering of: "Humphrey, come here a minute!" and the answering call: "Yes, Mary, I'm coming," followed by the sound of hurrying footsteps. Thus, though frightened of him, though almost hating him, the invalid would hardly allow her husband to leave her, if only for a day.

Still more was Mrs. Tonge frightened of her house—that home which she knew so intimately. But, in the same perverse manner, she would never quit it, even for a night. While suffering terribly from insomnia, and from that fear of darkness which, though it usually leaves us when our childhood is past, had never wholly left her, she was steadfast in her refusal to allow Nurse Gooch to sleep in the same room, thus lessening those nocturnal terrors by human companionship. On the contrary, the sick woman not only insisted on being alone, but was resolute in locking both the doors of her room, one of which led into her husband's bedroom, the other into the passage outside, so that had she been seized with sudden illness, which was not altogether unlikely, no help could have reached her. Thus, bolted securely within those four walls, she would indulge her broken spirit in an orgy of sleepless terror. The dogs slept downstairs: her only companion was Polly, noiseless now, but faithful as ever, sitting hunched up on his perch, his dome-like cage enveloped in a pall of grey felt; and, even had he sounded his bitter, head-splitting laughter, it would have seemed more sweet than the music of any southern nightingales to the poor invalid, tossing about on her bed. For the parrot, alone of the animal world, could give his mistress some feeling of momentary security.

Day would come at last, to bring with it an hour or two of grey, unrefreshing sleep. The afternoon she would spend knitting, seated in a large armchair in front of the fire, in her over-heated boudoir, crowded with strong-smelling flowers. Photographs of friends—friends whom she had not seen for years and had perhaps never really cared for—littered all the furniture, and clambered up the walls, over the fireplace, in an endless formation, imbuing the room with that peculiar, morbid tone of old photographs, yellow and glazed as death itself. Bustles, bonnets, then straw hats and leg-of-mutton sleeves, showed grotesquely in these little squares of faded, polished cardboard, set off by a palm tree in an art pot, a balustraded terrace, a mountainous yet flat background, or one of those other queer properties of the old photographic world. The wistful smiles on these pretty faces were now gone like her own, the smoothness of the skin was now replaced by hundreds of ever so small wrinkles, the fruit of care, sorrow, or some seed of ill-nature or bad temper that, undreamt of then, had now blossomed. The rest of open space on table, piano, or writing-desk was taken up by diminutive unconnected vases of violets, fresias or jonquils, their heavy breath weighing on the air like a cloud, seeming among these photographs so many floral tributes to dead friendship, each one marking the grave of some pretended or genuine affection. The room was overloaded with these vases; the flowers lent no grace to the room, no sweetness to the overburdened air. The Pomeranian yapped at Mrs. Tonge's feet, the Pekinese lay curled up in a basket, while at her elbow the parrot picked at a large, white grape, the stale odour of the bird's cage mingling with the already stifling atmosphere of the room, till it become almost intolerable. Here the invalid would sit for hours enjoying one of the thousand little grievances from which she was able to choose, turning it over and pecking at it like the parrot at his grape; or, perhaps, she would be gripped by one of the manifold terrors of her life. Then that supreme horror, the fear of death (which, as she grew older, claimed an ever greater part of her attention), grimaced at her from the scented shadows, till it seemed to her as if she sat there knitting endlessly her own shroud, and the vases of flowers transformed their shapes, rearranging themselves till they became wreaths and crosses, and the hot smell they exhaled became the very odour of death. Then she would ring again, calling for Nurse Gooch, but even that familiar footfall would make her shudder for an instant.

Her only pleasures now consisted in the tormenting of her even-tempered husband, or, in a lesser degree, of the poor young nurse—to whom she had now become attached in the same sense that a dog is attached to any object, such as a doll or an india-rubber ball, which it can worry. But Gooch, good and amiable, clean-looking rather than pretty, her face fully expressing that patience and kindness which were her two great qualities, won the affections not only of the invalid but of Colonel Tonge, and even of the servants—this latter no mean conquest when it is remembered that there is a traditional feud between servants and trained nurse, almost rivalling that other hereditary vendetta between nursery and schoolroom. Nurse Gooch was really fond of her patient, in spite of the maddening irritation of her ways: nor had she been unhappy during these eighteen months that had followed her luncheon at the Grove on that first winter day. For after the hardships of her own childhood, she appreciated this solid, very comfortable, home, while it presented to her a full scope for the exercise of those protective instincts which were particularly deep-rooted in her nature. Often, in a way, she envied Mrs. Tonge her kind husband and charming house, thinking how happy the invalid might have been had only her disposition been a different one. For in Colonel Tonge the young nurse could see nothing but consideration for his ill wife, and kindness indeed to everyone till, slowly, she formed in her own mind an image of him very different from that fashioned by his wife. To Nurse Gooch he was a model of suffering chivalry; to her his stature and heart seemed great, his importance equal to his own estimate of it. In fact, he became that very appealing combination—one which always fascinates the English people—a hero in public, a martyr in private life. And it was a source of great comfort for her to reflect that by keeping Mrs. Tonge in as good a mood as possible, or, to borrow a military phrase, by intentionally drawing the fire on to herself, she was able to some small extent to alleviate the trials of the husband. Then she could feel, too, in some mysterious manner, that he was grateful for it, that he began to take a pleasure in her society, in the knowledge that she understood his difficulties, applauded his moderation. Often they used to sit together, consulting with Dr. Maynard, a clever doctor, but one who lacked courage, and was in the habit of giving way to his patients. Gradually, therefore, if any new symptom showed itself, if any new problem arose regarding the invalid, it was with the nurse and not with the doctor that Colonel Tonge would first come to talk it over.

Existence at the Grove, though each day appeared to her encompassed in the span of an hour, so that she was continually finding herself landed, as if by some magic carpet of the fourth dimension, at the corresponding time of the next day, yet seemed eternal; even the state of the sick woman, though her nerves became ever more affected, appeared to be stationary. Outside there was the flat, placid life of the countryside to be watched, the punctual revolution of the seasons. First came the ice-green glitter of the snowdrops, frosting the grass of the park with their crystal constellations; then these faded, withered, turned yellow, deepened to the butter colour of the daffodils that ousted them, flowers swaying their large heads under the spring winds, transparent, full of the very colour of the sun; and, almost before you had time to observe it, they would flush to a deep purple, would be transformed into anemones, the centre of their dusky blossoms powdered with pollen, black like charcoal dust, or would adopt that velvet softness of texture which distinguishes the rose from other flowers; and summer would be in its full flame. Then, inside the Grove, you found good food, punctual hours, a calm routine broken only by the outbursts of Mrs. Tonge, or by the bitter cackle of the parrot, its feathers green with the depth of the tropical forest, its eyes wary and knowing. It looked cunning, as if in possession of some queer secret—some secret such as that of the parrot encountered in Mexico by the traveller Humboldt—a bird which alone in all the world possessed a tongue of its own, since it spoke a language now extinct. For the tribe who talked it had been killed to a man in the course of America becoming a Christian continent, while the bird had lived on for a century.

The summer was a particularly hot one, and as it burnt to its climax Mrs. Tonge's irritable nerves inflicted an increasing punishment on those around her. The Colonel, who was drawn away on various long-promised visits to old friends and taken to London several times on the business of his estate, left the Grove more than usual this July, so that the full brunt of any trouble in the house fell upon Nurse Gooch, who would often have to shut herself up in her room and, strong-minded, well-trained woman though she was, cry like a hurt child, so intolerable was the strain imposed upon her by the invalid. The latter soon realized when she had made the tactical error of being too disagreeable—or, perhaps, one should say of concentrating a day's temper in one short hour, instead of spreading it thinly, evenly, over the whole of the sun's passage, so that looked back upon, it should tinge the day with some unpleasant colour in the minds of her companions or servants. And being possessed of a certain charm or a false kindliness, which she could exert whenever it was necessary to her, she was soon able again to engage the nurse's pity and affection.

"Poor thing," Gooch would think to herself. "One can't blame her for it. Look how she suffers." But however true was this reflection, it was the sick woman who was still the chief opponent of any plan for the mitigation of her sufferings. Though her sleeplessness became worse, though the prospect of those long, dark hours threw a shadow blacker than the night itself over each day, yet she still refused to allow Nurse Gooch to rest in the room with her; while Dr. Maynard, who should have insisted on it, was, as usual, completely overborne by his patient.

It is difficult to describe. though, how much Mrs. Tonge suffered, locked in her room during those sultry nights, for their darkness appeared to cover a period easily surpassing the length of any wintry night. As she lay there, her limbs twitching, memories dormant in her mind for forty years would rise up to torment her. Her parents, her old nurse (all dead how many summers past!) would return to her here in the silence. All the disappointments of her life would revive their former aching. Once more she would see the gas-lit ballrooms in which she had danced as a girl, and the faces of men she had forgotten half a lifetime ago. Then, again, she would see her wedding. All these memories would link up, and coalesce in feverish waking dreams of but a moment's duration, but which would yet seem to hold all eternity in their contorted perspectives. Wide awake now, she would recall her longing for children, or ponder upon one of her thousand little grievances, which took on new and greater dimensions in these hours. Here she was . . . with a parrot as her only friend . . . in this everlasting blackness. The thought of death would return to her, death that was at the end of each turning, making every life into a blind, hopeless cul-de-sac. Long and hard she would fight this spectre of finality, against which no religion had the power to fortify her spirit. Then, after midnight, new terrors began, as the Grove woke up to its strange nocturnal life. Footsteps would sound outside, treading stealthily, stealthily on the black, hollow air; the furniture in the room, cumbersome old cupboards and chests of drawers, would suddenly tattoo a series of little but very definite hard sounds upon the silence, as if rapping out some unknown code. But when everything was swathed in quiet once more, this new absence of noise would be worse, more frightening than were the sounds themselves. It would smother everything with its blackness; everything would be still . . . waiting . . . listening! The silence, from having been merely a form of muffled sound, or perhaps a negation of it, became itself positive, active—could be felt and tested by the senses. There it was again, that creaking—as if someone was listening . . . someone certainly . . . someone standing on a loose board, crouching down in the darkness outside, afraid to tread for fear of waking one. Then would follow a distraction. A new code would be rapped out as something tapped on the window-pane . . . tap-tap-tap, like a mad thing. Only the wind with that branch of ivy, she supposed. There it was again . . . tap-tap . . . like a mad thing trying to get into her room . . . tap-tap . . . into her very head, it seemed! Outside the house a dog would bark once, menacingly, and then its rough voice would die suddenly, as if silenced. Footsteps would tread again down the long passages, footsteps more distinct than ever this time. And once or twice they lingered stealthily at the bolted door; the handle would creak, grasped very carefully, turned by an invisible hand; and was there not the sound of a smothered, animal-like breathing? The wolf-at-the-door, the wolf-at-the-door, she says to herself in that fevered mind, where it seems as if two people, two strangers, were carrying on a whispered conversation of interminable length. Then silence comes once more; an unequalled stillness pours into the room, and into the corridors outside, so that the tapping, when it returns, takes on a new quality, rippling this quiet blackness with enlarging circles of sound, as when a stone is cast into a small pool. Tap-tap-tap . . . again tap. Perhaps she is only dead, being fastened into her coffin. Tap-tap . . . they are nailing it down, tap-tap; and she lies dead in the silence for ever. Then far away the taps sound out again, and the coffin is unnailed. But this time it is the parrot rapping upon the bars of his dome-like cage with his hard beak; and she is reassured. Grey light clutches again at the swathed windows, and the furniture of the room grows slowly into its accustomed shape; the things round her fall back again into their familiar contours, and are recognizable as themselves, for in the night they had assumed new positions, new shapes, strange attitudes . . . and the poor nervous creature lying on the rumpled bed falls asleep for an hour or two.

But as the light drips stealthily in, filling the black hollows of room and corridor, the housemaids, warned by Nurse Gooch to be more than usually quiet, scratch gently in the passage outside like so many mice, scratch with a gentle feeble sound that must inevitably rouse anyone—even a person who sleeps well by habit and is at that moment deep-rooted in slumber. For this timid, rodent-like noise is more irritating to the strongest nerves, will awaken more surely than any of that loud, sudden music to which we are accustomed—that music of blows rained accidentally but with great force upon the fragile legs and corners of old furniture or brittle carving of ancient gilded frames—blows delivered with the back of an ever so light feathery brush. Thus Mrs. Tonge would open her eyes upon one more hot and calm morning.

As she lay there, in the semi-darkness, she could hear faint voices sounding in the passage. Soon after she has rung her bell, Nurse Gooch comes in with the letters, as clean and kind as is possible for a human being to be, bright as are all trained nurses in the early morning; too bright, perhaps, too wide awake, and already making the best of it. Her hair has a dark golden colour in it under the light, and gleams very brightly under the cap she is wearing, while she talks in an even, soothing voice. As she goes down the corridor towards the invalid's room, the housemaids take her passing presence for a signal that they may resume that noisy bustle of cleanliness with which they salute each day. Suddenly motes of dust whirl up into the air beneath their brushes, turning the already searching rays of the sun to columns and twisted pillars of sparkling glass that support this heavy firmament, pillars prism-like in the radiant array of their colour. As the housemaids, bent nearly double in their long white print dresses, move slowly over the carpet, brush in one hand dust-pan in the other, their movements break up these columns, so that the atoms that compose them fall through the air like so many sequins, and are violently agitated; then these take on new shapes, and from pillars are converted into obelisks, pyramids, rectangles, and all the variety of glittering forms that, bound by the angles of straight lines, can be imposed upon this dull air and earth by the lance-like rays of the morning sun.

In the room she still lies in bed, turning over the unopened envelopes of her letters. Gooch goes to the window and talks to the parrot. As she uncovers the cage the bird breaks into its metallic laughter, that rattles down through the open window into the shrubbery, like so many brassy rings thrown down by a juggler, for they curve in again at the pantry window, where John the footman is standing in an apron, cleaning the silver with a dirty-looking piece of old yellow leather and some gritty rose-pink paste. As he polishes the convex mirror formed by the flanks of the silver bowl, while his face reflected in one side assumes a grotesque appearance, the contorted trees and twisted perspective of lawn and garden show in the other. The second housemaid peeps in. "Oh, you do look a sight!" she cries, bridling with laughter, pointing to the bowl in his hand. "I may be a sight," he says, "or I may not, but I'm not a blarsted slave, am I?" "Well, you needn't answer so nasty," she says. "It's not that, it's that parrot—'ark at it now. I shall be glad when 'e comes back; one can't do no right in this place. Everything is wrong. First it's one damn' thing, then another. Nurse sticks it like a soldier," he says, "but I stand up for my rights! I'm not a slave, I'm not, that I should stand there letting that blarsted parrot screech at me like a sergeant-major on a parade ground, and her talking a lot of nonsense. I'd like to wring its bloody neck, I would—they're a pair of them, they are!"

And certainly—Nurse Gooch herself had to admit—the invalid was this summer more than ever exacting. For many months past she had worried her husband about a summer-house, for which she had formed one of those queer, urgent longings that sick people consider themselves free to indulge. The hut had stood there in the woods, year after year, unnoticed, falling to damp decay, when, as if given new eyes, Mrs. Tonge saw it for the first time, and determined to make it her own. Here, she felt, it would be possible to sit quietly, rest peacefully, in an atmosphere different from that of the Grove, and perhaps find that sleep denied her in any other place. As the summer-house was in a very dilapidated condition, she asked her husband to have it repaired for her, but met with a very unexpected opposition. The Colonel, used as he was to furthering every plan of his sick wife, absolutely ignored this new entreaty. Which fact, unfortunately, only strengthened her determination, and made her persist in her caprice.

There was, in reality, some danger in letting Mrs. Tonge remain alone for a long period in a spot so remote from the house—she refused, again, to allow anyone to wait with her in this solitude—for though, as is the habit of permanent invalids, she might live for many years, yet she was a nervous, delicate woman, very liable to a sudden attack of illness, and here no help could reach her. But Dr. Maynard, with his customary inability to say "No" to a patient— or, perhaps, because he felt that the rest she hoped to obtain here would be more valuable to her than any unexpected attack of illness would be dangerous—gave his sanction to the new scheme. Colonel Tonge, however, still urged the doctor to forbid it, making a strong protest against what he considered this folly, and himself steadfastly refused to have the place touched up in any way, or even swept out. The invalid changed her tactics: from anger she passed to a mood of plaintive injury. "I know, Humphrey," she moaned at him, "that you only go on like that because you hate to think that I am having a peaceful moment. What harm *can* there be in going to the summer-house? It doesn't hurt you, does it?"

The Colonel, patient as ever, would show no sign of ill-temper, putting the case as reasonably as he could. "Mary, my dear, it is really very unwise and foolish of you. I know how much unemployment there is, how unsettled is the countryside. You should see some of the tramps that are brought up before me on the Bench. That summer-house may seem deep in the woods, but it is very near the high road. You can never tell who will come into the park. Anyone can get in. There's no lodge near that gate. I tell you, my dear, it isn't safe. I can't think how you can be so silly. It's folly, sheer folly!"

Mrs. Tonge cried a little. "I'm not afraid of tramps or motor-cars, or of anything on a road. But I know you'd do anything to prevent my getting any rest, Humphrey. I believe you'd like me to go without any sleep at all, as long as it didn't worry you. I know you're only waiting for me to die." . . . And the poor little man, discomfited, walked away. He was always so patient . . . like that . . . and kind, it made Nurse Gooch feel a great pity for him. But she thought he was wrong in this particular instance—wrong ever to oppose the invalid's wishes, however seldom he did so; and knowing her influence with him, she persuaded the Colonel to say no more about it, though he still seemed a little uneasy. Yet so great had become his reliance on the young nurse's judgment, that she easily induced him to pretend to his wife that he now thought his opposition had been mistaken.

But Mrs. Tonge could not be deceived. She knew perfectly well that he did not really approve, and it therefore gave her an increased pleasure to rest in the summer-house. Getting up later than ever in these hot months of the year, she would go there every afternoon. She forbade her two pets to be with her, so that a piteous, plaintive yapping filled the Grove each day after luncheon; only Polly, devoted Polly, was privileged to share this new solitude. Curiously enough, she did not feel frightened here. The rather ominous silence of the woods held no menace for her; she was happier among these dank shadows than in her own bedroom or placid flowering garden; and, whether from perversity or from some form of auto-suggestion, it was a fact that when the nurse walked out to the hut to bring the sick woman back to the house for tea, she often found her in a slumber more peaceful than any she had enjoyed for years.

Between two and three o'clock each fine afternoon a queer procession could be seen walking over the lawn, between the beds of flowers that lay like embossed embroidery among the sleek grass. First of all came Mrs. Tonge, never glancing aside at flower or tree, her upright carriage and slow-moving walk bestowing an almost ritual air on the proceedings; then followed the uniform-clad figure of the nurse, holding newspapers and a small cluster of three or four grapes for the parrot in one hand, while from the other dangled the sacred dome. The grapes, transparent, jewel-like, catching the prevailing colour, which was that of the penetrating glow of sunlight through green leaves, focused the eye as they moved along, till they seemed like some mystic regalia, even drawing the eye away from the more metallic colouring of the parrot, who, as he was borne along, shrieked continually, taking an obvious pleasure in scaring the poor timid birds of the English countryside by a display of flaming plumage and alien, rather acrid, laughter. Slowly they passed over the shrill, water-smooth lawns, where single high trees stood up fleecy against the sky, or, overburdened by the full weight of summer, trailed their branches right down upon the fragrant ground, into the dark woods cloudy with foliage and rank with the smell of tall nettles, elder-trees, bracken, and all those things that grow in unkept places. No bird-song sounded now in this ultimate unfolding of the seasons, and the little path that led winding through this wilderness lay like a curling green ribbon, of a brighter hue than the surrounding shrubs and velvety with moss, from which weeds sprouted up at the corners like small tufts of feathers. This untidy ribbon, lying without purpose across the woodland ground, led to the rustic hut which the caprice of some former mistress of the Grove had caused to be built here, rather pointlessly, some ninety years ago. Under a round roof, sloping down from its centre, and covered with the rough bark of trees, it lay mouldering beneath the structure of branches which hung motionless, as if cut from cardboard, on the heavy air. Sponge-like, it seemed, in its dampness, like some fungus lying about at the foot of a tree. Great knots of ivy clung to the upper part of the door, while, where the peeling bark had fallen away, were revealed arrangements of rusty nails, geometrical, but growing like thorns out of the wood. No view was framed in the pointed spaces of the two windows, except the light which trellised itself with the shadow of green leaves along the ground, or, flooding a stretch of bracken, played first on one leaf, then on another, bringing out unexpected patterns, making each bent-back leaf, as it was touched, the centre of some shifting arabesque design such as is woven in Eastern carpets.

The parrot would be placed on the dingy, bark-covered table; a grape would be half-peeled, and pressed, like a melting jewel between the bars of the cage. The wire dome would then be draped ceremoniously with grey felt; the invalid would lie back in her long chair, a rug over her knees, the countless newspapers which it was her habit to read placed at her side; and Nurse Gooch would walk back briskly through the dark stillness of the wood out again into the droning odorous languor of the garden.

As Mrs. Tonge rested in her long chair, she found, certainly, a peace otherwise denied to her in the grim world of a sick woman's fancy. No argument, she determined, should ever persuade her to give up this siesta. Day followed day, each warm and bright-coloured as the other; only the leaves became a little ranker in their scent, the woods yet more silent. But, sometimes, as she was on the border of sleep, already seeing the queer avenues of that land which she could so seldom reach, while through its landscape she could still distinguish the more rational, familiar features of her real surroundings, a sound like a rushing wind, or as if gigantic wings were beating on the taut drum-like fabric of the air, would startle her for a moment, and, looking round, she would see the tall stiff trees lift up their canvas branches, caught by a false breeze, as a motor-car passed between the two high hedges that concealed the road. Above this hidden white scar a high whirling column of dust would dance for a few seconds, as if it were some jinn of the air made visible for the moment; or, again, she would be lulled by the kindly, cooing voices of the country people, which floated over to her, for, as her husband had pointed out, the road was in reality very near the summer-house. But these things did not appear unpleasant to her; and, in any case, how much better were these explicable sounds than that state of suspended animation, alternating with a sudden show of life, which she had grown to dread so much at night in her own room!

The hot weather continued, and with it the life of the Grove. Colonel Tonge, as we have remarked, was away this summer more than was his wont, but the routine of the invalid, the nurse, and the servants repeated itself almost automatically. Every afternoon Nurse Gooch would walk out with the patient to the hut and would leave her there, only returning in time to fetch her back to the house for tea. One afternoon, when the Colonel was expected home from a short visit to Major Morley, an old friend and brother-officer whom, though a near neighbour, he saw very seldom, Mrs. Tonge suddenly made up her mind to stay out in the summer-house for tea, telling the nurse to bring it out to her at five o'clock. Now, though there was nothing very original or startling in this idea, Gooch, who in matters relating to an invalid did not lack a certain subtlety, at once expostulated—not, indeed, from any feeling of disapproval—but because she well knew that the sick woman would in reality be deeply disappointed if her nurse seemed pleased, or even satisfied, with this new break away from the normal programme. The nurse, therefore, succeeded in putting up a show of anxiety, saying such things as that the Colonel would be hurt and annoyed at finding his wife absent on his return. Finally, pretending to be persuaded against her better judgment, she agreed to bring tea out to the summer-house at five o'clock; then, placing the parrot's cage on the table, she covered it up, completed her ritual, and walked back to the house through the hot, strangely sultry, afternoon.

Mrs. Tonge felt an unaccustomed luxurious ease steal over her as she lay stretched out on her couch reading her papers, though perhaps perusing them less carefully today than was her custom. As a rule, she read them from cover to cover—births, deaths, marriages, sales, advertisements of all kinds; and while these journals represented every shade of political opinion, she was quite unmoved by their varying propaganda. She regarded them, in fact, as her own form of relaxation. This afternoon, however, she could not fix her attention on them. She peeled an amber, honey-scented grape for Polly, who mumbled back lovingly but softly. What a difference even an hour's sleep makes! She wondered when Humphrey was coming back, feeling that she had been rather hard with him lately—in fact, for some time past. With a sudden impulse of affection the image she had formed of him in her own mind was broken, and he became to her again the young man whom she had loved. She determined that she would be nicer to him; and certainly she felt a little better today. The afternoon in the summer-house seemed just warm enough . . . and quiet . . . nicely quiet, she thought. Slowly, almost contentedly, and for the first time for many years without any fear, any nervous feeling, she stretched her limbs until every nerve in her body became quiet, and sighing gently, let sleep wash over her tired limbs, her worn-out mind, in soft delicious little waves.

But, though the dampness of the hut may have tempered the afternoon heat for Mrs. Tonge, it seemed very breathless outside. Even Nurse Gooch, as she sat sewing in her usually cool room, felt rather overcome. Oh, how hot it was! And the house was very still. As a rule you heard the servants chattering, moving through the passages; the jingling of silver or the rattling clatter of plates would reach you from pantry or kitchen. But today there was no noise—not a sound, except the hot insect-like droning of the sewing-machine, as she bent over it, running the needle along the white edge of the new linen, which filled the room with a rather stifling scent. But directly she stopped, even for an instant, silence flooded the room. Well, one can't look after a case like this for eighteen months without feeling odd oneself sometimes, she supposed! Yet there was something queer about the stillness. There must be going to be a storm, she thought.

No sound came in from farm or stable at this high-up, open window, on a level with the motionless green cradles of the birds; but down below on the lawn a single leaf would suddenly burst out into a mad fluttering, as if trying to indicate the secret of this general alarm, and then be still, too still, as if it feared to be caught in an act of rebellion. . . . In the flower-beds, then, a single violet-coloured blossom would wave out wildly, flicker for an instant like a tongue of flame, then float once more stiffly upon the glazed heat. She was quite glad to finish her sewing, get the tea ready, and leave the house. But the air outside was even hotter than within—suffocating—so that one could not breathe, and as she passed out into the furtive silence of the woods she seemed separated from the world she knew. If I go on like this, she said to herself, I shall soon be the next invalid! Yet the walk seemed longer than it ought to be, so that she was continually being confronted with little twistings in it which she did not remember, though she had trodden this path at least four times a day for several months past. Still she knew, of course, that it must be the right one. But, somehow or other, she was startled this afternoon by things that usually she would not notice—the ordinary, rather inexplicable rustlings of the woodland, for instance. Doubtless these were audible yesterday as today, but as a rule she did not heed them; and once or twice, certainly, it seemed to her that she heard a peculiar scampering, as of a hurrying through thickets, or the dragging crackle of twigs and brambles as they released their clinging hold on invisible garments. It was with a distinct feeling of relief, then, that after what seemed quite a long walk, she caught sight of the summer-house round the next turning. It had a very human, friendly look to her this afternoon; yet it belonged so much to these woods, this soil, that it was like a large mushroom growing out of a taller green tangle. The invalid did not call out to her, even the parrot was silent—an indication, usually, that its mistress was asleep. (How queer it is the way she can sleep here, and nowhere else!) Nurse Gooch cried out cheerfully "Wake up, wake up! I've brought you your tea!" Still there was no answer, and, skirting the blind corner of the hut, carrying the tray in front of her, she was already standing in the low doorway before she had even cast a glance at its dark interior. Thrown suddenly into the quiet smallness of the summer-house, where she was at such close quarters with everything, almost within an arm's span of each wall, she was unable to breathe for a moment. An overwhelming sensation of nausea took possession of her, so that she felt that she, too, would fall upon that terrible floor. Yes, though the whole universe swung round, her trained eye observed the slaughter-house details. There lay the murdered woman, her head on one side, her skull crushed by some ferocious blow, her face twisted to a mask of terror—that queer unreasoning terror which had never left her. Dumb, blinking in its overturned cage, the parrot was hunched up, its feathers clotted together with blood. Clutching the bird's cage as if to save it from some fresh disaster, Nurse Gooch rushed wildly out of the summer-house into the motionless woods.

* * *

As she approached the Grove, her own sense of discipline asserted itself, forcing her to slow down her pace, to set her mind a little more in order. But now it was, actually, that the full shock came to her, for in that sudden blind moment of fear, when her limbs had melted one into the other, when her heart had bounded to her very lips, she had been unable to think, had experienced no feeling except an endless surprise, pity, and disgust. Afterward curiosity, as well, intervened, and she began to wonder who had done this thing, and why such a brutal fate had engulfed the poor, timid, elderly woman. And then she was forced to steel her soul for the next ordeal: she would have need of every particle of strength in mind and body, since it devolved upon her to break the news. Through the library window she could see Colonel Tonge standing by the empty fireplace, and even while she was still labouring under the blow that had befallen her, she dreaded telling him of it as the not least awful incident in this terrible adventure—nearly as overwhelming, indeed, as had been the actual moment of discovery. Her respect, and fondness even, for him, her knowledge that his had not been a happy marriage, only made the task a more difficult one to face and endure.

With an unexpected nervous susceptibility the Colonel seemed to feel the burning, panting breath of tragedy almost before she had spoken. Perhaps something out of her control manifested itself in her face, in her air; but as she entered, he looked at her with eyes as fearful as her own, and it seemed as if he, too, were mastering his emotions to confront something that he dreaded. "Go on, go on," he said, "what is it?"

.   .   .   .   .

Month followed month, and he still shut himself up in his room, till he became so changed in looks, in manner, as hardly to appear the same man. All pride, all self-importance had left him. The spring had gone out of his walk, the jauntiness out of dress and carriage. Every hour of the day he loaded himself with reproaches—for not having been firmer, for not having absolutely refused to allow his wife to stay out there alone—for having been away at the time of the tragedy. Gooch would hear him, unable to sleep at night, walking about the passages, pacing up and down, up and down, till the first grey light crept in at the corners of blind and curtain. It was as if the spirit of sleepless terror that had haunted his wife had now transferred its temple to his body. Incapable of attending to the business of his estate, to which formerly he had devoted so much consideration, he now seldom left the house in the daytime, and, if he did, in whatever direction he might set out, his feet always led him sooner or later to the same place, and he would be startled, aghast to find himself in the woods again.

Anything that reminded him of his dead wife had to be hidden away. The two poor little dogs were removed by his married sister when she went home, after a quite unsuccessful attempt to cheer her brother and give him comfort. The parrot, now never laughing, never speaking, languished in an attic, attended only by Emily, the housemaid. The other servants, too, were kind to the bird, since it had for them a fatal attraction: not only was it connected with death, having about it the very odour of the cemetery, but was in itself the witness and only relic of a brutal crime, so that it possessed the charm popularly associated with a portion of hangman's rope, and, in addition, was a living thing possessed of a dreadful secret. But the parrot would never utter, and downstairs—where the conversation, however wide the circle of its origin, always in the end drew in on to one topic—they had to admit that Polly had never been the-same-like-since. Occasionally Emily would leave the door of the cage open, hoping that he would walk out or fly round as he used to do. But nothing could tempt him out of his battered dome. As for Colonel Tonge, he had never liked the bird, hating its harsh laughter, and this solitary, now silent, witness of his wife's end filled him at present with an unconquerable aversion.

Great sympathy was evinced everywhere for the poor widower, crushed under a catastrophe so unexpected and mysterious. But the public sympathy could do little to help him; and though some solution of the mystery might temporarily have distracted his mind, even if it could not have rallied his spirits, none was forthcoming. He went through all the sordid business associated with murder—inquest and interview; but the crime remained odd as ever in its total absence of warning, intention, or clue. Who, indeed, could have plotted to murder this invalid lady, possessed of few friends and no enemies? And what purpose was served by this intolerable brutality? It is true that, after a time, the police found a stained, blunt-headed club, obviously the weapon with which the fatal wound had been inflicted, buried deep in the bracken; but, in a sense, this discovery only removed the murder further from the public experience, in that the possible motive of theft was at the same time disposed of—for with this weapon were found the few rings, the gold watch, and small amount of money that the dead woman had about her, as she had lain asleep in the summer-house on that sultry August afternoon. The police, thinking it possible that these articles had been hidden from an impulse of fear, that the original motive had indeed been the ordinary one, arrested a tramp found wandering in the district, hiding himself at night under hedges and in the shelter of empty barns; but though he could not give a very detailed or convincing account of his doings on the day of the "Hut Murder"—as it was called—the evidence that connected him with the crime was not enough to secure his conviction. It remained, however, the impression of many people, among them of both Dr. Maynard and Nurse Gooch, that he was in reality guilty of the foul act of which he had been suspected. Colonel Tonge, though he followed every detail of the trial with a painful interest, could never be induced to discuss the possible guilt of the tramp, but it was noticeable that after the man's release his nervous condition became more than ever marked, which led them to conclude that, in his opinion too, the person accused should never have been acquitted.

The bereaved husband's insomnia troubled him sorely; he had no peace, no rest by day or night. The only person able to bring him relief, to lighten his burden even for a moment, was Nurse Gooch; so that Dr. Maynard felt it his duty, for once, to insist on her remaining at the Grove until the Colonel should display some sign of returning health and a reviving spirit. The nurse, for her part, had always liked, pitied, and admired him, while, by one of those curious human instincts, all the compassion, all the affection even, which she had given so freely to the dead woman, was now made over to her new patient. And then she, too, felt remorse, had things on her mind with which to reproach herself. How well she could understand and sympathize with his self-accusation! Why, conscious as she had been of her influence over him, had she not supported the Colonel's wise protest against his wife's use of the summer-house, instead of urging, as she had done, that it was a reasonable plan, and finally persuading him to withdraw his objection to it? Terribly she felt now the responsibility so foolishly incurred, that perhaps she was in part to blame for the tragedy, even in the matter of allowing the invalid to wait out in the summer-house for tea on that dreadful afternoon; and in the months that followed the murder it was one of the few pleasant things in her life to reflect that she could, by her presence and sympathetic understanding, lessen his misery ever so little, giving him for a little while a passing sense of comfort.

When, after many long, lonely months, he made her an offer of marriage, saying that life without her support would be to him an intolerable burden, she accepted his proposal, realizing that the interest she felt in him, the overwhelming pity that sometimes clutched at her heart, was but a disguise for love. Regardless of any difference in age or outlook, she hoped, by becoming his wife, to help and ease the remainder of a life, the unhappy tenor of which had now deepened into a more dreadful tone.

The honeymoon was spent in France, in order to make for them both a complete break from the background of their lives. But even among the lush meadows and rich trees of Normandy, away from any sting of association, Humphrey did not recover at once, as she had hoped, his old buoyancy. Listless, uneasy, restless, he would for hours be silent, wrapped in a melancholy that did not ordinarily belong to his temperament, while, in his broken slumber and sudden awakenings, his wife could detect the existence of a great well of sorrow that even her anxious affection could not plumb, a grief her love could not solace. The discovery of the extent of his affliction caused her further worry, made her dread their return to the scene of his past life. But as time passed it was obvious that his spirits were returning; and when he told her that during their absence the Grove had been entirely repainted and redecorated, she began to feel happier, hoping that it would seem to him like the beginning of a new life.

Almost two years to a day after the crime, they returned from their honeymoon, but Colonel Tonge did not seem conscious of any sense of anniversary, while she, naturally, would not mention it to him. But it made her feel a little uneasy.

As they drove back from the station, the new chauffeur quite by chance, by one of those dreadful inspirations which are only given to stupid people, drove the newly married couple down the concealed road near the summer-house, instead of taking them in by the near lodge. Colonel Tonge obviously experienced no emotion, but his wife felt for the moment as if she would be stifled between those two high hedges. How like was this afternoon to that other one! No leaf moved on any tree, no bird let its song trickle through the cloudy, too-dark leafage; the air was hot, motionless, and still, though through it ran those same secret tremors, inexplicable tremblings. For the new Mrs. Tonge the whole atmosphere was stained with memories.

Yet she soon forgot the uneasy promptings of her heart and mind in the pleasure she felt at the reception which awaited them. She had always been a favourite with the servants, and the latter could never forget the poor Colonel's sufferings, so that they had taken an especial care to give the newly wedded pair an inspiriting welcome. The Colonel stopped to talk with them, while Mrs. Tonge, eager to see what alterations had been made, stepped into the house alone. It looked charming, she thought, with the new paint smooth on the old walls; and, unable to repress a slight thrill of pleasure, which she felt to be wrong, though she could not quite exorcise it, at being for the first time mistress of a house—and such a lovely house—she walked on through the empty, gleaming rooms that led one into the other. The last room was the boudoir. She entered it softly, closing the door behind her, wishing to explore its impression to the full, for she wondered whether it would make her feel an usurper, a stranger in someone else's place. But no! it was a new room to her: gone was that dead look imparted by the yellow glaze of countless old photographs and by the spreading litter of trivial objects. And while she bore towards the dead woman no feelings but those of pity and affection, yet, being of a practical nature, she was glad that nothing remained of the old mistress—nothing that could call up painful memories. The room was quiet and restful; the long windows stood wide open on to the pleasant water-cool spaces of the lawn, that unfolded up to the borders of the wood where stood tall fleecy green trees, while under their blue shadows ran the murmur of shallow streams. The healthy scents of tree and grass, the peaceful watery sounds, and honey-gathering, contented drone of the bees as they hung over the flowers, drifted into the house, diffusing an air of ease and comfort. This was *her* house, *her* garden, *her* home, and she now had a husband to whom she was devoted. Why, then, should she ever allow her mind to dwell on the tragedies of the past? Was it not better to forget utterly, to obliterate the memory in her husband, by offering him all her love, till gradually these possessions to which he had been so attached became dear to him again? . . . But just then, behind her, she heard the thin voice of the dead woman crying out—a voice grey with fear and breaking. "Humphrey," it sighed, "what is it? Oh, my God!" . . . And then the sound of a heavy dumb blow and low moaning, followed by burst after burst of idiot laughter, as with a fluttering whirl of flaming green feathers the parrot flew up again to its empty attic.

THE END

A SELECTIVE BIBLIOGRAPHY [Chiefly of Shorter Pieces] FOR THE
ENTHUSIASTS OF THE FANTASTIC

GRANT ALLEN. *Twelve Tales.* (Grant Richards.)
JOHN ATKINS. *The Diary of William Carpenter.* (The Favil Press.)
STACY AUMONIER. *One After Another.* (Hutchinson.)
F. W. BAIN. *A Digit of the Moon and other Stories.* (Hurst & Blackett.)
HONORÉ BALZAC. *Droll Stories.* Illustrated by Gustave Doré. John (Camden Hotten.)
MAURICE BARING. *Half a Minute's Silence.* (Heinemann.)
MAX BEERBOHM. *Seven Men.* (Heinemann.)
E. F. BENSON. *Visible and Invisible.* (Hutchinson.)
STELLA BENSON. *I Pose.* (Macmillan.)
,, ,, *Living Alone.* (Macmillan.)
CONRAD BERCOVICI. *Between Earth and Sky.* (Cape.)
AMBROSE BIERCE. *In the Midst of Life.* (Chatto & Windus.)
,, ,, *The Monk and The Hangman's Daughter.* (Cape.)
,, ,, *Can Such Things Be?* (Cape.)
,, ,, *Ten Tales.* (First Edition Club.)
,, ,, *The Eyes of the Panther.* (Cape.)
ALGERNON BLACKWOOD. *The Empty House.* (Macmillan.)
,, ,, *The Listener.* (Macmillan.)
,, ,, *The Lost Valley.* (Macmillan.)
,, ,, *Incredible Adventures.* (Macmillan.)
,, ,, *Ten-Minute Stories.* (Murray.)
,, ,, *The Wolves of God.* (Cassell.)
,, ,, *Day and Night Stories.* (Cassell.)
,, ,, *The Dance of Death.* (Jenkins.)
,, ,, *Strange Stories selected by the author.* (Heinemann.)
HECTOR BOLITHO. *The House in Half-Moon Street.* (Jenkins.)
ELIZABETH BOWEN. *The Cat Jumps.* (Gollancz.)
JAMES BRANCH CABELL. *The White Robe.* (Lane.)
KAREL CAPEK. *Tales from Two Pockets.* (Allen & Unwin.)
LEWIS CARROLL. *Complete Works of,* edited by Alexander Woolcott. (Nonesuch Press.)
G. K. CHESTERTON. *The Man Who Was Thursday.* (Arrowsmith.)
,, ,, *The Innocence of Father Brown.* (Cassell.)
,, ,, *The Wisdom of Father Brown.* (Cassell.)
,, ,, *The Incredulity of Father Brown.* (Cassell.)
,, ,, *The Secret of Father Brown.* (Cassell.)
,, ,, *The Man Who Knew Too Much.* (Cassell.)
,, ,, *The Poet and the Lunatic.* (Cassell.)
JOHN COLLIER. *Green Thoughts.* (Joiner & Steele.)
WILKIE COLLINS. *After Dark.* (Chatto & Windus.)
JOSEPH CONRAD. *The Complete Short Stories of.* (Hutchinson.)
A. E. COPPARD. *Adam and Eve and Pinch Me.* (Cape.)
,, ,, *The Black Dog.* (Cape.)
,, ,, *Clorinda Walks in Heaven.* (Cape.)
,, ,, *Fishmonger's Fiddle.* (Cape.)
F. MARION CRAWFORD. *Uncanny Tales.* (T. Fisher Unwin.)
CLEMENCE DANE. *The Wandering Stars.* (Heinemann.)
WALTER DE LA MARE. *The Riddle.* (Faber.)
,, ,, *The Connoisseur.* (Collins.)
,, ,, *On the Edge.* (Faber.)
,, ,, *The Wind Blows Over.* (Faber.)
,, ,, *Ding Dong Bell.* (Selwyn & Blount.)
THOMAS DELONEY. *The Gentle Craft.* (Clarendon Press.)
,, ,, *The Cordwainer's Stories.* (Clarendon Press.)

THOMAS DE QUINCEY. *Selected Writings of,* edited by Philip Van Doren Stern. (Nonesuch Press.)
CHARLES DICKENS. *The Posthumous Papers of the Pickwick Club.* (Chapman & Hall.)
„ „ *Christmas Books.* (Chapman & Hall.)
„ „ *Christmas Stories.* (Chapman & Hall.)
VALENTINE DOBREE. *To Blush Unseen.* (Cresset Press.)
T. H. DOSTOEVSKY. *White Nights.* (Heinemann.)
„ „ *An Honest Thief.* (Heinemann.)
„ „ *The Gambler.* (Heinemann.)
ERNEST DOWSON. *Dilemnas.* (Leonard Smithers.)
CONAN DOYLE. *The Last Galley.* (Murray.)
LORD DUNSANY. *The Sword of Welleran.* (Allen & Unwin.)
„ „ *A Dreamer's Tale.* (Allen & Unwin.)
„ „ *Fifty One Tales.* (Allen & Unwin.)
„ „ *Tales of Wonder.* (Allen & Unwin.)
B. L. FARJEON. *The Mystery of Mr. Felix.* (Hutchinson.)
E. M. FORSTER. *Celestial Omnibus.* (Edward Arnold.)
DAVID GARNETT. *Go She Must.* (Chatto & Windus.)
„ „ *Lady into Fox.* (Chatto & Windus.)
RICHARD GARNETT. *The Twilight of the Gods.* (Lane.)
ELIZABETH GASKELL. *Right at Last.* (Oxford University Press.)
„ „ *Lizzie Leigh.* (Oxford University Press.)
GEORGE GISSING. *Human Odds and Ends.* (Sidgwick & Jackson.)
„ „ *The House of the Cobwebs.* (Constable.)
LE COMTE DE GOBINEAU. *The Crimson Handkerchief.* (Cape.)
GRAHAM GREENE. *The Basement Room.* (Cresset Press.)
ROBERT GREENE. *The Conny-Catching Tracts.* (Oxford University Press.)
NATHANIAL HAWTHORNE. *Tales selected by Carl Van Doren.* (Oxford University Press.)
LAFCADIO HEARN. *Kwaiden.* (Cape.)
MAURICE HEWLETT. *Lore of Proserpine.* (Macmillan.)
CLAUDE HOUGHTON. *Three Fantastic Tales.* (Joiner & Steele.)
RICHARD HUGHES. *A Moment of Time.* (Chatto & Windus.)
VIOLET HUNT. *Tales of the Uncanny.*
ALDOUS HUXLEY. *Limbo.* (Chatto & Windus.)
„ „ *Mortal Coils.* (Chatto & Windus.)
„ „ *The Little Mexicans.* (Chatto & Windus.)
„ „ *Two or Three Graces.* (Chatto & Windus.)
„ „ *Brief Candles.* (Chatto & Windus.)
„ „ *Twice Seven: Fourteen Selected Stories.* (The Reprint Society.)
PHILIPPE DE L'ILLE-ADAM. *Sardonic Tales.* (Cape.)
W. W. JACOBS. *Short Cruises.* (Methuen.)
„ „ *Night Watches.* (Chapman & Hall.)
„ „ *Sea Whispers.* (Hodder & Stoughton.)
HENRY JAMES. *The Lesson of the Master and Other Stories.* (Macmillan.)
„ „ *What Maisie Knew and Other Stories.* (Macmillan.)
„ „ *The Better Sort and Other Stories.* (Macmillan.)
„ „ *The Turn of the Screw and the Aspern Papers.* (Everyman Library.)
M. R. JAMES. *Collected Ghost Stories.* (Edward Arnold.)
GERALD KERSH. *The Extraordinary Dummy and other Stories.* (Heinemann.)
RUDYARD KIPLING. *The Phantom Rickshaw.* (Macmillan.)
„ „ *Life's Handicap.* (Macmillan.)
„ „ *The Jungle Book.* (Macmillan.)
„ „ *Debits and Credits.* (Macmillan.)
ALEXANDER KUPRIN. *The River of Life.* (Allen & Unwin.)
JAMES LAVER. *The Laburnam Tree.* (Cresset Press.)
D. H. LAWRENCE. *Collected Stories.* (Heinemann.)
J. SHERIDAN LE FANU. *In A Glass Darkly.* (Peter Davies.)
„ „ *The Purcell Papers.* (Bentley.)
RICHARD LE GALLIENNE. *Makers of Rainbow.* (Lane.)
MATTHEW G. LEWIS. *Tales of Terror.* (Routledge.)
„ „ *Tales of Wonder.* (Routledge.)

SAMUEL LOVER. *Legends and Stories of Ireland.* (Constable.)
EDWARD BULWER LYTTON. *The Haunted and the Haunters.* (Simpkin Marshall.)
ARTHUR MACHEN. *The Chronicles of Clemendy.* (Secker.)
SEUMAS MACMANUS. *The Chimney Corners.* (Irish Publishing Co.)
„ „ *Tales That Were Told.* (Talbot Press.)
R. H. MALDEN. *New Ghosts.* (Edward Arnold.)
W. S. MAUGHAM. *Orientations and Other Stories.* (Unwin.)
GUY DE MAUPASSANT. *Yvette and other Stories.* (Duckworth.)
„ „ *Stories from.* (Cape.)
„ „ *Short Stories.* (Dent. Everyman.)
ETHEL COLBURN MAYNE. *Inner Circle.* (Constable.)
„ „ *Come In.* (Chapman & Hall.)
CHRISTOPHER MORLEY. *The Haunted Bookshop.* (Doubleday Doran.)
WILLIAM MORRIS. *The World Beyond the World.* (Longmans.)
„ „ *The Roots of the Mountains.*
„ „ *The Well at the World's End.*
NEIL MUNRO. *The Lost Pibroch and Other Sheeling Stories.* (Blackwood.)
H. H. MUNRO ("SAKI"). *The Chronicles of Clovis.* (Lane.)
„ „ *Beasts and Super Beasts.* (Lane.)
THOMAS NASHE. *The Unfortunate Traveller and other Writings.* (Blackwell.)
OLIVER ONIONS. *Widdershins.* (Secker.)
„ „ *Ghosts in Daylight.* (Chapman & Hall.)
ELMORE ELLIOT PEAKE. *The Shape of Fear and other Ghostly Stories.* (Macmillan.)
HAROLD PEARSE. *Border Ghost Stories.* (E. MacDonald.)
PATRICK HENRY PEARSE. *The Mother and other Stories.* (Talbot Press.)
ELIZABETH STUART PHELPS. *Men, Women and Ghosts.* (Boston, U.S.A.)
EDGAR ALLAN POE. *Tales of Mystery and Imagination.* (Putnam.)
T. F. POWYS. *The White Paternoster.* (Chatto & Windus.)
„ „ *The House with the Echo.* (Chatto & Windus.)
„ „ *No Painted Plumage.* (Chatto & Windus.)
V. S. PRITCHETT. *The Spanish Virgin and Other Stories.* (Benn.)
SIR ARTHUR QUILLER-COUCH. *Old Fires and Profitable Ghosts.* (Dent.)
FORREST REID. *A Garden by the Sea.* (Talbot Press.)
ROGER RIORDAN AND TOZO TAKAYANAGI. *Sunrise Stories.* (Kegan Paul.)
F. ROLFE (BARON CORVO). *Stories Toto Told Me.* (Chatto & Windus.)
„ *In His Own Image.* (Chatto & Windus.)
JOHN RUSSELL. *Far Wandering Men.* (Butterworth.)
WILLIAM SANSOM. *Fireman Flower.* (Hogarth Press.)
OLIVE SCHREINER. *Dreams.* (T. Fisher Unwin.)
„ „ *Dream Life and Real Life.* (T. Fisher Unwin.)
ARTHUR SCHNITZLER. *Little Novels.* (Constable.)
SIR WALTER SCOTT. *Short Stories Introduced by Lord David Cecil.* (Oxford University Press.)
WILLIAM SHARP (FIONA MACLEOD). *The Sin-Eaters and Other Legendary Moralities.* (Heinemann.)
„ „ *The Dominion of Dreams.* (Heinemann.)
„ „ *The Laughter of Peterkin and Other Tales.* (Heinemann.)
SHCHEDRIN (M. E. SALTYKOV). *Fables.* (Chatto & Windus.)
MARY WOLLSTONECRAFT SHELLEY. *The Last Man.*
MAY SINCLAIR. *Uncanny Stories.* (Hutchinson.)
OSBERT SITWELL. *Triple Fugue.* (Duckworth.)
„ „ *Dumb Animal and other Stories.* (Duckworth.)
FEDOR SOLOGUB. *The Sweet Scented Name and Other Fairy Tales.* (Secker.)
„ „ *The Old House.* (Secker.)
JAMES STEPHENS. *Here are Ladies.* (Macmillan.)
„ „ *In the Land of Youth.* (Macmillan.)
ROBERT LOUIS STEVENSON. *The Merry Men.* (Macmillan.)
„ „ *New Arabian Nights.* (Chatto & Windus.)
J. F. SULLIVAN. *Queer-Side Stories.* (Downey.)
ARTHUR SYMONS. *Spiritual Adventures.* (Secker.)
RABINDRANATH TAGORE. *Hungry Stones.* (Macmillan.)
W. M. THACKERAY. *The Yellow Plush Papers.* Nelson.)

LEO TOLSTOY. *Twenty-Three Tales.* (Oxford University Press.)
„   „   *The Kreutzer Sonata.* (Oxford University Press.)
„   „   *Russian Tales.* (Oxford University Press.)
IVAN TURGENEV. *Dream Tales.* (Heinemann.)
„   „   *Knock, Knock and Other Stories.* (Heinemann.)
„   „   *The Two Friends.* (Heinemann.)
MARK TWAIN. *The Mysterious Island and other Stories.* (Harpers.)
H. A. VACHELL. *The Enchanted Garden.* (Cassell.)
JULES VERNE. *Dr. Ose's Experiments and other Stories.* (Routledge.)
„   „   *The Mysterious Island and other Stories.* (Routledge.)
H. RUSSELL WAKEFIELD. *A Ghostly Company.* (Cape.)
„   „   *Ghost Stories.* (Cape.)
EDGAR WALLACE. *Sanders of the River.* (Ward, Lock.)
„   „   *People of the River.* (Ward, Lock.)
„   „   *Bosambo of the River.* (Ward, Lock.)
H. G. WELLS. *The Plattner Story and others.* (Benn.)
„   „   *Tales of Space and Time.* (Macmillan.)
„   „   *Twelve Stories and A Dream.* (Macmillan.)
„   „   *The Country of the Blind and other Stories.* (Macmillan.)
EDITH WHARTON. *Tales of Men and Ghosts.* (Macmillan.)
OSCAR WILDE. *The Happy Prince and other Tales.* (Duckworth.)
„   „   *A House of Pomegranates.* (Methuen.)
VIRGINIA WOOLF. *A Haunted House and other Stories.* (Hogarth Press.)
W. B. YEATS. *The Celtic-Twilight.* (Macmillan.)
„   „   *The Secret Rose.* (Macmillan.)
EMILE ZOLA. *Stories for Ninon.* (Secker.)

www.ingramcontent.com/pod-product-compliance
Ingram Content Group UK Ltd.
Pitfield, Milton Keynes, MK11 3LW, UK
UKHW041951230426
12048UKWH00008B/262